To my darling Alexander, in the hope that the Balkans lives on in your soul as you conquer the world.
    To my mother, Lidia, for everything.
    For Keva, Lepa, and all the loving, strong, stubborn, fearless Balkan women who came before.

IRINA JANAKIEVSKA

THE BALKAN KITCHEN

RECIPES AND STORIES FROM THE HEART OF THE BALKANS

Hardie Grant
BOOKS

Introductivon 6
A Personal Note 28

DORUČEK ♦ Breakfast 30

FURNA ♦ From the Oven 48

MEZE ♦ For Sharing 80

LAŽICA ♦ On the Spoon 108

RUČEK ♦ Lunch 122

ZEMJA ♦ From Land 154

VODA ♦ From Water 180

BLAGO ♦ Sweets and Desserts 200

ŠPAJZ ♦ From the Larder 234

Glossary 262
Sources and Further Reading 265
Acknowledgements 266
About the Author 270
Index 271

Introduction

The culinary education of this Balkan child started with a small piece of dough. Kneaded into oblivion with an overzealous amount of flour, somehow shaped into a swirl and baked alongside my mother's *pita*, it was proudly displayed to all the members of my family, and stubbornly nibbled despite being so tough as to be almost inedible. At around four years old I progressed to chopping walnuts and vegetables for a variety of uses, and to the endless pitting and peeling of fruit for *slatko* and other preserves – all under the kind but watchful eye of my maternal grandmother, Lepa, whose insistence that everything be prepared to her meticulous standards would have given any Michelin-starred chef a run for their money. Lepa was a banker, or more precisely the head of the supervisory and audit function of the national bank. She was married to Dragi, an actor who everyone knew as Amfi (after amphitheatre). In many ways opposites, they were deeply in love with each other their whole lives, impossibly beautiful and famously glamorous. My grandmother's family was from Kumanovo, a city in the northern part of North Macedonia, and my grandfather's family was from the capital, Skopje. They met and fell in love in a Skopje from a bygone era, one that was devastated and forever changed by the earthquake of 1963. They loved to host: my grandfather, always the actor, loved to entertain and make people laugh, and my grandmother loved to impress with her beautifully prepared food. My childhood as their grandchild was idyllic. When not getting in the way in the kitchen or being otherwise adored, I would accompany my grandfather to the theatre for his rehearsals.

My grandmother's mother, Paraskeva (or Keva), was left widowed young. She owned a finishing school where she instructed young women preparing for marriage in artisanal crafts such as sewing, embroidery and crochet. With the advent of communism this was deemed a capitalist pursuit, and her business was appropriated. She subsequently retrained and worked as a hospital nurse. Keva was an excellent cook and particularly exceptional baker. Keva's sister, Rosa, and Rosa's husband, Kiro, were partisans, and Keva was often called upon to shelter various members of the resistance movement. Keva and Rosa's father, Milan, was a baker. My father's family are Vlach, an ethnic community that are dispersed across the south-western Balkans (including North Macedonia, northern Greece,

Keva, 1930s

Lepa and Dragi, c. 1950s

southern Albania, southwestern Bulgaria, Serbia and Romania) and who speak Vlaški – a term that encompasses two variants of an eastern Romance language, Aromanian and Meglenoromanian. The family of my paternal grandmother, Ariadne, came from both Thessaloniki (in Greece) and Bitola (in south-western North Macedonia). She grew up in Bitola, where her father was the French consul, but then spent part of her young married life in Sarajevo until the family moved back to Skopje. Her husband, my grandfather Ilija, had a metalworking business that spanned the region – Skopje, Sarajevo, and Thessaloniki. He too was considered a capitalist and after the Second World War, they lost nearly everything except one shop in the Old Turkish Bazaar in Skopje. My grandfather's family hailed from Kruševo (a town in central North Macedonia that is one of the highest altitude towns in the Balkans). It is famous for the Ilinden Uprising, where the short-lived attempt to overthrow Ottoman rule in Macedonia began in 1903. The uprising was crushed and my grandfather's family had to escape to Skopje with my grandfather, a baby at the time, smuggled in a saddle, because his father, my great-grandfather Dimitar, had manufactured cannonballs and other arms used for the uprising. Both sides of my family remain rooted to North Macedonia, but have been and still are dispersed across the Balkans, including in Montenegro, Serbia, Slovenia and the rest of the world. In short, my family is a true Balkan microcosm.

I was born in Skopje, at a time when the country was known as the Republic of Macedonia and was part of the Socialist Federal Republic of Yugoslavia. I was very much a child of the 1980s, and significantly a child of the Yugoslav 1980s. Although Tito had died by the time I was born, I grew up like most other Yugoslav children my age celebrating him and his legacy, waving a Yugoslav flag and wearing a Yugoslav Partisan hat as a Tito pioneer, celebrating Yugoslavia's sporting glories, proud of its status as a non-aligned leader in the world and learning about what was hailed as a multi-ethnic, multi-religious and multi-cultural country, where rising above ethnicity, religion and political beliefs to celebrate commonality and diversity was encouraged. Yet the Yugoslav dream was beginning to unravel by the mid-1980s, with economic and political problems, food and energy shortages and the emergence of populist politicians such as Franjo Tuđman (in Croatia) and Slobodan Milošević (in Serbia).

My parents separated in the late 1980s (eventually divorcing) and my mother, an architect who foresaw the gathering storm in Yugoslavia, found a job in Kuwait, which allowed us to move there to seek a better life. We left Kuwait in 1990 because of the invasion of Kuwait by Iraq but returned in 1993 following the dissolution of Yugoslavia and the outbreak of the Yugoslav wars. My mother still lives and works in Kuwait.

I happened to come of university age in 2001, when North Macedonia was amid an escalation of violence between Macedonians and Albanians that was threatening to escalate into full-blown civil war. Having studied in an international English school in Kuwait, I was in the fortunate position of having the option to study elsewhere in the world

Introduction

while the situation in North Macedonia remained uncertain. I chose continued exile from my home and came to London to study international relations and history, and over time began to specialise in the interplay of the history of the Cold War, the Balkans and the former Yugoslavia. I suppose on some level I needed to make sense of what happened to the country I was born in that no longer was, and understand why and how Yugoslavia shattered so tragically, plunging the region into the various Yugoslav wars of dissolution in the 1990s and the political, social and economic turmoil that continues in various guises to this day. As I graduated, nationalist politics had started to take hold of my country and the Balkans more widely. The various Yugoslav republics were plunged into 'transitions' – political, economic, geographical and existential – which were intended to ensure their survival and define their respective identities in a post-Yugoslav world, but in most cases resulted in demagogues taking hold. Similarly, various other nation-states of the Balkans also saw an opportunity to recreate their respective identities and assert agendas.

I could not see a future for myself there. A large corporate law firm took a gamble on me and sponsored me through law school with a job waiting for me at the end. Corporate law – with all the glamour of working in the City of London, at the forefront of legal innovation in the field – was initially a career I fell into gratefully because it offered an escape to a viable future: stability, financial security and a chance to stay in Great Britain and succeed on my own terms and merit. As a migrant to Great Britain, I had everything to prove, I also met and fell in love with Peter, my now husband, which sealed my decision to stay. Corporate law was an all-consuming career, which, especially after the birth of our son Alexander, became unsustainable.

Mum and I, Skopje, early 1980s

◆   Introduction

The Balkan Kitchen

In the summer of 2011, I sat on the floor in the corridor of my grandmother Lepa's empty apartment and wept. A few days earlier she had been hit by a driver on a pedestrian crossing and passed away shortly after while I was on the plane from London to Skopje. I was heartbroken, inconsolable, and felt, perhaps a like bit like that corridor, transient. Not knowing where to go or what to do with my grief. The bookshelf in front of me held our family's most treasured books and, on one shelf, my grandmother's recipe books. I thought that by looking through them I could trick myself into thinking she was still there, busily cooking something beautiful that tasted of love, longing and memories.

Grandma and I, mid 1980s

She had known, without me really telling her, that I was deeply unhappy (over)working as a corporate lawyer in London. The last thing my grandmother said to me when I was there for Easter before she passed away was that, unlike her generation, I had a choice: I could do something I loved that would fulfil my soul. Her generation had survived world wars and their dreams were sacrificed for survival – and to build another collective dream, of socialist Yugoslavia. She had wanted to be a musician, but with the shortages of cadres in all areas required to reconstruct a functioning society out of the ravages of the Second World War, she became a banker. She wanted more for me – everything she had sacrificed.

All this ran through my mind as I picked up her 1956 edition of the *Veliki Narodni Kuvar* (Great National Cookbook) by Spasenija Pata Markovic, its fading olive-green cover torn but lovingly repaired, pages marked and full of her recipes that had been scribbled in old school notebooks or on fragments of scrap paper, collected or created over time. All the signs of a cookbook that had been well used and loved. I happened to open it on a page with a recipe for *Grijaž torta s čokoladom*, a walnut praline cake with chocolate, next to which she had written 'Princess' and 'For Irina' with a date two weeks after the day I was born. This is the cake that has now become Alexander's cake. I imagine she first made it for the day I came home from the hospital, to celebrate the arrival of her grandchild into this world. For my grandmother, cooking beautiful food and feeding people was the ultimate manifestation of love. It struck me then that I would never again be able to learn from her and understand the intricacies of everything she did in the kitchen, some of which must

1956 edition of Veliki Narodni Kuvar by Spasenija Pata Markovic

have seemed so obvious to her that she did not write it down.

In that moment, the idea of the Balkan Kitchen flew into my mind and has refused to give me peace since. I knew then that I needed to set out on a journey to teach myself to cook like the inspiring women and men in my family, and to recreate the recipes lovingly documented by them as well as the flavours so vividly preserved in my memories. In this way, I thought they would somehow always be with me. I did not realise it then, but cooking was to become my way of dealing with grief, with what we call *taga* – a sorrow, a yearning, a love for a person, a time, a place. I have heard it said that home is where your eyes first see sunlight. Even though I had left out of choice, there was an irrepressible pull to my place of birth, to the Macedonian sun, to the Balkans. Threads that kept me firmly woven to my South East European homeland. Cooking became a way for me to be at home anywhere in the world. Sharing my food became a way to share a part of myself with people I loved so that they could experience the tastes of my childhood and understand me and where I came from. It was a way they, too, could taste and fall in love with the flavours preserved in my memories. It has, in recent years, also become a way for me to teach my son where a part of him comes from. His eyes may have first seen British sunlight, but his soul carries those threads of Balkan flavours and memories.

◆ Introduction

I knew, too, that I had to write – not just about my family's enduring love affair with food, our memories and stories, but about the people of the Balkans, what Balkan cuisine means to us and how it carries the weight of the often difficult and painful but at the same time beautifully culturally rich and unique history of the Balkans. How we, uprooted repeatedly from the Balkans at various points throughout history because of occupation, wars or other social, political or economic upheaval, carry the Balkan Kitchen in our souls wherever we have chosen to put down new roots.

Along the way, this project took on a greater significance for me. It became a journey of historical investigation to understand the history behind the food of my childhood. To truly understand the origins and the current state of Balkan cuisine, I needed to unravel how Balkan cuisine had, over time, acquired its complex influences, layers, flavours and textures. Unpicking the ever-present historical threads that food carries with it is not always easy. In the Balkans, some of these threads are lost in history and memory, or have become nearly invisible, their origin undocumented or simply changed by the prevailing political, religious or national narrative at any given point in history. But echoes of these threads remain, and in many ways, despite years of research and travels across the region, this is a journey that has only just begun.

It also became a mission of documenting the cuisine of a region I love, one that is fast disappearing with the passing of older generations and the exodus of each successive generation, or being otherwise modified, appropriated or altered for political or nationalist purposes. It became a mission of helping others like me, members of the Balkan diaspora who find themselves adrift around the world and hungry for the food they grew up with, to recreate the flavours of their memories wherever they are in the world.

In 2015 my husband Peter bought me a website domain as a present in a bid to encourage me to share my journey with the world. Shortly after, the Balkan Kitchen website and social media channels were born. I started to document my journey and my findings, accompanied by passable food photos. Social media gave me the most incredible community around the world of people from or in love with the Balkans and its cuisine. We shared memories, stories and recipes and connected on a deeply personal level. By late 2019, I finally took my grandmother's advice and made another choice: to scale back my legal career in order to have more time to follow my heart and write.

Mum and I

Introduction

Grandma and I, early 1980s

Ariadne and Ilija, c. 1920s

Mum and Dad, late 1970s

'The Balkans'

The etymology of the word 'Balkan' is complicated. It is thought to be an Ottoman Turkish word for a wooded mountain range, and it likely therefore originated as a reference to the mountain range now known as the Balkan Mountains, but then known by locals in Slavic as Stara Planina (old mountain), among other names. It is possible that the Ottoman Turkish word has a Farsi root – *bālkāneh* or *bālākhāna* meaning 'high above' or 'proud house', though there are related words in other Turkic languages too. Non-Ottoman sources used the term Haemus (or Aemus, or similar variants) for the same mountain range, all derived from the ancient Thracian term for mountain ridge, *saimon*. It is conjectured that the Thracian term made its way into ancient Greek and took on a new meaning – *haima* (blood), thought to be a reference to the ancient Greek myth of Zeus battling and spilling the blood of the Titan Typhon over the mountains. It is possibly this that inspired another popular myth around the meaning of Balkan: a literal translation from modern Turkish of *bal* (honey) and *kan* (blood). The conceptualisation of a specific 'Balkan' region emerged within the Ottoman Empire at the turn of the 19th century so this remains a myth, though many would say it is an appropriate metaphor for these predominantly mountainous lands of abundance and millennia of bloodshed.

Delineating the contours of 'the Balkans' is even more complex, largely due to the confluence of various geographical, historical and political descriptions. A long-standing geographical misconception – that the Balkan Mountains stretched unbroken from the Black Sea in Bulgaria to the Adriatic Sea, whereas in fact the mountain range peters out in modern-day eastern Serbia – led a German geographer, Johann August Zeune, to coin the term 'Balkan Peninsula' in 1808. However, that concept remains disputed, and the delineation of a Balkan Peninsula is just as unclear as that of 'the Balkans'. To date, there is no real geographical, historical, or political consensus on where the borders of either lie, and no real consensus as to which nation-states, or peoples, are included in the undefined and potentially indefinable boundaries of the Balkans.

In simplistic and practical terms, the Balkans lie in South East Europe, between the Adriatic Sea in the north-west, the Black Sea in the north-east, the Turkish Straits in the east and the Aegean Sea in the south. As for the northern land border, some would argue that this is marked by the Danube River up to Vienna, but many Slovenians or Istrians would not consider themselves Balkan. In short – the delineation of what constitutes the Balkans remains just as obscure now as it has always been.

To my mind, it is most helpful to think of the Balkans as a mutable region, and one which, in current global-map terms comprises nation-states born out of the demise of the former Yugoslavia – Bosnia and Herzegovina, Croatia, Kosovo, Montenegro, North Macedonia, Serbia and Slovenia, as well as Albania, Bulgaria, and parts of Greece, Romania, Hungary and Turkey.

The scope of this book is, for practical reasons, limited to the area comprising the former Yugoslavia, with the occasional glance and descriptive overspill towards the rest of the Balkans (and sometimes further afield) to give clarity to the influences on the cuisine, and to illustrate any similarities or differences between dishes, to the extent I have been able to discover them. Yugoslavia is of course not synonymous with the Balkans and vice versa, but unlike the cuisines of the rest of the region, it remains woefully underexplored and misunderstood.

Introduction

There were several major languages spoken across the former Yugoslavia, including Serbo-Croat, Slovenian, Macedonian and Albanian, and many regional dialects. However, Serbo-Croat was the only language taught across all the republics and autonomous provinces of former Yugoslavia. My mother tongue is Macedonian, but I grew up also understanding and speaking Serbo-Croat. Following Yugoslavia's dissolution, Serbo-Croat devolved into four separate standards – Bosnian, Croatian, Montenegrin and Serbian. In this book my default language is Macedonian, but I use a mixture of languages to name dishes or ingredients, including Albanian, Bosnian, Croatian, Montenegrin, Serbian, Slovenian and occasionally Turkish or other international languages to indicate the possible origin or influence on a dish, or to demonstrate how words from other languages have been used or adapted into the various languages of the region – what I sometimes refer to as 'Balkanised'. Often, words from other languages are 'misused' – a dish may have the same name as, for example, an existing Turkish dish, but is in reality either a completely different dish or significantly different to the other. Where a dish is named in one of the languages, this is explained and I have often chosen the language most appropriate for the dish – that is, the language/dialect of the area most typically associated with it. Where a dish transcends modern national and linguistic boundaries, I also provide some of its other names in other relevant languages or dialects, but for obvious reasons I cannot list all names.

A POTTED HISTORY

The Balkans are ancient lands, where Europe meets Asia. They have been both the birthplace of ancient civilizations and the thoroughfares of empires.

The area has been inhabited from as early as the Palaeolithic Period. One of the earliest known settlements in the region is Lepenski Vir, located on the banks of the Danube, dating to around 9500–6000 BCE.

Agriculture arrived in the Balkans around 6000–7000 BCE and various Neolithic cultures, such as the Starčevo-Körös-Criş culture, the Vinča culture and the Karanovo culture developed in the region. The impact of the introduction of agriculture (the cultivation of early forms of wheat and legumes) to the Balkans was profound and, in many ways, continues to influence the cuisine to this day. It allowed for the establishment of more permanent Neolithic communities along the fertile floodplains of the Balkan rivers (the Danube in the north, Drava and Sava in the north-west, Drina and Morava in the centre and Vardar in the south), as well as along the coastal areas along the Adriatic, Ionian, Aegean and Black Seas. These cultures are known for their advancements in agriculture, including the cultivation of cereals like wheat and barley, legumes, and the domestication of animals like cattle, sheep and goats, as well as the consequent emergence of more sophisticated trading networks. They also paved the way for the emergence of more complex civilisations with the advent of the Balkan Bronze Age around 3300 BCE and the development of civilizations such as the Minoans and Mycenaeans in the Aegean. The Illyrians, Thracians and Dacians had established their respective cultures in the region by 1000 BCE, which broadly overlapped with the emergence of ancient Greece between 1200–900 BCE, culminating with the golden age of classical Greece by 400 BCE. Between 356–323 BCE, Alexander the Great conquered the various Greek city-states and during his reign extended the Macedonian empire to include much of the Balkan Peninsula, Asia Minor, Egypt and beyond, bringing about the spread of Hellenic culture across vast territories of the known world at the time. Alexander the Great's conquests ushered in the Hellenistic period, which ended with the completion of the Roman conquests of the Balkans by around the 1st century CE. Around the 4th century, the Roman Empire was divided into east and west, with the Eastern Roman, or Byzantine Empire, centred in Constantinople.

The Balkans remained an integral part of the Byzantine Empire for several centuries, and pre-existing pagan traditions and beliefs melded with Eastern Orthodox Christianity. Byzantine presence in the region was turbulent and Constantinople faced periods of expansion, contraction and conflict. Celts arrived, both as mercenaries for hire and occasionally invaders, around the 5th century. Between the 6th and 8th centuries, the region faced further incursions from newly arrived tribes of Avars, Slavs and Lombards, along with the Turkic Bulgars. The arrival of Slavic tribes to the region displaced (often to the safety of the mountains) or assimilated much of the indigenous population and therefore had a significant and lasting impact on the ethnic, cultural and linguistic mosaic of the region. By the 9th century, the Byzantine Empire was experiencing a period of revival in the Balkans under the Macedonian dynasty, but by the 10th century, it was facing a threat from the newly emerging First Bulgarian Empire, and by the 11th century, from the Seljuk Empire. Constantinople managed to retain some semblance of control, but by the 12th century, the Byzantine Empire was again facing a double threat, this time from the Second Bulgarian Empire and the Crusades. With the 1204 sacking of Constantinople, and consequent fragmentation of the Byzantine Empire, various states and Latin crusader kingdoms were established across the Balkans and Constantinople never fully regained control of the Balkans. Ottoman Turkish incursions into the Balkans started as early as the 14th century, and by 1453, Constantinople had fallen to the Ottomans, marking both the end of the Byzantine Empire and the start of a long period of Ottoman rule in the Balkans. By the later part of the 16th century, the Ottomans had managed to win control over nearly the entire Balkan Peninsula. In much of the region, the Ottomans either co-opted or destroyed the local aristocracy, but did not eliminate the communities they ruled over. Instead, in exchange for loyalty and regular tax payments, the Ottomans permitted a high degree of discretion to pre-existing local religious and community leaders, thereby guaranteeing the survival of these (predominantly Christian Orthodox) communities. Survival, however, often came at a heavy price. The Ottomans implemented a system of *devşirme* – the practice of taking children, primarily boys, from Christian families to serve in various positions in the Ottoman state. The children were often (but not always) forcibly separated from their families and converted to Islam, then taken to Constantinople to receive education and training. Some went on to staff the elite Janissary corps and others went on to serve in high administrative or bureaucratic positions within the Ottoman Empire, often returning to govern in the region they originally hailed from. This was one of the most effective tactics used by the Ottomans to integrate the diverse Balkans and consolidate their role in the region. From the Balkan perspective, this was a heart-rending burden and one that has woven deep sorrow into much of the literature and music of the region.

The Ottomans also introduced Islam to the region, which found large numbers of converts, particularly among Albanians and Bosnians. Muslim converts were concentrated in towns rather than the countryside or the mountains of the Balkans, which once again offered some sanctuary from foreign rule. Consequently, cosmopolitan urban centres of commerce formed, in which adherents of different faiths and carriers of various cultures coexisted peacefully side by side, allowing for an incredible interpenetration of influences. This religious variety was further enriched with the arrival of the Jews expelled from Spain in the late 15th century, who settled in Ottoman-controlled lands with the encouragement and permission of Constantinople. This Ottoman organising principle – by religion – slowed the development of a national consciousness. Religious, ethnic, linguistic and cultural differences did not prevent the people of the Balkans from living together in relative peace under Ottoman rule.

From the late 17th century onwards, Ottoman control over the Balkans began to wane. This, coupled with increasingly desperate and misguided attempts to cling onto Balkan territory, started to create a power vacuum in the region, the result of which was political anarchy and violence – an environment rife for the emergence of irredentist movements and new nation-states, as well as bids by the great (read: Western) powers, other European states and the new South East European nation-states to profit from the dissolution of the Ottoman Empire. The Habsburgs (rulers of what was to become the Austro-Hungarian Empire by 1867) took the opportunity to step in and expand into the Balkans and encouraged the further intermingling of people across the Balkans to fill lands depopulated by war and the flight of Turkish settlers. As the line of imperial control between the Habsburgs and the Osmanlis shifted, migrants from the south, predominantly identifying as Serb, were encouraged to move and protect the new frontiers, such as Krajina. The Habsburgs established a protectorate in Bosnia and Herzegovina in 1878 and eventually annexed it by 1908.

Throughout the 19th century and start of the 20th century, new Balkan nation-states came into being. Greece, Serbia and Bulgaria, unshackled from empire at a point in history where imperialist ideologies and agendas dominated political thought and policy, modelled themselves on the European powers. They sought to extend their power and influence across the Balkans through any means necessary, including military force, while often overtly supporting different guerrilla and irredentist movements that were fighting the Ottomans (and each other). Vying with each other for regional dominance, they pursued policies of expansion towards Balkan territory still under Ottoman control. However, the process of ethnic and religious homogenisation that had taken place in Western Europe had not occurred in the Balkans under Ottoman rule. Balkan-born, but often European-educated, elites leading the new wave of national consciousness and the birth of Balkan nations were trying to impose Western ideas of the nation-state – in which the nation was often imagined as a historically continuous and homogenous group with a shared ethnicity, language, culture and religion – onto a non-heterogenous, multi-ethnic, multi-religious, multi-cultural and multi-linguistic Balkan mosaic.

A series of events at the start of the 20th century precipitated a negative perception of the Balkans. Alexander I, King of Serbia and his wife were assassinated by a group of army conspirators in Belgrade in May 1903, which sent shockwaves through the European aristocracy. In August 1903, the Internal Macedonian Revolutionary Organisation rebelled against Ottoman rule, leading to a temporary liberation of the Republic of Kruševo. The uprising was crushed, but the so-called 'Macedonian Question' (how to carve up the strategically and economically important historic region of Macedonia, including the port of Thessaloniki, between Serbia, Bulgaria and Greece) became internationalised (and continues to rear its head to this day).

Meanwhile, the Ottoman Empire was crumbling. Various reform movements aimed at modernising the Ottoman Empire came together under the banner of the 'Young Turks'. Following the Young Turk Revolution of July 1908, the Young Turks seized power. Their attempts to revitalise the ailing Ottoman Empire (including constitutional, military, educational and industrial reforms) had some success internally, but their disastrous foreign policy ultimately led to its dissolution.

The two Balkan Wars of 1912–13 were a significant factor in the retreat of the Ottoman Empire from Europe. October 1912 saw the outbreak of the First Balkan War with Montenegro declaring war on the Ottoman Empire. A consequent alliance between Bulgaria, Greece, Montenegro and Serbia saw the expulsion of the Ottoman Empire from Macedonia and Thrace and the loss of almost all of its European territories, including Crete, to the alliance of Balkan states as well as the newly created Albania (following the Treaty of London in May 1913). This was soon followed by the Second Balkan War in June 1913, fought between Bulgaria and the remaining Balkan states (including Romania), largely over the division of Macedonia. Bulgaria attacked Serbia, which in turn allied with Greece to drive back Bulgaria. The Ottoman Empire intervened against Bulgaria and recovered part of eastern Thrace, including Edirne.

The Balkan Wars led to the establishment of a new balance of power in the region, with Bulgaria emerging defeated and intent on recovering territory, and Serbia and Greece emerging enlarged and confident. Montenegro and Romania gained territory and Macedonia was carved up. Albania emerged as an independent state (because neither Italy nor the Habsburgs wanted to allow Serbia to control the Adriatic). In June 1914, Archduke Franz Ferdinand was assassinated in Sarajevo, which was perceived as triggering the outbreak of the First World War, imperial collapse and socialist revolution. By the end of the First World War, Serbia, Montenegro, Romania and Greece were on the 'winning side' and Bulgaria, together with Hungary, Austria and the Ottoman Empire, were treated as defeated. All Balkan nation-states emerged dissatisfied with the outcome: the 'winners' felt they had been insufficiently rewarded and the 'losers' that they had been treated too harshly. The Kingdom of Serbs, Croats and Slovenes was born in 1918 out of the ashes of the Austro-Hungarian and Ottoman Empires. Its formation cut across several highly problematic and contentious First World War agreements, and the new state faced territorial disputes not of its own making (including with Italy over certain parts of the Adriatic – Trieste, Istria, Pula and Rijeka/Fiume). Nominally intended to represent Serbs, Croats and Slovenes (and Bosnians and Macedonians), it purported to (aggressively) take up the cause for all South Slavs during the interwar period, but in reality it became a Greater Serbian state with the eventual imposition of a royal dictatorship in 1929, when it became the Kingdom of Yugoslavia, ruled by Alexander I, King of Yugoslavia. King Alexander was assassinated in 1934, and the fragile framework lumbered on. Initially, King Alexander's successor, Prince Paul, tried to maintain neutrality, but he faced mounting pressure to join the Axis powers. In March 1941, a coup within the Yugoslav government overthrew Prince Paul, who had been inclined towards Axis cooperation. The new government, led by King Peter II and a group of officers, sought to strengthen ties with the Allies. This move led to swift retaliation by the Axis powers, who invaded Yugoslavia in April 1941. The invasion resulted in a rapid and tumultuous defeat for the Yugoslav armed forces. The country was subsequently dismembered, with various parts occupied by Nazi Germany, Italy, Hungary and Bulgaria. Resistance movements emerged, most notably the Yugoslav Partisans led by Josip Broz Tito, who played a pivotal role in both the Yugoslav resistance and victory over fascism and the liberation of Yugoslavia, as well as the defeat of Nazi Germany and the Axis. The complex dynamics and rivalries of the Second World War in the territory of Yugoslavia eventually contributed to the post-war creation of the Socialist Federal Republic of Yugoslavia. The new Yugoslavia (in many respects a successor to the interwar Kingdom of Yugoslavia) was formed in 1945. It was a federation composed of six republics: Bosnia and Herzegovina, Croatia, Macedonia, Montenegro, Serbia and Slovenia, and two autonomous provinces: Kosovo and Vojvodina. Yugoslav federalism was intended to offer a solution to (and, in retrospect, temporary respite from) the territorial rivalries of the region.

Domestically, Yugoslavia was a multi-ethnic and multi-religious state allowing a high degree of cultural and political economy for the constituent republics. It was also a unique experiment in socialism, adopting a form of self-management that aimed to combine elements of central economic planning with worker self-governance. Internationally, Yugoslavia pursued a policy of non-alignment during the Cold War, maintaining relations with both the Western and Eastern bloc. Tito served as the leader of Yugoslavia from its formation until his death in 1980, and his legacy remains a complex subject. The Yugoslav system faced various challenges, which increased after Tito's death, including ethnic tensions, economic difficulties and political rivalries between the republics. These ultimately culminated in the early 1990s and contributed to the disintegration of Yugoslavia and the subsequent wars, which were complex, interrelated and have left lasting scars on the region and its people.

In June 1991, Slovenia and Croatia declared their secession from Yugoslavia. In Slovenia's case, this led to the Ten-Day War with the Serb-dominated Yugoslav People's Army (JNA). Slovenia emerged victorious, independent and relatively unscathed, largely because of its distinct culture and history and more ethnically homogenous population. In autumn (fall) 1991, war (now known as the Croatian War of Independence) also broke out between Croatia and the JNA and lasted until a ceasefire was agreed in January 1992 (the Vance Peace Plan) and a United Nations (UN) Protection Force (UNPROFOR) was deployed to monitor the peace and new borders. Skirmishes nevertheless continued between Croats and Serbs into 1995.

Meanwhile, Macedonia declared its independence in September 1991. It managed to avoid entanglement in the wars of succession but faced challenges with Greece over the recognition of its sovereignty and name (and is now known, as of 2019, as North Macedonia). The complex multi-ethnic nature of Macedonia resulted in mounting tension between the Macedonian majority and Albanian minority (specifically the Albanian National Liberation Army), eventually escalating to near civil war in 2001, which was resolved with the Ohrid Framework Agreement. Bosnia and Herzegovina declared independence in April 1992, but fighting broke out between Bosnia and Herzegovina's multi-ethnic population comprising Bosniaks (Bosnian Muslims), Bosnian Serbs and Bosnian Croats. This deteriorated into a war, during which indiscriminate shelling, systematic ethnic cleansing and atrocities were committed on all sides, but in particular by paramilitary Bosnian Serbs and the JNA against Bosniaks – the most devastating being the siege of Sarajevo and the Srebrenica genocide. The Bosnian war of independence ended in November 1995 with the Dayton Peace Accords establishing a complex political structure in Bosnia and Herzegovina – a Bosniak-Croat federation and a Bosnian Serb Republic, with Sarajevo remaining as the undivided capital city.

Following the outbreak of the Bosnian War, the remaining entities of former Yugoslavia – Serbia and Montenegro – formed a new political union known as the Federal Republic of Yugoslavia (FRY), which included the still autonomous province of Kosovo and purported to be the successor state to the former Yugoslavia, but it was never recognised as such. In 2003, the FRY became the State Union of Serbia and Montenegro, which was in turn dissolved when Montenegro declared its independence in June 2006, leaving Serbia and Kosovo.

In Kosovo, growing pressure from the majority ethnic Albanians for greater autonomy had previously resulted in a civil war in 1998, once again with atrocities committed on all sides. As a response to a Serbian military offensive against the Kosovo Liberation Army, NATO launched a bombing campaign against Serbia in March 1999, prompting the then Serbian president, Slobodan Milošević, to order a retaliatory campaign of ethnic cleansing of Kosovar Albanians. NATO intervention eventually led to the withdrawal of Serbian forces and the establishment of a NATO-led international peacekeeping force in Kosovo (KFOR), which is gradually handing over responsibilities to the Kosovo police and other authorities. Tensions between Albanians and Serbs in Kosovo continue, with sporadic violence breaking out (such as in March 2004). Kosovo declared its independence from Serbia in February 2008, but although a significant number of countries around the world recognise its independence, Serbia does not.

Balkanism and 'Balkan cuisine'

In her seminal work *Imagining the Balkans*, Maria Todorova coins the term 'Balkanism'. It refers to a concept situated within ongoing theoretical debates in relation to orientalism and post-colonialism in which the imagined Balkans have often served as the European 'other', a repository of negative characteristics upon which a positive and self-congratulatory image of the 'European' could be built.

The origins of this conceptualisation of the Balkans can be traced back to discourse surrounding the region in the 19th century. The dissolution of the Ottoman Empire and the events leading up to the outbreak of the First World War, including the Balkan Wars, resulted in clichés and stereotypes about the 'Orient' becoming attributed to the Balkans. The region became synonymous with instability and violence and was infamously known as the 'powder-keg' of Europe. This stigmatisation gathered momentum throughout the 20th century, though temporarily paused between 1945 and 1991 for the lifespan of socialist Yugoslavia.

While the painful fragmentation of Yugoslavia impacted the Balkans negatively, it did not plunge the entire region into war. Nevertheless, constant use of the word Balkan when referencing the Yugoslav wars of the 1990s rekindled the indiscriminate use of old derogatory stereotypes about the region and its history as unstable, unpredictable and violent. 'Balkan' became, once again, a heavily loaded term, one that was synonymous with the former Yugoslavia, fragmentation ('Balkanisation') and internecine conflict. To be Balkan was to be bloodthirsty, murderous, backwards. Former Yugoslavia – and we, the Yugoslavs – became defined for posterity solely by our conflicts.

In the face of such prejudice – and during the fallout from political, economic and social turmoil – the championing of our cuisine has been low priority. Yet, in recent times, cuisine has started to be deployed across the whole Balkan region as a nationalist fig leaf. Many people in the Balkans (and even the reigning governments) have formed strong opinions about so-called national dishes, which are analysed through the lens of ethnic nationalism and regional geography and are deployed for various populist purposes – debates about the ownership of *ajvar*, sour cabbage *sarma*, *ćevapčići* or *štruklji* being notable examples. In popular culture across the region, dishes that traverse political borders have been proudly presented as the exclusive invention of modern 'national' identities. Despite the relatively fixed nature of the current borders of Balkan nation-states (ongoing political tensions relating to North Macedonia, Kosovo and Bosnia and Herzegovina notwithstanding), longstanding questions of identity, language, ethnicity, territorial claims rooted in history and irredentist aspirations can become, directly or obliquely, the object of discussion through food. Seeking to 'liberate' or reunify any part of a 'nation' left outside the current borders of a nation-state through the myth of a national cuisine is culinary nationalism.

Admittedly, there are clear benefits to defining or delineating cuisines, dishes or food products along national lines. For example, for existing nation-states, it can serve as a bastion against cultural appropriation. For nation-states denied self-determination or whose very reason for existence is still being challenged on historical, geographical, political, cultural, ethnic, religious, linguistic or other grounds, food becomes a way of preserving identity – a way of claiming and ensuring the continued psychological, emotional and spiritual (if not geographical) existence of a nation. Although the concept of a national cuisine, like the nation-state it attaches to, is a myth, it would be remiss to underplay the importance of food in the intricacies of identity – real or imagined. Food can also be attached to cultural, ethnic or religious groups, and this may be even more meaningful than a delineation along national – or nationalistic – lines. Much of our perceived identity as humans is inextricably linked to the lands we emerge from and the bounty from those lands that has ensured our survival, both physical and cultural and spiritual. At a time in our global history of unprecedented migration, forced or voluntary, when so many are uprooted from the land they call home, food becomes the thing that can travel with us.

Yet food, which transcends any modern physical political borders is, or rather should be, inherently anti-nationalist. The relatively recent emergence of nation-states in global history means that delineating cuisine or dishes along national lines can have the effect of negating history that predates the establishment of the nation-state, thus trivialising the interconnectedness of ancient foodways. Food remains an artifact that evidences and preserves the past more stubbornly than anything.

It is for these reasons that in my Balkan kitchen I do not cook Bosnian, Croatian, Kosovan, Macedonian, Montenegrin, Serbian or Slovenian food. With the greatest curiosity, respect and love, I cook and write about 'Balkan cuisine', trying to discover and describe the intricacies of the origins of a dish, its historical layers of identity, the ancient foodways it has taken into, through or out of the Balkans, its association with the modern myth of nation-states and current political boundaries and, perhaps more meaningfully, its significance to various cultural, ethnic, geographic, linguistic, religious or other groups.

There is of course no such thing as a homogenous Balkan cuisine. As a concept it is inherently supranational and as elusive as the contours of the Balkans. However, in its implicit regionalism lies (some) salvation. For me, it is a necessary artifice, a safe space from which to explore and celebrate both the commonality across, and the culinary diversity of, the Balkans without falling prey to the problematic delineation of cuisine along national lines and inadvertently perpetuating nationalist or political agendas. I am certainly guilty of Todorova's Balkanism, but I am the other, writing from within my 'otherness', attempting to take ownership of the symbolic othering of the Balkans in order to (perhaps naively) reclaim the word Balkan and turn it into something positive, so that through food I can explore and celebrate the incredible cultural and culinary wealth of the region.

A UNIQUE CULINARY CROSSROADS

So, what then is 'Balkan cuisine'? It is the culmination of waves of human evolution and migration, the product of both nascent civilisations and occupying empires that have traversed through or dominated the region, either fleetingly or for prolonged periods of time. This is not uniquely Balkan. There are many parts of our world that have been the thoroughfares of human history. But what is unique is the sheer variety of influences found in the Balkans at any given point in history, which over time have created an extraordinarily profuse Balkan heterogeneity – in all respects, but especially the cuisine.

It is a cuisine born at a crossroads of human history, on the line of demarcation between the Hellenistic and non-Hellenistic world, the Eastern and Western Roman Empires, Byzantine Orthodox Christianity and Roman Catholicism, a Muslim Ottoman Empire and a Christian Western Europe. The Balkans have been the non-aligned buffer between the communist 'East' and the capitalist 'West' and, most recently, the 'other' Europe on the doorstep of the European Union. A frontier where ideas and ideologies were born or arrived, intermingled, were adapted and hybridised, and which remained or continued their travels and influence in all directions. A place where baklava and syrup-soaked sweets so beloved across the Levant sit comfortably alongside the creamy cakes and pastries of Central Europe – in each case transformed into something distinctly Balkan. Where the Ottoman penchant for wrapping and stuffing vegetables, greens and fruits has taken on a life of its own – often combined with the Balkan obsession for fermentation, such in sour cabbage *sarma*. Where *burek* has many meanings, depending on where you are in the region. Where the mixture of civilisations produced different results depending on the length of exposure to a relevant influence – for example, the southern Balkans, which remained under Ottoman rule longest, retain more of a Levantine flavour in their cuisine. Where traces can be found from across the world: Europe, the Levant, Persia, Asia and the Americas, the latter in the corn, tomatoes, peppers and beans introduced via the Columbian Exchange and Ottoman Empire.

The cuisine obviously differs across the region, reflecting the distinct natural conditions, flora and fauna, climate, topography, socioeconomic and political factors, culture, ethnicity, religion, family traditions and preferences of each area. The climate and topography ranges from Mediterranean in the south and along the Adriatic – allowing olives, figs, grapes and many sun-loving fruits to flourish – and temperate across the central arable and forest regions, to extremely harsh and bitterly cold across the rugged mountains. Successive waves of migration into the region of more dominant or less peacefully inclined cultures, or the arrival of conquering armies or empires, displaced a large part of the indigenous population, driving them from the fertile lowlands into the mountains, which offer not only wild game, but extensive upland grazing. These mountains became sanctuaries of survival, centres of herding (allowing the production of delicious cheeses, dairy and meat products), oases of microcultures and havens for all, including outlaws and freedom fighters.

This combination of the Mediterranean, Adriatic and mountain ranges makes for unique terroirs across the region that are particularly suitable for wine production, both of international and indigenous grape varieties, the latter including whites such as Temjanika, Žilavka, Smederevka, Morava, Malvazija, Graševina, Assyrtiko and Krstač and reds such as Vranac, Plavac Mali, Kaštelanski Crljenak, Dingač, Prokupac, Teran, Kallmet, Babić and Mavrud.

Grain and livestock dominate the vast, fertile Pannonian Plain. Coastal areas are naturally dominated by fruits of the sea. Inland areas use freshwater fish from the rivers and lakes and, of course, meats, which are cured, smoked, grilled, slow-roasted or otherwise slow-cooked.

In the southern regions, sunflower oil forms the basis for cooking; in coastal regions, olive oil. As you move inland and north towards Central Europe, lard reigns supreme, but it is used throughout the region for baked goods, religious affiliations permitting. Some parts are characterized by the production and use of wheat, others by millet, rye, corn, rice or buckwheat. Breads and grains form the basis of the Balkan diet, supplemented heavily by dairy and fresh fruits and vegetables (though immediate geographic reality has an influence on the local diet, with coastal areas varying significantly). Lush fruits and vegetables dominate the entirety of the region; they are eaten seasonally and preserved for winter. Greens and herbs are gathered for cooking as well as medicinal purposes.

Different socioeconomic factors have resulted in a distinction between the food enjoyed in urban areas versus more rural areas. Different religions – Christian, Muslim, Jewish – as well as different ethnicities each have food uniquely associated with their respective customs and traditions.

As a repository of many cultural, ideological, religious, political and other exchanges and confrontations, the Balkans have not only birthed but also absorbed many diverse culinary traditions, resulting in one of the most dynamic, multi-layered, complex and, therefore, in my opinion, interesting cuisines in the world. The plethora of influences has created a delicious amalgamation. The unifying culinary ethos is undoubtedly one of *cucina povera*: using all the bounty off

the land (cultivated or foraged); treating humble ingredients respectfully and with ingenuity; eating seasonally and preserving overabundance for periods of scarcity; wasting nothing. It is adaptation out of necessity, a stubbornness of spirit born out of millennia of historical criss-crossing, empires, oppression, adversity, wars, poverty and massive exoduses from the region. Something truly special and delicious created out of almost nothing. But it is also something more, it is *cucina sopravvivenza* – a cuisine that has, despite everything, survived. It is high time the Balkans takes its rightful place as one of the most unique culinary crossroads in the world.

Introduction

A Personal Note

Selecting which recipes made it into the book was by far the hardest task of writing it. The recipes that made the cut are intended to be representative of the kinds of dishes found across the Balkans, or else they are particularly unique ones, or simply ones I loved most. There are many others I wish I could have included, other aspects of our cuisine I wish I could have covered and more stories to be told.

I make no claim that this cookbook is a historical study or that these are 'authentic' or 'traditional' recipes because what is authentic or traditional to one family may not be to another, especially in a region as diverse and multifaceted as the Balkans. Instead, I have tried my best to describe some of my findings on how dishes are made, variations of them, stories, myths or customs surrounding them, or their history to the extent I have been able to uncover it with any certainty. Any omissions or mistakes are my own. I have also tried to describe how and why I deviate – often because I have needed to adapt traditional and time-consuming methods to a busy working life or substitute indigenous ingredients that are not often available internationally, but sometimes simply because of personal taste.

This book is, above all, my love letter to the Balkans, told through recipes and stories. My hope for *The Balkan Kitchen* is that it makes you fall as hopelessly in love with the Balkans, its people and its cuisine as I am.

BREAKFAST

DORUČEK

The breakfast culture across the Balkan region is as varied, vibrant and diverse as its landscape and ranges from the simple, such as *popara* (stale bread rehydrated with milk, to make a kind of bread porridge), to the elaborate.

For many, the day begins with a fortifying cup of coffee. The further south you go, the more likely that cup of coffee is to be Turkish (or Serbian/Bosnian/Macedonian/Greek or even 'oriental' coffee, as more modern nation-building sensibilities now dictate). Children begin with warmed milk – sometimes with caramel or cocoa – yoghurt or juice.

My favourite childhood breakfasts were a comforting bowl of either polenta or *tarana*, cooked with a little butter and a generous grating of *sirenje* cheese over the top. Otherwise, I might have *griz*, a porridge made from semolina and milk, which I loved sweetened with a little sugar and topped with a dusting of cinnamon and perhaps a drizzle of wild honey. Often, we would have a selection of freshly baked goods – a slice of *burek*, *simit pogača*, *gevrek* (bagels, similar to Turkish *simit)*, or a variety of *kifli* or other sweet or savoury breads and pastries from our favourite bakery. These would always be bought first thing in the morning and either eaten on the go with drinking yoghurt or *ayran*, which is considered by many a mandatory accompaniment for baked goods, or be brought home and made part of a spread featuring all manner of sweet and savoury accompaniments: various cheeses and cured meats, eggs, tomatoes, peppers, olives and homemade preserves – from *ajvar* to *pekmez* or even *slatko*. Wonderfully fresh bread, still warm from the oven, with quince, green fig or sour cherry *slatko* and a hard, salty cheese, remains one of my favourite breakfasts.

Things like *palačinki*, *uštipci* or apples in *šlafor* were reserved for weekend breakfasts, to be enjoyed at leisure while spending time together.

Seasonal fruits were always on offer and would accompany any breakfast – or any meal, for that matter. In the summer, my grandmother and I often started and ended our day eating bread, *sirenje* and crisp, cold watermelon, bought fresh from the field from the back of the farmer's roadside truck.

What are now thought of as more 'traditional' breakfasts across the region reflect a time when for many people, breakfast was an opportunity to 'load up' and line the stomach with the kind of hearty food that could keep you going for an entire day of hard labour – from fields to mountains via factories and mines. In Croatia, you would find the utter comfort of *Zagorski žganci* served with *cvarci*. Serbia and North Macedonia boast *kačamak* – a maize-based porridge that some love to combine with cheese, *kajmak* or yoghurt.

In Bosnia and Herzegovina, you will find *ječmenka*, a porridge made from barley cooked with milk, sugar and a hint of cinnamon. In Montenegro, *kaštradina*, cornmeal porridge served with smoked and dried mutton, is a staple. Slovenia's *ajdova kaša* and *ajdovi žganci* feature buckwheat with a variety of toppings. Kosovo and Albania delight in *flija* or *fli* – pancake batter and yoghurt or *kajmak* baked layer by layer under a *sac*, while in North Macedonia you will find a similar dish called *gjomleze* baked under a *vrshnik*, as well as *pitulici*, in which the layers are pre-baked and then layered with *sirenje* before being baked once more.

Really, the recipes included in this chapter may be eaten any time of day. At home, we often have a variation on the theme of eggs and tomatoes for a light supper. It was a lucky day indeed when my grandmother or mother had baked something the day before and I could have leftover Pita, Milibrod or perhaps Kifli with one of the mezes that can be found in For Sharing.

**MAKES 16–20
(SERVES 4–6)**

Palačinki

2 medium eggs
400 ml (14 fl oz/generous 1½ cups) whole (full-fat) milk
150 ml (5 fl oz/scant ⅔ cup) sparkling water
1 tablespoon sunflower oil
200 g (7 oz/1⅔ cups) plain (all-purpose) flour, sifted
2 teaspoons caster (superfine) sugar
½ teaspoon fine sea salt
20–25 g (¾–1 oz) unsalted butter, for frying

OPTIONAL TOPPINGS
fresh fruit
chocolate spread
homemade *dzem*, marmalade, pekmez or slatko (see pages 246–251)
ground nuts
lemon juice and sugar
cheeses
smoked or other deli meats

There are few things that better encapsulate childhood in the Balkans than a stack of freshly made *palačinki* (or *palačinke*) at grandma's house. They are our version of crêpes. We have them sweet, savoury, stuffed and baked or stuffed and fried. The latter variety is a favourite starter at weddings, usually stuffed with cheese and ham and then breaded and deep-fried and served with a variation on tartar sauce. The women in my family have always added sparkling water to the batter. It makes them beautifully light and airy and I dare not mess with inherited wisdom. I like them savoury with white cheese, or with a simple topping of ground walnuts, lemon juice and sugar. If you have greater self-restraint than we do and you happen to have leftover *palačinki*, my great-grandmother, Keva, would roll them with a little raw cacao and sugar, arrange them in a saucepan, cover with milk and simmer gently until the milk was nearly all absorbed. When I do this I also drizzle a little melted dark chocolate over the top before serving.

Crack the eggs into a large bowl and whisk lightly. Add the milk, sparkling water, oil, flour, sugar and salt and whisk until smooth. Cover and leave to stand for at least 30 minutes.

Heat a medium (approximately 20 cm/8 inches diameter) non-stick frying pan on a medium-high heat.

Add a little butter to the pan and tilt it so the butter coats the surface. Pour in a ladle of batter and tilt the pan so the batter spreads evenly over the base. Cook for 1–2 minutes, or until small holes appear on the surface, the edges start to come away from the sides and the underside is lightly browned. With a butter or palette knife, loosen and flip the *palačinka* over. Cook for a further minute or until cooked through. Serve warm with your choice of topping.

Note
Stack the *palačinki* while they are still hot so they do not stick together. They keep well covered either at room temperature for a day, or 2–3 days in the refrigerator. To reheat, microwave them in a stack for around 30 seconds.

 Breakfast

**MAKES 20-24,
(SERVES 2-4)**

Priganice

10 g (½ oz) fast-action dried yeast
1 tablespoon caster (superfine) sugar
75 ml (2½ fl oz/5 tablespoons) lukewarm whole (full-fat) milk
175 g (6 oz/scant 1½ cups) plain (all-purpose) flour
½ teaspoon fine sea salt
1 medium egg, lightly beaten
50 ml 3½ tablespoons) lukewarm water
1 tablespoon rakija (or šljivovica, orahovača or rum)
sunflower oil, for frying

'Ah! But you are ours!' That is what Vojka Sekulić said to me when I told her where I came from. We were staying at her house in Perast, Montenegro, because I was doing a series of open water swims around the Bay of Kotor. That morning, before we set out on the boat, she had made the most delicious *priganice*. That is what these fried delights are called in Montenegro, but they are variously known as *fritule* in Croatia, *miške* in Slovenia, *tiganici* or *uštipci* in North Macedonia, *petulla* in Kosovo and Albania and variations on *uštipci* elsewhere across the Balkans (confusingly *uštipci* is also a term used for meatballs flavoured with cheese in Leskovac, Serbia). They are made in countless ways, but the unifying theme is a deep-fried enriched dough, similar to a doughnut, which can be flavoured with citrus peel or spices (or anything), and eaten sweet or savoury. They are very popular for breakfast, but you can also find them as street food snacks.

I told her that the *priganice* tasted just like my grandmother's (this recipe). She hugged me, and when she found out I was from North Macedonia she uttered that phrase that has stuck with me ever since. So much is encapsulated in those words. It implies an inherent understanding, a shared history and love that transcends political boundaries. Belonging. We had them with her homemade wild sour cherry slatko, honey and beautiful fresh *Pljevaljski sir* (a hard white sheep's or cow's milk cheese from Montenegro). For the rest of the week, she went above and beyond to make the most incredible breakfasts, intent on exceeding herself, just like all the other Balkan women I know. *Ti si naša* – you are ours.

Note

You can scrape the batter into a piping bag and pipe the mixture into the oil, using scissors to snip pieces off at regular intervals. This will give you slightly more uniform *priganice*, but I rather like the spoon technique as it results in uniquely charming shapes. You can also use this batter to make what are known as *mekici* in North Macedonia – a palm-sized version that is stretched out as it is dropped into the oil to fry. Flavour the dough with lemon or orange zest if you like, as well as spices such as ground cinnamon, cloves and nutmeg. The alcohol is important as it prevents the *priganice* absorbing too much oil. My friend Alexandra Alexandrova Oberstar's mother, Zora, used *orahovača* in her *fritule* (see page 257) instead of *rakija*, which gives a wonderful flavour.

In a small bowl, mix together the yeast, sugar and milk, then set aside for 5–10 minutes until frothy.

Sift the flour and salt into a separate large bowl. Make a well in the middle and add the yeast mixture, egg, half the water and the *rakija*. With an electric whisk, beat until smooth and aerated. The consistency should be a thick batter (like raw choux pastry). If it is too thick and it is difficult to stir, add more of the water. Cover and set aside to rest for at least 30 minutes.

Pour the oil into a medium deep saucepan until it is one-third full. Heat over a medium-high heat until the oil reaches 175°C (350°F) or a little batter dropped into it sizzles immediately.

Using a teaspoon, scoop out a large marble-sized amount of batter, then use another teaspoon to shape it into a ball before carefully dropping it into the hot oil. Fry the *priganice* in batches of 4–6 (don't overcrowd the pan), for 2–3 minutes, turning occasionally, until they are puffed up and golden brown. Lift them out with a slotted spoon and place them on a tray lined with paper towels to drain. Serve warm, with sweet or savoury accompaniments.

 Breakfast

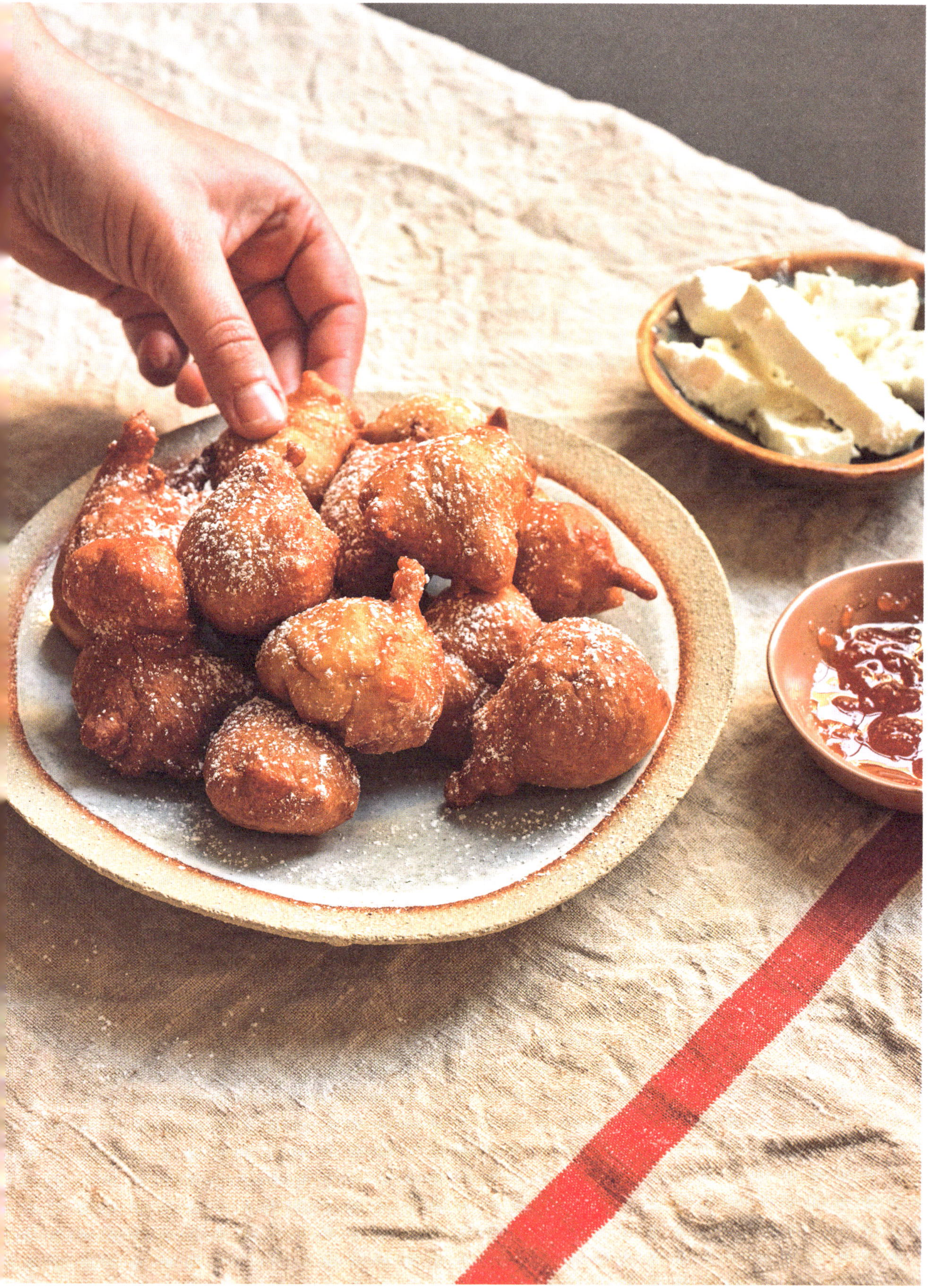

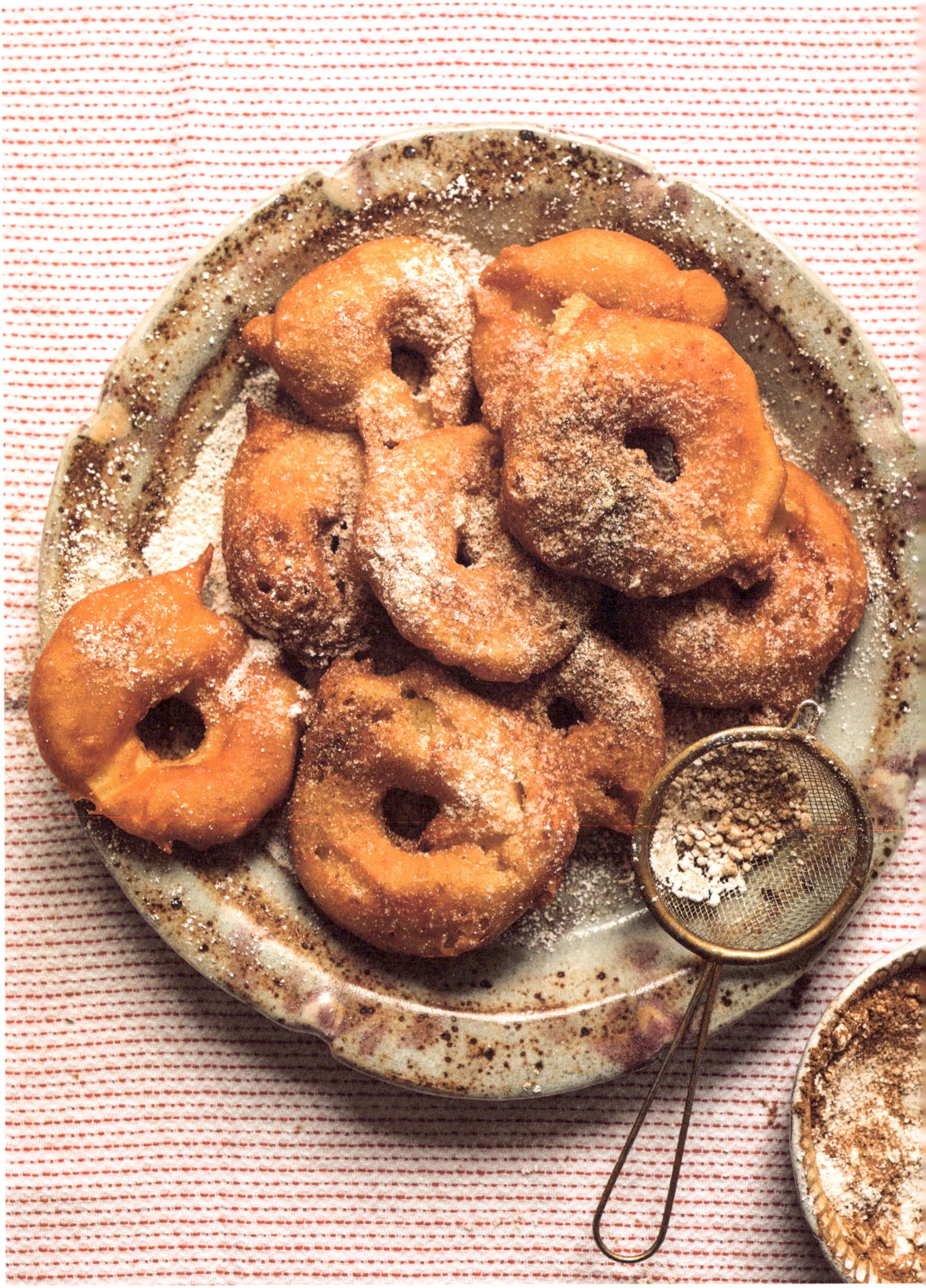

SERVES 4

Apples in Šlafor

125 g (4½ oz/1 cup) plain (all-purpose) flour
1 medium egg
100 ml (3½ fl oz/scant ½ cup) whole (full-fat) milk
25 g (1 oz) unsalted butter, melted and cooled
½ teaspoon baking powder
1 teaspoon caster (superfine) sugar
¼ teaspoon ground cinnamon, plus extra for dusting
½ teaspoon vanilla bean paste
1 teaspoon lemon zest
1 teaspoon rum (optional)
⅛ teaspoon fine sea salt
sunflower oil, for frying
2–3 eating (dessert) apples, peeled, cored and sliced in 1 cm (½ inch) thick rings
icing (confectioners') sugar, for dusting

Perhaps the most appropriate name for a weekend breakfast, these are apples in dressing gowns (*šlafor* or *šlafrok* being adaptations of the German word, *schlafrock*). It was a happy weekend indeed when my mother made these as a special treat. They would also work very well as a dessert with ice cream, but for me these are the perfect thing to eat on a weekend morning, still wearing your pyjamas and dressing gown.

First, prepare the batter. Mix together the flour, egg, milk, butter, baking powder, sugar, cinnamon, vanilla, lemon zest, rum (if using) and salt in a large bowl and beat with an electric whisk until well combined and smooth. Cover and set aside to rest for at least 30 minutes.

Pour 2 cm (¾ inch) oil into a medium frying pan. Heat over a medium-high heat until the oil reaches 175°C (350°F) or a little batter dropped into it sizzles immediately.

Drop the apple slices into the batter and coat them well. Lift out four to six coated slices and place them in the pan, frying for 2–3 minutes on each side until they are slightly puffed up and golden brown. Lift them out with a slotted spoon and place them on a tray lined with paper towels to drain. Repeat with the remaining apple slices. Dust the apple fritters with icing sugar and a pinch of cinnamon. Serve warm.

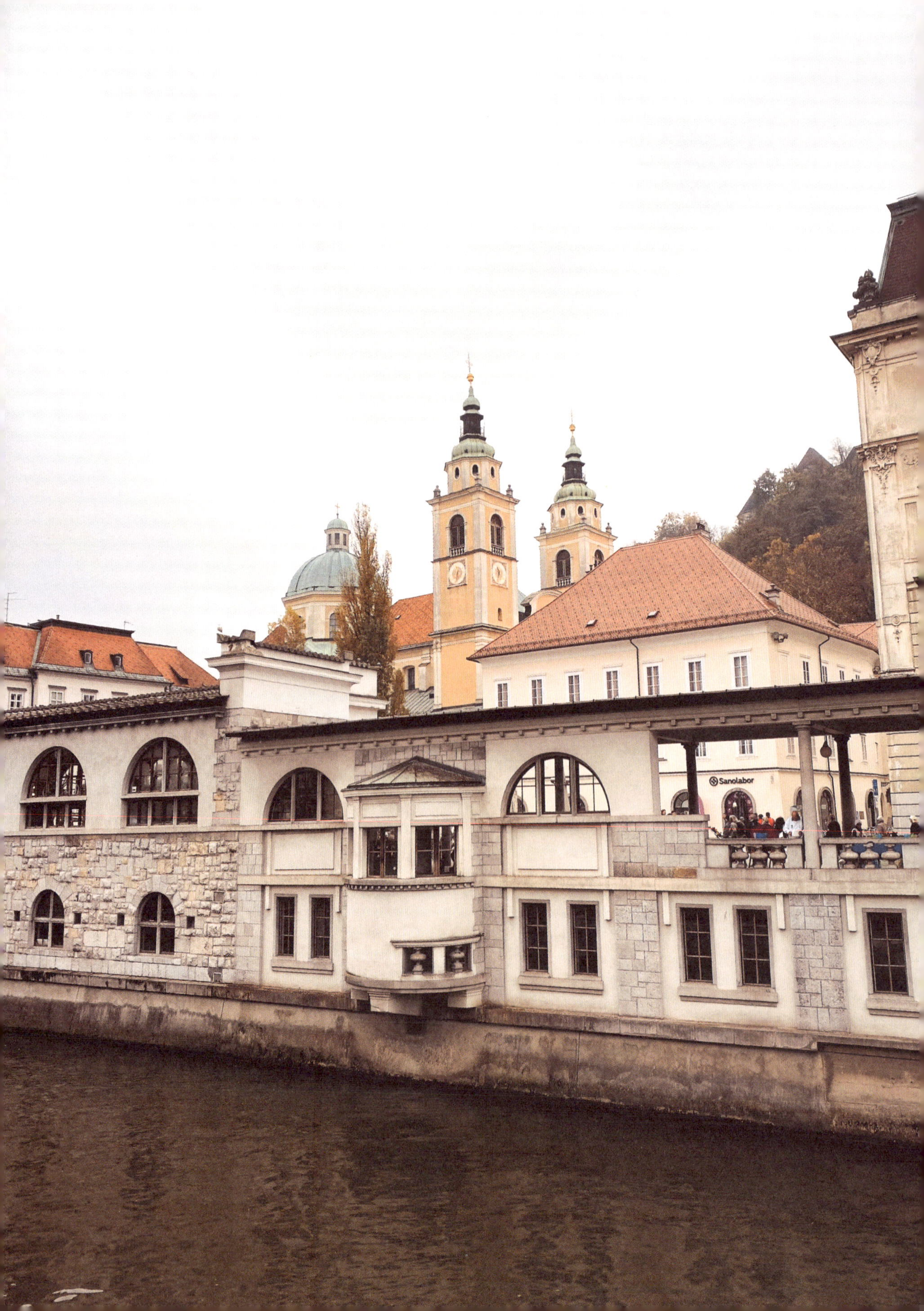
Sanolabor

SERVES 12–14

Pumpkin Štrukljí

300 g (10½ oz/2 cups) buckwheat flour
1 teaspoon fine sea salt
300 ml (10 fl oz/1¼ cups) boiling water
1 teaspoon sunflower or pumpkin oil, plus extra for brushing
1 medium egg, lightly beaten
80–100 g (2¾–3½ oz/scant ⅔–generous ¾ cup) plain (all-purpose) flour, plus extra as needed and for dusting

FOR THE FILLING
500–600 g (1 lb 2–1 lb 5 oz) grey-skinned pumpkin (such as Crown Prince), deseeded and cut into 10 cm (4 inch) chunks, or 1 x 425 g (15 oz) tin of pumpkin puree
50 g (1¾ oz/scant ½ cup) ground walnuts
100 g light brown soft sugar
1½ tablespoons ground cinnamon
1 teaspoon ground nutmeg

FOR THE TOPPING
30 g (1 oz) unsalted butter
40 g (1½ oz) set honey
¼ teaspoon ground cinnamon
¼ teaspoon sea salt flakes

Note
The dough is incredibly versatile, so feel free to experiment with different fillings. A simple cottage cheese, sour cream, egg and tarragon filling works really well here, served with some breadcrumbs lightly toasted in butter.

Štrukljí are perhaps one of the most loved dishes in Slovenia and north-western Croatia. They are rolled dumplings typically made from wheat or buckwheat flour and they can be made with a very wide variety of fillings, from sweet – such as apples, poppy seeds, walnuts – to savoury – such as *skuta* (a young curd or cottage cheese), tarragon and so on. They can be steamed, boiled, baked or fried and are often served as an accompaniment to meat and gravy or one of Slovenia's hearty soups and stews. Croatia's *Zagorski štrukljí* from the Zagorje region are a particularly delicious variant, filled with cheese and baked in a sour cream sauce. Once a festive dish reserved for special occasions and popular among the 17th century urban elites, *štrukljí* have become an everyday dish.

On my last trip to Ljubljana, I spent the day wandering the city in search of the iconic buildings designed by Jože Plečnik. Seen as the father of Slovenian architecture, Ljubljana owes a significant part of its design identity to him. You will also find his iconic buildings in Belgrade, Vienna and Prague. In Plečnik's covered market along the Ljubljanica River, reminiscent of something from Venice, there are a number of humble Slovenian restaurants, bakeries, fishmongers and butchers. Tucked under the arcazdes is a place called Moji Štrukljí Slovenije which has taken the art of *štrukljí* to another level, using combinations of any kind of dough and filling you can imagine. They more than fuelled my exploration of Ljubljana. Taking inspiration (and liberty) from them, here is my version.

Preheat the oven to 180°C fan (400°F).

First, make the filling. Place the pumpkin flesh side up in a roasting tin and bake in the oven for 40–50 minutes or until the flesh is tender. Remove from the oven and allow to cool, then scoop out and roughly chop the flesh. You should have 400–425 g (14–15 oz). Put the pumpkin flesh, walnuts, sugar, cinnamon and nutmeg into a large bowl and mix well to combine.

To make the dough, sift the buckwheat flour into a large bowl. Add the salt and pour over the boiling water. Stir well with a wooden spoon until there are no lumps and the mixture comes together into a dough. Set aside to cool. When cool to the touch, add the oil and egg and sift in 80 g (2¾ oz/scant ⅔ cup) of the flour. Mix everything again to form a soft dough. If the dough is too wet and sticky, add the rest of the flour.

Lightly dust a work surface with plain flour and tip out the dough. Knead for 6–8 minutes or until you have a smooth, soft and pliable dough. Place the dough back in the bowl and brush the surface with a little oil, then cover and set aside to rest in a warm place for at least 30 minutes.

Once the dough has rested, tip it out onto a well floured work surface and roll it out into a large neat rectangle, about 32 x 40 cm (12½ x 16 inches) and no more than 5 mm (¼ inch) thick. Spread the filling evenly over the dough so that it is completely covered, but leaving a 3 cm (1¼ inch) gap along one long edge. Starting from the other long edge, roll the dough up tightly. Cut the log into two equal pieces. Brush two large pieces of cling film (plastic wrap) with oil and wrap each roll tightly in the cling film, making them as neat and cylindrical as possible. Twist the edges of the cling film to seal and either tie a knot or use a little kitchen twine to tie the edges of the cling film securely.

Breakfast

Recipe continued overleaf ↪

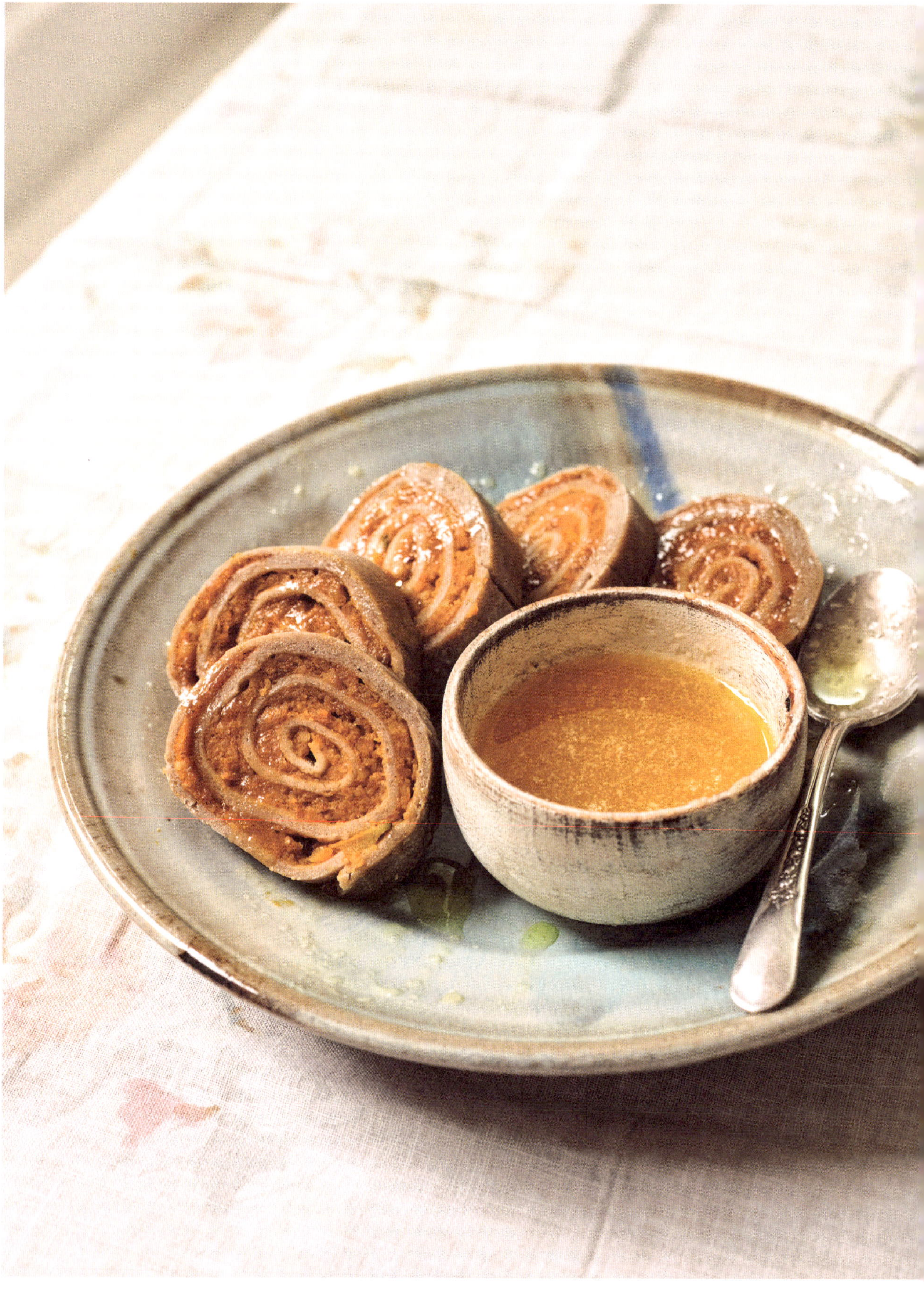

Bring a large saucepan of water to a gentle simmer over a medium heat and add the rolls. Cook for 25 minutes. Remove and allow to cool.

To make the topping, melt the butter in a small saucepan over a medium-high heat. Remove from the heat, then add the honey, cinnamon and salt and mix well. Pour into a small serving bowl and set aside to cool slightly; it will thicken as it cools.

To serve, unwrap the rolls and slice into 2 cm (¾ inch) thick slices, spoon a little of the honey butter topping over each spiral.

Breakfast

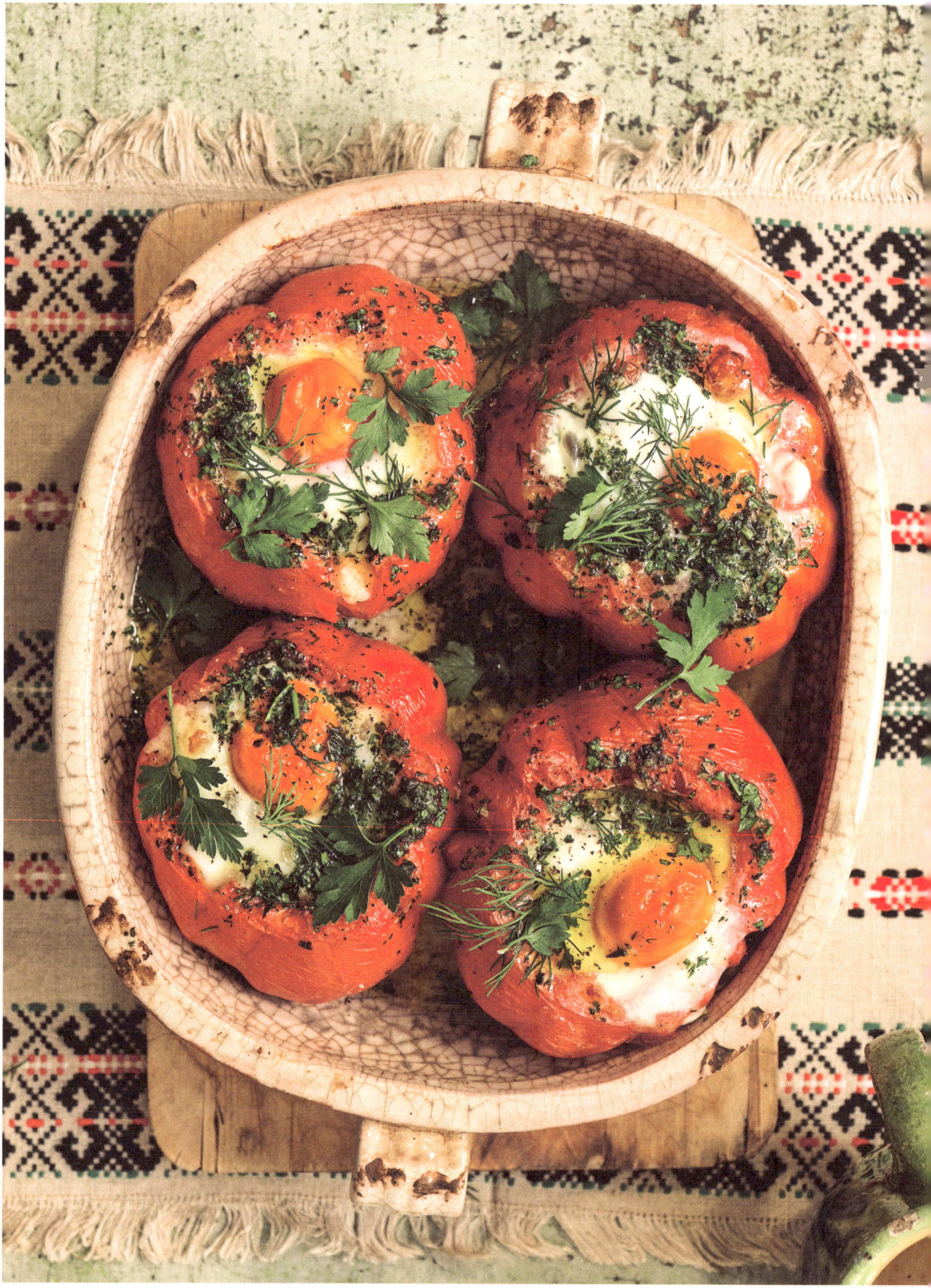

SERVES 4

Eggs and Tomatoes

4 large ripe beef (beefsteak) or bull's heart tomatoes
20 g (¾ oz) čvarci (or smoked ham), plus extra to serve
40 g (1½ oz) kashkaval (or Cheddar), grated
2 tablespoons olive oil, plus extra for drizzling
1–2 garlic cloves, crushed
10 g (½ oz) fresh soft herbs, such as parsley, oregano, dill and mint, leaves/fronds picked and finely chopped, plus extra to serve
½ teaspoon sea salt flakes, plus extra to serve
4 medium eggs
freshly ground black pepper

Eggs and tomatoes are a staple in any Balkan kitchen. A family favourite for many is *kajgana* – something between scrambled eggs, an omelette and a frittata. Lightly whisked eggs are rippled through whatever vegetables happen to be in season: from greens such as young *blitva* (Swiss chard) and bountiful alliums (leeks, spring onions/scallions) to peppers and tomatoes. Or, the eggs might be cooked with *sataraš*, a stew of onions, tomatoes and peppers. Add any of the beautiful cheeses from across the region and you have not just breakfast, but a quick meal for any time of day. I particularly loved an Istrian variant of wild *šparoge* (asparagus) braised in a little extra virgin olive oil with eggs added almost as an afterthought.

One of my favourite takes on this theme is eggs IN tomatoes. This is colloquially known in North Macedonia as 'mother-in-law's eyes' – though I cannot trace the origin or reason for the name. I suppose it comes from days when young brides would have moved into the home of their husband's family and were constantly under the watchful eyes of their mother-in-law. I prefer to think of them as the sun caught in a tomato. The flavour of Balkan tomatoes is indescribable and difficult to replicate. They are lush, baked to perfection in the summer sun, especially in more sun-drenched parts of region. We use them for everything, eat them with everything. If you are like me, you eat them like apples, the tomato juices dribbling down your arms. Local tomato variants of *volovo srce* (bull's heart) or *jabučar* (literally 'apple tomato') at the peak of their summer ripeness are huge and would comfortably hold an egg (or three). Use the biggest tomatoes you can find. If they aren't quite ripe yet, let them bask in the sunshine on your windowsill for a day or two before using them.

Preheat the oven to 180°C fan (400°F). Line a medium baking tray (pan) with baking parchment.

Carefully cut out the core of each tomato, keeping them whole and taking care not to pierce the skin. Using a teaspoon, scoop out as much of the pulp, seeds and juice as you can (reserve it for sauces). Place the tomatoes in the baking tray.

Distribute the *čvarci* and cheese evenly between the tomatoes.

Combine the oil, garlic, herbs, salt and a generous grind of black pepper in a small bowl and mix well. Drizzle a teaspoon of the oil mixture into each tomato. Carefully crack one egg into each tomato (feel free to beat the egg lightly if you prefer).

Bake in the oven for 30–35 minutes or until the tomatoes are tender and the skin blistered, with the eggs just set. Serve with a drizzle more of the oil over each tomato (serving the rest alongside), a pinch of salt and scatter some roughly chopped *čvarci* and fresh herbs on top.

Note
Use *duvan čvarci* if you can find them.

Breakfast

SERVES 4-6

Kačamak

1 litre (34 fl oz/4¼ cups) water
½ tablespoon fine sea salt
100 g (3½ oz) pork fat (or ghee)
350 g (12 oz) finely ground cornmeal

FOR THE ČVARCI CRUMB

50 g (1¾ oz) čvarci (or smoked ham), finely chopped
1 teaspoon Aleppo pepper
½ teaspoon chilli (hot pepper) flakes (optional)
¼ teaspoon sea salt flakes
freshly ground black pepper

TO SERVE

100 g (3½ oz) cheese of your choice, or more to taste
200 g (7 oz/generous ¾ cup) plain set yoghurt, or more to taste

Imagine yourself in a cosy wooden cabin, looking out onto incredible views of snow-covered peaks. It's a crisp but sunny winter's day, with the freshest mountain air. You've just had the best sleep, perhaps ever. This savoury porridge is your breakfast, made with pork fat rendered from home-reared pigs and served with the freshest white mountain cheese and yoghurt. Some *kajmak* (a Balkan clotted cream, see page 261) too, perhaps. Simple, nutritious, hearty and incredibly filling – you are ready for a day of mountaineering or skiing, or just general frolicking in the snow. Kačamak. I often wonder about the name – it may be derived from the Ottoman Turkish word for 'escape' (*kaçmak*), but is that an allusion to rebels against the Ottoman Empire hiding in the mountains and evading capture, or to the cooking technique of allowing steam to escape through the cornmeal? In Montenegro, it is made with *Žuti Jarik* (Yellow Jarik) corn, a hardy mountain flint corn, thought to be one of the oldest varieties of corn in the Balkans. In eastern Serbia and parts of Bulgaria, you find *Svrljig* or *Svrljiški belmuž*, a porridge made with *Svrlig* white cheese curds and Beli Osmak corn (grown in the mountainous areas of Bosnia and Herzegovina, Croatia, Slovenia and Serbia). In North Macedonia, corn porridge is also known as *bakardan*, after the Bakardan peak of the Shar Mountains. You might also come across it as *pura* in Croatia. In Bosnia, Montenegro, Kosovo and Albania, you can also find a version of *kačamak* called *tučenjak* ('beaten' or 'pounded') made with potatoes and a little bit of cornmeal, which I believe was born out of necessity (when flour of any type would have been scarce). The potatoes and cornmeal are beaten until smooth, which requires some serious arm muscle. In Montenegro, I have also eaten a version of *kačamak* layered with cheese and scrambled eggs, and there is also a dish called *cicvara*, where the cornmeal is cooked with milk (and sometimes *kajmak*). In Serbia, it is often served with delicious smoked meats or *slanina* (smoked and cured pork belly), pork crackling and *kajmak*. In Slovenia and Croatia, it is also known as *žganci*, and is made from cornmeal or buckwheat (in Slovenia this then becomes *Ajdovi žganci*).

Bring the water to the boil in a large, heavy-based saucepan and add the salt. Reduce to a gentle simmer and add half the pork fat.

When the fat has melted and the water is gently simmering again, add the cornmeal. It should almost form a 'lid' over the simmering water. Do not stir. Use the handle of a wooden spoon to make 3–4 holes in the cornmeal so that the water can gently simmer through the holes. Cook for at least 20 minutes without stirring – you should start to see the water seeping through the air holes.

Meanwhile, prepare the pork crackling crumb. Dry-fry the *čvarci* in a small, dry frying pan over a medium heat for 6–8 minutes or until most of the fat has rendered down and the *čvarci* are crisping up. Remove from the heat and add the Aleppo pepper, chilli flakes (if using), salt and black pepper. Transfer to a small serving bowl and set aside.

In the same frying pan, melt the rest of the pork fat, then set aside.

Return to the *kačamak*. Once there is no dry cornmeal left in the saucepan (the water has seeped through completely), reduce the heat

Breakfast

to medium and start stirring using the handle of a wooden spoon (this will require some muscle). As you stir, break up the cornmeal to ensure there are no dry bits left. Keep doing this for 10–15 minutes, or until there are no dry patches in the mixture and it has an almost firm, playdough-like consistency that is starting to turn into a crumb.

Spoon out the *kačamak* into a serving dish. As you spoon it out, drizzle over a little of the pork fat and break up the *kačamak* with your spoon to create large crumbs.

To serve, sprinkle the pork crackling crumb and half the crumbled cheese over the *kačamak*, serving the rest alongside with the yoghurt.

Breakfast

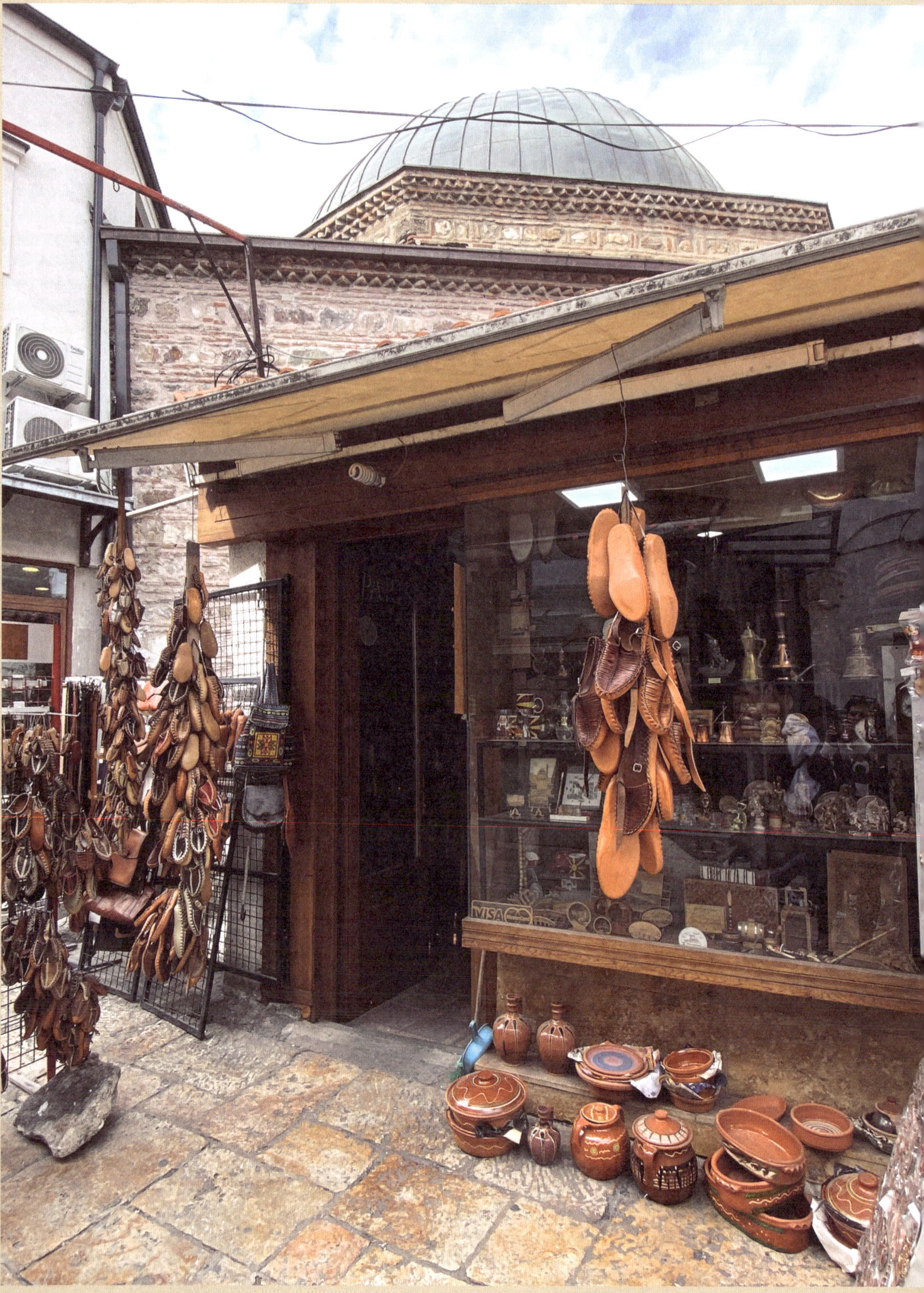
VISA

Teškoto

The beats of the *tapan* drum summon him. He is clad in white trousers edged in elaborate black embroidery, which are tucked into gaiters and traditional leather *opinci* on his feet. A beautiful sash of black, white and red wool is tied around his waist. His intricately embroidered *elek* (vest) drapes over his crisp white shirt, and he is wearing the traditional *kapa* on his head. The *tapan* beats again. He interlocks one arm with another young man who has just come home to North Macedonia from America, to get married, like him. In his other arm, he holds a red handkerchief, which he twirls in the air as he leads the dance. The men arrange themselves in a half-moon around the *tapan* player, who taunts them with a few more beats. Suddenly the *zurli* – oboe-like trumpets – sound. Then the wooden *kavals* (flutes). Slowly he raises one *opinok*-clad foot and holds it suspended in mid-air, like a heron, until the *tapan* player deigns to release them with a full beat. It is a game of musical cat and mouse. A competition – can the men hold on until the next *tapan* beat, and who can hold on longest, the young men or the woodwind players? A series of half-beats, a brief respite, as the men masterfully arch their legs sideways, then behind. A full beat. Release. Now the other foot. And repeat. All as if moving in slow motion until a sudden burst of syncopated 7/8 time signature – one two, one two, one two three – and the young men squat down together, arms still interlocked, then leap back in the air on one foot. He is now the one taunting the *tapan* player as he leaps on top of it. He feels the rhythm reverberating through his body. It is the rhythm of his heartbeat. *Teškoto oro* – the heavy, difficult dance. He understands that heaviness, that longing for home. But he is here for now. Until he must leave again, he will dance, his heart light as air. He leaps off the *tapan*, almost floating down. Suddenly the rhythm gathers speed. He starts to pull his fellow *pečalbari* energetically round in a circle, then one by one they break off, swirling, bounding from leg to leg, either high up in the air or as close to the ground as possible, competing with the *tapan* and the *zurla,* feeling the music deep in their soul.

Breakfast

FROM THE OVEN

FURNA

My great-great-grandfather, Milan, was a *furnadžija* (a baker), who owned a *furna* (an oven, but a word that was synonymous with bakery) in Kumanovo, North Macedonia. My grandmother remembered him as a serious, strong, tall and imposing man who was not to be trifled with. He spoke a Macedonian Kumanovo dialect, Serbian, Greek, Ottoman Turkish, Hebrew and French – as was customary for many merchants, tradesmen and artisans at the turn of the 19th century in the region. He was known for being someone fair and honest to a fault, so much so that family legend asserts that he shot a Turk for cheating him in business – a bold move, given Macedonia was still part of the Ottoman Empire at the time and repercussions could have resulted in his own death. He was also known as a healer, with an innate ability to fix all manner of musculoskeletal issues, including re-setting dislocated and broken bones, with his strong baker's hands. People would reportedly come from very far just to see him. He worked hard, preparing fresh dough every day and working from the middle of the night. As well as supplying Kumanovo with fresh bread and other baked goods, the *furna* was also, in those pre-oven-in-every-home days, the focal point of the community. Women would bring, or sometimes send their children with, prepared meals in their variously shaped earthenware dishes (depending on the type of meal) and hand them over to be slow-baked in the bakery's wood-fired oven, returning to pick them up later. While the role of bakeries has naturally evolved over the past century or so, many famous old bakeries remain across the region, along with a bakery in every neighbourhood.

Bread is an integral component of the Balkan diet and has been for a very long time, as a result of a history of grain cultivation and baking practice in the region. Archaeologists in Serbia have unearthed remnants of bread that date back to the Vinča culture, one of the earliest Neolithic cultures in Europe, suggesting that these early inhabitants of the Balkans were grinding grains and baking bread as part of their dietary as well as ritual habits. To this day, breads and pastries are present at every meal, and there is a type of bread to mark every significant occasion, as well as for important events in the calendars of the respective religions of the Balkans.

There is a remarkable variety of techniques, flavours and textures to be found in Balkan baking – and each tells a unique culinary story. From the countless types of *poğaça* (the word an adaptation of Italian *focaccia*), which at its most basic is a kind of round, savoury loaf made from myriad types of flour but which also includes more elaborate examples that are either adorned or filled with seeds, spices or various sweet or savoury toppings. To the iconic: *kifli* or *kifle*, crescent-shaped pastries that loved across the Balkans; *somun* from Bosnia and Herzegovina; *pirun* from Montenegro, a dense maize loaf enriched with cheese or olives; *potica* from Slovenia; *proja*, a light cornbread enjoyed in various forms across the region; *burek* in its various guises across Bosnia and Herzegovina, North Macedonia and Serbia; and *soparnik* from Croatia. To deep-fried deliciousness: the *krofne* of Serbia and Croatia, to be filled with jams, marmalades or custard and dusted lightly with sugar; *petulla* from Kosovo – doughnuts enjoyed with a dusting of sugar and a drizzle of honey; and *mekici* from North Macedonia – enriched dough, deep-fried and enjoyed with sweet or savoury accompaniments.

The Balkan people's ability to make bread or pastries out of seemingly anything has been of paramount importance to survival in the region throughout history.

SERVES 8–10

Štrudla

75 g (2½ oz) unsalted butter (or margarine), melted and cooled
275–325 g (9¾–11½ oz) filo pastry sheets (10 sheets)
60 ml (2 fl oz/¼ cup) sparkling water
icing (confectioners') sugar, to serve

FOR THE SOUR CHERRY FILLING

600 g (1 lb 5 oz) sour cherries, washed, stalks removed, stoned and cut in half (or 500 g/1 lb 2 oz frozen sour cherries, thawed)
1 tablespoon Vanilla Sugar (see page 261, or use shop-bought)
100 g (3½ oz/generous ¾ cup) fine semolina

FOR THE APPLE FILLING

600 g (1 lb 5 oz) eating (dessert) apples, peeled and coarsely grated (about 500 g/1 lb 2 oz grated apple)
1–2 tablespoons light brown soft sugar (optional – if your apples are sour)
100 g (3½ oz/1 cup) ground walnuts (or ground almonds/almond meal)
1 tablespoon ground cinnamon
1 teaspoon lemon zest plus 1 tablespoon juice

Notes

If you can't find sour cherries, use the same quantity of sweet cherries but omit the sugar and add 1 teaspoon lemon zest and 2 tablespoons lemon juice to the mix.

The use of semolina to counter the natural juiciness of the fruit in baking is widespread across the region. You can replace the semolina with ground nuts, as I do for the apple. This works with any summer fruit.

The štrudla keeps well stored in an airtight container at room temperature for up to 2 days.

Like its Austrian cousin, Balkan *štrudla* consists of thin, flaky pastry wrapped around any number of sweet fillings, including sour cherries, apples, pumpkin, poppy seeds and nuts – I have given you my two favourite sweet filling options here. The word *štrudla*, however, is also used for any sweet yeasted and enriched dough rolled very thinly and then twirled with a sweet filling into a log, such as Milibrod (see page 74) or Potica (see page 76). For me, of using ready-made filo is really a cheat's Pita (see opposite), and if you feel no inclination to roll pastry for Pita or the Sarajevo-style Burek (see page 54), do this instead and for this amount of filo pastry use the same quantities of one of the suggested savoury fillings for the Pita, Sarajevo-style Burek or Soparnik (see page 62) or the sweet filling for Milibrod, Potica or the Pumpkin Štruklji (see page 39).

There are many stories surrounding the origins of strudel, including that the art of Ottoman confectionary, specifically baklava pastry, made it into Austro-Hungary as early as the 15th century and was then adapted and merged with existing Austro-Hungarian pastry techniques and preferences. Perhaps my favourite theory is that it was Balkan cooks who took the art of hand-stretched *burek* dough to the Austro-Hungarian court's kitchens – a plausible one given Austro-Hungarian control over Bosnia and Herzegovina. Whatever the truth, to me it represents a very successful example of culinary soft power in action. While the Ottoman and Habsburg empires continued their political, religious and military stand-off for centuries, pastry travelled further than their armies ever could, traversing the Balkans on its journey in both directions.

Prepare your chosen filling. For the sour cherry filling, place the prepared cherries in a colander over a bowl and set aside for 15 minutes to drain. Reserve the juice to drink. Transfer the drained cherries to a medium bowl and add the sugar and semolina and mix to combine.

For the apple filling, squeeze the grated apple, capturing the juice in a small bowl. Reserve the juice to drink. Place the apple in a medium bowl with the sugar (if using), ground walnuts, cinnamon, lemon zest and juice and mix to combine.

Preheat the oven to 180°C fan (400°F) and brush a 24 x 32 cm (9½ x 12½ inch) baking dish or tin (pan) with some of the butter.

Place one sheet of filo on a clean work surface and brush lightly with butter, then place another sheet on top and brush it lightly with butter too. Place a fifth of the filling along the short side of the filo sheet (which should be about the length of your baking dish), then start rolling, tucking in the edges at the end. Place the roll seam side down in the prepared baking dish. Repeat to make four rolls. Brush the tops of the rolls with more butter. With a serrated knife, pre-slice the rolls at 8 cm (3¼ inch) intervals, then spoon the sparkling water over the rolls.

Bake in the oven for 35–40 minutes, or until golden brown and the base of the rolls is cooked through. Remove from the oven and allow to cool in the dish for 10 minutes before dusting with icing sugar to serve.

▲▲▲ From the Oven

Pita

Unlike Middle Eastern *pita*, Balkan *pita* is, for lack of an appropriate translation, a pie made from pastry similar to but not quite the same as filo pastry (the dough sheets do not require drying but are used immediately). In composition, *pita* is almost always made with finely milled flour (typically wheat, though other flours are used across the region, such as buckwheat). *Pita* can be unleavened, made with flour, water, salt, oil and perhaps a little acid (vinegar or lemon juice) to strengthen the gluten and improve the elasticity of the dough so it can be manipulated more easily. Or it can be leavened with yeast or made with eggs or drinking yoghurt, or any of combination of them, which makes the *pita* fluffier. Regardless of which dough is used, there are two main techniques used for forming the *pita*: stretching and stacking. Unleavened dough is typically hand stretched and used to make *burek* (such as the Sarajevo-style Burek on page 54 or for the other type of *burek* loved across the region that I describe on page 58), or for other types of *pitas*. Leavened dough is typically stacked, meaning that a rolled-out pastry sheet is folded over itself like the petals of a carnation closing. As it bakes, the heat separates the stacked layers, puffing up the dough and creating a laminated, flaky and light texture. The stacking technique is known as *katmer* (the Turkish word for carnation) and I have predominantly come across it in North Macedonia, but that is not to say it isn't found in other guises across the rest of the Balkans – and of course, Turkey, for example in the Anatolian dessert made with pistachios also called *katmer*.

My mother has an even cleverer method for creating *katmer* pastry by stacking rolled out circles of dough that are then rolled out together into one dough sheet to be used to make Baklava (see page 208), which you could also use to make this *pita*.

Once rolled out, a *pita* can be shaped however you like, with the filling either layered (pastry, filling, pastry, filling and so on) or rolled (pastry rolled around the filling). If rolled, the rolls can be arranged in rows, as in this recipe, or coiled/swirled, as the Sarajevo-style Burek on page 54, or made into other intricate shapes – a cook's imagination is the limit.

Pita is an umbrella term as *pitas* are often described according to their filling. For example, in North Macedonia, a *pita* filled with spinach will either be called *pita so spanak* (pita with spinach) or *zelnik* (meaning with any *zeleniš*/greens such as spinach, nettles, spring/collard greens or Swiss chard). A *pita* with *sir* (white cheese) will be a *sirnica* in Bosnia and Herzegovina and Serbia. A pita with leeks will be *pita so pras/praz* or *prasiluk*, and so on. In our home, a *pita* with sauteed leeks and sauerkraut was often made for Badnik (Christmas Eve), a fasting day in the Christian Orthodox calendar.

After a lifetime spent watching my grandmother and mother make *pita*, eagerly waiting while the delicious smells emanating from the oven taunted me, impatiently poking it with a finger once out of the oven to check whether it was cool enough to eat, eating most of it merely minutes after it emerged from the oven with yoghurt, it is unsurprising that this is my ultimate comfort bake.

▲▲▲ From the Oven *Recipe overleaf* ↪

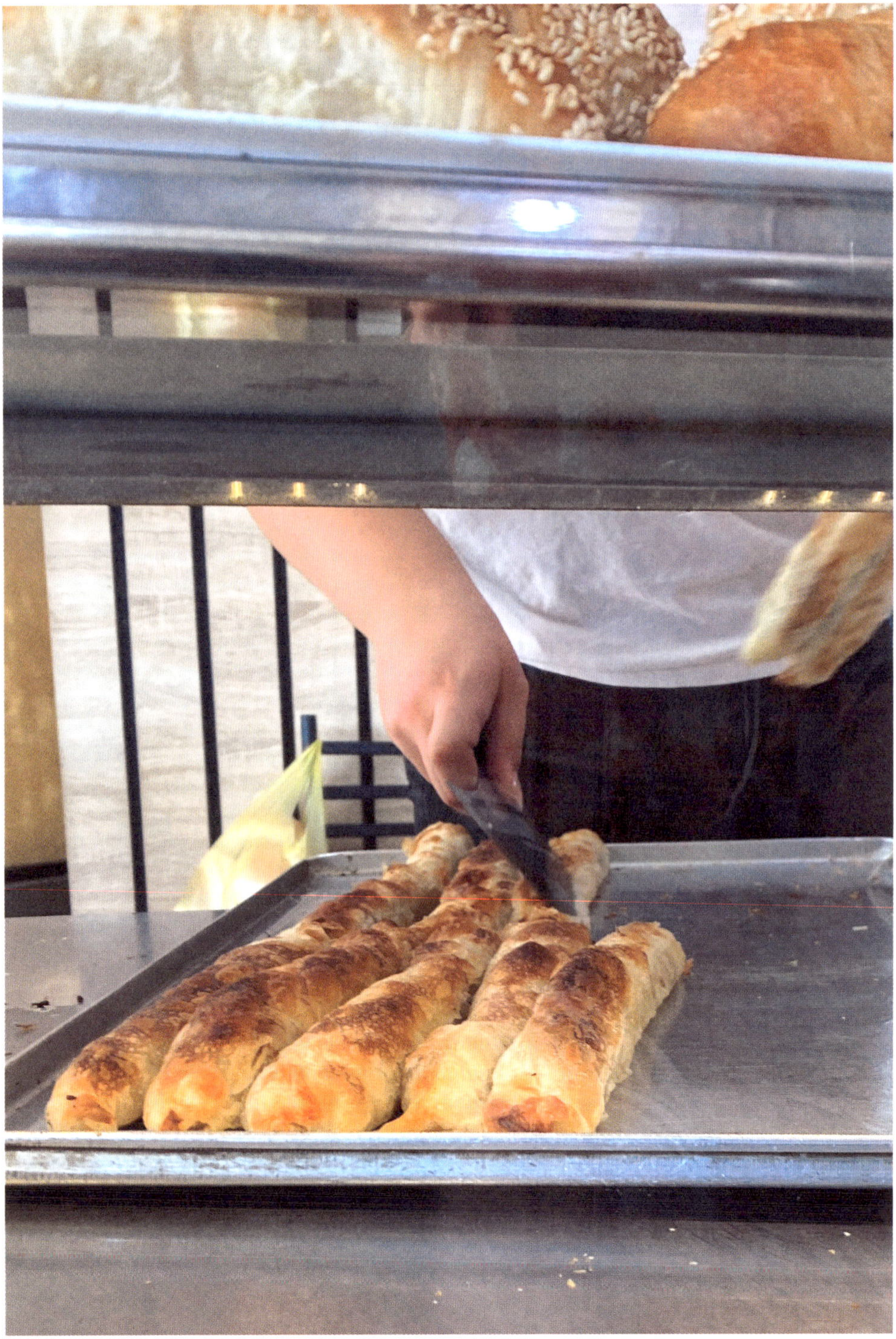

SERVES 6–8

Pita

10 g (½ oz) fast-action dried yeast
1 teaspoon caster (superfine) sugar
240 ml (8 fl oz/1 cup) lukewarm water
200 g (7 oz/1⅔ cups) strong white bread flour
200 g (7 oz/1⅔ cups) plain (all-purpose) flour, plus extra for dusting
1 teaspoon fine sea salt
100 g (3½ oz) unsalted butter (or pork fat or a mix of both), melted and cooled
1 medium egg, lightly beaten, for brushing

FOR THE SPINACH OR NETTLE FILLING

400 g (14 oz) spinach or nettles, washed and any large stalks removed and discarded
200 g (7 oz) white cheese (or feta), finely crumbled
2 eggs, lightly beaten
¼ teaspoon freshly grated nutmeg
½ teaspoon sea salt flakes
freshly ground black pepper

In a small bowl, mix together the yeast, sugar and water, then set aside for 5–10 minutes until frothy.

Sift the flours and salt into a large bowl. Make a well in the middle of the flour, pour in the yeast mixture and mix together with a fork until you have a shaggy dough. Tip out the dough onto a clean work surface (scraping out the sides of the bowl) and start to bring it together with your hands. Knead, dusting with a little flour if you need to, until the mixture comes together into a smooth, shiny and elastic ball of dough that springs back when touched. Place back in the bowl, dust lightly with flour, cover and set aside in a warm place to rise for at least 1 hour, or until the dough has doubled in size.

For the spinach or nettle filling, plunge the washed greens into a large bowl of boiling water for 1 minute if using spinach or 3–4 minutes if using nettles until soft and wilted. Drain the greens and immediately place them in a bowl of ice-cold water for 30 seconds, then drain again, squeeze out the water, roughly chop them and transfer to a bowl with the cheese, eggs, nutmeg, salt and a grind of black pepper, then set aside.

Preheat the oven to 180°C fan (400°F) and line a 42 x 30 cm (15½ x 12 inch) baking tray (pan) with baking parchment.

Once risen, transfer the dough to a lightly floured work surface. Dust a rolling pin with a little flour and roll out the dough as thinly as you can into a large circle about 50 cm/19½ inches in diameter. With a pastry brush, grease the surface with around two-thirds of the butter. Place a light bowl (about 25 cm/10 inches in diameter) in the middle of the pastry sheet but do not press it down. Using a knife or pastry cutter, slice the pastry sheet into seven wedges or petals, from the edge of the bowl to the edge of the pastry sheet. Remove the bowl; you should have what looks like a flower in bloom. Take one petal and fold it over the circle in the centre, stretching it by hand to fit over it as neatly as possible. Repeat it for all the petals, folding them over the central circle. You should end up with a smaller pastry disc made of layers that is about 25 cm (10 inches) in diameter. Lightly dust the top of the pastry, your work surface and rolling pin with flour again, then carefully roll out the pastry into a rectangle, about 60 x 42 cm (23½ x 15½ inches), the shorter side of which fits the longest side of your baking tray. Cut it widthwise into five or six strips. Brush the middle of each strip with the rest of the butter, then divide the filling evenly between the strips of dough, placing it in the middle all along the length of each piece. Fold over the sides of each dough strip to encase the filling, then pinch together the seam and both ends to seal. Repeat for all the dough strips.

Gently transfer each strip onto the baking tray, placing them seam side down next to each other (leaving about ½ cm/¼ inch gap between them). Brush the top with the beaten egg, then bake in the oven for 30–40 minutes, rotating the tray once halfway through, until golden and cooked through. Remove from the oven and leave to cool for about 10 minutes, then serve warm or at room temperature.

From the Oven

SERVES 4-6

Sarajevo-style Burek

425 g (15 oz/scant 3½ cups) strong white bread flour, plus extra for dusting
½ teaspoon fine sea salt
2 tablespoons sunflower oil, plus extra for greasing and brushing
250 ml (8 fl oz/1 cup) lukewarm water
10 g (½ oz) unsalted butter
50 ml (1¾ fl oz/3½ tablespoons) boiling water
cold drinking yoghurt, to serve

FOR THE MEAT FILLING

500 g (1 lb 2 oz) minced (ground) beef or veal
1 onion, grated or very finely chopped
2 garlic cloves, very finely chopped
1 teaspoon sunflower oil
1 teaspoon vegetable bouillon powder
½ teaspoon sea salt flakes
¼ teaspoon ground black pepper

FOR THE POTATO FILLING

600 g (1 lb 5 oz) waxy potatoes, peeled, coarsely grated and water squeezed out
1 onion, finely chopped
10 g (½ oz) chives, finely chopped (optional)
1 teaspoon sunflower oil
1 teaspoon vegetable bouillon powder
½ teaspoon sea salt flakes
½ teaspoon freshly ground black pepper (or white pepper), or more to taste

I am watching Mersiha Kevelj-Panjeta chop her homegrown tomatoes. She does it the Balkan way, with a small vintage paring knife with a wooden handle worn perfectly to the shape of her hand, which she moves deftly around a tomato held in the other hand. As the blade ends on the thumb, perfect pyramid shaped pieces of tomato fall in the decorative floral plate below to be joined by onions, a little oil, vinegar, salt and pepper. This salad will accompany the *dolma* and *burek* we made together. We are waiting for the *burek* to finish baking. It is taunting us with its aroma. Mersiha checks it and spoons a little water and butter mixture over it for the last few minutes of baking. I steal a tomato piece. Then another. Mersiha laughs knowingly. They taste incredible. Mersiha and her husband Mustafa grow them in the garden of their home, where they also run Bosnian cooking lessons. Earlier, I had admired that year's bounty – most of it now either turned into winter preserves or stored in Mersiha's perfectly organised freezer: bags of young Swiss chard, small light green bell peppers ready for *dolma*, tomatoes, herbs, everything. Mustafa and my husband, Peter, are discussing Bosnian winemaking in the background while sampling an exceptional one. I tell Mersiha that cooking with her feels like I have found family I never knew I had. As I look out of the window of their home, night is enveloping the peaks of the wild mountains that surround Sarajevo, and below, the city starts to glimmer with lights. I want to ask them about their experience of the war, the siege, the aftermath. But these questions break somewhere around the region of my heart before I can voice them, and anyway, I feel the answer to these unspoken questions. They survived. As did Sarajevo because of the resilience and sacrifice of its people. Instead, we sit, break *burek* together and speak of happier things.

Many people in Bosnia and Herzegovina will say that the only pastry that may be called *burek* is one filled with meat, onion and seasoning and made using the technique in this recipe, while across the rest of the Balkans, this recipe is also thought of as *pita so meso* (pita with meat). In Bosnia and Herzegovina, this pastry technique combined with any other filling warrants the name of *pita so...* (pita with...) the relevant filling, or is named after the filling, as in the previous recipe. A pita filled with *krumpir* or *krompir* (potato) is known as *krompiruša* (see second filling option). It is famously heavy on the black pepper but use white pepper if you prefer a gentler, earthier heat.

From the Oven   *Recipe continued overleaf*

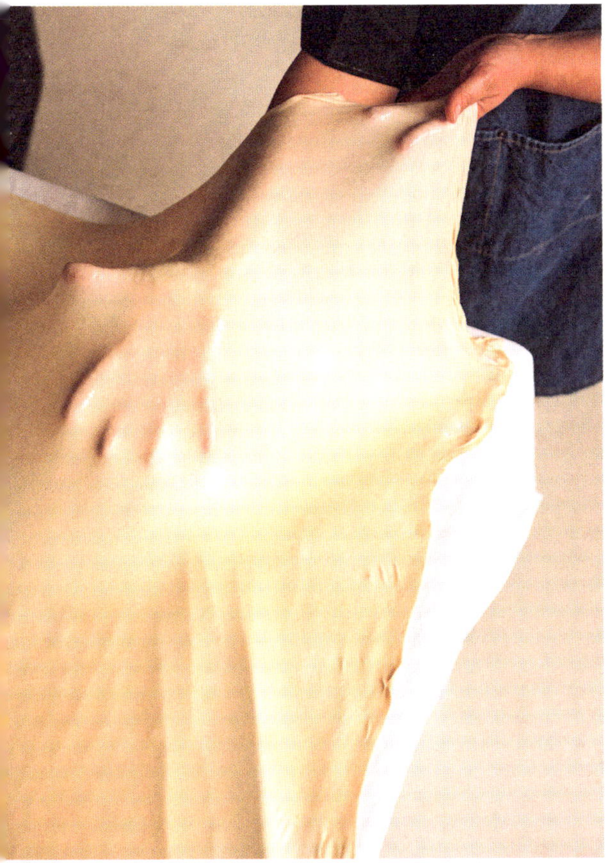
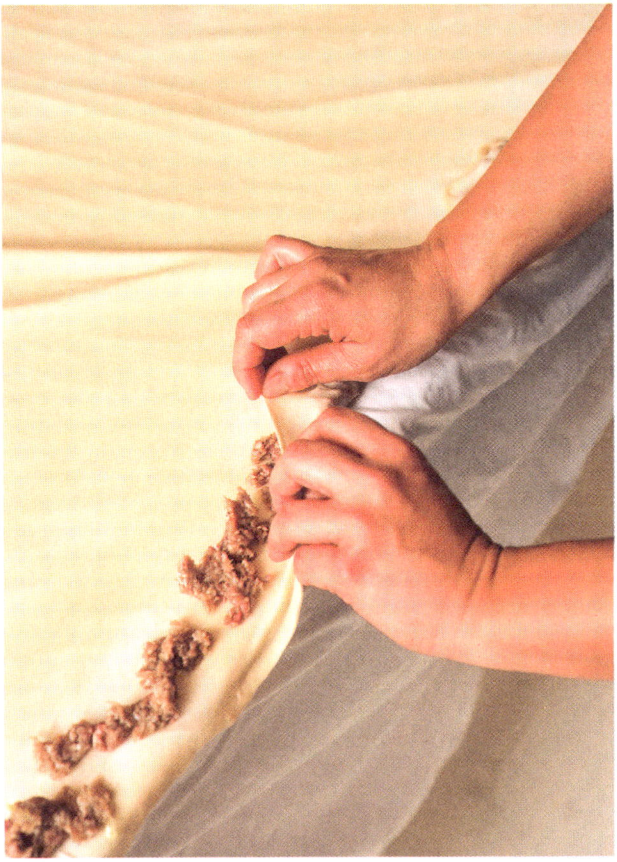
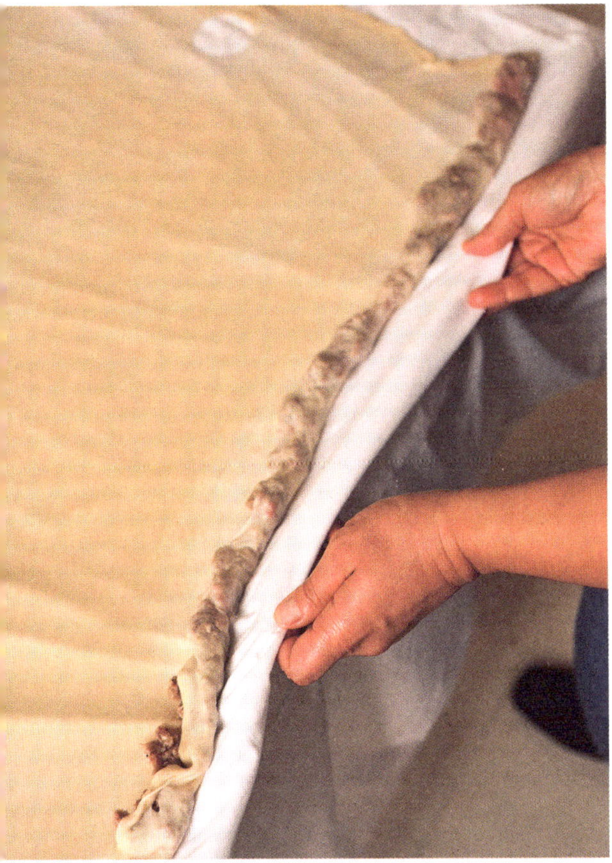
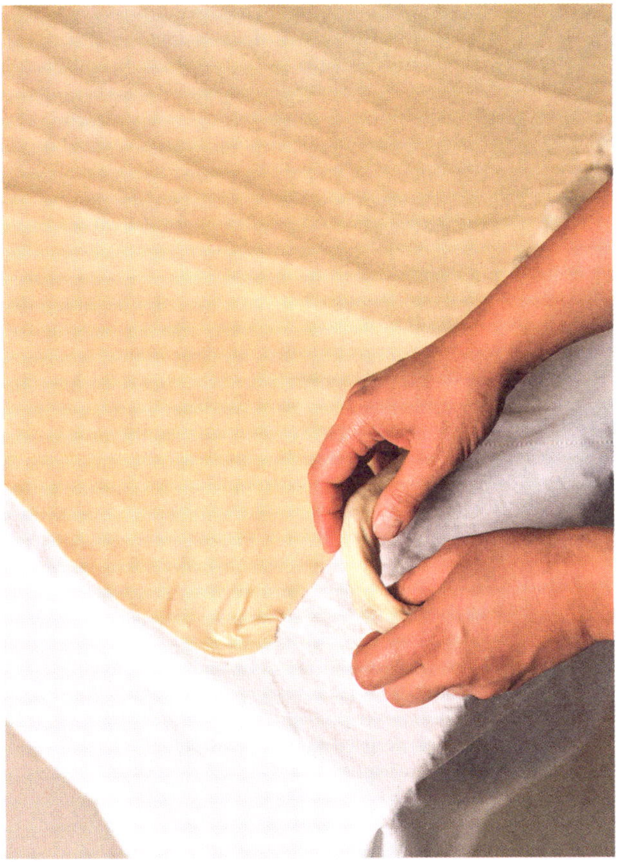

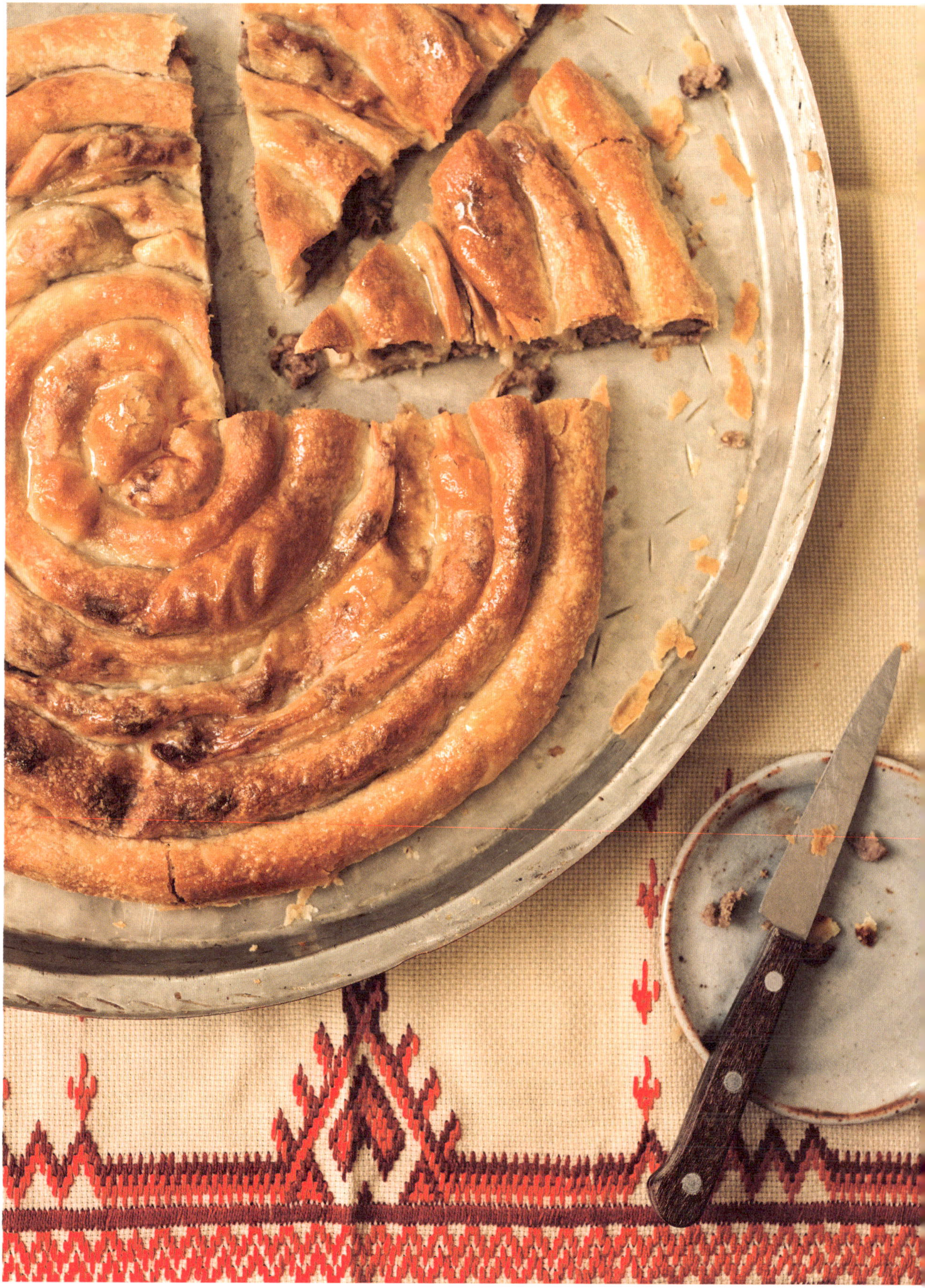

Sift the flour and salt into a large bowl. Add the oil and water, then use a fork (or your hands) to bring the mixture together into a shaggy dough. Tip out the dough onto a lightly floured work surface (scraping out the sides of the bowl) and knead for 5–6 minutes until you have a smooth dough. Shape into a ball, return to the bowl, then brush the top with oil, cover and set aside to rest in a warm place for at least 30 minutes.

Next, prepare your filling of choice. For the meat filling, combine all the ingredients in a large bowl and knead the mixture with your hand until well combined, then set aside. For the potato filling, combine all the ingredients in a large bowl and mix together until well combined. Drain any excess moisture, then set aside.

Preheat the oven to 200°C fan (425°F) and line a large baking sheet with baking parchment.

Working in a warm room (ideally around 24°C/75°F, but at least 21°C/70°F), cover a large table with a clean cotton tablecloth. Lightly dust a section of the tablecloth with flour and tip out the dough onto it. The dough should feel elastic. Give the dough a gentle knead and shape it back into a ball. Dust the top of the dough with flour, then dust an *oklagija* (long, thin rolling pin) with flour if you have one, or a regular rolling pin if you don't, and slowly start to roll out the dough, always pushing from the middle outwards to the edges, into as large a circle as you can (at least 50–60 cm/20–24 inches diameter). Brush the top of the dough with oil, making sure you cover all of it, then let it rest for 10–15 minutes.

Once rested, gently lift one side of the dough and, using the palm of your hand, gently start to stretch the dough from the middle outwards. Work slowly and use the balls of your fingertips, not your nails. Work all the way around the dough until it is paper-thin and practically transparent. Don't worry if there are one or two little rips here and there, but if you are getting too many, pause, brush the dough with a little more oil and let it rest for 5–10 minutes before you continue hand-stretching. The dough should reach the edge of your table and overhang, creating a rectangle roughly 100 x 80 cm (3¼ x 2½ feet). Use your fingertips to either stretch the edges or slightly trim any doughier overhanging pastry.

Place a line of filling along one of the longer edges of the dough and then, using the edge of the tablecloth, gently roll it over itself 2–3 times. Cut off the roll from the rest of the sheet with a knife, and then swirl it, seam side down, into a spiral and place on the prepared baking sheet (it's easiest if you swirl it directly on the baking sheet). Repeat with the remaining dough and filling, swirling the pastry rolls around to fill the baking sheet. Brush the top of the *burek* spiral with oil and use your hand to flick a little water (no more than 1 tablespoon) over the *burek* and baking sheet. Transfer to the oven to bake for 20 minutes.

Meanwhile, melt the butter in the boiling water. After 20 minutes of cooking time, remove the *burek* from the oven and reduce the temperature to 180°C fan (400°F). Drizzle half the water and butter mixture over the *burek*, then return it to the oven to bake for a further 15 minutes until golden brown. Turn the oven off, drizzle the rest of the water and butter mixture over the *burek*, and allow the *burek* to rest for 5 minutes in the warm oven before serving with a glass of cold drinking yoghurt.

▲▲▲   From the Oven

A Tale of Two Bureks

We found a letter from my great-grandmother, Keva, to my grandmother that starts 'Lepa, when I die ...' In the letter she sets out her practical wishes for after her passing. She was a religious woman but was adamant that she did not want any of the 'fuss' required by Eastern Orthodoxy around remembrance and All Souls' Day. Instead, she wanted my grandmother to buy half a *burek*, ground Turkish coffee and a bag of sugar and gift them to some poor old woman, from time to time. (It is a testament to the cultural significance of *burek* that it is considered an essential.)

The majority of people assume that Balkan *burek* is Ottoman and therefore the same as Turkish *börek* – and of course, there are undeniable similarities. But as with many origin stories, the *burek* origin story is incredibly complicated and it is difficult to attest to its exact origins without undermining the interconnectedness of ancient foodways. Variations on dough manipulated into a myriad of shapes with some sort of filling can be found in most cuisines around the world.

Here is a summary. At some point before the 7th century, the nomadic Turks of Central Asia started to try to replicate the fluffy texture of the thick oven-baked breads they obtained from town bakeries and markets, but adapted to the realities of their nomadic lifestyle. They emulated the structure of bread by layering sheets of dough as many times as possible before stuffing it with savoury fillings comprised of the limited foodstuffs available to them – meat and butter and cheese made from milk from their herds, foraged wild greens and grains, which they could buy or barter for in the markets. They then cooked the layered dough on a *saj* – a domed flat-iron griddle, suspended over an open fire or placed on hot stones.

As the Turkic tribes migrated (the Gökturks from Siberia to the Aral Sea, the Khazars across the Caucasus and the Bulgars to modern day Ukraine and down to Bulgaria), their pastry creation spread with them and was adapted as needed.

In the 11th century, the Seljuks (an Oğuz/Ghuzz Turkic tribe) started to take over lands formerly controlled

From the Oven

by the Byzantine Empire, including eastern Anatolia. They eventually invaded south-western Asia and established control over Mesopotamia, Syria, Palestine and most of Iran. The Seljuks brought the pastry with them, and along the way it possibly met and merged with the Byzantine *plakous*, a sort of flat cake that may have in turn descended from the Roman *placenta*, which may have in turn descended from the Hellenic *plakous* – two sheets of pastry, stuffed with honey and cheese or chopped nuts (though many would say these are the ancestors of baklava). The pastry's arrival in Iran is also possibly the point in time when it begins to be referred to as *börek* – a combination of the Farsi root *bûrak*, which referred to any dish made with *yufka* (a delicately thin pastry sheet, sort of like filo), and the Turkic root *bur*, meaning to twist, an allusion to the way in which thin sheets of dough have to be manipulated to produce a layered effect.

Then came the Mongol conquests of the 13th century, during which (like all 'progressive' conquerors), they adopted the things they liked and adapted them to their preferences. This nomadic pastry continued its travels through central Asia and reached the courts of Mongol-ruled China. Here it seems to have taken on a sweet element – *cakaril pirak* – with walnuts and honey (again, similar to *plakous* and perhaps an early form of baklava).

Finally, we arrive at the Ottomans, who in the 14th century began to emerge as the dominant Turkic tribe and started to conquer lands and expand their influence into the Balkans. Adrianople (Edirne) was captured in 1362 and Serbia in 1386. The influence of the Ottomans then extended into Anatolia, Northern Greece and led to the eventual fall of Constantinople in 1453. The rest, as they say, is history. The Balkans (and much of the territory of former Yugoslavia) remained under Ottoman control until the late 19th and early 20th century, and were the site of much to-ing and fro-ing between the houses of Habsburg and Osmanli.

In the Balkans during the 14th century, the most popular meat was mutton or pork. Corned pork was an important export from the mountainous regions between the Neretva River and Kotor. There are documents explaining the preparation of various types of *pita* bread filled with these meats, which may have been prototypes of *börek*. They could also be adaptations of Greco-Roman-Byzantine versions.

Börek became highly fashionable in Ottoman Istanbul, and it was present at the Sultan's dining table in the 15th century. The dish is first mentioned in relation to the former Yugoslav territories as being present in Skopje (in 1452), followed by Sarajevo and Novi Pazar (in 1489). Of course, as Ottoman influence over their conquered lands extended, so did their cuisine and customs, but at the same time, indigenous foods and customs were assimilated into the Ottoman culture. *Börek* began to merge with local ingredients and pre-existing techniques and preferences and assumed various new forms and, consequently, various new names. Also, we cannot forget the potential impact of the Ottoman practice of taking children from the Balkans to staff the Janissary corps (if they were boys) or the harems (if they were girls). These children (many of whom would go on to become important Ottoman viziers, begs or other officials) would have taken with them the memory of local food and customs. It is therefore reductive to say that *burek*, as we know it in former Yugoslavia, was an entirely Ottoman installation in the region, since there was significant cross-fertilisation and culinary influences travelled in all directions from and to Istanbul. Given the particularly strong foothold of the Ottoman Empire across the Balkans, *börek* (or *burek*, as it is known across the Balkans) has retained very strong roots in the region, especially (and predictably) in areas that remained

From the Oven

under Ottoman control longer – Serbia, Kosovo, Bosnia and Herzegovina and North Macedonia. Indeed, the Sarajevo-style *burek* on page 54 is still known in Turkey as 'Bosnian *börek*'.

As to the question of where you can find the best *burek* in the Balkans today remains a matter of very serious (and delicious) debate, from Skopje to Belgrade via Sarajevo and Banja Luka, down the many cities along the Adriatic coast. There are two schools of *burek* thought.

Most Bosnians will tell you that the only pastry you are allowed to call *burek* is one filled with meat and onions. It is made of unleavened dough, which is hand-stretched, then rolled around a filling and twisted into a spiral. The best *burekdžinice* (*burek* bakeries) still use a *sač* to cook their *burek*. This cooking device is similar to the Turkic *saj*, but the *burek* is cooked under (rather than over) the iron dome of the *sač*. The dome is covered in coal embers, infusing the pastry with a wonderful flavour. With any other filling, it is known as *pita*, and named after its contents.

In the rest of the former Yugoslavia – especially North Macedonia, Serbia and Kosovo – *burek* is again made from unleavened dough, which is stretched until paper-thin and then layered with a filling. It is usually cooked in round baking dishes and tipped out upside down. Typically, when buying *burek* from a bakery, you would ask for an eighth, quarter or half of a round, depending on your appetite and stomach capacity. The filling can be anything: cheese, spinach (or other greens) and cheese, meat or vegetables.

The history of *burek* is one of necessity, migration, evolution, adaptation and reinvention. It is a question of geography, a way of living. Its nomadic origins are perhaps the reason it has persevered.

It is in its conceptualisation a food created to be transportable and transported anywhere. An item designed to be versatile and able to sustain you in periods of scarcity – just dough with a little bit of foraged greens or whatever else you could find. This is why versions of it have taken root across so many lands, cultures, ethnicities and religions. This is why it has survived millennia of poverty, wars and conquest, displacement and migration – and why it will continue to do so.

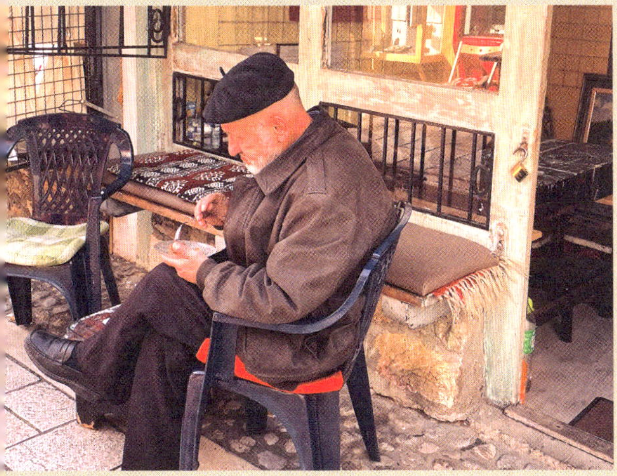

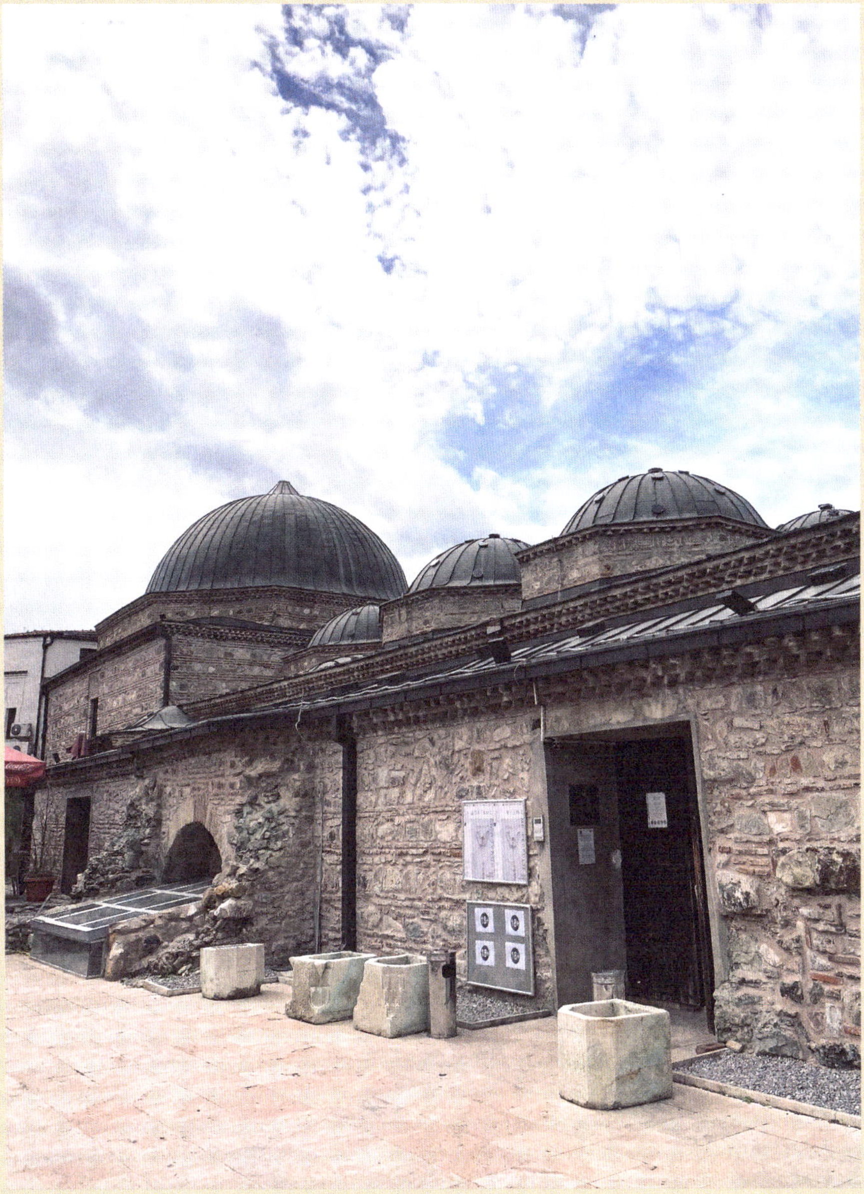

SERVES 4-6

Soparnik

400 g (14 oz/1⅔ cups) '00' flour, plus extra for dusting
½ teaspoon fine sea salt
200 ml (7 fl oz/scant 1 cup) lukewarm water
30 ml (2 tablespoons) extra virgin olive oil, plus extra for greasing

FOR THE FILLING

500 g (1 lb 2 oz) Swiss or rainbow chard (or baby spinach), washed
2 tablespoons olive oil
100–120 g (3½–4¼ oz) spring onions (scallions), roughly chopped
1 teaspoon sea salt flakes
freshly ground black pepper

FOR THE TOPPING

60 ml (2 fl oz/¼ cup) extra virgin olive oil
10 wild garlic (ramsons) leaves or 2–3 peeled garlic cloves
10 g (½ oz) fresh parsley, leaves and stalks

Note

It is not usual to fry the chard stalks and onion – in fact, large stalks are usually not used at all in the filling, but I don't like to waste them. If you have access to young chard, simply use the stalks fresh combined with the rest of the filling ingredients, but squeeze any excess moisture out first. Spinach is a good substitute for young Swiss chard, but try it with any greens you like.

Poljički soparnik (also known as *zeljanik* or *uljenak*) is a pie with very humble origins from the Poljica region of southern Dalmatia. It has now become a treat for special occasions that is loved all over Croatia (and beyond). What makes it unique is the cooking technique: typically prepared to be at least 1 metre (3¼ feet) in diameter, *soparnik* is baked directly on a traditional Croatian *komin* (outdoor live-fire oven) with the top of the *soparnik* covered in ashen charcoal made from old grape vine or olive wood. As soon as the *soparnik* inflates, a hole is poked into the middle to let the air out and the ashes are then gently dusted off with a broom. The top is then brushed with garlic and olive oil and the pie is cut into rhomboid pieces. My version is very much an homage. I use the two preheated baking sheets as an attempt to simulate a *komin* in a domestic oven – though, of course, you can try baking it under hot coals if you have an outdoor wood oven and are confident handling live fire.

Sift the flour and salt into a large bowl. Add the water and oil, then use a fork to bring the mixture together into a shaggy dough. Tip out the dough onto a lightly floured work surface (scraping out the sides of the bowl) and knead for 3–4 minutes until smooth. Return to the bowl, brush with oil, then cover and set aside to rest for at least 30 minutes.

Meanwhile, make the filling. Remove the stalks from the chard and chop them finely (roughly the same size as the spring onions) and set aside. Roughly chop the chard leaves and place them in a clean bowl.

Heat the oil in a medium saucepan over a medium-high heat. Add the spring onions, chard stalks and salt and fry for 5–6 minutes until they have softened but retain a little bite. Add them to the chard leaves along with a generous grind of black pepper and mix well to combine. Set aside to cool slightly, draining any excess liquid.

Preheat the oven to 180°C fan (400°F) and place two large baking sheets in the oven to heat up.

Divide the dough into two equal-sized pieces and shape into balls. Dust your work surface and rolling pin lightly with flour. Roll each ball of dough out into a 36 cm (14 in) circle. Place one circle on a large piece of baking parchment. Spread the filling over it, leaving a 3 cm (1¼ inch) border. Place the other circle of dough on top, then fold over the edges and crimp to encase the filling. Prick holes to allow air to escape.

Remove the baking sheets from the oven. Carefully transfer the *soparnik* on its baking parchment onto one of the hot baking sheets. Cover the *soparnik* with another sheet of baking parchment and place the other hot baking sheet over the top. Place this in the oven and bake for 20 minutes – it should puff up in the middle and lifting the baking sheet with it. After 20 minutes, remove the top baking sheet and parchment and bake for 10–15 minutes until golden brown and cooked through.

To make the topping, place all the ingredients in a food processor and blend until smooth. As soon as the *soparnik* comes out of the oven, brush it with the topping, serving the rest alongside in a small bowl.

▲▲▲ From the Oven

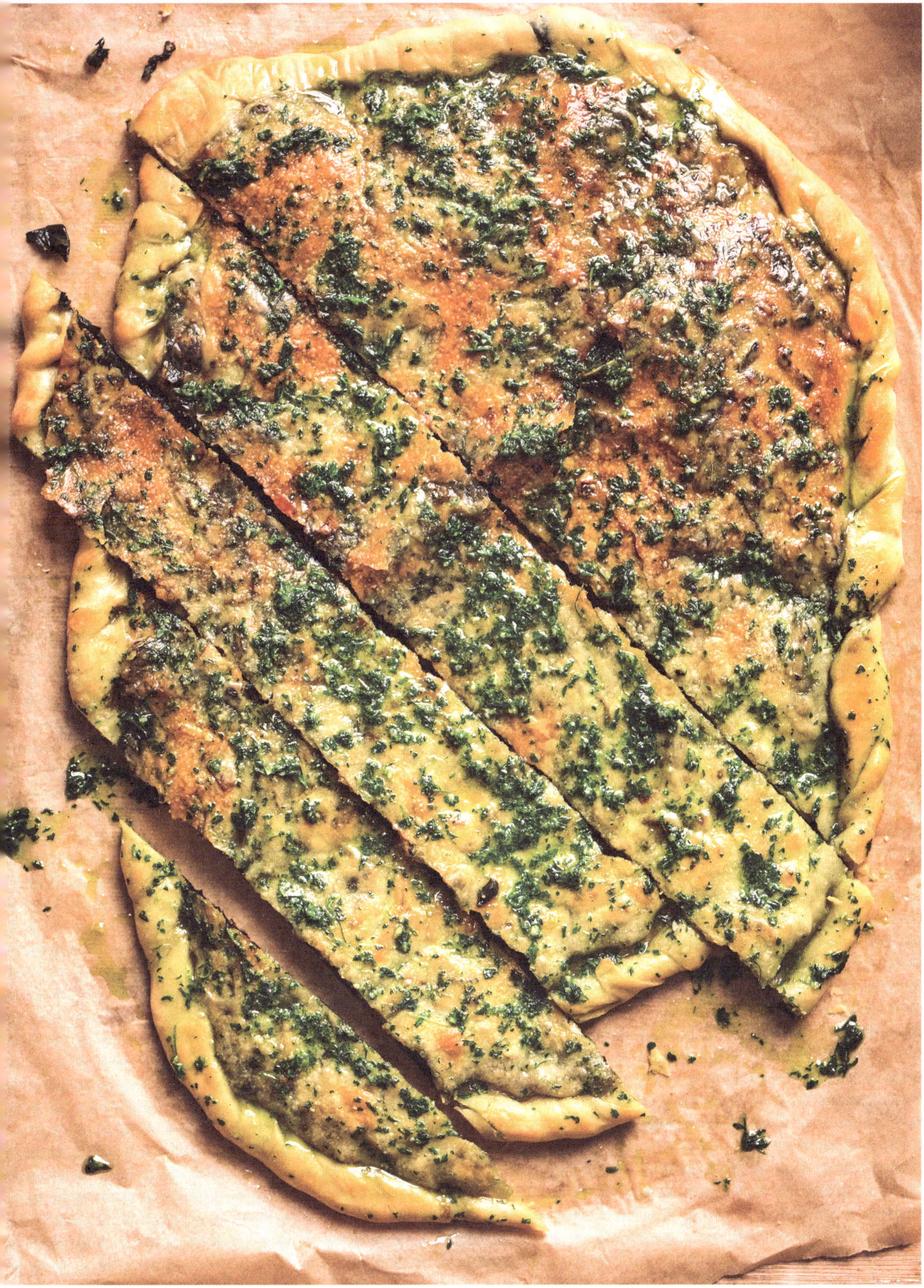

SERVES 8 (OR 4 WITH SECONDS)

Gibanica

3 medium eggs, lightly beaten
200 ml (7 fl oz/scant 1 cup) whole (full-fat) milk
200–225 ml (7–7½ fl oz/scant 1 cup) sparkling water, plus extra as needed
½ teaspoon baking powder
300–400 g (10½–14 oz) cow's or sheep's milk white cheese (or feta), crumbled
50–60 ml (1¾–2 oz/scant ¼–¼ cup) sunflower oil (or melted margarine or unsalted butter or a combination of any)
500 g (1 lb 2 oz) filo pastry sheets (14–16 sheets)
1 tablespoon sesame or nigella seeds (optional)

Gibanica is a cheese and egg filo rag pie that features regularly on a Balkan table for breakfast, brunch, lunch or dinner. It is sometimes called *sirnica* (because it contains cheese) and is also known as *banica* in Bulgaria, *guzvara* in Serbia and Croatia and *patsavroupita* in Greece. Its composition varies; in Serbia, for example, it is often made with *kajmak* (Balkan clotted cream, see page 261) and makes for a deliciously indulgent treat. This is my mother's recipe and it is a very forgiving one, even if (or especially if) you have less than ideal dry filo sheets. Feel free to play around with the amount or type of cheese – but steer clear of melty cheese. Use fresh, thin filo – often labelled as filo or '*kore*' (pastry sheets) for baklava – if you can find some in your local Turkish, Mediterranean or, if you're lucky, Balkan shop. For a savoury treat, serve the *gibanica* with cured or smoked meats, cheeses, vegetable preserves and fresh salad. For a sweet treat, sprinkle with a little cinnamon and sugar or drizzle over a little honey.

Place the eggs, milk, 200 ml (7 fl oz/scant 1 cup) of the sparkling water and the baking powder in a large bowl and whisk to combine. Add the cheese and 1 teaspoon of the oil into the egg and cheese mixture and mix well, then set aside.

With a pastry brush, brush a 32 x 24 cm (12½ x 9½ inch) baking dish with a little of the oil. Line it with a filo sheet (scrunching it a little and ensuring it reaches up the sides of the baking dish). Brush with oil and repeat with two more filo sheets. Then, take a filo sheet and, with your hands, scrunch it into the egg and cheese mixture, scoop it out and place it loosely in the baking dish, making sure to take some crumbled cheese with you as you lift it out. Repeat, distributing the scrunched up filo sheets and cheese mixture evenly in the tin, until you have used up nearly all the mixture (especially any crumbled cheese) and all but three of the filo sheets. Fold over the filo sheets from the sides of your baking dish and place a filo sheet (again, slightly scrunched) over the top. Brush oil over it and then pour over any remaining egg and cheese mixture. Place another filo sheet on top and brush with a little of the oil, then repeat with the final filo sheet. Brush any remaining oil over the top.

Using a serrated knife, cut through the filo sheets carefully to make 8–12 slices, taking care not to press down or pull the filo sheets as you cut. Drizzle the rest of the sparkling water along the cut lines. Give the tin a gentle shake to distribute the liquid around – it should be quite wet, and you should just about see liquid around the corners and up to the top layer of filo, but the *gibanica* should not be submerged in liquid. If it looks too dry, drizzle a little more sparkling water into each corner and give the *gibanica* another gentle shake.

Allow to stand and absorb some of the liquid for 15–30 minutes while you preheat the oven to 180°C fan (400°F). Sprinkle the sesame or nigella seeds over the top (if using), then bake in the oven for 40–50 minutes until golden brown, puffy and the middle is set. Allow the *gibanica* to cool for 30 minutes before slicing it along the pre-cut lines to serve.

▲▲▲ From the Oven

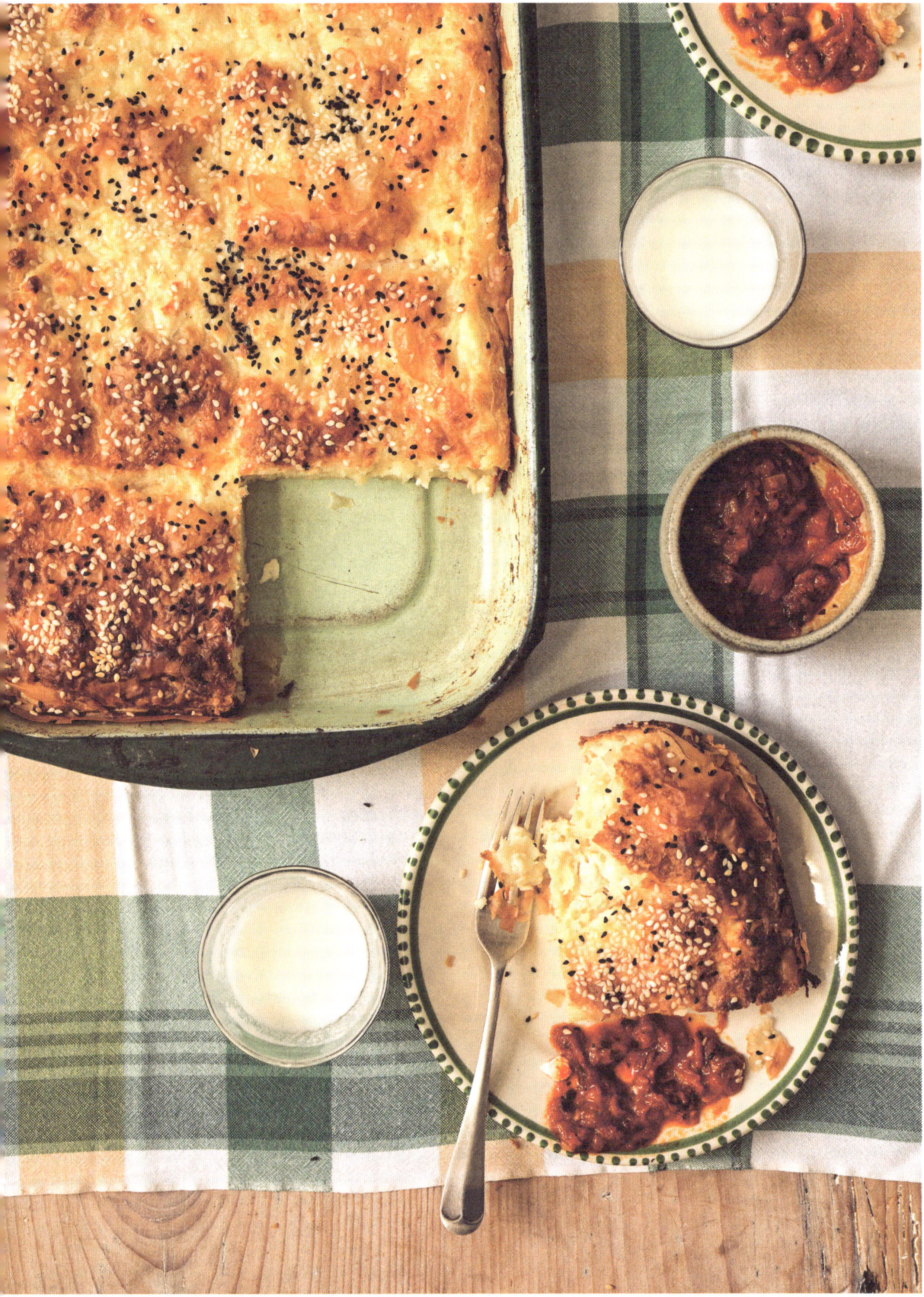

MAKES 2 LARGE OR 4 SMALLER FLATBREADS

Somun

1 teaspoon fast-action dried yeast
1 teaspoon caster (superfine) or granulated sugar
200 ml (7 fl oz/scant 1 cup) lukewarm water
250 g (9 oz/2 cups) strong white bread flour, plus extra for dusting
½ teaspoon fine sea salt
1 tablespoon nigella or sesame seeds, for sprinkling (optional)

Somun (as it is known in Bosnia and Herzegovina) or *lepinja* or *lepinje* (meaning little breads, as known across the rest of the region) is a traditional flatbread and our equivalent of Levantine pita bread. Many stories surround its origins, including that it was brought by, or created for, Ottoman soldiers on campaign through the Balkans who needed a portable bread that could be filled with a variety of things. Another is that the first somun was made in Sarajevo by a man whose family name was Somun and who was the quartermaster to Gazi Husrev-Bey, a famous governor of the Bosnian sanjak (Ottoman administrative district) in the 16th century seen by many as the father of Sarajevo. This recipe takes inspiration from the Bosnian version, usually prepared larger and flatter, and is especially popular during Ramadan when people will queue for their somun topped with nigella seeds. Serve it with *Pljeskavici* (see page 172) and *Ćevapi* (see page 176), where I suggest you cut it in half and grill it over the *roštilj* to soak up the cooking juices.

In a small bowl, mix together the yeast, sugar and water. Set aside for 5–10 minutes until frothy. Sift the flour and salt into a separate large bowl. Make a well in the middle of the flour, then add the yeast mixture. With a fork, mix until everything is well incorporated and you have a shaggy, wet, and sticky dough. Cover and leave to rise somewhere warm for 1–1½ hours, or until doubled in size.

Once risen, knock back the dough. With your fingertips or a fork, lift the edge of the dough furthest from you and pull it over the centre of the bowl. Turn the bowl by 90 degrees and repeat. Repeat six more times and re-form the dough into a ball. Cover and leave to prove a second time for 1–1½ hours, or until doubled in size.

Tip out the dough onto a lightly floured work surface, scraping down the bowl's sides. Dust the top lightly with flour, then divide it into two or four equal-sized pieces. Using well-floured hands, shape each into a ball, pinching any ends together. Place each ball (pinched side as the base) on your surface. Place the sides of your hands around the ball and firmly press them against its base while lifting and rotating it, repeating until a smooth, taut surface forms. Repeat with the remaining three pieces. Line a large baking sheet with parchment and dust with flour. Place the dough balls onto the baking sheet, spaced well apart, and prove, uncovered, somewhere warm for 35–45 minutes until doubled in size.

Preheat the oven to 230°C fan (475°F) or as hot as it will go. Using your fingertips, flatten each dough ball out into a circle about 12–15 cm (5–6 inches) in diameter, taking care not to knock all the bubbles out. Make a criss-cross pattern over the top with a lightly floured dough scraper or a palette knife. If using, sprinkle the nigella or sesame seeds over the top. With your hand, sprinkle some water over the top. Bake in the oven for 10–12 minutes, or until light brown, puffed up and hollow-sounding when tapped on the base. Remove from the oven and transfer to a wire rack to cool a little. Serve warm.

See photo on p. 173 and p. 177 ▲▲▲ From the Oven

SERVES 4-6

Old Bread Bake

2 tablespoons olive oil
2 large eggs, lightly beaten
250 g (9 oz/1 cup) plain yoghurt
¼ teaspoon baking powder
1 teaspoon dried oregano
1 tablespoon chopped fresh parsley leaves (or other soft herbs – optional)
50 ml (1¾ fl oz/3½ tablespoons) sparkling water
¼ teaspoon sea salt flakes
300 g (10½ oz) stale bread, cut into 1–2 cm (½–¾ cm) cubes
75 g (2½ oz) kashkaval (or mild Cheddar), cubed
75 g (7½ oz) white cheese (or feta), crumbled
25 g (1 oz) Parmesan or pecorino, grated (optional)
freshly ground black pepper

Centuries of empires, wars and poverty have taught the people of the Balkans how to make the most out of every last morsel of food. The current re-focus by the rest of the world on zero food waste is something that has long been genetically hardwired in us. My mother and I would occasionally catch my grandmother meticulously trimming distinctly furry or suspiciously green looking parts off very old bread. If we dared suggest to her that she could perhaps discard this bread and use the fresh bread we just bought, she would matter-of-factly respond that bread was often the only thing she had to eat in the periods immediately before and after Second World War and that she could never bring herself to throw it away. Consequently, our family has a deep love of bread and an even deeper obsession with never wasting it. My incredibly clever and resourceful mother came up with a really useful way to transform any collection of forgotten bread odds and ends (and any miscellaneous bits of cheese you may have in the refrigerator) into what I call, perhaps unfairly, 'old bread bake'. She would often make this as a weekend treat in lieu of *gibanica* (see page 64). It is not dissimilar to an Italian *strata*. We often have it for breakfast, but it makes for a lovely light lunch paired with a fresh salad.

Preheat the oven to 200°C fan (425°F).

Grease a 24 cm (9½ inch) round deep-sided baking dish or tin (pan) with half the oil.

Pour the rest of the oil into a large bowl. Add the eggs, yoghurt, baking powder, oregano, parsley, sparkling water, salt and a good grind of black pepper to the bowl and whisk to combine. Add the bread to the mixture and stir well to coat the bread. Next, add the cheese and mix well so the cheese is evenly distributed.

Transfer the mixture to the prepared baking dish and gently press down. Top with the Parmesan (if using) and bake in the oven for 25–30 minutes until golden brown. Serve warm.

Note

I use any combination of bread, such as sourdough, baguette, multigrain, seeded, brioche – really anything. If you like a little bit of crunch, add some toasted and roughly chopped nuts or seeds. Equally, feel free to experiment with the herbs and spices you use or add any dry-ish deli bits you have left in the refrigerator, such as olives, cured meats or sun-dried tomatoes. For the cheese, use a mix of hard and salty (for example white cheese, feta or halloumi) and soft and melty (such as *kashkaval*, mozzarella or Cheddar).

From the Oven

Grandma's Savoury Cake

SERVES 8-10

125 ml (4 fl oz/½ cup) sunflower oil, plus extra for greasing

1–2 boiled or steamed carrots (about 75 g/2½ oz), finely chopped

1 sweet long green or red pepper (about 75 g/2½ oz), finely chopped (or 1–2 celery stalks)

100 g (3½ oz) smoked ham, finely chopped

100 g (3½ oz) white cheese (or feta), crumbled

20 g (¾ oz) fresh parsley, leaves picked and finely chopped

275 g (9¾ oz/scant 2¼ cups) self-raising (self-rising) flour, plus extra for dusting

3 medium eggs

150 ml (5 fl oz/scant ⅔ cup) kefir

100 g (3½ oz/⅔ cup) finely ground cornmeal

¼ teaspoon fine sea salt

freshly ground black pepper

Note

This mixture also works well as savoury muffins. Divide the mixture between 12 muffin cases and bake at 180°C fan (400°F) for 30–35 minutes or until the tops are golden brown and a skewer comes out clean. This keeps well in an airtight container at room temperature for up to 2 days; after a day, warm it in the microwave for 10–15 seconds to freshen it up.

This is the last recipe my grandma wrote down for me. In April 2011, as I was leaving for the airport to fly back to London, she pressed the piece of paper in my hand. Shortly after, she passed away suddenly. On the back of the recipe she had written: 'Grandma loves you. Don't be scared, I'm sure you will succeed.' I have always felt, and will always feel, that she was writing me more than just a recipe for savoury cake, but rather her last piece of advice to me – her recipe for the rest of my life.

This recipe is really a variant of the Balkan cornbread known variously as *proja* or *projanica* (in Serbia, Croatia and North Macedonia) or *proha* or *uljevak* in Bosnia and Herzegovina. There are hundreds (if not thousands) of variants of it across the Balkans, especially from areas across the region famous for growing local varieties of corn, such as the Sulova corn from Albania's south-eastern regions (which is used to make *pispili*, a corn and spinach bread) or Kosovo white corn (which is used to make *leqenik*, which is similar to *pispili*). Many recipes are simply cornbread flavoured with local cheeses, but they can be more elaborate and enriched with various alliums and greens (especially courgettes/zucchini, spinach, nettles or leeks). Cornbread can be a meal on its own, accompanied by a variety of fresh salads, meze, preserves, pickles or serving boards of *suvomesnati* (dried, smoked or cured meats) and cheeses. Or, it is simply eaten in lieu of bread.

Preheat the oven to 190°C fan (400°F). Grease a 900 g (2 lb) loaf tin (pan) with a little oil, then coat in flour and tip out any excess or line with baking parchment.

Place the chopped carrots, pepper, ham, cheese and parsley in a medium bowl and mix well. Add 3 tablespoons of the self-raising flour to the savoury mixture and mix well to coat everything in flour.

Crack the eggs in a separate large bowl. Using an electric whisk, whisk the eggs for 2–3 minutes on high speed until they are well aerated, have doubled in size and are pale and frothy. Add the kefir and oil and mix for 15–30 seconds to combine. Sift the rest of the flour, the cornmeal, salt and a good grind of black pepper into the wet mixture and fold it in with a spatula. Next, fold in the vegetable mixture, ensuring that it is well distributed but do not overwork it. Pour the mixture into the prepared tin and distribute it evenly, making sure there are no air pockets, then bake in the oven for 60–75 minutes, turning around halfway through, until the top is golden brown and a skewer inserted into the centre comes out clean. Allow to cool in the tin for 10–15 minutes, then transfer to a wire rack to cool completely before slicing and serving.

▲▲▲ From the Oven

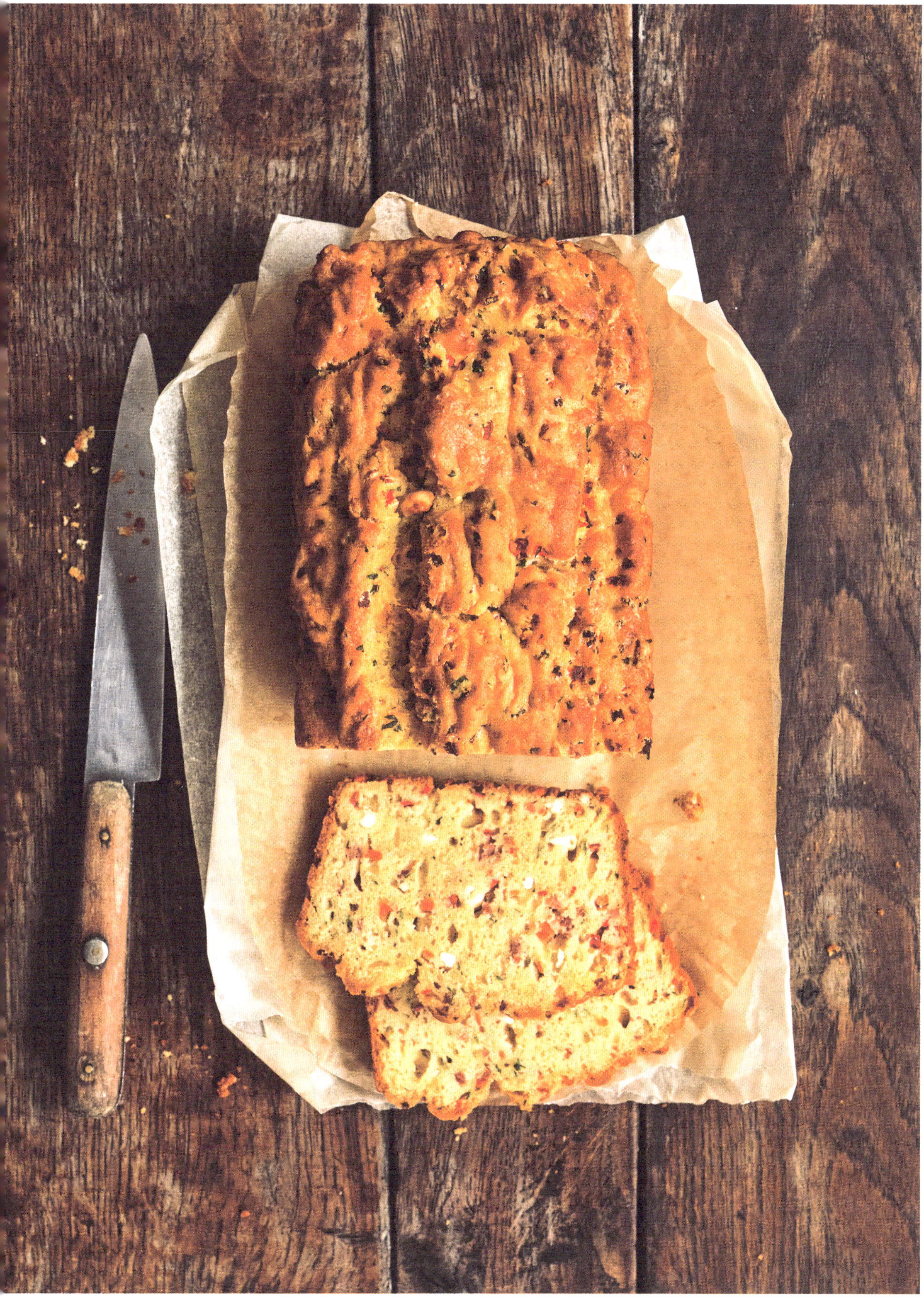

**MAKES
16 KIFLI**

Kifli

10 g (½ oz) fast-action dried yeast
1 tablespoon caster (superfine) sugar
125 ml (4 fl oz/½ cup) water
125 ml (4 fl oz/½ cup) kefir
100 ml (3½ fl oz/scant ½ cup) sunflower oil, plus extra for brushing
400 g (14 oz/scant 3¼ cups) strong white bread flour, plus extra for dusting
½ teaspoon fine sea salt
1 medium egg, lightly beaten
1 tablespoon sesame or nigella seeds (optional)

FILLING IDEAS
100 g (3½ oz) white cheese (or feta), crumbled
80 g (2¾ oz) kashkaval (or mild Cheddar), cut into 1 cm (½ inch) cubes) combined with 40–50 g (1½–1¾ oz) smoked ham, cut into 1.5 cm (¾ inch) cubes
80 g (2¾ oz) rosehip or apricot jam (jelly)
80 g (2¾ oz) Plum Pekmez (see page 247)

Every child who grew up in a Balkan household will remember *kifli* or *kifle* at every family feast and celebration. They are, I suppose, our croissants and very similar to Austrian kipferl, in shape if not in composition, as the name suggests. Savoury versions of them are always served alongside generously filled serving bowls of beautifully decorated salads (especially Ruska Salata, see page 84) and serving boards laden with cured and smoked meats and cheese, preserves and pickles. Sweet versions are as much of a treat, filled with any homemade preserves such as *dzem* or *pekmez* or marmalade, or the iconic Eurocrem, the former Yugoslav version of another famous chocolate spread that is still loved across the region. This base recipe will work for any savoury or sweet filling you like. I've given some suggestions below, but use whatever you fancy – just don't overfill them with sweet fillings or they leak. They are also beautiful unfilled in lieu of dinner bread rolls.

In a small bowl, mix together the yeast, sugar and water, then set aside for 5–10 minutes until frothy. Add the kefir and oil and stir well to combine.

Sift the flour and salt into a large bowl. Pour in the wet ingredients, then use a fork or spatula to mix until combined. Tip out the dough onto a lightly floured work surface and knead for 8–10 minutes until you have a soft dough.

Transfer to a large clean bowl brushed with a little oil, then brush a little oil over the top of the dough. Cover and set aside in a warm place to prove for 1–1½ hours, or until doubled in size.

Once risen, divide the dough in two equal-sized pieces.

Roll out one half of the dough into a large circle, about 30 cm (12 inches) in diameter. Using a pastry cutter, cut the circle into eight wedges. Place a marble-sized amount of filling at the wider end of one of the wedges, then roll once to cover the filling, press lightly and tuck in the edges, then gently stretching the wedge and continue to roll it, like a croissant, tucking in the tip of the wedge at the base. Repeat with all the wedges. Roll out the second half of the dough and repeat.

Place the rolls on two large baking sheets lined with baking parchment, spaced at least 2 cm (¾ inch) apart. Set them aside to rest and rise a little for 20 minutes.

Preheat the oven to 180°C fan (400°F). Brush the rolls with the beaten egg and sprinkle with the sesame or nigella seeds (if using). Bake in the oven for 20–25 minutes until golden brown and hollow-sounding when tapped on the base. Remove from the oven and transfer to a wire rack to cool slightly. Serve warm or cold.

From the Oven

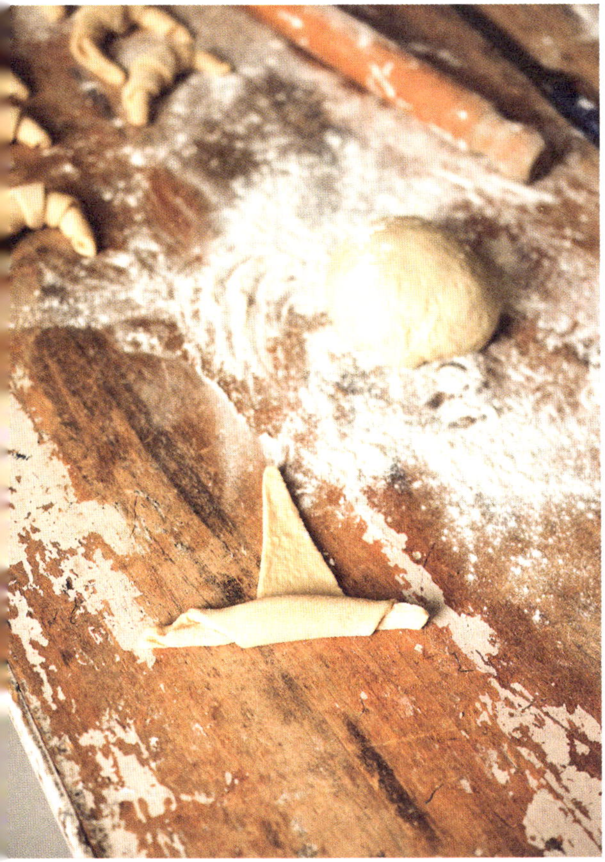
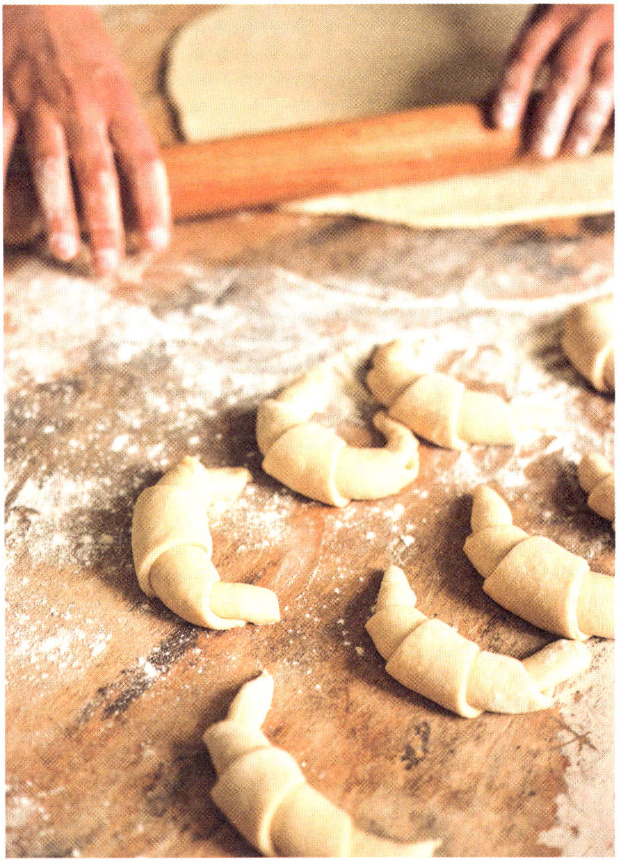
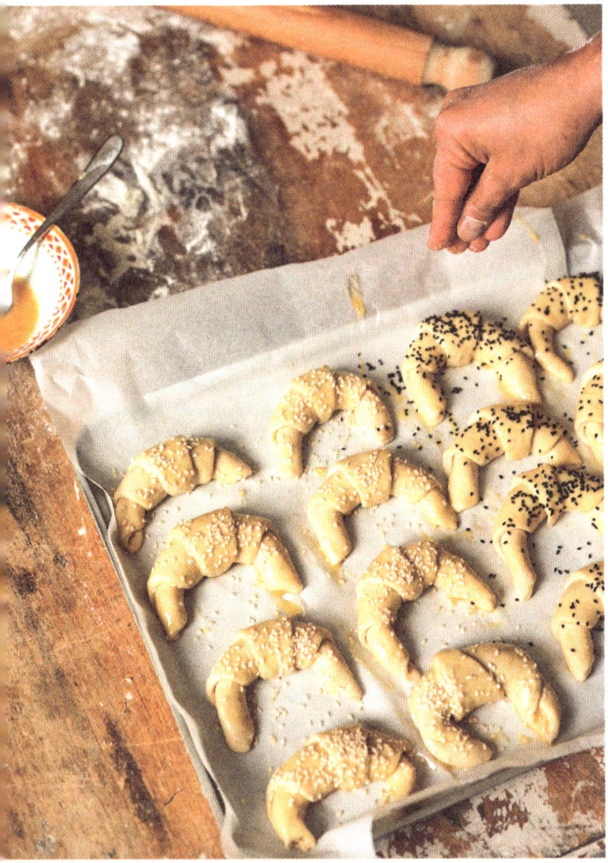
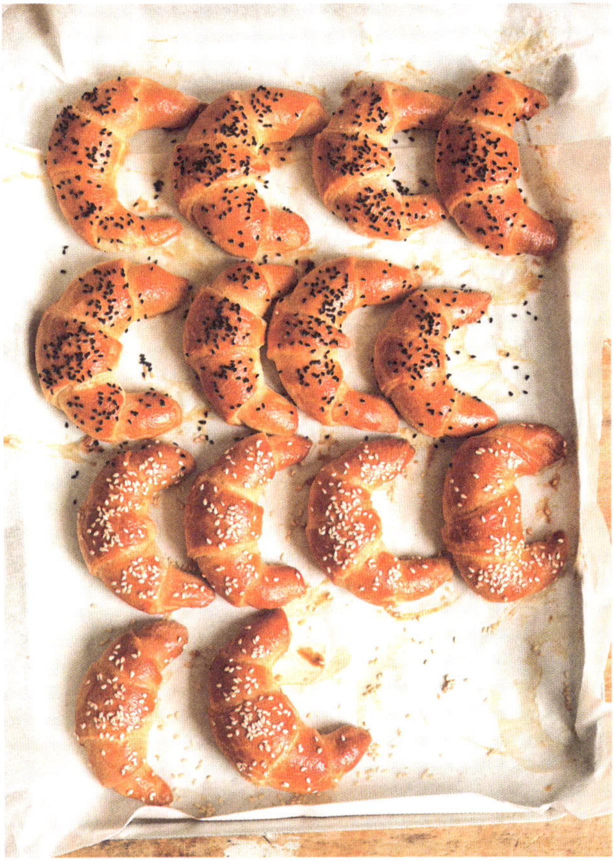

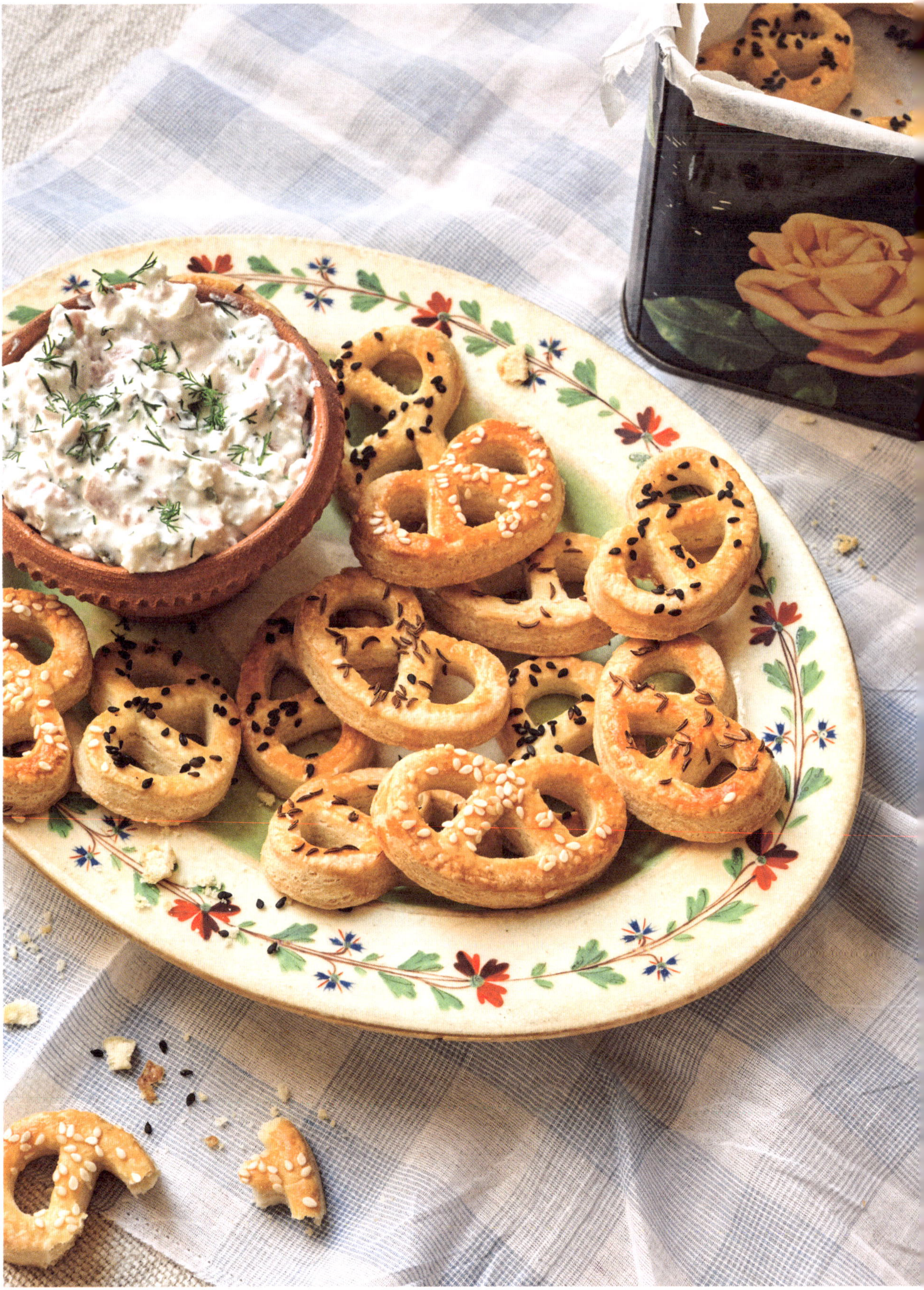

Solenki

MAKES 60–70 STICKS

450 g (1 lb/scant 3⅗ cups) plain (all-purpose) flour
1 teaspoon baking powder
1 teaspoon fine sea salt
200 g (7 oz) pork fat or ghee
3 medium eggs
120 ml (4 fl oz/½ cup) whole (full-fat) milk
2 tablespoons caraway or sesame seeds

Solenki could be translated literally as 'little salties' or perhaps better, 'little savouries'. In one cupboard in the kitchen, my grandmother kept a collection of old – now antique – tins that would have formerly housed sweets from one of Yugoslavia's iconic brands, Kraš. But for as far back as I can remember, they were always repurposed and filled with baked treats. Sometimes sweet, sometimes savoury, always something little she could serve at a moment's notice to welcome guests, comfort those longing for family living far away from or to serve as a little welcome home snack to those of us returning at long last. These little bites – especially when topped with caraway or sesame – were always my favourites. She sometimes cut them out with a small, custom-made pretzel-shaped cutter, which I still treasure, but cut them into any shape you like. I've suggested sticks as they are easiest. They work well as accompaniments to an aperitif.

Preheat the oven to 180°C fan (400°F) and line two large baking sheets with baking parchment.

Sift the flour, baking powder and salt into a large bowl. Add the pork fat or ghee and, using your hands, rub the fat into the flour until well incorporated and the mixture resembles coarse sand. Alternatively, you can do this in a food processor for 1–2 minutes.

Put 1 egg and 1 egg yolk into a small bowl and whisk until frothy. Add the milk and stir to combine. Add the wet ingredients to the dry mixture and mix (or pulse) to combine.

Tip out the dough onto a lightly floured work surface. Knead for 2–3 minutes until the ingredients are well combined and the dough comes together, but don't overwork it.

Lightly dust your work surface and rolling pin with flour again, then roll out the dough to form a large rectangle, about 30 x 40 cm (12 x 16 inches) and 3 mm (less than ¼ inch) thick. Using a serrated pastry cutter, cut out batons about 1 x 8 cm (½ x 3¼ inches). Using a butter or palette knife, gently lift them and place them on the prepared baking sheets. Press together any scraps of dough and roll them out again, cutting out more batons as before. Continue until all the dough has been used up.

Beat the remaining egg and use it to brush the tops of the pastry, then sprinkle with the caraway or sesame seeds. Bake in the oven for 22–24 minutes or until the batons are golden brown and their bases are crisp. Remove from the oven and transfer to a wire rack to cool. These will keep well stored in an airtight container at room temperature for up to 4 weeks.

Note
Served with Galička Salata on p. 81

From the Oven

MAKES 8 BUNS

Milibrod

7g (¼ oz) fast-action dried yeast
25 g (1 oz) caster (superfine) sugar
125 ml (4 fl oz/½ cup) lukewarm whole (full-fat) milk, plus extra for brushing
275 g (9¾ oz/scant 2¼ cups) strong white bread flour, plus extra for dusting
½ teaspoon fine sea salt
1 medium egg, lightly beaten
25 g (1 oz) unsalted butter, melted and cooled

FOR THE POPPY SEED FILLING
150 g (5½ oz/scant 1 cup) poppy seeds, ground
100 g (3½ oz/scant ½ cup) vanilla or caster sugar
2 teaspoons vanilla bean paste
50 g (1¾ oz/scant ⅛ cup) raisins
150 ml (5 fl oz/scant ⅔ cup) hot milk
1 teaspoon lemon zest

FOR THE APRICOT GLAZE
2 tablespoons Apricot Đzem (see page 247, or use shop-bought)
2 tablespoons lemon juice
1 tablespoons water

Milibrod is a type of sweet yeasted bread that in the Balkans is typically eaten at Easter. The name is likely derived from the German *milchbrot*, though in composition it is closer to Austrian *streizel* and Jewish *challah*. In North Macedonia it is also known as *kozinjak* and is often flavoured with sultanas (golden raisins), raisins or other dried fruits. There are so many variations of sweet yeasted breads across the Balkans. They can be baked like as a loaf, plaited or rolled (like the *potica* on page 76) and filled with various fillings – walnuts and poppy seeds being the most popular, but also jam, *pekmez*, marmalade, any other ground nuts or chocolate. In Croatia, Serbia and Bosnia and Herzegovina it is called *povitica* if rolled. When rolled and filled with walnuts, it is variously known as *orehnjača*, *orahnjača* and *orahovnjaca*. With poppy seeds, it becomes a *makovnjača*. Rolled, it is also often called *štrudla*.

This recipe for the dough comes from my godmother, Zore Bukleska. It is so versatile that I make it quite often, not just around Easter. This technique of twisting and making small knots is a little on the tricky side, but well worth the effort.

In a small bowl, mix together the yeast, sugar and milk, then set aside for 5–10 minutes until frothy.

Sift the flour and salt into a large bowl. Add the yeast mixture, egg and butter and then use a spatula to mix and bring the dough together, scraping down the sides of the bowl as you do. Tip out the dough onto a lightly floured work surface and knead for about 10 minutes until it comes together in a smooth, elastic dough that springs back when touched. Alternatively, if you have a stand mixer, combine as above and beat the mixture first on a low speed until the flour is incorporated and then on a medium speed for 10–12 minutes, pausing to scrape down the sides, until the dough comes together.

Place the dough into a clean bowl and cover tightly. Either prove in the refrigerator overnight (or for at least 8 hours), or leave in a warm place to prove for 1½ hours, or until the dough has doubled in size. If you prove it in the refrigerator, take the dough out of the fridge at least an hour before use so that it comes back to room temperature, otherwise it will be difficult to roll out.

Meanwhile, make the poppy seed filling. Put the poppy seeds, sugar, vanilla, raisins, milk and lemon zest into a small saucepan and cook over a medium heat for 8–10 minutes, stirring constantly, until the mixture has visibly thickened. Remove from the heat and set aside to cool.

Once the dough has risen, tip it out onto a lightly floured work surface. Using a lightly floured rolling pin, gently roll it out into a roughly 48 x 32 cm (19 x 12½ inch) rectangle. Spread the filling evenly over the dough with a spatula or palette knife. With the longest edge closest to you, fold over one third of the rectangle into the centre (as if closing a book) – you should have one third of the rectangle and filling still exposed. Fold over the other side of the rectangle so that no filling is exposed. With a knife, cut the dough widthwise into eight even strips. Take each dough strip and gently stretch and twist it around 3–4 times. Pinch one end of the strip together with the other (so you have a little circle) and twist it into a figure of eight. Repeat with the rest.

▲▲▲ From the Oven

Preheat the oven to 180°C fan (400°F). Line a large baking sheet with baking parchment and place the knots on the prepared baking sheet. With a pastry brush, brush each gently with a little milk. Set aside to rest for about 30 minutes.

Once rested, bake in the oven for 20–24 minutes, or until the buns are dark golden brown and hollow-sounding when tapped on the base.

While the knots are baking, prepare the glaze by heating the jam, lemon juice and water in a small saucepan over a medium heat for 1–2 minutes until the glaze is the consistency of runny honey. At this stage you can, if you prefer, sieve it (to remove any chunkier bits of apricot jam), but this is not necessary. Brush the knots with the glaze as soon as they come out of the oven, then place them on a wire rack to cool.

▲▲▲ From the Oven

Potica

SERVES 32-36

10 g (½ oz) fast-action dried yeast

175 ml (6 fl oz/¾ cup) lukewarm whole (full-fat) milk, plus extra for brushing

100 g (3½ oz/scant ½ cup) caster (superfine) sugar

550 g (1 lb 3¾ oz/scant 4½ cups) strong white bread flour, plus extra for dusting

¼ teaspoon fine sea salt

100 g (3½ oz) unsalted butter, softened, plus extra for greasing

2 large eggs and 1 egg yolk, lightly beaten

1 teaspoon vanilla bean paste

1 tablespoon lemon zest

1 tablespoon orange zest (optional)

1–2 tablespoons milk

FOR THE WALNUT AND CAROB FILLING

50 g (1¾ oz/scant ½ cup) sultanas (golden raisins)

2 tablespoons Orahovoča (see page 257) or rum

1 medium egg white

100 g (3½ oz/scant ½ cup) caster (superfine) sugar

120 ml (4 fl oz/½ cup) single (light) cream

200 g (7 oz/2 cups) ground walnuts

3 tablespoons carob bean powder (or raw unsweetened cacao powder)

1 tablespoon ground cinnamon

1 tablespoon lemon zest

1 tablespoon orange zest (optional)

Potica, a close cousin of *milibrod*, is one of Slovenia's most iconic baked treats. The name means 'little path' but is also derivative of the verb *poviti* (to wrap/roll up in Slovenian). Traditionally, *potica* is cooked in a round ceramic bundt baking dish called a *potičnik*. The first known recipe for *potica* – consisting of a thin pastry rolled with walnuts and honey – is found in the 17th-century writings of a Carniolian intellectual, Janez Vajkard Valvasor. In Slovenia, it is thought that if you can make *potica*, you can call yourself a good cook. Each Slovenian family is likely to have a recipe that has been passed down for generations. Traditionally prepared for festive occasions like Christmas, the favoured filling is still walnut, but there are now over a hundred other types of sweet or savoury fillings available: various nuts, seeds, spices and herbs for sweet versions and various cheeses, cured meats and herbs for savoury ones. There is a *potičnica* (potica cake shop) on Lake Bled that was established to preserve and teach the tradition of *potica*-making in Slovenia, which serves some very exciting flavours. I was especially taken with their sweet *skuta* (young curd cheese) and tarragon filling, but a walnut filling is, for me, hard to beat. As for carob – it is something that was widely used in the region in lieu of the once more expensive cacao. The earliest handwritten recipes I have from my great-grandmother reference carob, and like many children around the Mediterranean and Middle East to which this tree is native, I grew up playing our equivalent of conkers with carob bean pods.

In a small bowl, mix together the yeast, milk and 1 tablespoon of the sugar, then set aside for 5–10 minutes until frothy.

Put the rest of the sugar into a large bowl and sift in the flour and salt, then stir to combine. Add the butter, eggs, vanilla and zest. Pour in the yeast mixture, then use a spatula to combine (scraping down the sides of the bowl as you go). Tip out the dough onto a lightly floured work surface and knead for 5–6 minutes until the ingredients are just combined into a smooth dough that moves easily on the surface without sticking and springs back when touched.

Place the dough into a large clean bowl and cover. Set aside in a warm place to prove for around 2 hours, or until the dough has doubled in size.

Meanwhile, make the filling. Place the sultanas in a small bowl, add the Orahovoča or rum and set aside. In a separate bowl, whisk the egg white with an electric whisk, adding the sugar gradually until a stiff mixture forms. Add the cream and mix for 10 seconds just to combine it with the egg white mixture. Add the sultanas, ground walnuts, carob powder, cinnamon and zest and mix well to combine. Set aside.

Generously grease a 24 cm (9½ inch) *potičnik* (if you have one) or bundt tin, dust it with flour and shake out any excess.

Once the dough has risen, turn it out onto a lightly floured work surface. Using a lightly floured rolling pin, roll it out into a rectangle around 48 x 60 cm (19 x 23½ inches). The longest side needs to be the approximate length of the circumference of the *potičnik*. Spread the filling evenly over the surface of the dough with a spatula or palette knife, leaving a border of 5–6 cm (2–2½ inches) along one long side. Starting from the opposite long side, tightly roll up the *potica*. Place the roll in the prepared tin, seam side down, stretching it gently to ensure the ends meet. Cover and leave to rise again for 1½–2 hours, or until nearly doubled in size.

Preheat the oven to 170°C fan (375°F).

Brush the top of the risen *potica* with milk, then use a skewer or long toothpick to prick holes at regular intervals all the way around it, ensuring you go all the way down to the base.

Bake the *potica* in the oven for 40–50 minutes until golden brown (turning it around if needed to ensure an even bake). Allow it to cool completely in the tin before removing and slicing to serve.

From the Oven

Pastrmajlija

MAKES 4 PASTRMAJLIJA (SERVES 4 AS A MAIN OR 8 AS A SIDE)

10 g (½ oz) fast-action dried yeast
2 teaspoons caster (superfine) sugar
400 ml (14 fl oz/generous 1½ cups) lukewarm water
600 g (1 lb 5 oz/generous 4¾ cups) strong white bread flour, plus extra for dusting
2 teaspoons fine sea salt
1 tablespoon sunflower oil, plus extra for brushing
20–30 g (¾–1 oz/¼ cup) semolina or polenta (cornmeal), for shaping

FOR THE TOPPING

400 g (14 oz) pork loin or fillet (tenderloin), cut into small (no bigger than 1 cm/½ inch) cubes
1 tablespoon sweet paprika
1 teaspoon sunflower or olive oil
1 teaspoon smoked sea salt flakes
40 g (1½ oz) pork fat
4 medium eggs (optional)
freshly ground black pepper

Note
Swap the pork for other meat of your choice and use ghee or olive oil instead of pork fat. The dough works well as a pizza base too.

Across the Balkans, this is thought of as 'Macedonian pizza'. One of the greatest culinary rivalries within North Macedonia is which city makes the best *pastrmajlija* – Štip, Sveti Nikole, Veles or Kratovo. The differences between them are in the artistry of the dough and toppings. I refuse to take sides because frankly choosing is akin to choosing a favourite child. *Pastrmajlija* is so-called because it would have originally been made with *pastrma*, an air-dried cured meat that you find not only in the Balkans but across the Levant – Turkey, Armenia, Lebanon, Egypt and Iraq to name a few. In the Balkans, *pastrma* is typically made from mountain lamb or mutton, or sometimes goat. *Pastrmajlija* is an obvious cousin to Turkey's *pastirmali pide*, but in North Macedonia, *pastrmajlija* is, nowadays, more commonly made with pork and pork fat with the addition of egg, and for some, white cheese. Feel free to adapt it to your preference (as I have slightly), but there is an unwritten rule that you must have it with spicy pickled peppers or any other spicy pickle and a drink of cooling yoghurt.

Ideally, prepare the topping the night before so it has time to marinate, but you can also prepare it just before you make the dough. Place the cubed pork, paprika, oil, smoked sea salt and a good grind of black pepper into a medium bowl, cover and marinate in the refrigerator overnight, or for as long as you can.

To make the dough, place the yeast, sugar and water in a jug (pitcher) and stir to combine. Set aside for 5–10 minutes until frothy.

Sift the flour and salt into a large bowl. Make a well in the middle and add the oil and the yeast mixture. Using a fork, mix well until the flour and liquid comes together into a shaggy dough.

Tip out the dough onto a lightly floured surface (scraping out the sides of the bowl). Knead for about 10 minutes, or until you have a smooth, soft dough that moves around easily on the surface and springs back lightly when touched. If the dough is too sticky, rather than adding more flour, wash your hands, lightly dust them with flour and continue kneading. Shape the dough into a ball. Brush the bowl and the dough with a little oil, transfer the dough to the bowl and cover, then set aside in a warm place to prove for 1–1½ hours, or until doubled in size.

Tip out the dough onto a lightly floured work surface and divide it into four equal-sized pieces. Shape each piece into a ball, then cover and allow to rest for a further 15 minutes.

Preheat the oven to 220°C fan (475°F) and place two baking sheets in the oven to heat up.

Sprinkle the semolina over your work surface. Using your fingers, gently flatten each dough ball into a disc, then either use a rolling pin lightly dusted with flour or with your hands to stretch the discs out into oval, about 12 x 30 cm (13 x 12 inches). Using your fingers, gently flatten the centre of each oval and shape the edge to create a higher edge so you end up with a kind of dough boat. Place two of the pieces on a sheet of baking parchment and do the same for the other two. Distribute the cubed pork equally between the dough ovals, dotting the pork fat between the cubed pork.

Carefully transfer each sheet of baking parchment onto the preheated baking sheets and bake in the oven for 10–12 minutes, rotating them

From the Oven

if necessary to ensure they cook evenly on all sides. Remove from the oven, dip a pastry brush in the melted pork fat of each *pastrmajlija* and brush the edges of the dough with it. If you like, crack an egg into each *pastrmajlija*, taking care it does not spill over the edge.

Return to the oven and bake for a further 3–4 minutes, or until the egg is set to your liking and the base of each *pastrmajlija* is lightly golden brown and cooked through. Remove from the oven and serve hot.

▲▲▲ From the Oven

FOR SHARING
MEZE

This chapter contains only a fleeting glimpse of the kinds of small, flavourful dishes that are typically served as meze across the Balkans. Sometimes they are the precursors to the meal – intended to whet the appetite for both more delicious food to come and conversation. They are necessary accompaniments to a little glass (or two, or more) of something fortifying, such as the spirit *rakija* or a delicious local wine, which are meant to be sipped little by little, while leisurely snacking on the meze on offer. Sometimes they are simply side dishes, served alongside the main meal. For special social occasions and family celebrations and parties – birthdays, engagements, weddings, *slava* (a family saint's day celebration), Easter, Christmas, Eid – they are always included as part of a beautifully arranged table of *ordever* (a Balkanisation of the French *hors d'oeuvre*), alongside homemade breads and pastries and sharing boards and platters laden with a wide array of *suvomesnati* (air-dried, smoked or other cured meats) and cheeses.

Suvomesnati would typically include *Njeguški pršut*, a famous dry-cured ham similar to prosciutto from Njeguši in Montenegro, or more generally *pršut* from across the Balkans including Istria and Dalmatia and *Kraški pršut* (from Slovenia); *suva govedina*, dried beef from Montenegro; *Srem* salami from Serbia; *kulen* (from Croatia and Serbia), a spicy, fermented sausage, primarily made from pork and flavoured with paprika and garlic; *Češnjovka*, a cured pork and garlic sausage from Croatia; *slanina*, a Serbian-style bacon made from pork belly, cured with salt and spices, then air-dried; *suvi vrat*, air-dried and smoked pork neck or loin from Serbia; *sudzuk*, a type of air-dried, spicy sausage made from ground meat, usually beef, and seasoned with garlic, paprika, and other spices (variants of which you will find in North Macedonia, Kosovo and Bosnia and Herzegovina); and *pastrma*, a seasoned, air-dried beef or mutton found in North Macedonia, Kosovo and Bosnia and Herzegovina.

Cheeses across the region vary greatly in flavour, texture and production methods, often influenced by the unique local landscape, fauna and cultural practices, imparting distinct flavours on each. Cheeses that would typically be served include: *beli sir* or *sirenje*, a white brined cheese similar to feta, which can range from young and mild in flavour to aged, strong, crumbly and salty; *sirenje* or *kashkaval* from the Šar Mountains (which span North Macedonia, Serbia and Kosovo); *Pule* (*magareci*), a rare and highly prized cheese made in Serbia from a combination of donkey's milk and goat's milk; any of the delicious cheeses produced in Bosnia and Herzegovina, such as *Travnički*, *Livanjski*, *Vlašićki* or *Hercegovački*; any of the cheese produced in Croatia, for example *Paški sir*, a special hard cheese from Pag Island and *Škripavac*, a soft, fresh cheese loved in Zagreb and known for its squeaky texture; *Lički sir*; from Slovenia; *Tolmic/Tolminski sir*, a semi-hard cheese from the Tolmin area of western Slovenia; *Tavžentroža* and *Planika*; and of course Kajmak.

The offerings of course vary by region. For example, along the coasts you will also find marinated or grilled sardines or other tiny fish from the Adriatic. These dishes are all about sharing: food, conversation and life.

SERVES 4-6

Shopska Salata

1 banana shallot or onion, halved and thinly sliced

2–3 large beef (beefsteak) tomatoes, halved and sliced

1 large cucumber, halved lengthwise and sliced

6–8 roasted, fried or grilled long green peppers (see page 97), peeled and roughly chopped (optional)

20 g (¾ oz) fresh parsley, leaves picked and roughly chopped, plus a few picked leaves to serve (optional)

50 g (1¾ oz) sheep's milk white cheese (or feta) coarsely grated or crumbled

FOR THE DRESSING

3 tablespoons sunflower or extra virgin olive oil

1 tablespoon red wine vinegar

1 teaspoon sea salt flakes, or more to taste

freshly ground black pepper

Shopska salad is iconic across the region, but it is claimed as the national salad of Bulgaria. Purportedly 'invented' in the mid-1950s, one of the earliest recipes for it was published in a pamphlet by Balkantourist, Bulgaria's state tourism board, promoting tourism to Bulgaria's Black Sea. The salad is thought to represent the colours of the Bulgarian flag, and is named after a mountainous region called Shopluk that transcends the modern national borders of Bulgaria, North Macedonia and Serbia. This region is inhabited by an ethnic group called the Šop or Shopi – highlanders traditionally engaged in mountain herding – who would have made beautiful sheep's milk *sirenje* with the milk from their mountain-grazing herds. It is very likely that some form of this salad pre-dates the first published recipe – it would not take a huge leap of imagination to etymologically go from Shopluk or *Shopska salata* to Turkish *çoban* salata (Turkey's famous shepherd's salad) or vice versa. It likely originated as a humble shepherd's salad made from ingredients that are plentiful across the region, and was very likely consumed across the region in some guise long before any recipe existed for it. With the addition of fried green peppers, it is nowadays referred to as 'Macedonian' salad in North Macedonia. It is unashamedly simple, allowing the naturally beautiful ingredients from the region to shine. One mouthful of crusty bread, torn off in haste and dunked into the salad juices and I am instantly transported to anywhere in the Balkans in summer.

Place the shallot or onion in a bowl and cover with cold water. Leave to stand for 5 minutes, then drain. This takes away the sharpness of raw onions.

Combine the drained shallot or onion, tomatoes, cucumbers and roasted peppers (if using) in a large bowl.

In a small bowl, combine all the ingredients for the dressing and whisk together until the salt dissolves. Pour the dressing over the salad and toss gently to coat the vegetables. Sprinkle the parsley over the salad (if using) and sprinkle the cheese over the top. Top with the picked parsley leaves to serve.

Note

The dressing for this salad is optional. In the Balkans it is usually served on the side so that you may dress the salad to your preference: either just seasoned with no dressing at all, or just oil or just vinegar, or a mixture of both. Often, people rely on the juiciness and natural acidity of summer tomatoes to be the dressing. I love it with roasted, fried or grilled peppers, but feel free to leave them out or use raw diced peppers if you like.

For Sharing

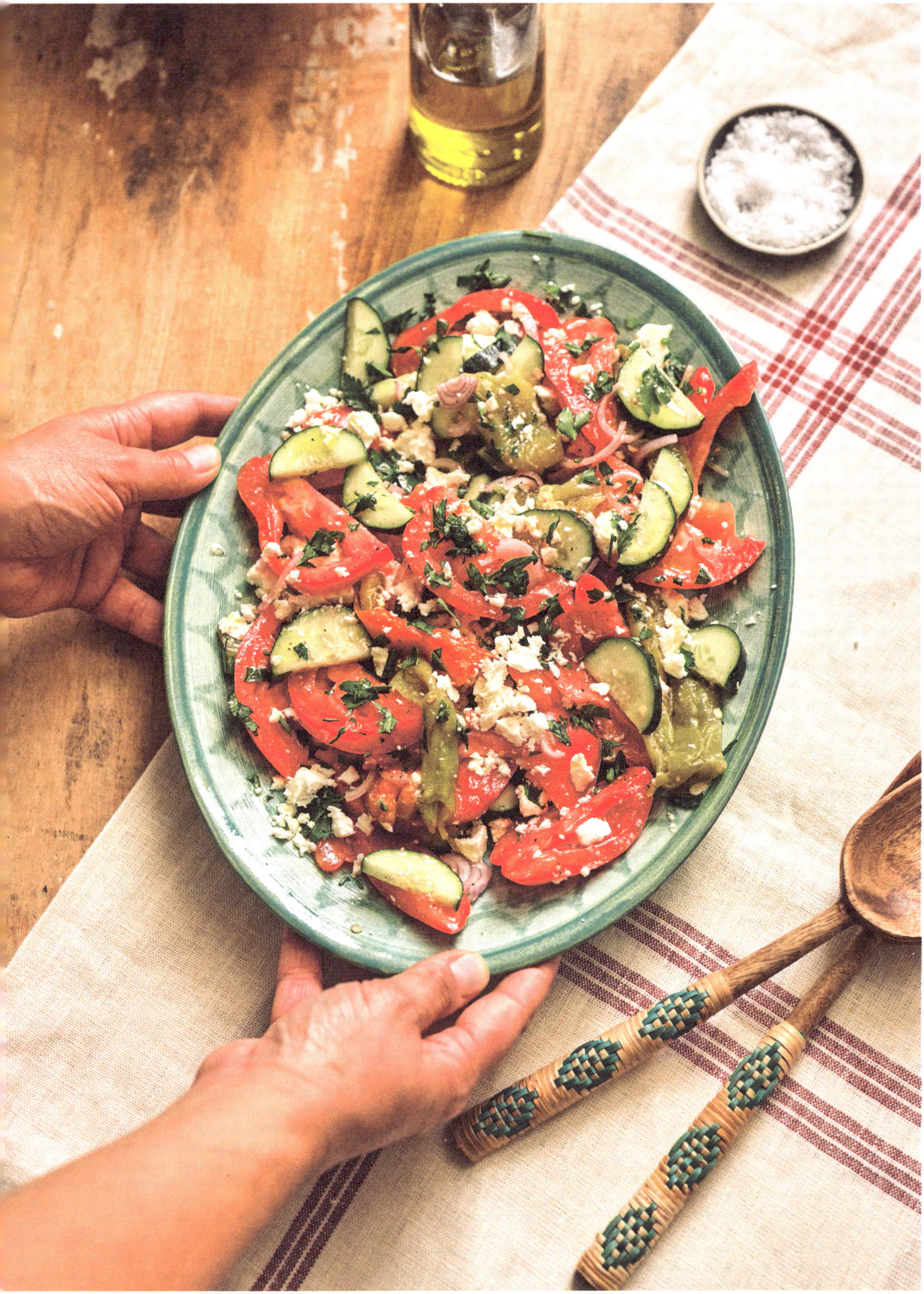

SERVES 6-8

Ruska Salata

450 g (1 lb) waxy potatoes, boiled in their skins, peeled and finely diced

400 g (14 oz) carrots, peeled, boiled or steamed and finely diced

200 g (7 oz/1⅓ cups) fresh or frozen peas, boiled or steamed

300–400 g (10½–14 oz) chicken breast or thigh, poached or roasted and finely diced

3 hard-boiled eggs, finely diced (reserving one egg yolk for the top)

200 g (7 oz) gherkins (pickles) or cornichons, finely diced

100 g (3½ oz) kashkaval (or mild Cheddar), finely diced (optional)

350–400 g (12–14 oz/1⅓–1⅔ cups) mayonnaise, or more to taste

½ teaspoon Dijon mustard

2 tablespoons lemon juice

1 teaspoon sea salt flakes, plus extra as needed

20 g (¾ oz) fresh parsley leaves or dill, finely chopped, plus extra to serve

freshly ground black pepper

Russian salad. Salade Olivier. *Macédoine de legumes* (in France). Known by various names and eaten around the world including in Iran, India, Turkey and, of course, the Balkans. In the Balkans, it is iconic. A salad that is present on every feast table, for any occasion. New Year's Eve celebrations are unthinkable without an elaborately decorated bowl of it. Each family has their own version, but there are some general guidelines: the Balkan version of Russian salad has poached chicken, vegetables (carrots, potatoes, sometimes cauliflower), hard-boiled eggs, tinned peas, maybe herbs, all coated in copious amounts of mayonnaise. Gherkins (pickles) are obligatory. Everything else is personal preference. A variant, known as 'French salad', uses ham, usually smoked.

In my kitchen it is the perfect way to use up leftovers – surplus vegetables from making bone broth, any leftover roasted or slow-cooked meats (beef, pork or game). I often cook extra chicken, carrots and potatoes when making chicken soup (see page 110) and use these for *Ruska salata*. In summer I use fresh cucumber and up the amount of lemon juice, in winter I use pickled cucumbers. Sometimes I leave out the meat and dairy entirely, and other times I cut the mayonnaise with natural yoghurt for a lighter version. I encourage you to experiment and create your own ideal version of *Ruska salata*. Here is mine.

Put the potatoes, carrots, peas, chicken, eggs, gherkins and cheese (if using) in a large bowl and mix well to combine.

In a separate small bowl, combine the mayonnaise, mustard, lemon juice, salt and a good grind of black pepper. Whisk to create a sauce, then add the herbs and mix well.

Spoon the sauce over the diced vegetable and meat mixture and stir gently to coat everything. Taste it and add more salt or black pepper if you like.

Place the salad in a large serving bowl, grate the reserved egg yolk over the top and decorate with fresh herbs to serve. This keeps well for up to 4 days stored in an airtight container in the refrigerator.

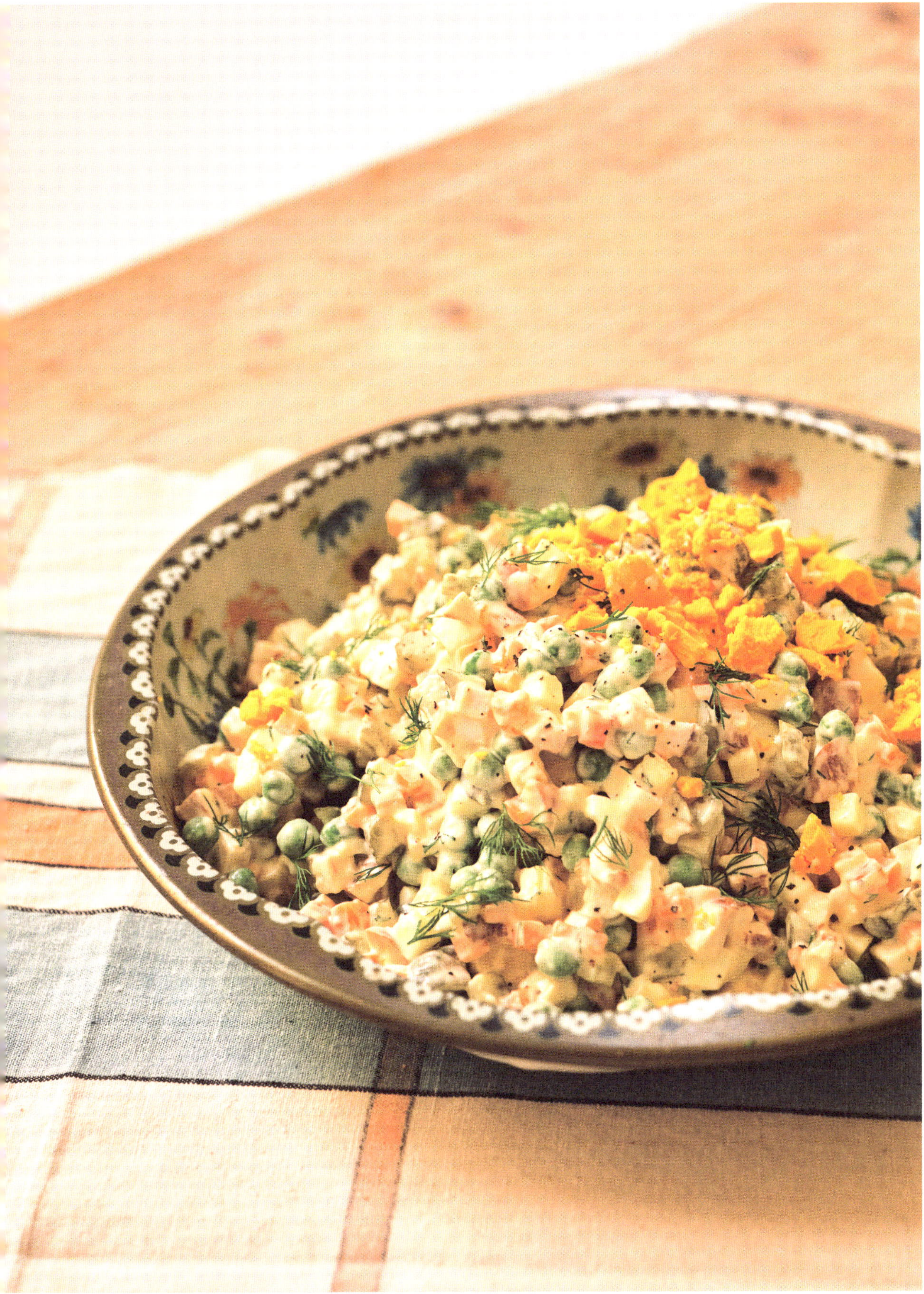

SERVES 4-6

Tarator

250–300 g (9–10½ oz) cucumbers
1 garlic clove, crushed
½ teaspoon sea salt flakes, plus extra as needed
1 teaspoon white balsamic vinegar (optional)
1 teaspoon dried mint, plus extra to serve
10 g (½ oz) fresh mint, leaves picked and finely chopped, plus extra to serve
10 g (½ oz) fresh dill, fronds picked and finely chopped, plus extra to serve
300 g (10½ oz/1¼ cups) plain set yoghurt, or more to taste
20 g (¾ oz) walnuts, lightly toasted and roughly chopped
freshly ground black pepper

FOR THE TOPPING (OPTIONAL)
1–2 garlic cloves, finely chopped
10 g (½ oz) fresh mint, leaves picked and finely chopped
½ teaspoon dried mint
½ teaspoon hot or mild Bukovo pepper (or Aleppo pepper)
½ teaspoon sea salt flakes
60 ml (2 fl oz/¼ cup) extra virgin olive oil

What we call *tarator* in the Balkans is not what is known as *tarator* in Turkey. That does not mean we do not have dishes that resemble Turkish-style *tarator* (see page 102), but for us, *tarator* is any variation on the theme of cucumbers, garlic and yoghurt. Our *tarator* is closer to Turkish *cacik* or Greek tzatziki. In the hellishly hot summers, especially in the southern Balkans, we add ice cubes to our *tarator* in an almost futile attempt to cool down, which makes it soupy. In Bulgaria and North Macedonia, it is intentionally often served as a raw, cooling yoghurt soup. The use of vinegar is controversial – blasphemous even – but I stand by it, as for me it enhances the sweetness of the cucumbers. For a full Balkan experience, have this with fresh warm crusty bread, while sipping from a *čokanj* (special shot glass) of *rakija* (brandy) and other mezes.

Coarsely grate the cucumbers, then take a handful of the grated cucumber and squeeze out as much of the water as you can over a small bowl (reserve it, it makes for a refreshing drink). Place the squeezed cucumber in a separate bowl and repeat until you have squeezed all the grated cucumber.

Place the garlic, salt and vinegar in a medium bowl and mix well to combine. Add the grated cucumber and the rest of the ingredients together with a good grind of black pepper and mix well. Check and adjust the seasoning to your taste. Store in an airtight container in the refrigerator until you are ready to serve.

To make the topping (if using), place the garlic, fresh and dried mint, Bukovo pepper, ½ tsp of salt and a good grind of black pepper into a small heatproof bowl. Heat the oil into a small saucepan over a high heat until it starts to smoke. Remove from the heat and immediately pour over the topping ingredients – they should sizzle. Set aside to cool.

To serve, place the tarator in a lipped serving bowl. Drizzle over some of the topping (if using) and serve the rest alongside. Sprinkle some fresh mint leaves (or dried mint) and dill fronds over the top.

Note

The *tarator* can be as thick or as liquid as you like. If you prefer yours thicker, simply use thicker Greek-style yoghurt. Equally, feel free to add more garlic, but before you adjust the amount of garlic, allow the mixture to sit for at least an hour in the refrigerator as the garlic flavour strengthens and comes through the longer it sits. The topping is completely non-traditional but this is how I love serving it for guests; feel free to simply top your *tarator* with a little dried or fresh mint and a drizzle of good oil.

For Sharing

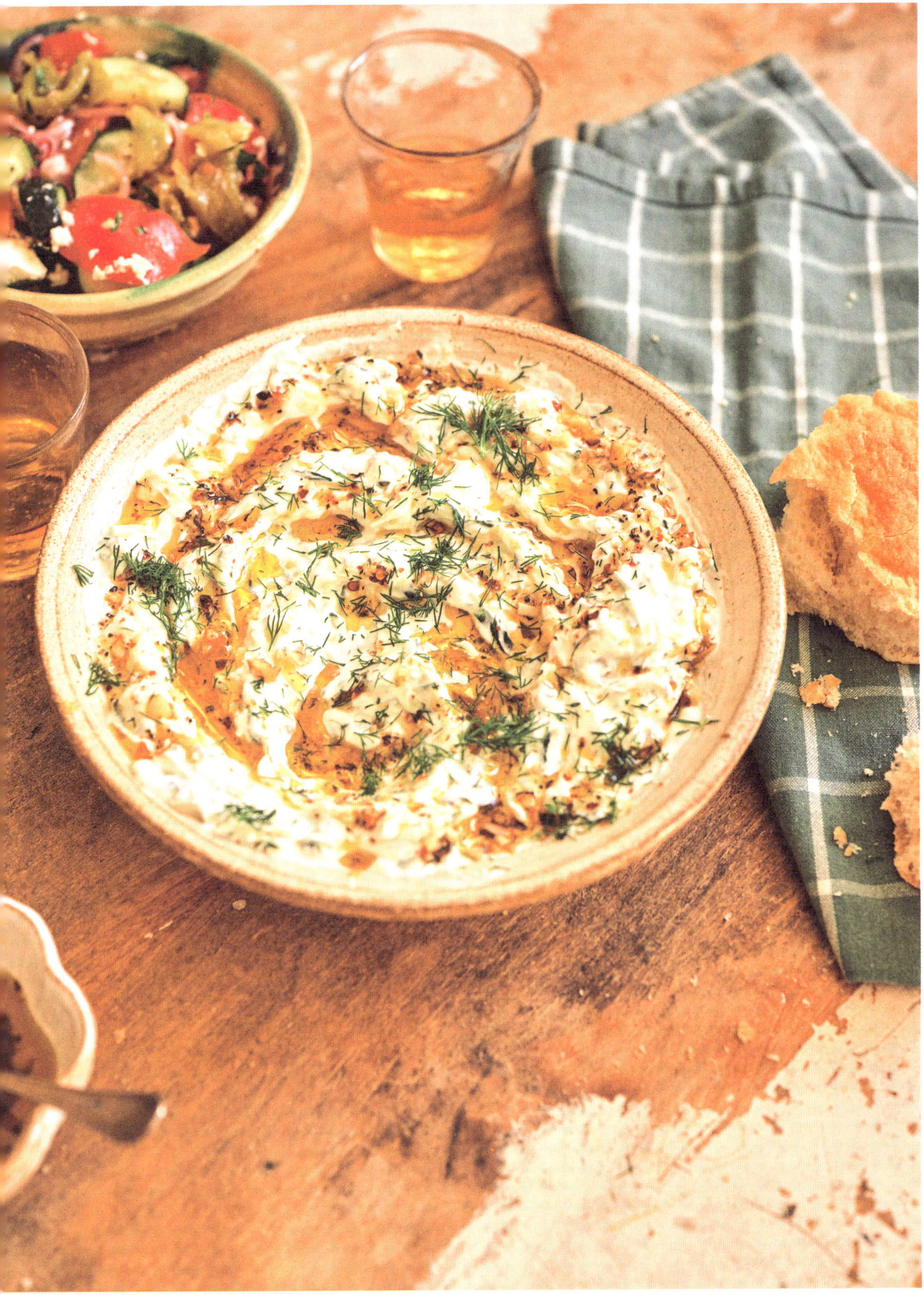

SERVES 4-6

Leek, Lemon and Olive Salata

1 large leek, halved lengthwise, washed and dark green leaves trimmed slightly, then finely chopped (about 150 g/5½ oz chopped leek)

40–50 ml (1¼–1¾ fl oz/3–3½ tablespoons) lemon juice plus 1 tablespoon zest

1 tablespoon sunflower or extra virgin olive oil

¼ teaspoon sea salt flakes

freshly ground black pepper

TO SERVE

1 lemon, sliced into half-moons

75 g (2½ oz) pitted black olives (ideally kalamata, and if you are using jarred olives, ideally packed in oil rather than brine), or more to taste

Leeks are used extensively in North Macedonia, both fresh in salads and for a wide variety of stews and pastry fillings, and to flavour certain types of smoked sausages. The most famously delicious local variety of leek is the Zrnovski leek, grown around the village of Zrnovci in the eastern part of North Macedonia. This lovely and easy leek salad – which I like to think of as leek ceviche – was frequently on our table during winter, making the most of the seasonal vegetable. I always associate it with Orthodox Christmas, because it is perfect for those who are either fasting due to observing the Nativity fast or vegan. Use the best-quality leeks you can find, ideally organic, as so much depends on their flavour.

Place the leek, juice and zest, oil, salt and a good grind of black pepper in a medium bowl, mix well to combine and set aside. Allow the leek to absorb the lemon juice for at least 30 minutes – it will start to soften. Garnish with the olives and lemon slices, then serve. This keeps well in an airtight container in the refrigerator for 1–2 days.

Note

Instead of olives, try dotting some Ljutenica over the lemon-marinated leek.

See photo on p. 90

For Sharing

SERVES 4-6

Galička Salata

250 g (9 oz/1 cup) set sheep's yoghurt (at least 3.5% fat), drained
½ teaspoon sea salt flakes
200 g (7 oz) sheep's milk white cheese (or feta), grated or crumbled
100 g (3½ oz) smoked, thick-cut ham, finely diced
50 g (1¾ oz) gherkins (pickles) or cornichons, finely diced
25 g (1 oz) walnuts, ground or finely chopped
1–2 garlic cloves, crushed (optional)
1 tablespoon extra virgin olive oil
10 g (½ oz) soft herbs, such as parsley, oregano or dill, finely chopped, plus extra to serve (optional)
freshly ground black pepper

Galičnik is a village on Mount Bistra in north-western North Macedonia famous for its surrounding countryside and nature reserves. The region has incredibly rich pastures for upland livestock grazing and is famous for its livestock trade and cheese, meat and wool production. The local *kashkaval*, *sirenje* and dairy products are particular specialities, which is likely why this salad is named after Galičnik, given it relies heavily on really good-quality sheep's milk yoghurt and cheese.

There was a strong tradition of *pećalba* (seasonal work) in Galičnik, where many young men would leave to make their fortune in larger towns and cities or go abroad to Australia or North America as skilled labourers and artisans – masons, carpenters, painters and, famously, *kopanicari* (wood carvers and church builders). They would be absent from Galičnik for months or even years at a time, trying to earn enough to support their existing or future families and sometimes returning having made a fortune. The tradition of the annual *Galička svadba* (wedding) held on St Peter's Day in July started for this reason – to allow all the returning *pećalbari* to wed, all on the same day, while they were home for the summer. During the wedding, the men of Galičnik dance the *teškoto* ('hard' or 'heavy') folk dance, a symbol for the harshness of life or perhaps the heaviness of their hearts at having to leave their homeland, sometimes never to return again.

Put the yoghurt and salt into a medium bowl and stir well to combine. Add the cheese, ham, gherkins, walnuts, garlic, oil, herbs and a good grind of black pepper and mix well. Garnish with fresh herbs to serve.

See photo on p. 72   For Sharing

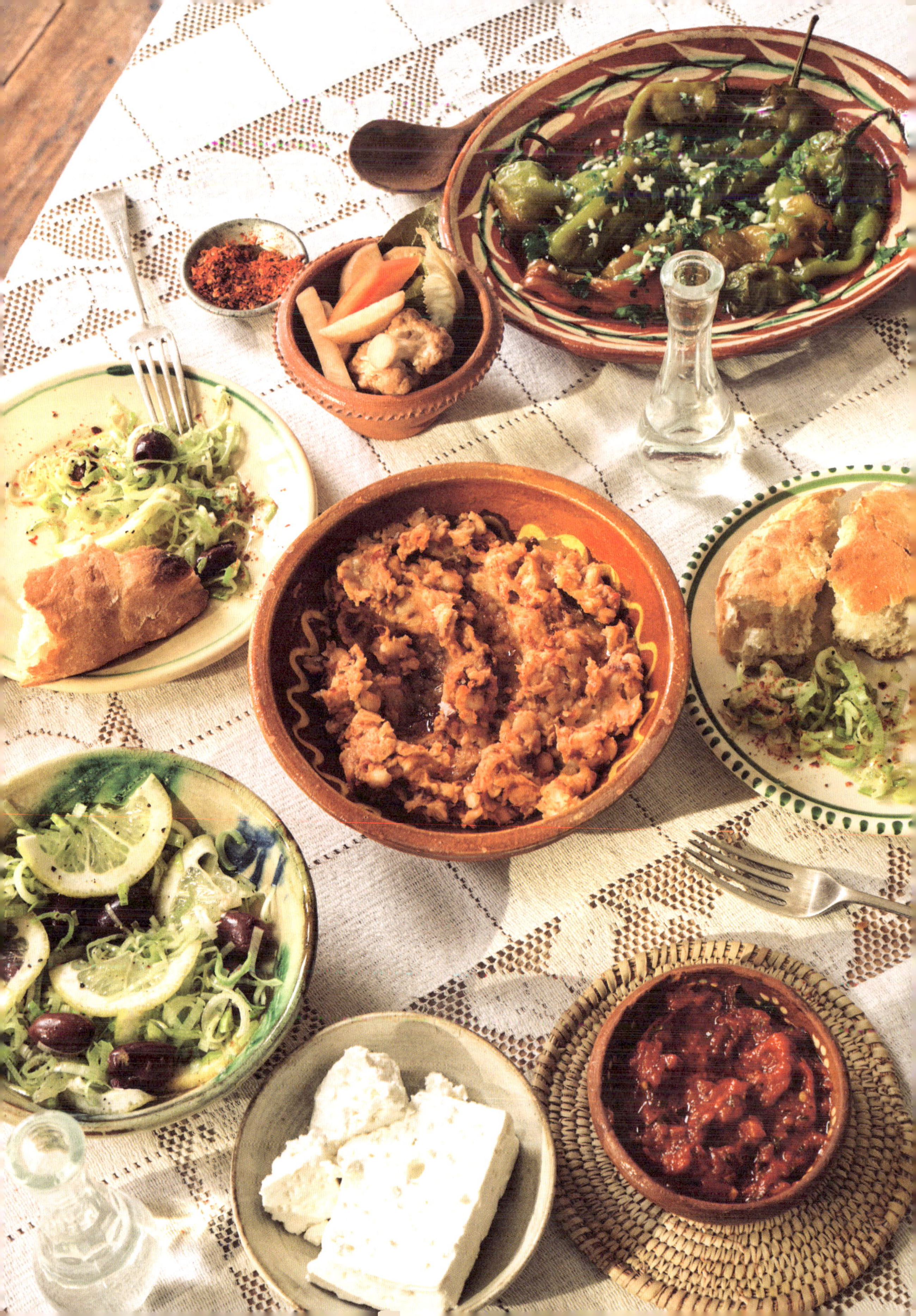

SERVES 4-6

Makalo

1 x 400 g (14 oz) tin of cannellini beans
1 small onion, peeled and quartered
150 ml (5 fl oz/scant ⅔ cup) water
1 tablespoon Dried Pepper Paste (see page 261)
1 garlic clove, crushed
½ teaspoon sea salt flakes, plus extra to serve
¼ teaspoon freshly ground black pepper
1 tablespoon extra virgin olive oil, plus extra to serve
Bukovo pepper (or Aleppo pepper), to serve (optional)

Makalo translates roughly to 'for dipping' or 'for scooping', which should be done with fresh crusty bread. There are many versions of makalo, including one made from just garlic and oil, closely resembling Levantine toum. This version is also known as *tućen pasulj* (pounded beans), *meljanac* and *papula*. It is a humble vegan meze using two iconic Balkan ingredients – beans and dried peppers. It can also be made with boiled potatoes instead of beans, if you prefer. I make *makalo* when I cook a big batch of beans for Tavče Gravče (see page 150), but below is a method for 'pimping' tinned or jarred beans to mimic the flavour of that long, slow cook when I am in a rush to make this and haven't got a batch of beans on the go.

Put the beans and their liquid into a small saucepan with the onion and water and simmer over a medium-high heat for 10–12 minutes until the onion has softened and the bean cooking liquid has thickened. Drain the beans and discard any bean skins that have separated. Reserve the bean cooking liquid and onion to thicken and flavour soups.

Next, place the beans, dried pepper paste, garlic, salt and pepper into a mortar. Use a pestle to crush them into a paste. Don't overdo it – it's good to keep a little texture in the beans. Add the oil and stir to combine.

To serve, top with an extra drizzle of oil, some more sea salt flakes and a little Bukovo pepper.

Note
Instead of the dried pepper paste, use 1–2 teaspoons Bukovo pepper or Aleppo pepper flakes, depending on how much heat you like.

For Sharing

SERVES 4-6

Pindžur

- 250–300 g (9–10½ oz) aubergine (eggplant)
- 200 g (7 oz) red Romano peppers (or sweet long green peppers)
- 320—360 g (1¼–12½ oz) ripe beef (beefsteak) tomatoes
- 2–3 garlic cloves, peeled
- 1 tablespoon sea salt flakes
- 50 ml (1 ¾ fl oz/3½ tablespoons) good-quality sunflower or olive oil, or more to taste

For me, this is summer in North Macedonia on a plate. Tomatoes, aubergines (eggplants) and sweet long peppers that taste like sunshine are abundant. One of the many, many creative ways we use them is in *pindžur*, a fresh summer relish prepared predominantly across the southern Balkans. Unlike *Ajvar* (see page 239), *pindžur* is eaten fresh (and also contains tomatoes). This preparation also differentiates it from *Ljutenitsa* (see page 241), although confusingly some call spicy *pindžur*, *ljutenitsa*. *Pindžur* is meant to be made and eaten immediately, or, even better, the next day, when the flavours have had time to get to know each other a little better. Use the ripest tomatoes you can find. In summer, use fresh, ripe tomatoes roughly chopped rather than roasting them alongside the aubergine and peppers – it gives the dish a lightness and acidity that is so welcome in the summer heat. It tastes best when you crush everything together – indeed, pounding all the ingredients together in a pestle and mortar while making sure the vegetables retain a little bit of texture is what makes it *pindžur*.

Place a griddle pan over a high heat. Prick the aubergine all over with a fork and, once the griddle pan is very hot, char the aubergine, turning occasionally, for 25–30 minutes, or until the skin is blistered and blackened all over. Transfer it to a wire rack with a plate or tray placed underneath and leave to cool.

Meanwhile, char the peppers and tomatoes for 20–25 minutes until their skins have blistered and started to blacken. If your griddle pan is big enough, you can do all the vegetables at the same time. Transfer the charred peppers and tomatoes to a plate, cover with a lid and leave to cool.

Once the vegetables are cool to the touch, cut the aubergine in half, scoop out the flesh and roughly chop it. Peel the peppers, remove the stalks and seeds and roughly chop the flesh. Peel and roughly chop the tomatoes.

Put the garlic and salt into a mortar and crush with a pestle until you have a smooth and almost creamy paste. Slowly start to add the roasted chopped vegetables and continue pounding and stirring with the pestle until you have a rough paste that still retains some of the texture of the vegetables. Transfer to a bowl and add the oil. Set aside for at least 30 minutes before serving, to allow the vegetable mixture to absorb the oil.

When ready to serve, transfer to a serving bowl and drizzle with a little extra oil to serve.

Note

You can also roughly chop the tomatoes, place them in a medium saucepan with a pinch of salt and braise them for 3–4 minutes on a medium-high heat to reduce some of the liquid. If you are firing up your barbecue, use it to char the aubergine, peppers and tomatoes – it gives them a nice smoky flavour. You can also roast the vegetables in an oven – place them on a baking sheet lined with baking parchment, prick the aubergine (as above), and roast them for 40–45 minutes at 200°C fan (425°F).

If you don't have a large enough pestle and mortar, chop everything as finely as you can and combine in a bowl.

For Sharing

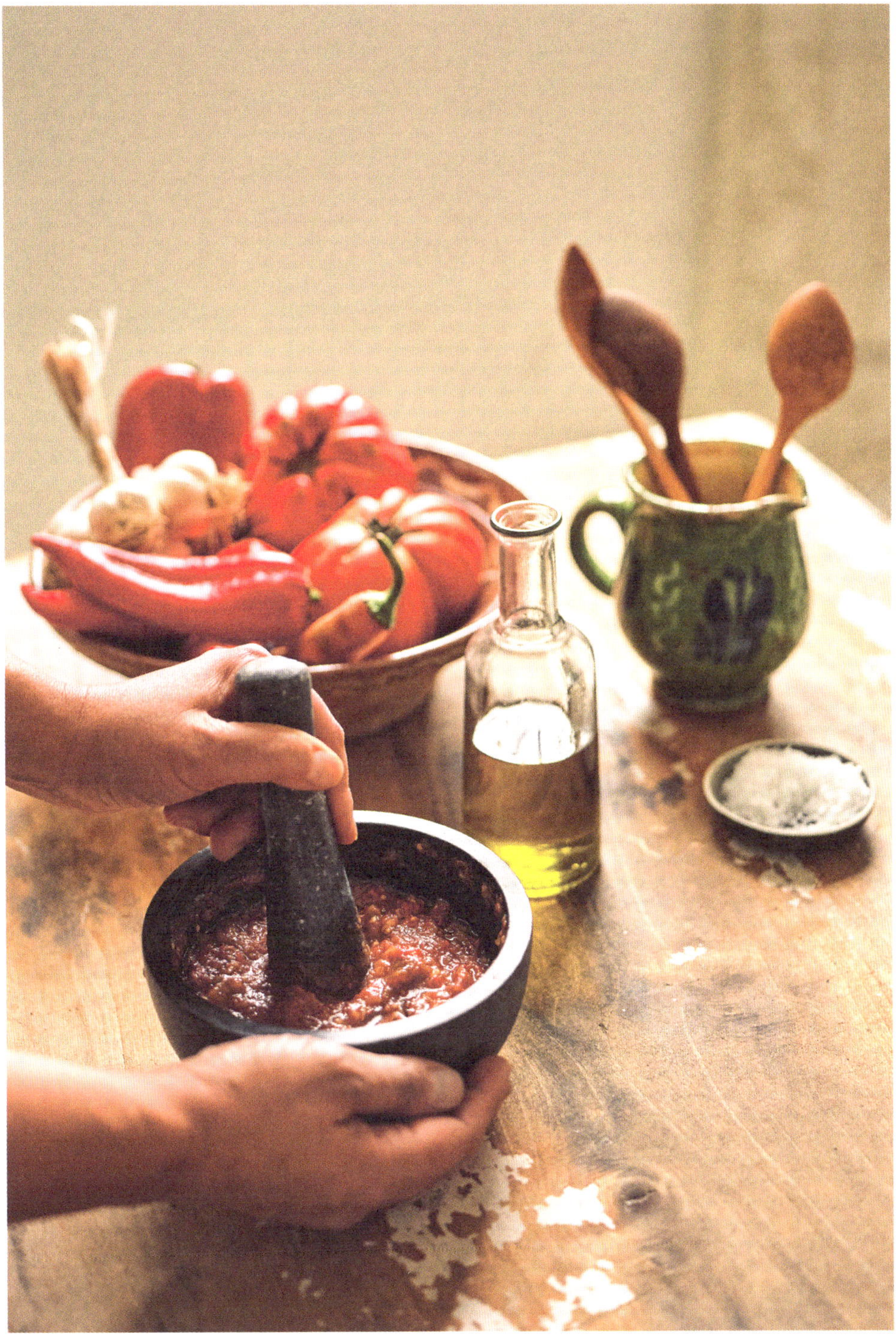

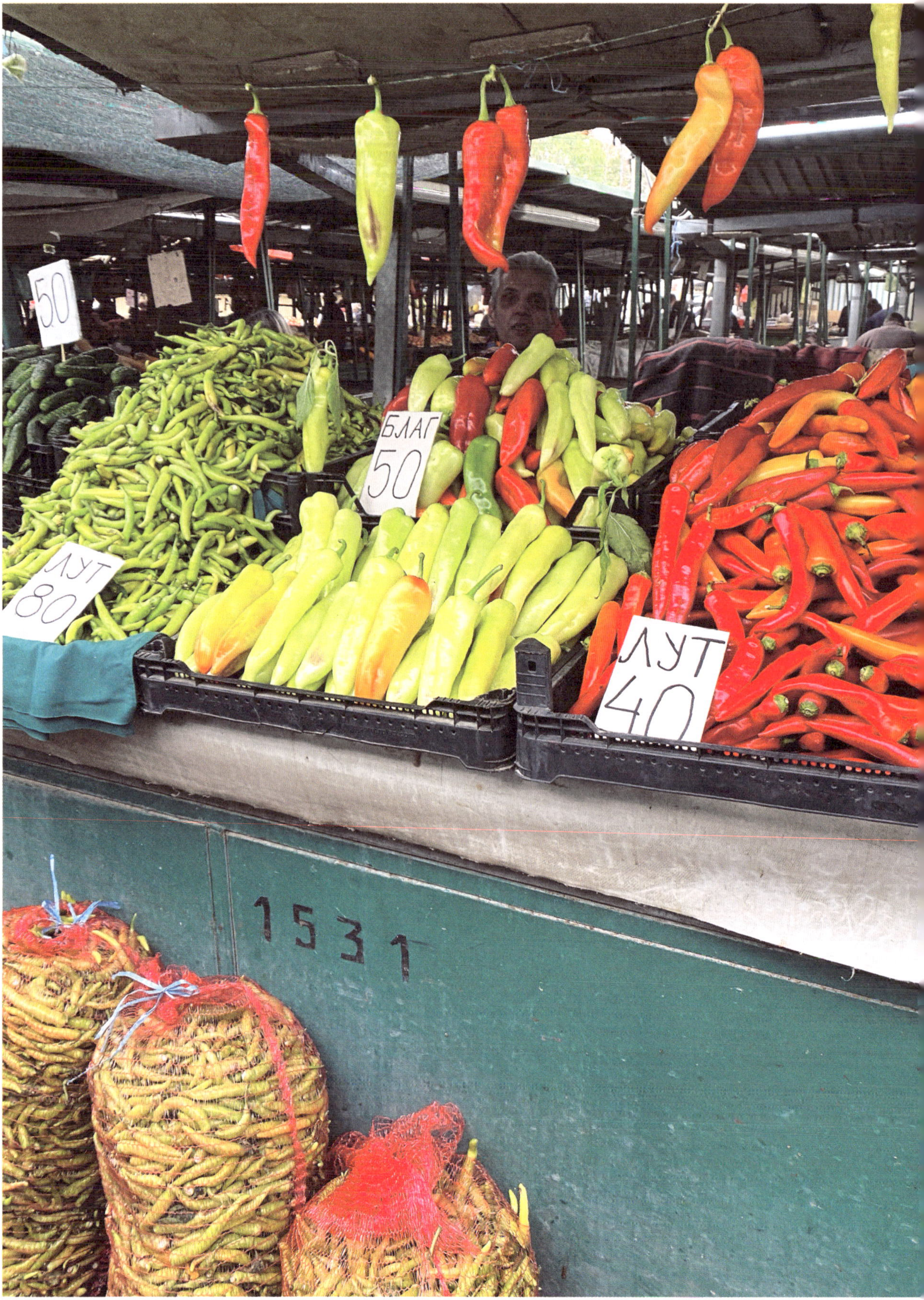
50
БЛАГ
50
ЛУТ
80
ЛУТ
40
1531

Peppers, Two Ways (of Many)

It is unthinkable to sit down for a meal in the Balkans without peppers being present in some form or another. A barbecued or fried pepper or two always accompany a platter of grilled meats, but they are so much more than a side show. Often, they are *the* show. Served with good crusty bread and salads, cheeses and meats, they can be a meal on their own. Here are two variations that are on constant rotation in my kitchen.

Stuffed and baked

SERVES 4 AS A MAIN OR 6-8 AS A SIDE

2 tablespoons olive oil, plus extra for brushing
1 kg (2 lb 4 oz) sweet long green peppers or mixed yellow, orange or red Romano peppers, stalks trimmed
400 g (14 oz) unsalted urda
2 medium eggs, lightly beaten
50 g (1¾ oz) spring onions (scallions), finely chopped
20 g (½ oz) fresh parsley, leaves picked and finely chopped
1 tablespoon nigella seeds
sea salt and freshly ground black pepper
Ajvar (see page 239) or Ljutenitsa (see page 241), to serve

Piperki so urda, or peppers with *urda* (a young, unsalted curd cheese) is a firm summer favourite across the region and I have had countless iterations of it. Sweet or spicy long peppers stuffed and then fried; or fried, peeled, stuffed, breaded and fried again; or fried and then baked in a sort of custard of *urda* and sour cream. I had a particularly delicious version of it in Prizren in Kosovo, with the spiciest barbecued peppers covered in a custard of the freshest and creamiest *urda* and then chargrilled (broiled). I like stuffing the peppers and then baking them. The custard is often nothing more complicated than *urda* seasoned with salt and pepper and bound with egg, but flavour it however you like. Here is one option.

Preheat the oven to 200°C fan (425°F) and brush a large baking dish (that fits the peppers snugly in a single layer) with oil.

Cut around the stalks of the peppers, creating a sort of lid. Set the lids aside. Deseed and devein the peppers, taking care not to pierce the skin.

In a bowl, combine the *urda*, eggs, spring onions, parsley, nigella seeds, olive oil and salt and pepper to taste.

Spoon the filling into each pepper, taking care not to overfill and leaving 1 cm (½ inch) gap from the top. Place the lid on each pepper. Arrange the filled peppers in the prepared baking dish. Brush the skins of each pepper with a little oil.

Bake in the oven for 30–35 minutes until the filling is set and the peppers are cooked through, softened and blackened in places. If you like, you can gently peel some or all of the skin off the peppers before serving, but I generally don't bother.

Serve hot or cold, with ajvar or ljutenitsa on the side.

For Sharing

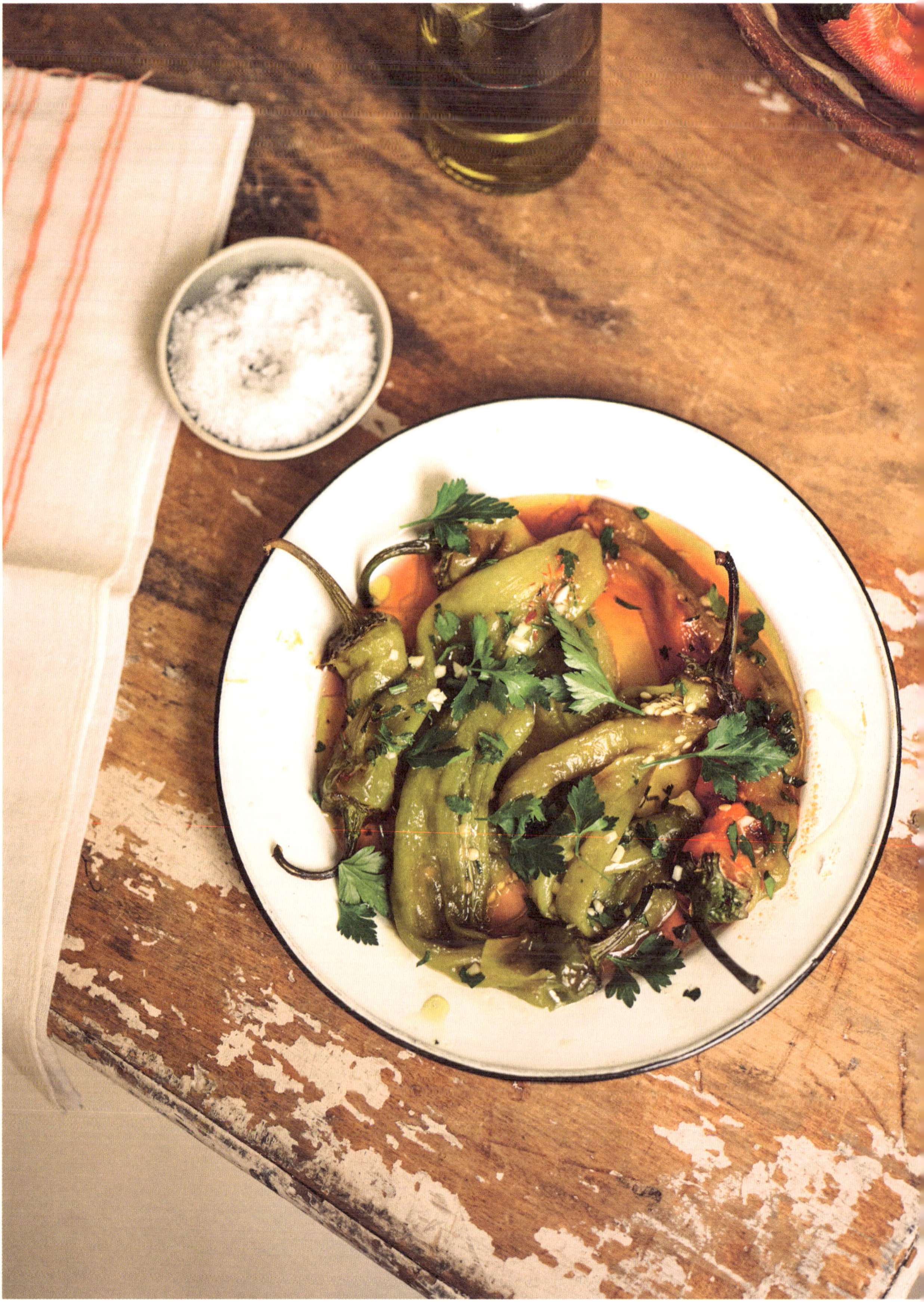

SERVES 4-6

Fried and marinated

2 tablespoons sunflower or other neutral oil, for frying

1 kg (2 lb 4 oz) sweet long green peppers or mixed yellow, orange or red Romano peppers, stalks trimmed

FOR THE MARINADE

1–2 garlic cloves, finely chopped

2 tablespoons red wine vinegar

1 teaspoon sea salt flakes, plus extra to serve

4 tablespoons extra virgin olive oil, plus extra to serve

20 g (½ oz) fresh parsley, leaves picked and finely chopped, plus extra to serve

freshly ground black pepper

From late summer and well into autumn (fall), the stalls of the food markets across the Balkans are laden with the freshest varieties of peppers. As soon as the oppressive heat of the day has abated (it would be madness to attempt to fry during the day), it is impossible to walk past the invariably open window of someone's kitchen without catching a tantalising whiff of peppers cooking, either just for that evening's meal or – very likely – a big batch cook in progress, using up that week's haul of peppers from the market. For me, as a Macedonian, no smell is more ubiquitous or mesmerising than that of *prženi* (fried) peppers – especially sweet long green peppers at the peak of their season. They need nothing more than a very simple vinaigrette, and when served with good crusty bread and white cheese, they become a lovely summer meal. They are also a useful staple to have to serve alongside heartier dishes, such as the Tavče Gravče on page 150.

Heat the oil in a large, lidded sauté pan over a high heat and add the peppers. Cover with the lid and fry for around 20 minutes, carefully turning them over from time to time with tongs to ensure the peppers are cooked through, softened and blackened in places on all sides. You may need to fry them in batches.

Transfer the peppers to a large lipped serving plate and cover with a lid or plate to steam as they cool, which makes for easier peeling. When cool to the touch, carefully peel the peppers, keeping them whole (stalks and seeds included) as much as possible. Discard the peel but keep all the juices and place the peeled peppers and juices back in the plate.

Make the marinade while the peppers are cooling. Put the garlic, vinegar, salt and a good grind of black pepper into a small bowl and mix well with a small whisk. Keep whisking as you add the oil. Pour the marinade over the peppers, scatter with the chopped parsley and gently mix the peppers. Cover with a lid or large plate and leave to marinate for at least 1 hour, or overnight in the refrigerator.

To serve, finish with a good drizzle of olive oil, a scatter of parsley leaves and a sprinkle of salt. These will keep well in an airtight container in the refrigerator for up to 1 week.

Note

If you are not a fan of frying, you can either barbecue or roast the peppers. To roast them, place them on a large baking tray (pan) lined with baking parchment, spaced out as much as possible. Roast them at 220°C fan (475°F) for 20–25 minutes, turning over halfway through the cooking time, or until they are cooked through, softened and blackened in places on all sides. Cool, peel and marinate as above.

For Sharing

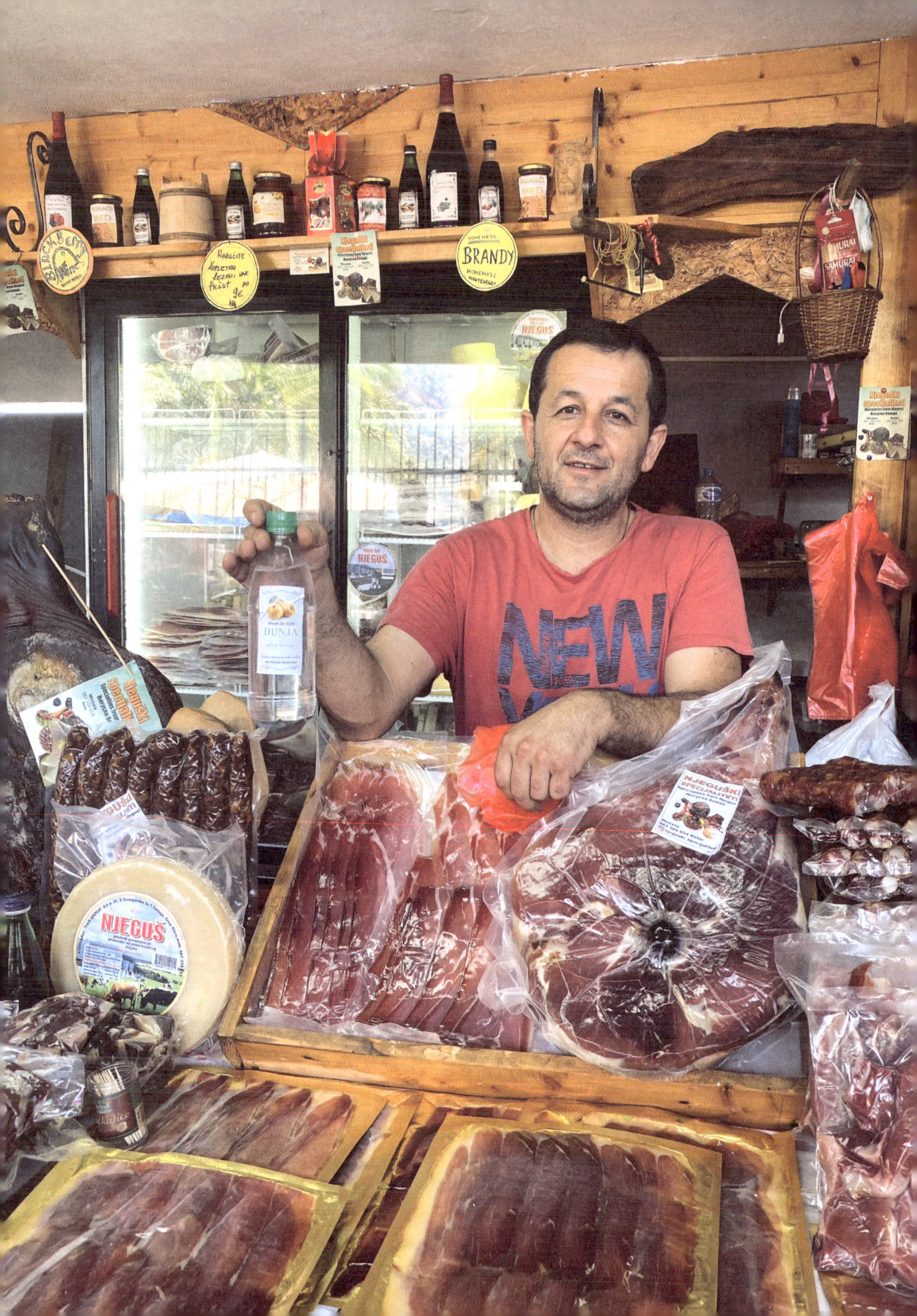
BRANDY
NJEGUŠ
DUNJA
NEW
NJEGUŠKI SPECIJALITETI
NJEGUŠ

Kufer

I am idling by the baggage carousel and wondering what would happen if my *kufer* (suitcase) was accidentally taken home by someone else. What would they think if instead of their carefully packed clothes and shoes they found an old ice cream box. Would they open it, to find fermented cabbage leaves, prepared and portioned in stacks of 10, then carefully wrapped? Or vine leaves? Or perhaps a selection of *sitni kolači* (bite-sized sweet treats)?

Would they unravel the travel towel to reveal the bottle of *rakija* (fruit brandy)? A specially aged vintage from my Uncle Simo that he made the year of my graduation and which survived him by nearly 20 years. It is labelled by my grandmother, in Cyrillic, with a date and a warning sign: *za mačkanje* (for rubbing). Translation: do not drink this (or drink it with extreme caution as it may burn your insides) but certainly use it topically to stave off pneumonia, neutralise insect bites, sterilise anything. Then there are the jars. Homemade sauces and preserves such as *ajvar, ljutenitsa, slatko*. I would like to think their curiosity would get the better of them and they would sample them and become incontrovertibly hooked on the essence of the Balkan larder.

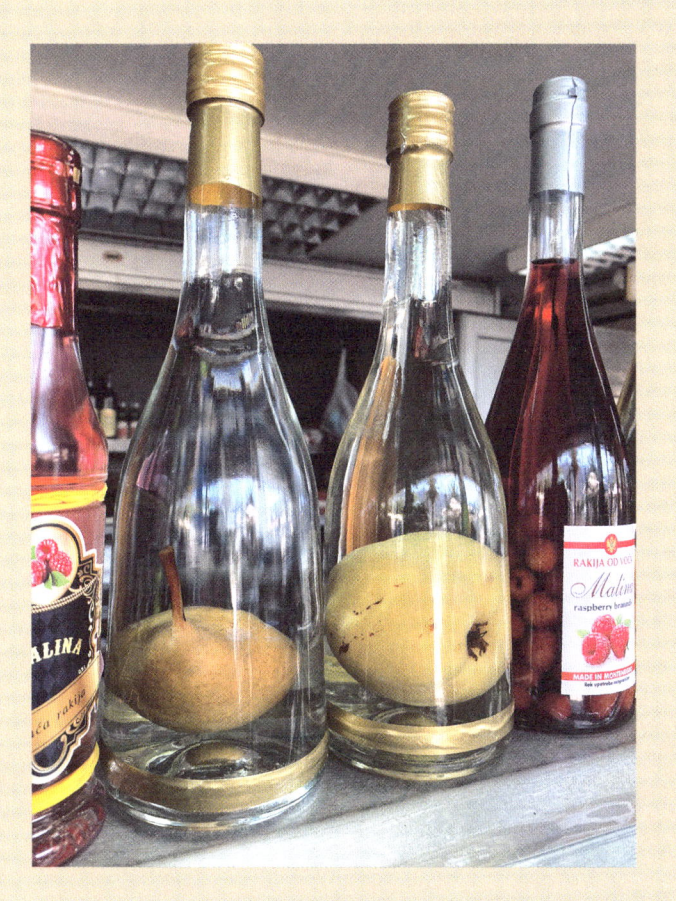

And the fruits and vegetables! My goodness, what on earth would they think of all of those? A Skopje *jabucar* tomato, because after indulging my taste buds one last time, I am convinced that this year I will manage to dry the seeds properly and grow these tomatoes that taste of home in my London garden. Peppers: a wide selection of fresh ones, their stalks carefully wrapped with slightly damp kitchen towel to help ease their voyage; little packages of dried *vrtka* peppers or Pirot peppers from Serbia; garlands of dried red ones; the special *vezenki* peppers from Macedonia. Would they know what to do with them? Would they think to cook them with the Tetovo beans – yes, those ones in the paper bag right next to the dried peppers? Under the packs of sweet paprika and dried Bukovo pepper. I consider whether next time I travel I should leave a note or perhaps recipe detailing how the contents are best consumed.

For Sharing

It would be a lucky traveller indeed if their journey coincided with my return from Istria. Then, they would also find carefully wrapped bottles of the golden-green hued olive oils made from *bjelica* and *buža* olives. A Teranino liqueur and fig-leaf wine made by a friend. Wild *šparoge* (asparagus) I bought in the market in Pula. Or, if they happened upon my suitcase coming back from Serbia or Montenegro, would they break open the vacuum-packed bags of *duvan čvarci* (pork crackling/rind floss) from Valjevo, or the *Njeguški pršut* (dry-cured ham) I tried in a market in Kotor and travelled to Njeguši for?

Whenever this lucky traveller happens upon my suitcase, they will find dried bunches of mountain herbs, or linden, or St John's wort, perfuming the entire suitcase, including my great-grandmother's hand-woven textiles, crochet and embroidery, prepared for her, my grandmother's and my mother's dowry chests (as was custom). There would be photographs stolen from albums, too. Some I've never seen before but want to look at forever. Precious letters that I look at time and again. I can almost see them as they are being written by the people I loved who are no longer with me.

Would this careless traveller who did not check the travel label understand what it would mean to me if I was never reunited with this suitcase? Fragments of a life, of a homeland, that I transport with me, little by little, to a part of the world where I have built a new life. Why do I do this? Because I fear forgetting. Forgetting the flavours. Forgetting my ancestors. I fear the threads that tie me to the Balkan soil loosening and eventually snapping. I fear floating around the world endlessly, never belonging, never being able to anchor again. I fear ... what would happen to those lands if we all leave?

My suitcase arrives. I thank the travel gods, cease silently cursing my imaginary, careless, suitcase-stealing fellow traveller, and start planning how best to use the contents this time, in order to put off forgetting for a little while longer. At least until I am back on Balkan soil once more and can refill the suitcase with more fragments of my Balkan life.

For Sharing

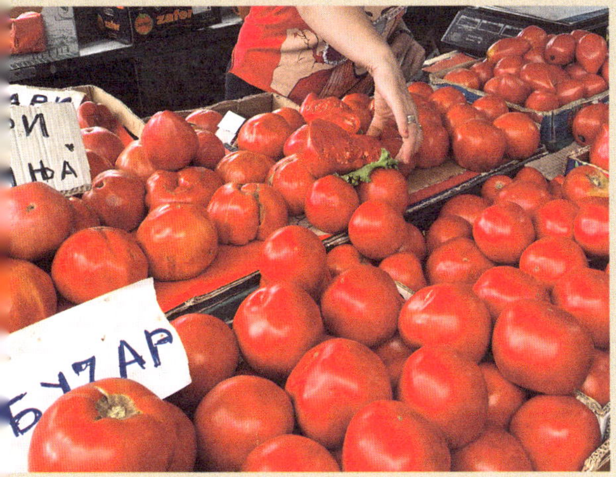

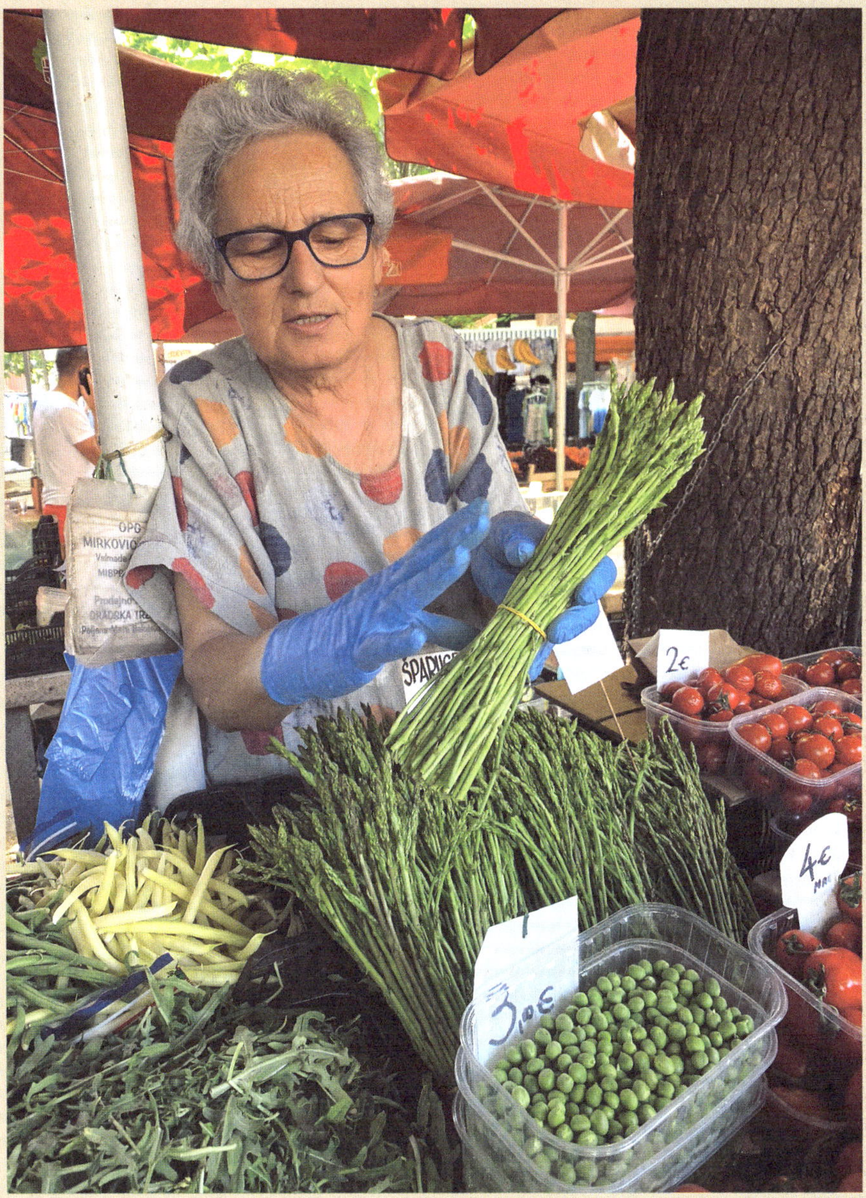
2€

SERVES 4

Aubergines in Walnut Sauce

750 g (1 lb 10 oz) aubergines (eggplants), cut into 1 cm (½ inch) thick slices
3–4 tablespoons extra virgin olive oil
1 teaspoon sea salt flakes

FOR THE WALNUT SAUCE
75 g (2½ oz) walnuts
150 ml (5 fl oz/scant ⅔ cup) water
2 garlic cloves, peeled
½ teaspoon sea salt flakes
1 tablespoon extra virgin olive oil, plus extra to serve
10 g (½ oz) fresh parsley, leaves picked and roughly chopped
freshly ground black pepper

FOR THE PICKLED CHILLIES
2–3 red or green chillies, thinly sliced
1 teaspoon sea salt flakes
30 ml (2 fl oz/2 tablespoons) white balsamic vinegar

I often think of an invisible line across the Balkan Peninsula beyond which that noblest of the nightshade family, the aubergine (eggplant), is no longer queen of the Balkan kitchen. Where my imaginary line falls is an impossible delineation, but you are more likely to find infinite variations of aubergine dishes in the southern (hotter) parts of the Balkans, because aubergines need sunshine to reach their full flavour potential. My favourite aubergine dishes are often the simplest: fried, grilled on the barbecue or roasted slices of aubergine that are either soaked in a simple red wine vinaigrette with parsley and garlic as with the peppers on page 97 (which with added pickling liquid also works as a winter preserve) or mellowed with a garlic-infused yoghurt as with the courgettes (zucchini) on page 105.

This walnut sauce is a loose interpretation of something my grandfather often made. When staying at my grandparents' apartment, I would occasionally wake to the clanging of an ancient brass pestle and mortar, a sound not dissimilar to the gongs of a Buddhist monastery, and wander over to the kitchen to find my grandfather bent over the table concentrating over its contents: walnuts, garlic, parsley and old bread (soaked in water, with the water then squeezed out) with a little oil to make a parsley and walnut sauce, not dissimilar to Turkish *tarator* or Italian pesto. We use this kind of sauce as an accompaniment to many things, but especially grilled or fried vegetables, fish and meat. Using the pestle and mortar to extract flavour is wonderful. My way is very much a shortcut and cooking the walnuts slightly omits the need for bread – but I do, on occasion, channel my grandfather and make it as he did, and in the same pestle and mortar.

Preheat the oven to 200°C fan (425°F). Arrange the aubergine slices on two baking sheets lined with baking parchment. Brush them with the oil on both sides and sprinkle with the salt. Roast in the oven for 25–30 minutes, turning the slices halfway through the cooking time to ensure all the slices are golden brown and soft in the middle. Remove from the oven and set aside to cool.

Meanwhile, make the walnut sauce. Place the walnuts in a small saucepan with the water and cook over a high heat for 2–3 minutes just to soften the walnuts. Remove from the heat and set aside to cool slightly (reserving the cooking liquid), then transfer to a food processor with the garlic, salt and a good grind of black pepper and blend to a smooth paste. Loosen with 1–2 tablespoons of the walnut cooking liquid if you need to.

To make the pickled chillies, place the sliced chillies in a small bowl with the salt. Leave to stand for 10 minutes then add the vinegar.

To serve, arrange the aubergine slices on a large serving platter, slightly overlapping. Spoon the sauce over the aubergine slices and sprinkle with the parsley leaves. Drizzle a little extra virgin olive oil over the top. Dot a few pickled chillies over the top to finish, serving the rest alongside.

Note
Store the pickled chillies in a jar in the refrigerator for up to two weeks.

For Sharing

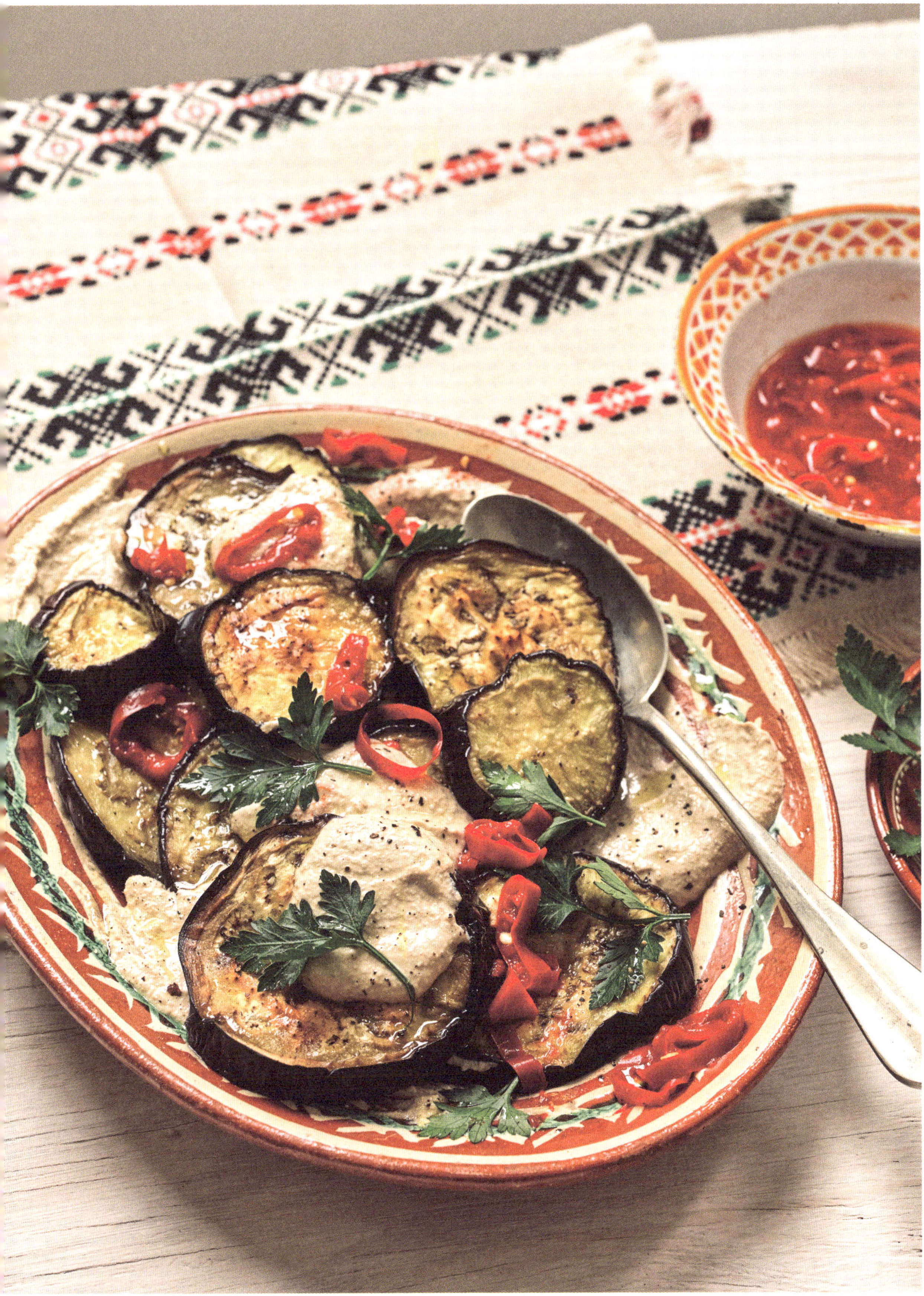

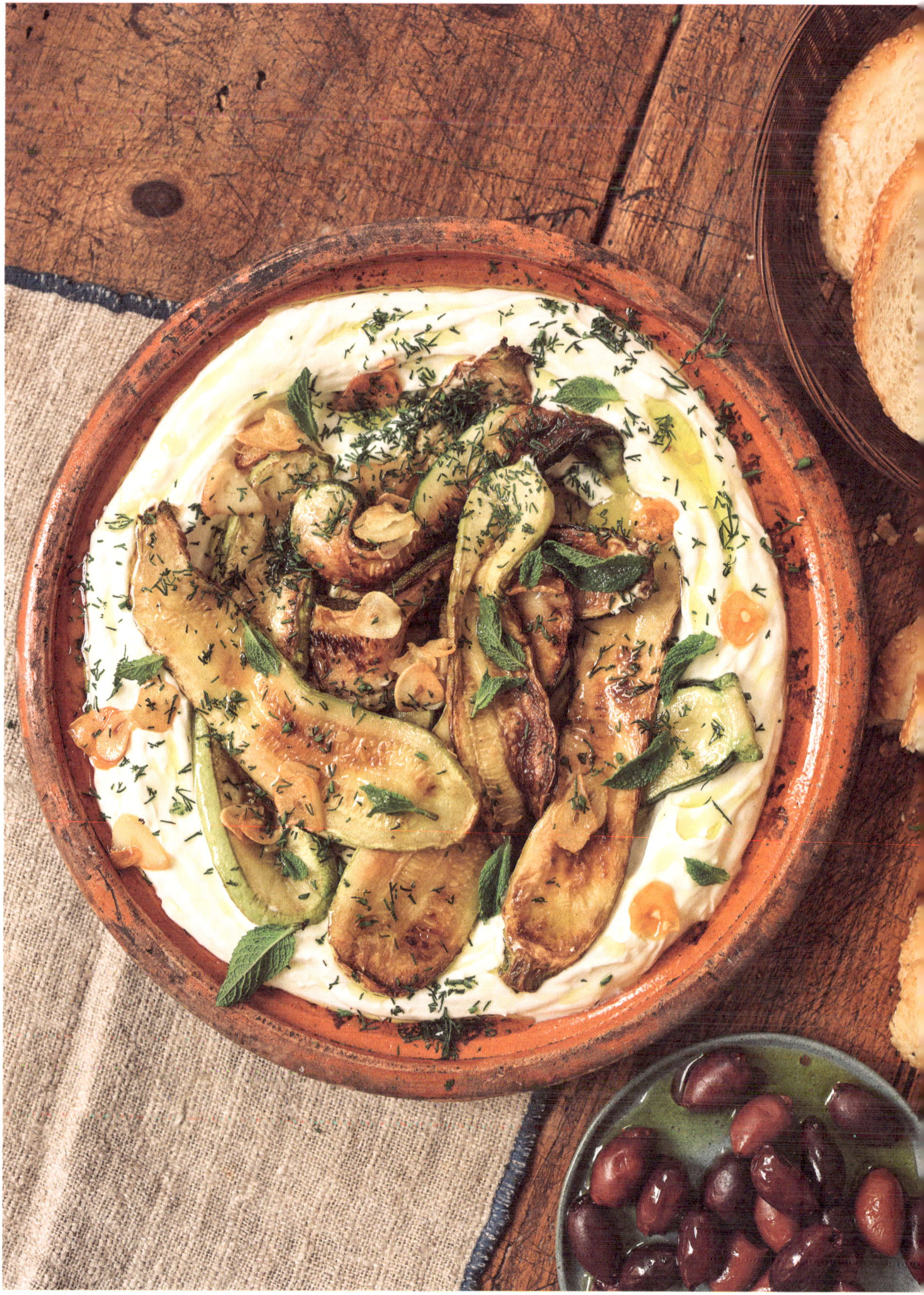

SERVES 4

Courgettes in Yoghurt Sauce

500 g (1 lb 2 oz) large courgettes (zucchini), sliced lengthwise into 1 cm (½ inch) thick slices
½ teaspoon sea salt flakes
2 tablespoons extra virgin olive oil
crusty bread, to serve

FOR THE YOGHURT SAUCE
200 g (7 oz/generous ¾ cup) plain thick-set yoghurt
2 garlic cloves, crushed
1 teaspoon lemon zest plus 1 tablespoon juice
½ teaspoon sea salt flakes
1 teaspoon extra virgin olive oil
10 g (½ oz) fresh soft herbs, such as parsley, mint and/or dill, leaves picked, to serve
freshly ground black pepper

FOR THE FRIED GARLIC (OPTIONAL)
60 ml (2 fl oz/¼ cup) extra virgin olive oil
6 garlic cloves, peeled and finely sliced
pinch of sea salt

There is something inherently soothing about the gentle union of vegetables and yoghurt. It's a union that is shared by the cuisines of the Balkans, Eastern Mediterranean, the Levant and beyond. Many of the variations on this theme have fewer than a handful of simple ingredients but are always astonishing in their elegant flavour. This way of cooking celebrates the beauty of the ingredients and the deep respect for them. Across the Balkans, courgettes (zucchini) are a summer staple in the kitchen: poached, stewed, roasted, fried, grilled on the barbecue or grated (shredded) and turned into fritters.

Sprinkle the sliced courgettes with the salt and place them in a colander over a bowl to capture any liquid. Set aside to drain for 15 minutes.

Preheat the oven to 200°C fan (425°F) and line a large baking sheet with baking parchment.

Pat the courgettes dry with paper towels, then brush them with the oil and spread out on the prepared baking sheet. Roast in the oven for 20–22 minutes, turning the slices over halfway through the cooking time, until the courgettes are soft in the middle and turning a deep golden brown. Alternatively, griddle the courgettes either on the barbecue or on a cast-iron griddle over a high heat for 10–12 minutes, turning over halfway through, until cooked and dark char lines have appeared across the courgette flesh.

Meanwhile make the yoghurt sauce by combining the yoghurt, garlic, lemon zest and juice, oil, salt and a good grind of black pepper in a small bowl.

To make the fried garlic, combine the oil and garlic slices in a small frying pan over a medium heat and cook for 5–6 minutes, or until the garlic just starts to turn crispy and golden. Remove from the heat and strain the oil through a sieve into a small heatproof bowl. Place the garlic slices on a small plate lined with paper towels and sprinkle with a pinch of salt.

Place half the yoghurt sauce on a lipped serving plate, then arrange the courgettes over the yoghurt. Spoon the rest of the yoghurt sauce over the courgettes then top with the herbs, a drizzle of the garlic oil and the fried garlic slices, serving the rest in small bowls alongside. Serve warm or cold with crusty bread for dipping.

Note
You can use 2 large aubergines (eggplants) or 8–10 baby aubergines sliced in half instead of courgettes, roasted as on page 102.

For Sharing

Street Corn

SERVES 4-8

4 corn cobs, husks and silk threads removed, halved
1 tablespoon sunflower or other neutral oil
fine sea salt

FOR THE TOPPING

75 g (2½ oz) Kajmak (see page 261, or use shop-bought or softened unsalted butter)
1 tablespoon lemon zest, plus extra to serve
1 tablespoon hot or sweet Bukovo pepper (or Aleppo pepper or sweet paprika), plus extra to serve
½ teaspoon smoked sea salt flakes
freshly ground black pepper

This is my attempt to recreate Balkan street corn at home. Picture the scene: it is summer. You are standing in the historic Turkish bazaar of Sarajevo. Or Skopje. Or by the sea in Split. Or Prizren. Or in the centre of any town across the former Yugoslavia. Very likely under an ancient monument ... or a brutalist masterpiece (depending on your architectural preferences). Or sitting on the pebbles overlooking the azure Adriatic. Or wandering by a lake or river. You see a small cart. It has a giant portable pot full of gently simmering corn on the cob, or a small portable barbecue with corn charring in its husks. You ask for corn, and you are handed your delicious specimen and offered a choice of a little butter or salt. Maybe some spicy dried red pepper, if you're lucky. Often, the seller has brought it straight from their field that morning. You eat it with its juices dribbling down your chin. Thank goodness for the cheap paper napkin. You wander off, and regret not getting another one. You wander back and do what you should have done in the first place.

Bring a large saucepan of salted water to the boil, then lower the heat to medium-high and add the corn. Cook for 10–12 minutes until the kernels are just soft when tested with a fork or sharp knife. Drain the corn, pat them dry with paper towels and brush on all sides with the oil.

Preheat the grill (broiler) to as high as it will go. Arrange the corn on a baking sheet lined with baking parchment and grill (broil) for about 20 minutes, turning over from time to time to ensure the corn in evenly charred on all sides.

Meanwhile, make the topping. Put the *kajmak*, lemon zest, Bukovo pepper, smoked sea salt and a good grind of black pepper into a bowl and mix to combine.

To serve, place the corn cobs on a serving platter with a teaspoon of topping over each, serving the rest in a small bowl alongside. Sprinkle some zest and Bukovo pepper flakes over the top.

Note

If you are firing up your barbecue, use it to cook the corn – gently peel back the husk (but don't remove it) and remove the silk threads, then brush the corn with a little oil and season with salt and pepper. Wrap them back up in their husks, then grill them on the barbecue, turning from time to time, until the husks are charred and the inside is cooked through and tender (about 20–25 minutes). To serve, peel back the husks and trim them, then serve with the topping as above.

For Sharing

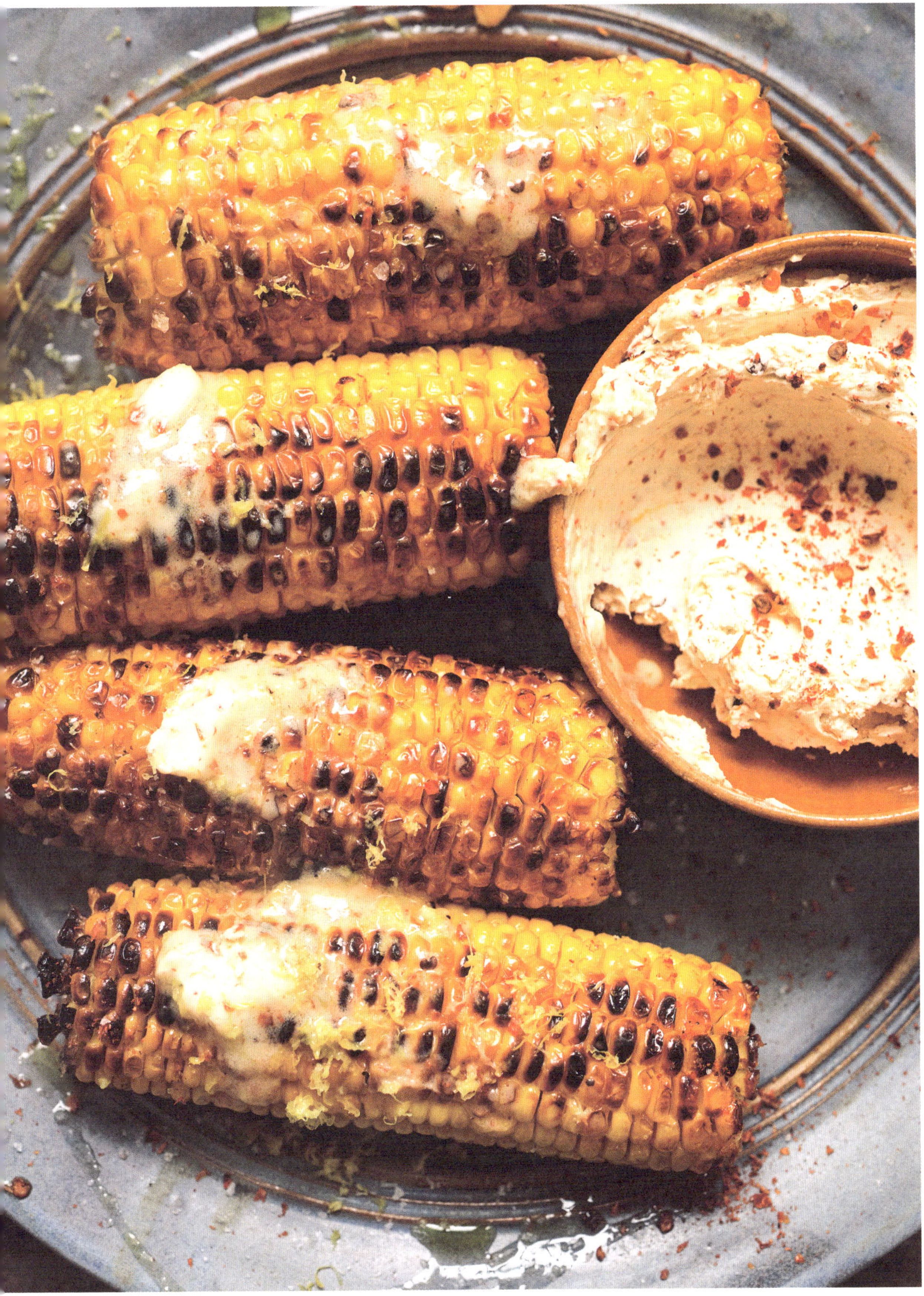

ON THE SPOON
LAŽICA

Family meals almost always begin with or include something *'na žlica'*, *'na kašika'* or *'na lažica'* – on the spoon. *Supa* (soup) and *čorba* (a thick soup) are an integral part of Balkan culinary traditions and each region has its own unique *supa* or *čorba* that reflects local ingredients and historical and cultural influences.

Supa is not čorba and čorba is not supa, although they can be made from the same ingredients and cooked almost in the same way. The key differences are in the consistency and historical influence. *Supa* is often a clear broth with a consistency that must be slurped off the spoon, rather than something that clings more stubbornly to it. *Supa* is often served before a meal, whereas *čorba* can be a meal on its own. Soups can, however, be thickened – with egg (as with Greek *avgolemono*), rice, pasta, potatoes, or, for lamb soups, yoghurt, to cut through the fattiness of the meat.

You are more likely to find *čorbas* in Serbia, Kosovo, North Macedonia, Montenegro and Bosnia and Herzegovina – areas controlled at various points by the Ottoman Empire for significant periods. The word itself is of Turkish origin, and elements of Ottoman culinary traditions are apparent in the *čorbas* of the Balkans, but they are adapted to suit local ingredients, flavour preferences and in some cases, cooking techniques. In Bosnia and Herzegovina, you will find *Begova čorba*, a creamy *čorba* made with chicken, okra and vegetables, thought fit for a *beg* (a nobleman or high-ranking official of the Ottoman Empire). There are also innumerable examples of bean *čorbas* all over the region, lamb *čorbas* (especially in North Macedonia, Kosovo, Montenegro and Bosnia and Herzegovina) and *riblja čorba* – thick fish soups, made with either local freshwater fish by inland communities or with fish, seafood and Mediterranean flair along the coastal regions. The picture is similar in areas not subject to Ottoman control. In Croatia you would find *Istarska maneštra* (a Balkanised minestrone) and *bograč*, a rich and thick meat and vegetable stew from the Baranja region, variants of which are also enjoyed in Slovenia. In Slovenia you will find *jota*, a thick soup made with sauerkraut, beans and potatoes, often flavoured with smoked pork and *matevž*, a thick mashed bean and potato soup, often served with roasted sausages.

There are also many wonderfully unique examples of soups across the region. I was most taken with *Istarska supa* (Istrian soup), the basis of which is typically red Istrian wine, made from indigenous Teran or Borgonja grapes, which is heated in *škundelice* (earthenware bowls) with a little pinch of sugar, maybe pepper and Istrian olive oil. One dips fresh or lightly fried bread into the wine soup.

All the recipes included here allow for deviation – think of them as a set of building blocks, to be adapted to what you have available. For some, however, such as *šketo*, an extra flick of sweet paprika or a little bit less parsley is as far as even the most sacrilegious gourmet would go before it turns into an example of something else entirely.

SERVES 4-6

Balkan Penicillin

1 chicken carcass plus 1 chicken leg (or any other chicken cuts on the bone, including chicken backbone from spatchcocking chicken)

3 litres cold water (100 fl oz/12½ cups), plus extra as needed

2 onions, quartered

1 long red or green pepper, deseeded and quartered

2 tomatoes, quartered

2 courgettes (zucchini), peeled and quartered

2–3 celery stalks, chopped into large batons

2–3 carrots, peeled and topped and tailed

20 g (¾ oz) fresh parsley, stalks separated and leaves finely chopped

2–3 sprigs of fresh thyme

2–3 bay leaves

1 teaspoon black peppercorns

300 g (10½ oz) waxy potatoes, peeled and chopped into 1 cm (½ inch) cubes

80 g (2¾ oz) Tarana (see page 260, or any pastina, such as vermicelli or orzo; optional)

1 teaspoon sea salt flakes

freshly ground black pepper

1 lemon, cut into wedges, to serve

Note

If you have a pressure cooker, use it to reduce the cooking time. Once you have reached the stage of adding the vegetables to the broth, transfer everything to the pressure cooker and cook on high pressure (on a soup setting if you have it) for 30 minutes.

There is a 19th-century Macedonian poem called '*T'ga Za Jug*' (Longing for the South) by Konstantin Miladinov, written while he was studying in Moscow but longing to be home and to see the beauty and the sun, the light of his southern European home. It ends with the line: 'As that sun sets, I may die.' I only understood it completely when, having grown up in the Balkans and then the Middle East, I moved to Britain for university and suddenly, inexplicably, overwhelmingly missed the warm light of home. This soup is a combination of several other types of soup from across the Balkans. Made and adapted by generations of women in my family, each of them adding their own twist, it was the first thing I cooked by myself, for myself. It is my Balkan penicillin, my light of home in a bowl, my taste of sunshine. It soothes and cures all ills, but especially a homesick soul.

Put the chicken carcass and leg into a large stockpot and add the water (making sure the chicken is submerged – add more if you need). Bring to a simmer over a medium-high heat. Do not allow the water to boil – as soon as it is close to doing so, pour in some cold water and immediately skim off any scum and impurities and discard them. Continue to do this for 25–30 minutes, or until the stock simmers clear without too much froth.

Add the onions, pepper, tomatoes, courgettes, celery, carrots, parsley stalks, thyme, bay leaves and peppercorns. Reduce the heat to medium, cover with a lid and simmer gently for 2–2½ hours, periodically topping up with water and skimming, if needed. When the chicken is falling off the bones, remove from the heat and allow to cool.

Strain the broth through a fine-mesh sieve into a large, clean saucepan, reserving the contents of the sieve. At this stage, either bring the stock back up to the boil and reduce by one-third, or remove about 1 litre (34 fl oz/4¼ cups) of the broth and store in a clean, airtight container in the refrigerator for other meals, such as the Chicken and Rice on page 158.

Reserve and set aside the chicken and cooked carrots from the sieve. Discard the bay leaves, peppercorns and thyme sprigs. Using a spatula (or soup spoon), pass the remaining cooked vegetables (onions, celery, tomatoes, peppers and courgettes) through the sieve directly into the saucepan containing the remaining broth. Shred the chicken, taking care to remove all bones, and slice the carrots, then add them back to the broth. Add the potatoes and *tarana*, the salt and a good grind of black pepper, then place the saucepan over a medium-high heat. Simmer for 10–12 minutes, or until the potato is cooked through, then add the chopped parsley leaves (reserve some to serve) and check and adjust the seasoning to your taste.

Serve in soup bowls with a sprinkle of the reserved chopped parsley and a generous squeeze of lemon juice.

On the Spoon

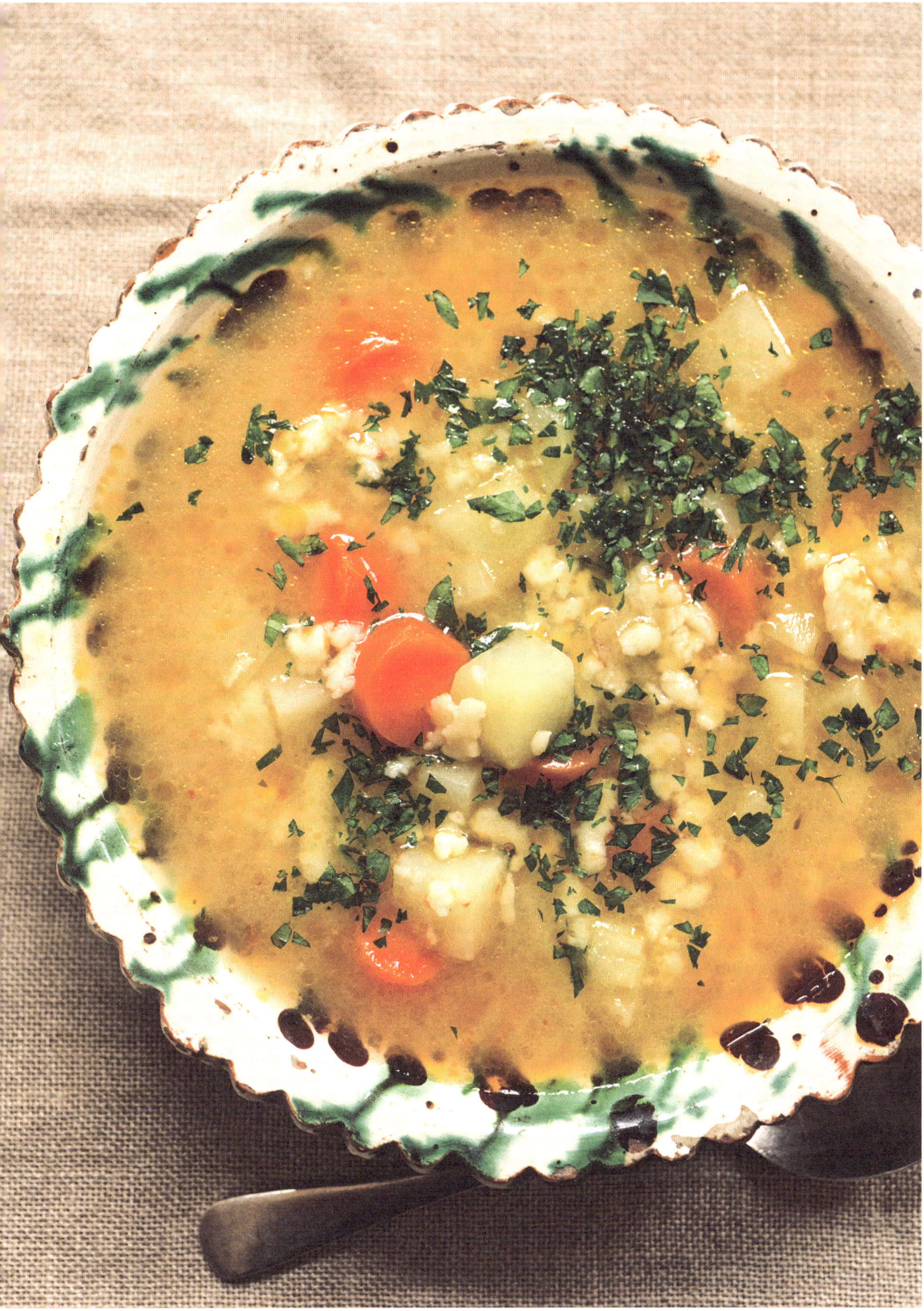

Juha with Knedle

SERVES 4-6

1 kg (2 lb 4 oz) beef or veal bones
200 g (7 oz) beef chuck steak
3 litres cold water (100 fl oz/12½ cups), plus extra as needed
2 onions, quartered
2–3 celery stalks, chopped into large batons
2–3 medium carrots, peeled and topped and tailed
1 parsnip, peeled and topped and tailed
10 g (½ oz) fresh parsley, stalks separated and leaves picked and finely chopped
2–3 sprigs of fresh thyme
2–3 bay leaves
1 teaspoon black peppercorns
300 g (10½ oz) waxy potatoes, peeled, halved lengthwise and sliced thinly
1 teaspoon sea salt flakes
freshly ground black pepper

FOR THE SOUP KNEDLE
1 medium egg, separated
¼ teaspoon fine sea salt
½ teaspoon sunflower or olive oil
60 g (2 oz) griz (or fine semolina)

Note
Instead of making *knedle*, feel free to use *fide* (egg vermicelli for soup) or any small pasta shape, such as Tarana (see page 260).

Although this is more commonly known as *juha* or *supa so knedle/knedli*, my son lovingly calls it 'cloud soup'. As a Balkan mother, this fills my heart with unspeakable joy for two reasons: firstly, he continues the long tradition of a Balkan child loving soup while also getting all the restorative and health benefits of bone broth, and secondly, I have succeeded in my mission of making the *knedle* as light as clouds while still holding their shape in the broth. The earliest cookbooks published in Serbo-Croat (as the language was called then, in what was to eventually become the Kingdom of Yugoslavia) appeared in the late 19th century and were translations of German or Austro-Hungarian cookbooks, so the influence on our cuisine is significant. *Knedle* is an obvious adaptation of the German *knödel* (bread dumplings), but in composition they are closer to an Austrian or Bavarian *grießnockerl* for soup. Bone broth (either beef, like this, or chicken) with *knedle* is deeply loved by nearly every corner of the former Yugoslavia, and it has a strong hold over our collective culinary consciousness and identity.

Put the bones and beef into a large stockpot and add the water (making sure the bones are submerged – add more if you need). Bring to a simmer over a medium-high heat. Do not allow the water to boil – as soon as it is close to doing so, pour in some cold water and immediately skim off any scum and impurities and discard them. Continue to do this for 25–30 minutes, or until the stock simmers clear without too much froth.

Add the onions, celery, carrots, parsnip, parsley stalks, thyme, bay leaves and peppercorns. Reduce the heat to medium, cover with a lid and simmer gently for 2–2½ hours, periodically topping up with water and skimming, if needed. When the beef pieces are tender enough to be cut with a spoon, remove from the heat and allow to cool.

Strain the broth through a fine-mesh sieve into a large, clean saucepan, reserving the contents of the sieve. At this stage, either bring the stock back up to the boil and reduce by one-third, or remove about 1 litre (34 fl oz/4¼ cups) of the broth and store in a clean, airtight container in the refrigerator for other meals such as the Elbasan Tava on page 166.

Reserve and set aside the beef pieces, cooked carrots and parsnip from the sieve. Discard the bones, bay leaves, peppercorns and thyme sprigs. Either keep the broth clear as is, or use a spatula (or soup spoon) to pass the onions and celery through the sieve directly into the saucepan containing the remaining broth. Shred the beef (removing any sinew or gristle) and slice the carrots and parsnip, then add everything back to the broth. Add the potatoes, salt and a good grind of black pepper, then place the saucepan over a medium heat and bring to a gentle simmer while you make the *knedle*.

Put the egg white into a bowl and add the salt. Whisk for 5–6 minutes, or until soft peaks form and it has more than doubled in size. Add the egg yolk, the oil and a generous grind of black pepper. Whisk for a few seconds until just combined, then fold in the *griz* until the mixture has an even consistency taking care not to lose the air from the egg whites. Once the soup is simmering gently, take a small teaspoon and dip it in the soup (to warm up the spoon). Then scoop a small amount of the *knedle* mixture

On the Spoon

(your teaspoon should be no more than a third full), roll it up the side of the bowl so it shapes naturally into a quenelle and place the teaspoon in the soup until the mixture falls off the teaspoon. Repeat until you have used up the *knedle* mixture.

Once all the *knedle* are in, add the chopped parsley (reserve some to serve) and simmer for 4–5 minutes until the *knedle* have more than quadrupled in size and are cooked through. Check and adjust the seasoning to your taste and serve in soup bowls with a sprinkle of the reserved chopped parsley on top.

On the Spoon

SERVES 4

Šketo

4 tablespoons sunflower or olive oil
500 g (1 lb 2 oz) lamb (4 loin chops or untrimmed best-end chops)
1 teaspoon sea salt flakes, plus extra as needed
600 ml (20 fl oz/2½ cups) hot water, plus extra as needed
4–6 spring onions (scallions), finely chopped
4–6 garlic cloves, finely chopped
1 tablespoon sweet paprika
1 tablespoon plain (all-purpose) flour
1 teaspoon vegetable bouillon powder
300 g (10½ oz) fresh parsley, thick stems removed and the rest finely chopped (leaves and stems)
freshly ground black pepper

TO SERVE
plain set yoghurt
crusty bread

A rather unusual dish, this is essentially a lamb *čorba* (thick soup). I have only ever encountered this in North Macedonia, Albania and Kosovo. In Albanian it is called *mish škeo*, meaning 'meat without vegetables'. In a book called *Tunel* (tunnel) by Petre Andreevski, two characters discuss *šketo*, one of them stating he's eaten it in Bitola (a city in the south-western part of North Macedonia), the other declaring he will travel to Bitola and ask around the whole city to get the recipe for it just so he can eat it. I imagine it as a dish born in times of hardship. Traditionally, it would be made with offcuts of lamb on the bone and whatever wild greens and herbs could be foraged (including wild parsley). To me, this humble dish is testament to the resourcefulness of the Balkan kitchen that something incredibly delicious created from not very much; a frugal amount of meat, padded out with greens and herbs. Nowadays, flat-leaf parsley is typically used, and it may sound a lot, but I have been conservative with the amount.

Heat 2 tablespoons of the oil in a frying pan over a medium-high heat. Season the lamb on all sides with the salt and a generous grind of black pepper. Add the lamb to the frying pan and brown evenly for 3–4 minutes on each side.

Transfer the browned lamb to a large, heavy-based saucepan for which you have a lid. Pour about 100 ml (3½ fl oz/scant ½ cup) of the water into the frying pan that you browned the lamb in and stir with a wooden spoon to deglaze the pan, then taste the liquid; if it's not bitter, pour it into the saucepan with the lamb. Set the frying pan aside for later. Pour in the rest of the water to cover the lamb, then place the saucepan over a medium heat, cover with the lid and gently simmer for 40–45 minutes, stirring occasionally to ensure the meat doesn't stick to the bottom. Add a splash of water if you need to, ensuring the lamb is always fully submerged in liquid as it braises.

Meanwhile, heat the remaining oil in the frying pan over a medium-high heat. Add the spring onions and fry for 3–4 minutes or until slightly softened but still retaining their colour. Add the garlic and fry for 1 minute. Then add the paprika, flour, vegetable powder and 1–2 tablespoons of the lamb cooking liquid and cook for a further 30 seconds while stirring well to combine. Pour this mixture into the saucepan with the lamb and stir well. Add the parsley and a little more water to cover everything, if you need to – but note the consistency of this should be that of a thick soup. Taste and adjust the seasoning to your preference. Continue to simmer gently, stirring occasionally, for a further 20–25 minutes, or until the meat is tender. Serve warm, with yoghurt and crusty bread on the side.

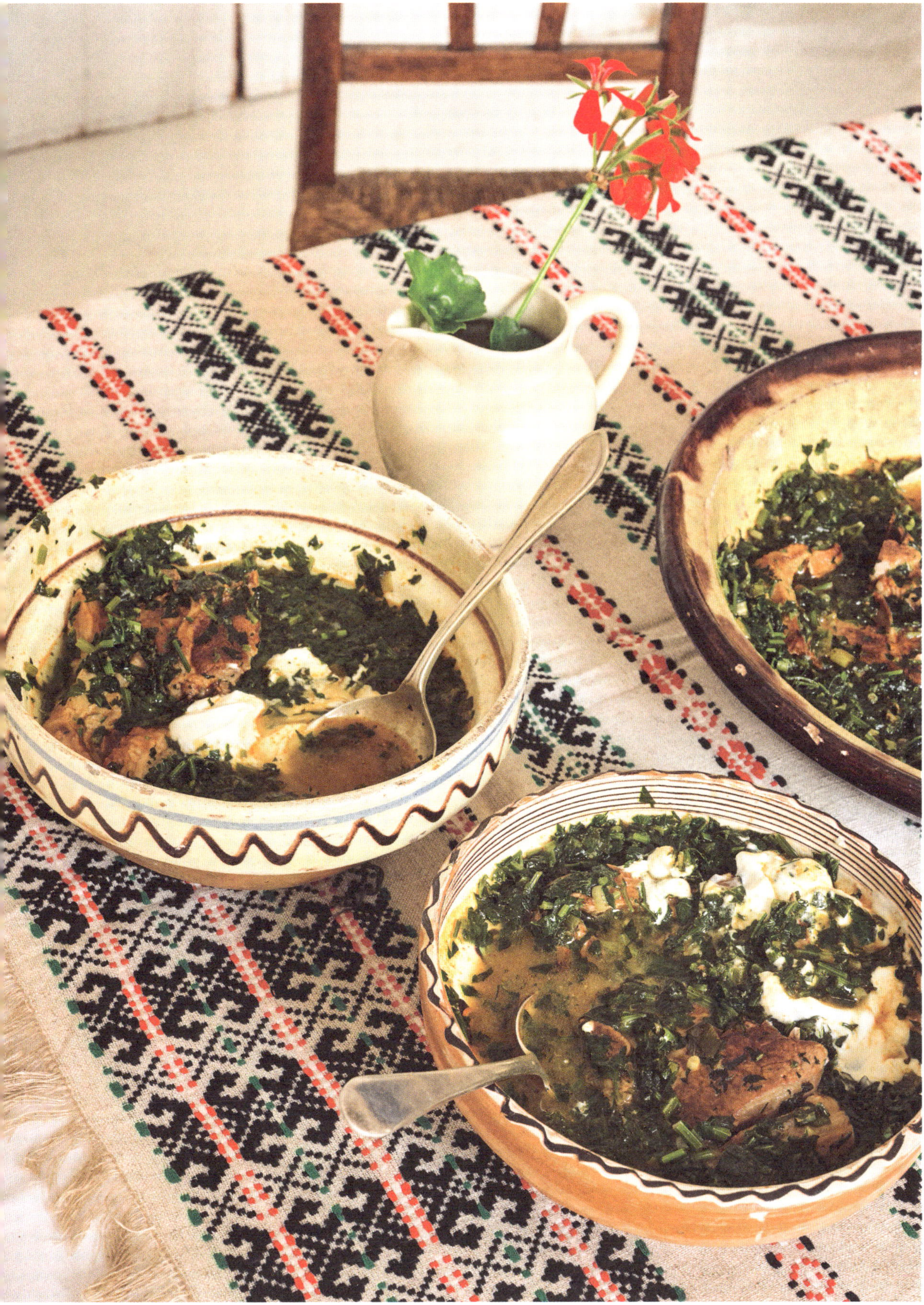

SERVES 4-6

Meatball Soup

FOR THE MEATBALLS

250 g (9 oz) minced (ground) beef (at least 10% fat)

1 medium egg, lightly beaten

25 g (1 oz/¼ cup) dried breadcrumbs (or panko breadcrumbs)

½ teaspoon vegetable bouillon powder

¼ teaspoon bicarbonate of soda (baking soda)

1 tablespoon tomato purée (paste)

½ onion, grated

1 teaspoon dried oregano

20 g (¾ oz) fresh parsley, leaves picked and finely chopped

¼ teaspoon sea salt flakes

2 tablespoons sunflower or extra virgin olive oil, plus extra for greasing

freshly ground black pepper

FOR THE SOUP BASE

2 tablespoons sunflower or extra virgin olive oil

½ onion, finely chopped

1 leek, washed, trimmed and finely chopped

2–3 celery stalks, finely chopped

2–3 carrots, peeled and chopped

½ teaspoon sea salt flakes, plus extra as needed

200 g (7 oz) tomato passata (sieved tomatoes) or 225 g (8 oz) beef (beefsteak) tomatoes, grated and skin discarded

1 tablespoon tomato purée (paste)

100 g (3½ oz/scant ½ cup) barley, washed and soaked in boiling water for at least 10 minutes, then drained

1 litre (34 fl oz/4¼ cups) beef or vegetable stock

20 g (¾ oz) fresh parsley, leaves picked and roughly chopped

My mother's meatball soup is, for me, the ultimate comfort food. Its composition varies with the seasons, but is constant in its speed, ease, practicality and nourishment of body and spirit. Serve with chunks of torn crusty bread and some cheese. It is a dish to be eaten together, discussing the day gone by, and if you are my son, intergalactic superheroes, meteors and dinosaurs.

First, make the meatballs. Place all the ingredients for the meatballs except the oil in a large bowl together with a good grind of black pepper. Use your hands to knead the mixture for 3–4 minutes until everything is well combined. Oil your hands lightly and divide the mixture into 24–28 large marble-sized meatballs.

Heat the oil in a large, lidded saucepan over a medium-high heat. Fry the meatballs for 4–6 minutes, or until they are browned all over – you may need to do this in batches. Once browned, transfer them to a plate and set aside while you prepare the soup base.

Add the oil for the soup base to the same saucepan along with the onion, leek, celery, carrots and salt. Cover and sweat the vegetables over a medium-high heat, stirring occasionally, for 16–18 minutes, or until they are soft, translucent and almost jammy. Add a splash of water to loosen the vegetables if they start sticking to the bottom of the saucepan.

Add the passata or grated tomatoes, tomato purée, barley, stock, the meatballs and a good grind of black pepper. Bring to the boil, then reduce the heat to medium, cover and simmer gently for 35–40 minutes. Remove the lid and allow to bubble for a further 5–10 minutes, or until the soup has reached your desired consistency. Taste and adjust the seasoning, if needed. Stir through the parsley just before serving.

SERVES 4-6

Ariadne's Nettle Chorba

500–600 g (1 lb 2 oz–1 lb 5 oz) young nettles
2 tablespoons olive oil, plus extra to serve
1 onion (or leek or 3–4 spring onions/scallions), finely chopped
½ teaspoon sea salt flakes
2 garlic cloves, crushed
¼ teaspoon chilli flakes, plus extra to serve
2 floury potatoes, peeled, halved and cut into 1 cm (½ inch) thick slices
750 ml (1 lb 10 oz) vegetable or chicken stock
freshly ground black pepper

TO SERVE
1 lemon, cut into wedges
20 g (½ oz) Parmesan, grated (optional)
crusty bread

My father's mother, Ariadne, famously made a wonderful nettle soup. I don't recall the flavour of it and all my mother can remember of the recipe is that it included 'the usual' (nettles and potatoes), so this is very much an homage to the memory of her nettle *chorba*.

The use of foraged greens was paramount to survival in the Balkans throughout history. From rebels fighting Ottoman control to partisans fighting for freedom during the Second World War, the wild landscapes – and in particular forests – of the Balkans have always provided both sanctuary and vital sustenance to those who would have had to use whatever was available for survival. Use the tops of the young spring nettles, before the plant flowers – and do use gloves to pick them. When they are in season, I use nettles as a substitute for spinach. They also freeze very well to be used the rest of the year.

Wearing gloves, wash the nettles well, pick off the leaves and plunge them into a bowl of boiling water for 3–4 minutes until soft and wilted. Drain and immediately place the nettles in a bowl of ice-cold water for 30 seconds, then drain again and squeeze out the excess water. Roughly chop the leaves and set aside.

Heat the oil in a large saucepan over a medium-high heat and add the onion and salt. Fry for 10–12 minutes, or until the onion is soft and translucent. Add the garlic and chilli flakes and fry for 30–60 seconds until fragrant. Add the potatoes and sauté them with the onion mixture for 2 minutes, stirring gently. Pour in the stock and simmer for about 10 minutes, then add the nettles and continue to simmer for a further 3–4 minutes.

Serve with a squeeze of lemon, a drizzle of olive oil, chilli flakes, Parmesan (if using) and crusty bread.

On the Spoon

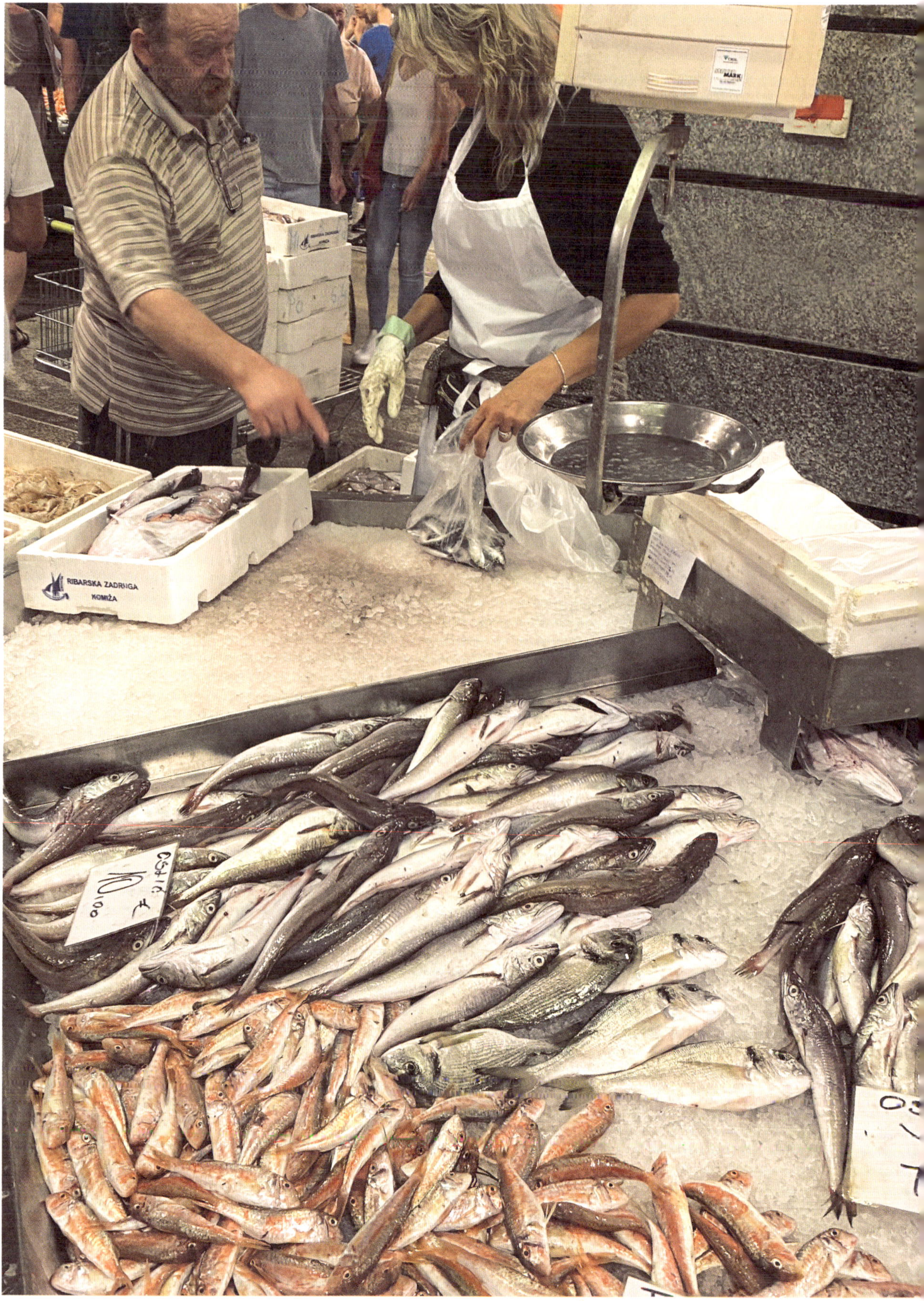
RIBARSKA ZADRUGA
KOMIŽA

Mejrema's Fish Soup

SERVES 4–6

2 tablespoons olive oil
1 onion, finely chopped
½ teaspoon salt
2–3 garlic cloves, finely chopped
300 g (10½ oz) skinless fish fillets (sole, sea bream or sea bass), cut into 3–4 cm (1¼–1½ inch) pieces
80 g (2¾ oz/scant ½ cup) long-grain rice, soaked for 30 minutes, then drained
10 g (½ oz) fresh parsley leaves, finely chopped
1 teaspoon vegetable bouillon powder
freshly ground black pepper
1 lemon, cut into wedges, to serve

FOR THE BROTH

2 kg (4 lb 8 oz) fish bones (sole, monkfish, sea bream, sea bass or red mullet, with 1–2 fish heads, or any cuttlefish or squid trimmings)
3 litres cold water (100 fl oz/12½ cups), plus extra as needed
1 onion, quartered
2–3 celery stalks, chopped into batons
2–3 carrots, peeled, topped and tailed
½ fennel bulb, cut into wedges
2–3 bay leaves
10 g (½ oz) fresh parsley stalks
¼ teaspoon black peppercorns

There is a beautiful island called Ciovo in the Trogir archipelago in Croatia. It was late summer and we were having lunch at the house of a family friend, Mejrema Reuter (an actress, artist, writer, all-round Renaissance woman and my former teacher – and forever inspiration). We sat on her balcony in the dappled shade of the olive and fig trees in her garden, which were bursting with fruit, cooled by a light Adriatic breeze that had picked up the scent of Ciovo's pines and lavender on its journey from the seashore. She had been to the fish market that morning especially for us and picked up *orada* (wild gilthead sea bream native to the Adriatic). Among other Dalmatian delicacies, she had made us her fish soup, adored by her beloved late husband, Carl. It was, and remains, the most beautiful and delicate fish soup I have ever eaten, and I have eaten countless variations all along the Balkan Adriatic coast from Montenegro to Istria. This is my attempt to recreate it, but I've gone down the alternative Dalmatian route of using rice rather than potatoes.

First, make the broth. Put the fish bones into a large stockpot and add the water (making sure the bones are submerged – add more if you need). Bring to a simmer over a medium-high heat. Do not allow the water to boil – as soon as it is close to doing so, pour in some cold water and immediately skim off any scum and impurities and discard them. Continue to do this for 15–20 minutes, or until the stock simmers clear. Add the onion, celery, carrots, fennel, bay leaves, parsley stalks and peppercorns. Reduce the heat to medium, cover and simmer gently for 20–30 minutes, periodically topping up with water and skimming, if needed.

Strain the broth through a fine-mesh sieve into a large, clean saucepan. At this stage, either bring the stock back up to the boil and reduce by one-third, or remove about 1 litre (34 fl oz/4¼ cups) of the broth and store in a clean, airtight container in the refrigerator for other meals, such as the Brodet on page 191.

Pick off any flesh from the fish bones and remove and slice the cooked carrots, then add both back to the pan. Discard the fish bones and the rest of the aromatics.

Next, make the soup base. Heat the oil in a medium sauté pan over a medium-high heat and add the onion and salt. Fry for 10–12 minutes, or until the onion is soft and translucent. Add the garlic and fry for 30–60 seconds, or just until you start to smell the garlic. Transfer the cooked onion and garlic mixture to the pan with the broth, deglazing the sauté pan with some of the broth.

Add the fish fillets, rice, parsley, vegetable powder and a good grind of black pepper. Simmer over a medium-high heat for 10–12 minutes, or until the fish and rice are cooked through.

Serve with a squeeze of lemon.

SERVES 6-8

A Bean Čorba

500 g (1 lb 2 oz/2½ cups) dry Tetovo beans (or white kidney, cannellini or haricot/navy beans)
1 teaspoon bicarbonate of soda (baking soda)
3 litres cold water (100 fl oz/12½ cups), plus extra as needed
3 tablespoons olive or sunflower oil
2 onions, finely chopped
2 garlic cloves, crushed
100 g (3½ oz) slanina (or smoked streaky/side bacon or smoked pancetta), cut into 5 mm (¼ inch) slices
2 tablespoons sweet paprika
1 tablespoon tomato purée (paste)
1 tablespoon vegetable bouillon powder
3–4 bay leaves
1–2 sprigs of fresh thyme
4–6 juniper berries
3–4 carrots, peeled and cut into chunks
1.2–1.4 kg (2 lb 11 oz–3 lb 1½ oz) smoked ham hock
300 g (10½ oz) Sour Cabbage (see page 245), finely shredded (or sauerkraut)
20 g (¾ oz) fresh soft herbs, such as parsley, mint or oregano, leaves picked and finely chopped, plus extra to serve
sea salt flakes and freshly ground black pepper
Aleppo pepper, to serve

Across the Balkans, bean *čorbas*, or thick bean soups, range from incredibly humble and stark – such as the so-called monastery *grah*, *grav* or *pasulj* favoured on Eastern Orthodox fasting days, where cooked beans can be flavoured with as little as sautéed onions and perhaps mint – to the hearty and decadent – such as *jota*, found in northern Croatia and Slovenia, which is a stew of beans, pork, sauerkraut or soured turnip and, in Slovenia, thick slices of *Kranjska klobasa* (Carniolian sausage). I grew up eating a bean *čorba* that consisted of cooked beans flavoured with *zaprška* (a kind of roux made from oil and sweet paprika, and sometimes flour and fried onions) similar to the Tavče Gravče on page 150. This version is closer to a Slovenian-style *jota*, minus the Carniolian sausage – though do use that in lieu of the *slanina* and ham hock if you can find it. Really, after cooking the beans, you can flavour it however you like, and I encourage you to make your own Balkan inspired bean *čorba*.

Put the beans and bicarbonate of soda into a large, heavy-based saucepan or stockpot and cover with water. Set aside to soak for at least 8 hours, or overnight.

Drain and cover with water again, then place the saucepan over a medium-high heat and bring to the boil. After 10–15 minutes, you should have a lot of scum on the top. Drain the beans again and rinse them under running water. Set aside.

Preheat the oven to 180°C fan (400°F).

Heat the oil in a large cast-iron casserole dish (Dutch oven) over a medium-high heat and add the onion. Fry for 5–7 minutes, or until soft and light brown, then add the garlic and cook for 30 seconds. Add the *slanina*, paprika, tomato purée and vegetable powder and stir to coat. Remove from the heat and add the drained beans, bay leaves, thyme, juniper berries, carrots, and a generous grind of black pepper and stir to combine, then nestle the ham hock among the beans. Pour in the fresh 3 litres (100 fl oz/12½ cups) water (or more to ensure everything is submerged), cover with a lid and transfer to the oven. Cook for 3½–4 hours, stirring occasionally and topping up with a splash of water if you need to, until the meat is falling off the ham hock. Remove the ham hock from the dish and place it on a large plate to cool. When cool enough to handle, peel off the skin and any excess fat and gristle and discard. Pick off all the meat and shred it roughly with your hands. Return the meat to the dish, along with half the sour cabbage and the herbs. Stir to incorporate. Discard the bones. Check and adjust the seasoning to your taste, bearing in mind the combination of ham hock and sour cabbage will be quite salty. Serve topped with more sour cabbage and sprinkled with Aleppo pepper and fresh soft herbs.

On the Spoon

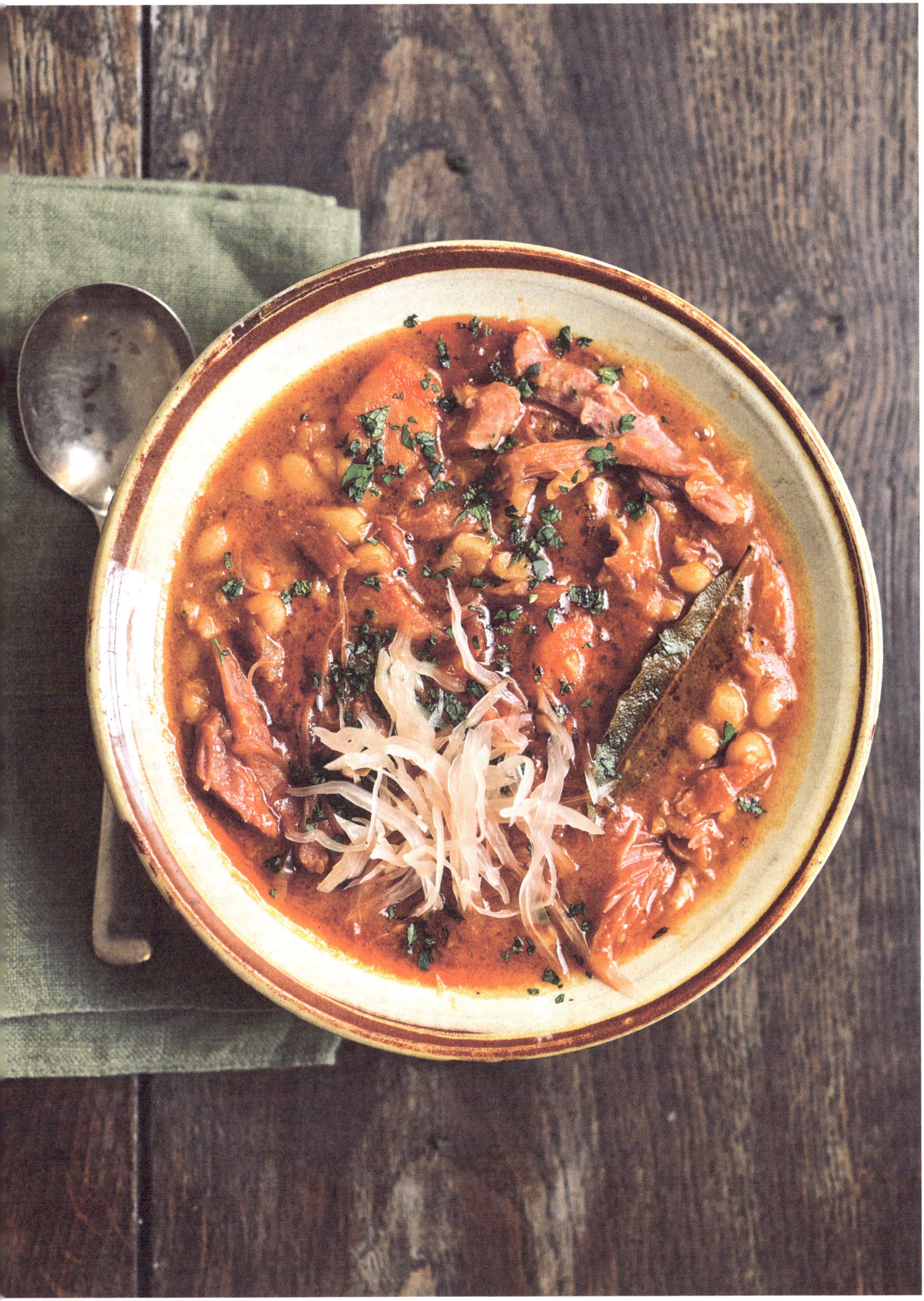

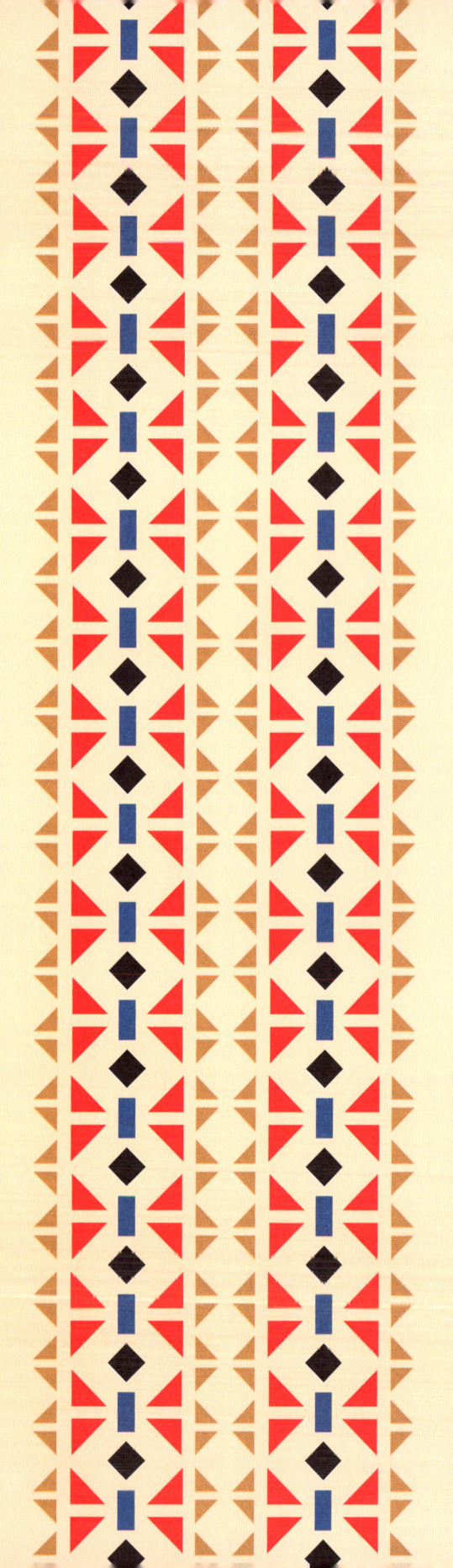

The 1946 Constitution of the Federal People's Republic of Yugoslavia, was, in many ways, a groundbreaking document for its time. It enshrined the principle of gender equality and explicitly recognised the equal rights of men and women, marking a significant step towards women's empowerment in the region. This constitutional commitment laid the foundation for subsequent legal and societal changes aimed at advancing women's rights and promoting equality throughout the former Yugoslavia. This, however, did not quite translate fully into society, which responded not with an equal division of responsibilities between the sexes, but an attempt to economise in what was seen as 'woman's work' in the domestic sphere. The infamous double burden on Yugoslav women was born, along with the stigma of *zaposlena zena-domacica* (a working woman-housewife). Efforts were focused on didactic instruction to women (through the medium of cookbooks published during the Yugoslav era) on economising housework, including time-saving techniques for cooking and an emphasis on how the working woman could ensure her family ate a healthy, balanced diet throughout the working week.

For many in former Yugoslavia, the working (and school) day ran from 7 a.m. to 3 p.m. This meant that the main meal of the day was *ruček* or *ručak* (lunch), which was typically eaten as a family around 4 p.m., once everyone had returned home from their respective days and came together to eat. For the significant number of women in former Yugoslavia

LUNCH
RUČEK

who worked (like my grandmother and my mother) and then came home and had to cook for the family, planning was essential. A busy working and domestic life meant lunch had to be something healthy, typically made in advance, which would last several days and could be finished off or reheated at the end of a busy day, topped up with an array of quick-to-put-together seasonal salads, cured meats and cheeses, breads and various preserves, ferments and pickles and other items from the *špajz*.

In our home, this manifested as time spent cooking as the sun set on the weekend: a large pot of *supa* or *čorba*, a weekly *mandža* (like the *Grašok* on page 124) or a *sarma* bubbling away. Otherwise, it might be the kind of meal that cooks and bakes at the same time, slowly, until the top has a golden or reddish (if paprika is involved) crust, its colours those of summer in full swing. When food needed to be topped up during the week, the principle was the same – prepare it the night before so it is ready for the next day. Bean dishes like Tavče Gravče were almost always reserved for Fridays, sometimes accompanied by fish, because Fridays tended to be fasting days. These dishes are, for me, the definition of comfort. Some of them are just as easily transformed into celebratory dishes for more special occasions or family gatherings, like the Drob Sarma or Podvarok. They are the kinds of dishes that are, dare I say, almost impossible to overcook. In fact, the longer they cook, the better. As I write this, I can almost hear the objections, comparisons and amicable debates – that's not what we have for *ruček* in my part of North Macedonia! In Sarajevo! Belgrade! Zagreb! Ljubljana! Podgorica! Well, of course not, because every family has a different formula for composing their weekly *ruček* rituals, based on the seasons, local ingredients and preferences. Along the coastal parts of Croatia and Montenegro you are more likely to have fish- and seafood-based *ručak*, using the fresh bounty from the Adriatic infused with Mediterranean flavour. Inland, a slow-cooked meat and vegetable dish is more likely, such as a *peka* or *kotlovina* in Croatia, or a roast lamb in the mountains of Montenegro. In Serbia, a delicious selection of grilled or roast meats might be on the menu. In Slovenia, hearty porridges, dumplings and stews can be found. In Bosnia and Herzegovina, it would be *burek* and perhaps *Bosanski lonac*. In Kosovo, they might eat a baked layered pancaked known as *flija*, accompanied by grilled meats and fresh mezes. The commonality that prevails across all is generally that *ruček* – as the most substantive meal of the day when the whole family comes together – is hearty, healthy and balanced.

Grašok

SERVES 4

3 tablespoons sunflower or olive oil
1 onion, finely chopped
½ teaspoon sea salt flakes
2–3 carrots, peeled and finely grated
3 tablespoons sweet paprika
1 tablespoon plain (all-purpose) flour
2 tablespoons tomato purée (paste)
1 x 400 g (14 oz) tin plum tomatoes
500 g (1 lb 2 oz) peas (fresh or frozen)
1 litre (34 fl oz/4¼ cups) vegetable stock (or more if you prefer it brothier)
30 g (1 oz) fresh parsley, leaves and tender stems picked and finely chopped
30 g (1 oz) fresh dill, fronds picked and finely chopped
1–2 lemon-scented geranium (*Pelargonium citrosum*) leaves (optional)
freshly ground black pepper
crusty bread, to serve

In the Balkans, many dishes are mononymous, which means the name of the vegetable is used as the name for the dish. In this case, *grašok*, *grašak* or *mahuna* are all names for green peas, but they are also understood to also mean a green pea *mandza* (the word appropriated from Italian *mangia* – to eat) which typically refers to a brothy stew. In our home some kind of *mandza* featuring whatever vegetables happen to be in season is a weekly ritual. The point of a *mandza* is that it can be made the day before, and finished off or reheated at the end of a busy day. This is a perfect spring *mandza* when green peas are in season, but it works just as well with frozen peas. Most families will pad this out with meat and potatoes for a more substantial meal, but I find it particularly delightful meatless. Interestingly, similar dishes exist across the Levant, the closest being an Egyptian dish – *bisala wa gazar* – which is a green pea and carrot stew made with paprika and tomatoes and various other spices, often eaten by Coptic Egyptians on fasting days. There are several variants across the Balkans; in North Croatia, *grashak cuspajz* uses a butter and flour roux as the sauce. This version is more of a southern Balkan one because of the liberal use of paprika and tomatoes. Increase the amount of liquid if you prefer it brothier rather than a thick soup.

Heat the oil in a large, heavy-based saucepan over a medium-high heat. Add the onion and salt and fry for 10–12 minutes, or until softened. Add the carrots and fry for a further 2–4 minutes until they start to soften. Then add the paprika, flour and tomato purée and cook for a further minute, stirring well to coat the onion and carrot mixture. Add the tomatoes (swilling out the tin with a splash of water) and stir, gently breaking them up with the back of your spoon. Add the peas, stock, half the parsley and dill, the geranium leaves (if using) and a good grind of black pepper. Reduce the heat to medium, cover with a lid and simmer, stirring occasionally, for 45–60 minutes, or until the sauce has reduced by at least a third and thickened to a consistency you like.

In the last few minutes of cooking, stir through the rest of the herbs (reserving some to serve). Serve warm with crusty bread (or any other accompaniment of your choice) and the remaining herbs.

Note

For a meat version, chop 500 g (1 lb 2 oz) stewing meat (such as beef chuck steak) into 2 cm (1 inch) cubes and brown it for 2–3 minutes. Remove the meat from the pan and cook the rest of the ingredients as above, then add the meat back in and transfer everything to an ovenproof casserole dish (Dutch oven) to slow-cook for around 2 hours at 180°C fan (400°F), or until the meat is tender enough to cut through with a spoon.

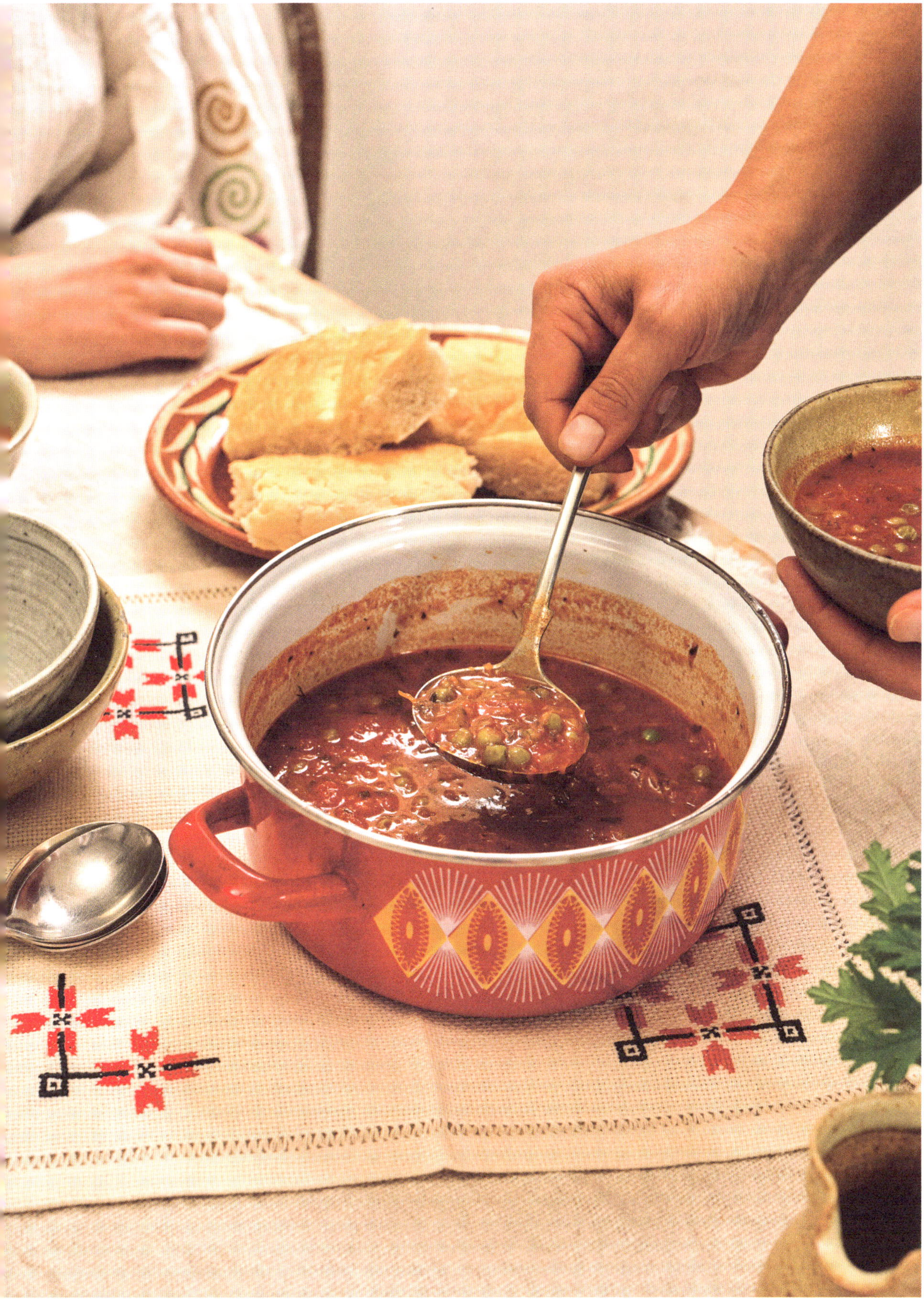

SERVES 8 AS A STARTER OR 4 AS A MAIN

Imam Bayildi

4 aubergines (eggplants; about 1–1.2 kg/2 lb 4 oz–2 lb 11 oz total)
75 ml (2½ fl oz/5 tablespoons) extra virgin olive oil, plus extra as needed and to serve
1 large onion, finely chopped
2 garlic cloves, finely chopped
2 tablespoons tomato purée (paste)
1 x 400 g (14 oz) tin of plum tomatoes (or 4 large beef/beefsteak tomatoes, finely chopped)
1 teaspoon caster (superfine) sugar
40 g (1½ oz) fresh parsley, leaves and tender stems picked and finely chopped, plus extra to serve
½ teaspoon dried oregano
1 teaspoon vegetable bouillon powder
400 ml (14 fl oz/generous 1½ cups) boiling water
sea salt and freshly ground black pepper

TO SERVE
white cheese (or feta)
plain set yoghurt
crusty bread

Imam bayildi – a dish so good that, according to legend, it once made an *imam* (holy man) faint from delicious delirium (either because the dish was so good or because of how much – at the time very expensive – olive oil his wife had used to make it). *Bayildi* means 'fainted', hence the dish's name. It is another Ottoman dish that is seen in various guises across the Balkans, Eastern Mediterranean and the Middle East. Though it contains just a handful of simple ingredients, they are treated beautifully, which allows their natural majesty to shine. The secret here is time. Time to drain the bitterness out of the aubergines (eggplants) with salt. Time to scoop out their delicious flesh and cook it down with onions and garlic until caramelised and sweet. Time to allow the tomatoes to infuse with the aubergine and cook down into a delicious jam-like consistency. Time to roast the aubergine shells with olive oil before they meet their delicious filling. Time to then bake everything down gently and slowly until the aubergine skin is silky and tender. Time.

This dish is close to my heart as it is one of the first dishes my mother taught me to cook. It then became the first dish I cooked for many friends, old and new, and for my husband, Peter. I'm convinced he fell in love with me because of my *imam bayildi*. There is a noble honesty to it – unashamedly simple, just aubergines and tomatoes, but with time and love, transformed into something truly majestic.

Cut the aubergines in half lengthways, score the flesh (keeping the skin intact) and salt generously. Place flesh side down in a colander and set aside for at least 1 hour – this drains any bitterness from the aubergines.

Rinse the aubergines and pat them dry with paper towels. Scoop out the flesh (again ensuring you keep the skin intact, so you are left with shells, like aubergine 'boats'). Chop the scooped-out flesh into roughly 1 cm (½ inch) cubes and set aside.

Preheat the oven to 200°C fan (425°F).

Place the aubergine shells in a large baking dish (about 22 x 30 cm /9 x 12 inches) and brush with 2 tablespoons of the oil. Roast in the oven for about 20 minutes, or until the skins start to soften and you start to see a little colour on the residual flesh. Remove from the oven and set aside. Reduce the heat of the oven to 180°C fan (400°F).

Meanwhile, prepare the filling. Heat the remaining oil in a large frying pan and fry the onion for 10–12 minutes until softened and lightly browned. Add the chopped aubergine flesh and cook for about 20 minutes until the flesh softens and you start to see a little caramelisation (loosen with 1–2 tablespoons more oil if the pan is looking too dry and the aubergine starts to stick). Next, add the garlic and tomato purée and cook for a further minute, or until you start to smell the garlic. Add the tomatoes (swilling out the tin with a splash of water if using tinned), the sugar, most of the parsley (reserving some to serve), the oregano, vegetable powder, ½ teaspoon salt and a generous grind of black pepper. Cook for 20–25 minutes, or until the mixture comes together into a thick sauce.

When ready, divide the filling between the aubergine shells. Don't be afraid to completely cover the shells if you have lots of filling. Deglaze the pan used to cook the filling with the boiling water, scraping up the cooking

Lunch

juices. Pour this carefully over the filled aubergines – they should be submerged in filling and liquid.

Cover the baking dish with foil and bake in the oven for about 2 hours, checking from time to time and topping up with a splash of water if you need to ensure the aubergines do not dry out. It is ready when the filling is thick and nicely browned and you are able to cut through the aubergine skin with a spoon. Remove the foil and bake for a further 10–15 minutes to crisp the top.

Before serving, scatter over the reserved parsley and drizzle with a little more olive oil. Serve warm with white cheese, yoghurt and crusty bread.

Lunch

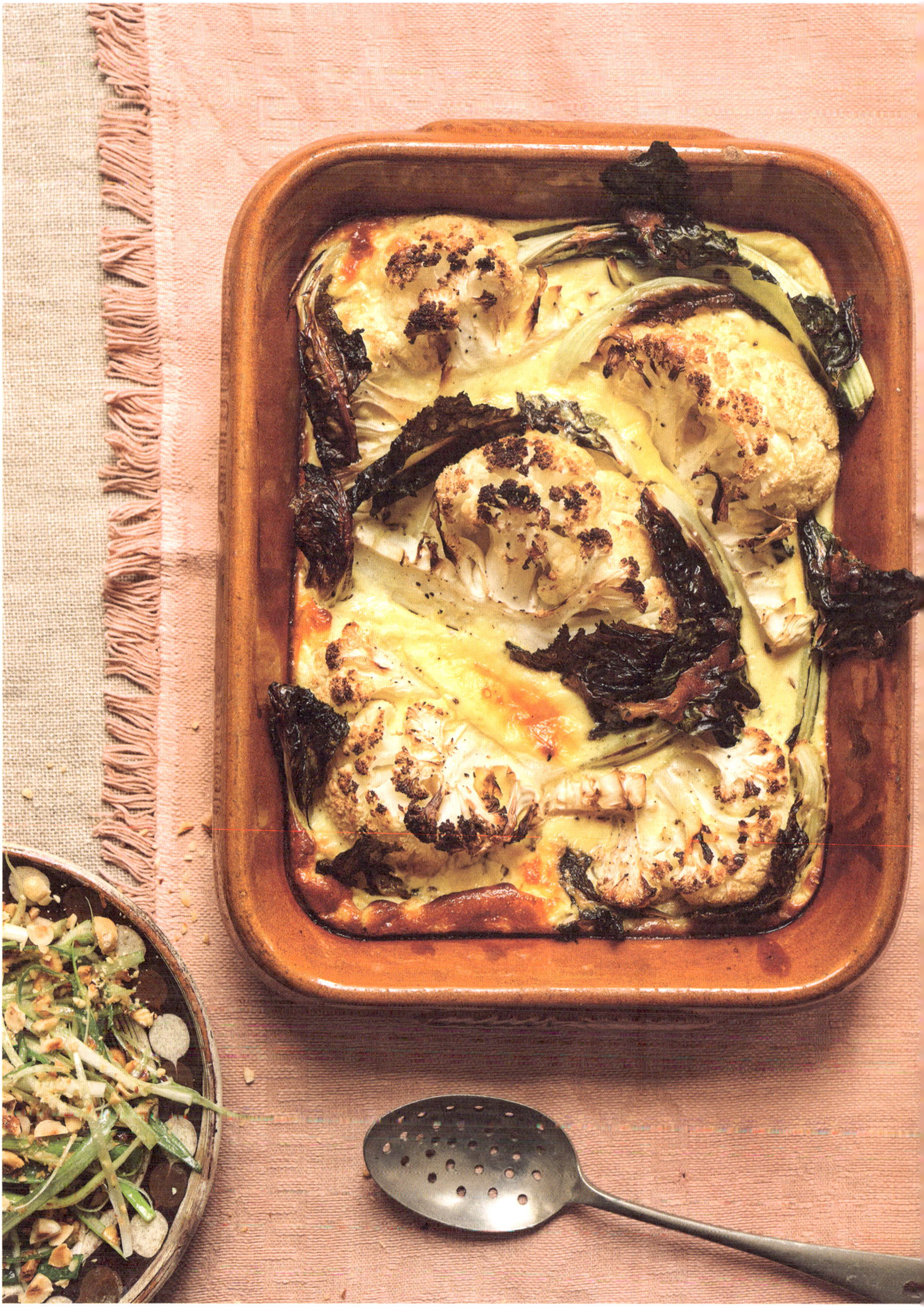

SERVES 4

Cauliflower Bake

1 large cauliflower (about 1.2 kg/ 2 lb 11 oz)
2 tablespoons extra virgin olive oil, plus extra for brushing
sea salt flakes
4 medium eggs
240 g (8½ oz/scant 1 cup) plain yoghurt
¼ teaspoon caraway seeds
freshly ground black pepper

FOR THE SPRING ONION SALAD

4–6 spring onions (scallions), washed and sliced into lengthwise into thin strips
30 g (1 oz/scant ¼ cup) blanched hazelnuts, lightly toasted and roughly chopped
1 teaspoon Bukovo pepper (or Aleppo pepper)
1 tablespoon extra virgin olive oil
¼ teaspoon sea salt flakes

I love cauliflower, and that's mostly down to my mother's ingenious way of preparing it, which is a sort of healthier version of cauliflower cheese. This was a simple and quick midweek meal for us, paired with a fresh salad, but it also works as a side dish. Mama would always parboil the cauliflower to make this dish, but I love roasted cauliflower (florets and leaves). I'll often have it on its own, just paired with some garlicky yoghurt and something spicy like Dried Pepper Paste (see page 261). I have combined this adult love of roasted cauliflower with my childhood treat.

Preheat the oven to 200°C fan (425°F) and line a large baking tray (pan) with baking parchment.

Separate the leaves from the cauliflower and trim them, discarding any that are too bruised. Cut the cauliflower head into 6–8 wedges. Pat the wedges and leaves dry, then transfer to the prepared baking tray. Coat them in the oil and sprinkle with a pinch of salt and a good grind of black pepper. Make sure everything is well spaced out on the tray, then roast in the oven for 20–25 minutes until a butter knife easily pierces the stalks and the cauliflower is golden brown with nicely charred edges.

Brush a 20 x 30 cm (8 x 12 inch) deep-sided baking dish with a little oil. Transfer the wedges and leaves to the baking dish, arranging them evenly in one layer. Reduce the oven temperature to 180°C fan (400°F).

Crack the eggs into a bowl and whisk until frothy. Add the yoghurt, caraway seeds, salt and a good grind of black pepper, then whisk until smooth. Pour the sauce over the cauliflower, then bake in the oven for 25–30 minutes, or until the sauce has puffed up, is just set and has a golden brown crust on top.

Meanwhile, make the salad. Place the spring onions in a bowl of iced water for 2 minutes, or until they curl up. Drain well and pat dry with paper towels, then transfer to a serving bowl. Add the hazelnuts, Bukovo pepper, olive oil, salt and a good grind of black pepper and toss to coat. Serve alongside the cauliflower bake.

SERVES 4 AS A MAIN OR 6-8 AS A SIDE

Spinach and Rice

2 tablespoons sunflower or olive oil
3–4 spring onions (scallions) or 1 onion, finely chopped
½ teaspoon sea salt flakes
1 tablespoon tomato purée (paste; or 1 medium tomato, peeled and grated)
750 ml (25 fl oz/3 cups) vegetable stock
1 tablespoon sweet paprika
125 g (4½ oz/generous ½ cup) risotto rice (arborio or carnaroli) or pudding rice
300 g (10½ oz) baby spinach (stalks removed if you have time)
freshly ground black pepper

TO SERVE
4–8 eggs, fried or poached (optional)
plain yoghurt
white cheese (or feta)
crusty bread

Spanak K˜ioriz is something I adored eating as a child and still do. My mother made it frequently, so to me it will always have that special taste of comfort and love. It is still something I ask her to make for me because, as is the way with comfort food from our childhood, it always tastes better when made by my mother's hands.

Really this is a sort of spinach risotto, very similar to Turkish *pirinçli ispanak* and Greek *spanakorizo* but with Balkan elements, specifically the use of sweet paprika and tomatoes. It is generally eaten as a hot meal, sometimes topped with fried eggs. Some like to bake the spinach rice in the oven and top it with eggs, almost like a shakshuka, and some like to add meat. I prefer the simplicity of making it risotto-style, then adding fried or poached eggs for a quick and healthy family meal.

Heat the oil in a large saucepan over a medium-high heat and fry the onion with the salt for 8–10 minutes, stirring occasionally, until soft and just starting to caramelise.

Reduce the heat to medium, add the tomato purée and 2 tablespoons of the stock and cook for 1 minute, stirring constantly, until well combined with the onion. Add the paprika and stir well to combine, taking care not to burn the paprika – loosen the mixture with a tablespoon or two more of the stock if you need to.

Next, add the rice and stir for 1–2 minutes until it is well coated in the onion, paprika and tomato mixture. Increase the heat to medium-high and add the vegetable stock a ladle at a time, stirring often, until the rice is nearly cooked – about 15 minutes. You may not need all the stock. If you need a little more liquid, just top up the stock with water.

Add the spinach and another ladle of stock or water and cook for a further 6–8 minutes, stirring occasionally, until the rice is cooked but retains a bite and the spinach has wilted down. Taste and adjust the seasoning, adding a good grind of black pepper.

Serve the rice with fried or poached eggs if you like, as well as yoghurt, white cheese and crusty bread on the side.

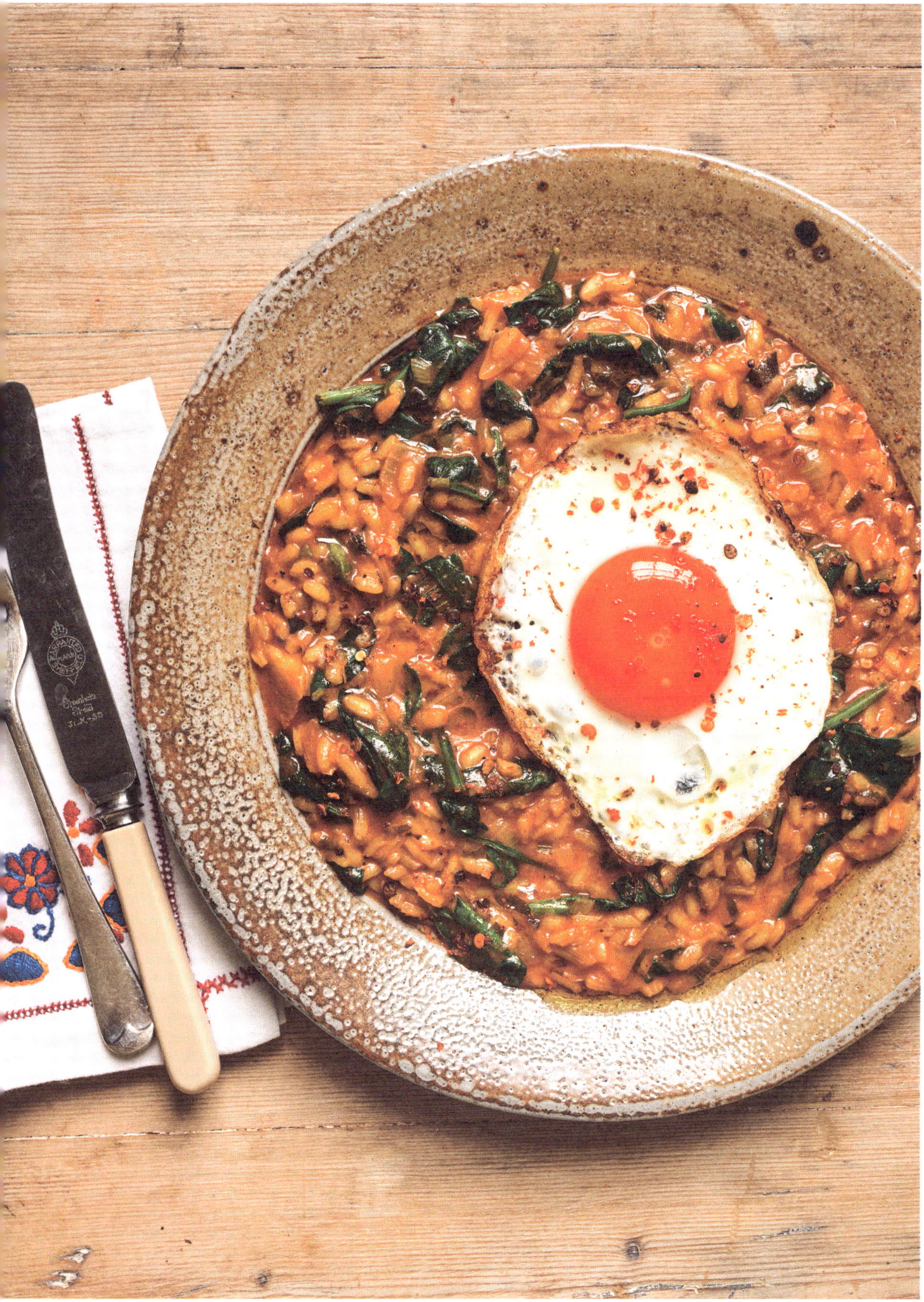

SERVES 4 AS A MAIN

Klepe

FOR THE DOUGH

350 g (12 oz/generous 2¾ cups) plain (all purpose) or '00' flour, sifted, plus extra for dusting

150 ml (5 fl oz/scant ⅔ cup) lukewarm water

1 medium egg

½ teaspoon sunflower oil, plus extra for brushing

½ teaspoon fine sea salt

20 g (¾ oz/scant ¼ cup) semolina or polenta (cornmeal), for shaping

FOR THE MEAT FILLING

350 g (12 oz) minced (ground) beef (or lamb or a mix of both)

1 teaspoon sunflower or olive oil

1 small onion, peeled and minced (ground) or very finely chopped

½ teaspoon sweet smoked paprika

1 teaspoon sweet paprika

1 teaspoon vegetable bouillon powder

½ teaspoon sea salt flakes

¼ teaspoon freshly ground black pepper

FOR THE CHEESE FILLING

25 g (1 oz) spring onions (scallions), finely chopped

400 g (14 oz) white cheese (or feta), crumbled

1 tablespoon nigella seeds

20 g (¾ oz) fresh parsley, leaves picked and finely chopped

¼ teaspoon ground black pepper

FOR THE YOGHURT SAUCE

150 g (5½ oz/scant ⅔ cup) plain set yoghurt

1 large garlic clove, crushed (or 2 if not making the wild garlic oil)

½ teaspoon sea salt flakes

FOR THE SPICED BUTTER

50 g (1¾ oz) unsalted butter

There are plausible historical theories that dumplings found their way to the Balkans from the imperial Chinese courts. Their exact journey is still subject to research and debate, but it possibly begins with the ancient Chinese steamed buns stuffed with meat called *mantou* (though *mantou* are nowadays plain steamed buns, with *baozi* resembling the ancient *mantou* more closely). These then developed in the Mongolian Empire around the 12th century, where the yeasted bun was replaced with a thin dough sheet. The resulting *manta* were either steamed or boiled (similar to a Chinese *jiaozi*). From there, the idea of a meat-filled dumpling travelled widely – following the Silk Road across central Asia and the Caucasus with Mongol and Turkic horsemen (though there are also theories that they may have travelled the other way from the Middle East). Migrating Turkic tribes brought the dumplings to Anatolia where they evolved into *manti* – spiced meat-filled dumplings, served with a garlic yoghurt sauce. With the rise of the Ottoman Empire, *manti* arrived in the palace kitchens at Topkapi – a recipe for steamed dumplings filled with spiced minced lamb and chickpeas (garbanzos), served with a garlic yoghurt sauce and sumac is recorded in the earliest Ottoman cookbook from the 15th century by Muhammad Shirvâni. As the Ottoman Empire expanded into the Balkans, *manti* almost certainly came along for the imperial ride – though when exactly is not known.

Whenever they made it to the Balkans, *manti* encountered local customs, ingredients and cooking preferences, and diverged in two ways. One retained the name but changed into something different to the Ottoman (and modern-day Turkish) *manti*. Balkan *manti* or *mantije* are little meat (or vegetable) parcels made with *burek* dough that are baked together as a sort of pull-apart bread. The other retained the idea of *manti* but changed the name and became what are known as *klepe* or *kulaci*, which are essentially meat-filled dumplings or – dare I say it – ravioli (given competing influences on the region from Venice). They are served with a garlic yoghurt sauce and topped with a sweet, paprika-infused butter. Unlike Turkish manti, these are not par-baked before being boiled. *Klepe* or *kulaci* are famously associated with Bosnia and Herzegovina but also parts of Croatia. They are typically filled with meat, but I have given an alternative if preparing these for vegetarians. The wild garlic (ramsons) oil is a non-traditional but delicious addition for spring. Feel free to omit it and simply add two crushed garlic cloves to the yoghurt sauce instead.

Lunch *Recipe continued overleaf*

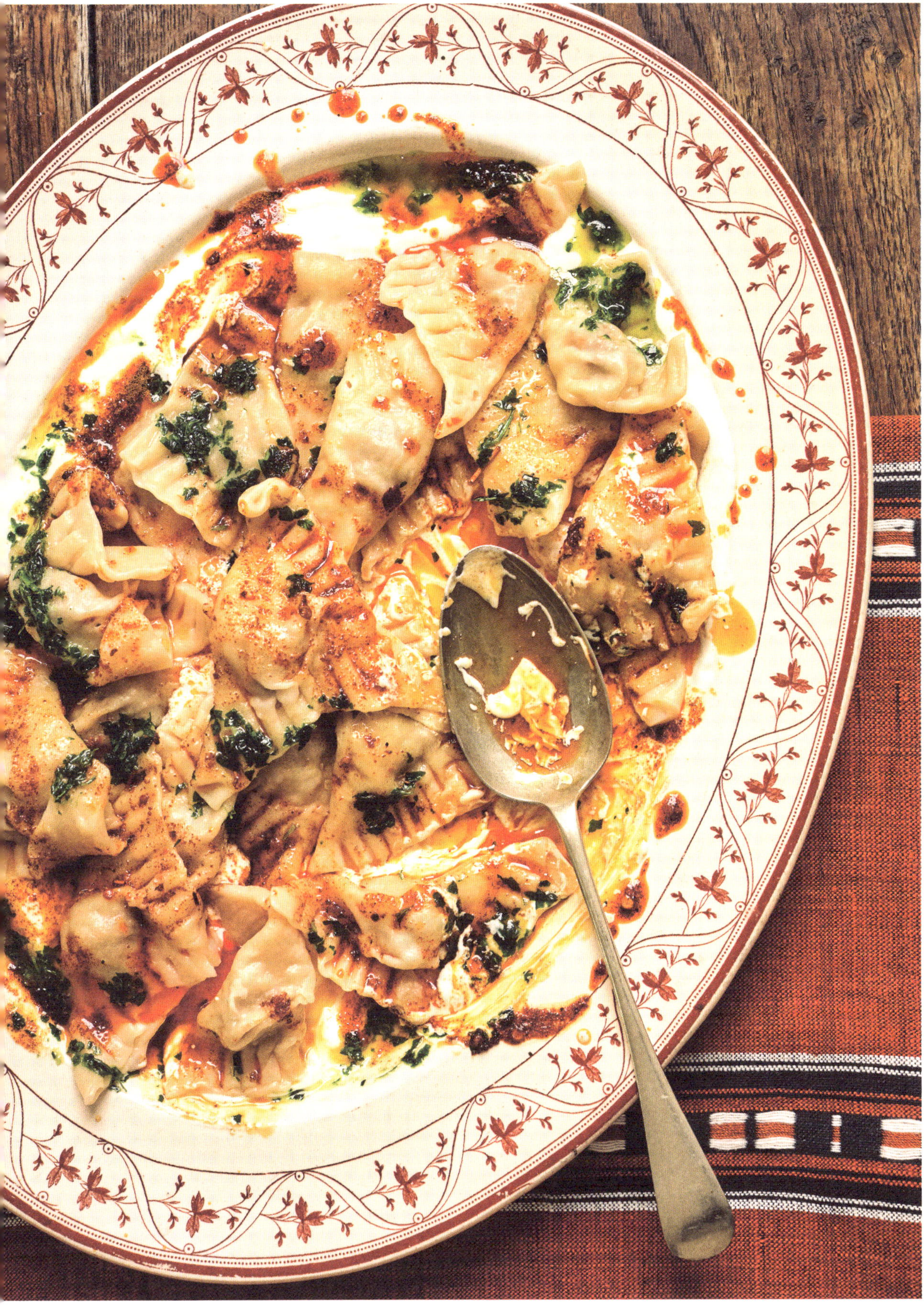

1 tablespoon sweet paprika
½ teaspoon Bukovo pepper
 (or Aleppo pepper)
¼ teaspoon sea salt flakes

FOR THE WILD GARLIC OIL (OPTIONAL)
75 ml (2½ fl oz/5 tablespoons) olive oil
10 g (½ oz) wild garlic (ramsons)
 leaves, washed

Put all the ingredients for the dough into a large bowl, then use a fork to bring the mixture together into a shaggy dough. Tip out the dough onto a lightly floured work surface (scraping down the sides of the bowl) and knead for 4–5 minutes, just until a smooth dough forms. Brush with oil and cover with the bowl, then leave to rest for at least 30 minutes.

Meanwhile, make your filling of choice. For the meat filling, combine all the ingredients in a medium bowl and knead with your hand for 3–4 minutes until well combined. For the cheese filling, combine all the ingredients in a medium bowl and mix well.

Next, dust the work surface with more flour and roll out the dough into a large 52 cm (24 inch) square, no more than 3 mm (⅛ inch) thick. Using a pastry cutter, cut the dough into 4 cm (1½ inch) squares. Place a marble-sized amount of filling in the middle of each square, then fold over into a triangle, pressing the edges together with a fork. Transfer the dumplings to a clean tray dusted lightly with semolina or polenta (to avoid them sticking).

To cook the dumplings, bring a large saucepan of salted water to the boil, then reduce to a gentle simmer. Lower the dumplings into the water in batches and cook for 5–6 minutes, or until they float. Once the dumplings float, give them an additional 2–3 minutes, then remove with a slotted spoon, draining well. Place them on a large serving plate and continue cooking the remaining dumplings.

While the dumplings are cooking, prepare the yoghurt sauce by mixing all the ingredients together in a small bowl.

To make the spiced butter, melt the butter in a small frying pan over a medium-high heat. When the butter starts to bubble (but is not browned), remove from the heat and add the sweet paprika, Bukovo pepper and salt. Stir, then pour into a small bowl and set aside.

To make the wild garlic oil, combine the oil and wild garlic in a food processor and blend until smooth, then transfer to a small bowl. You will not need all of it for this dish, but it keeps well in the refrigerator for up to 1 week.

To serve, spoon the yoghurt sauce over the cooked *klepe*, then spoon over the butter sauce and finally spoon over some of the wild garlic oil.

Note
The prepared *klepe* can also be frozen before cooking – freeze them on a tray or baking sheet, then once frozen, transfer them to a food bag or container.

**MAKES
24–32 ROLLS
(SERVES 6–8)**

Sarma od Kisel Kupus

It is early November, and at last cold enough to start fermenting the cabbages outdoors without them spoiling. My grandmother is preparing the giant plastic fermenting barrel designated for the annual ritual of making *kisel kupus* (sour/fermented cabbage) with its pour spout and various accoutrements – bricks (to elevate the barrel, leaving enough room to pour out the base of the brine), large sterilised stones (to weigh down the cabbages), a lid, plastic mats and covers, blankets and part of a hosepipe (to circulate the brine from time to time). And, of course, kilos and kilos of white cabbages, a handful of beetroot (beets) and salt. I watch as my grandmother and my uncle carefully layer the prepared cabbages (cored, then salted), a glimpse of purple beetroot here and there, and then finally pour in the brine. Once filled and weighed down, the barrel is carefully wrapped in the blankets to keep it warm for the initial fermentation stage and to protect it against frost. The barrel and its precious contents will be overwintering on my grandmother's tenth-floor balcony, overlooking a foggy and likely snow-covered Skopje. The cabbages will slowly ferment under her watchful eye, carefully tended, and hopefully will be ready just in time for New Year's Day and our Christmas in January, to start what I love thinking of as 'sour cabbage *sarma* season', until spring's arrival in late March. A version of this recipe, and a story about why it means so much to me, appeared in the *Guardian* in December 2020. That article – my first published piece of food writing – made this version of *sarma* even more special to me. In the Balkans, *sarma* (the Turkish word for 'wrapped') refers to a family of dishes that remain true to the culinary and etymological root of the word: leaves (including cabbage, vine, Swiss chard) wrapped around a filling of meat and rice, or vegetables, herbs or nuts (or any combination of these) and rice. *Sarma* is loved across the entirety of the region and enjoyed throughout the year in endless variations using whatever seasonal leaves are available.

Lunch   *Recipe continued overleaf*

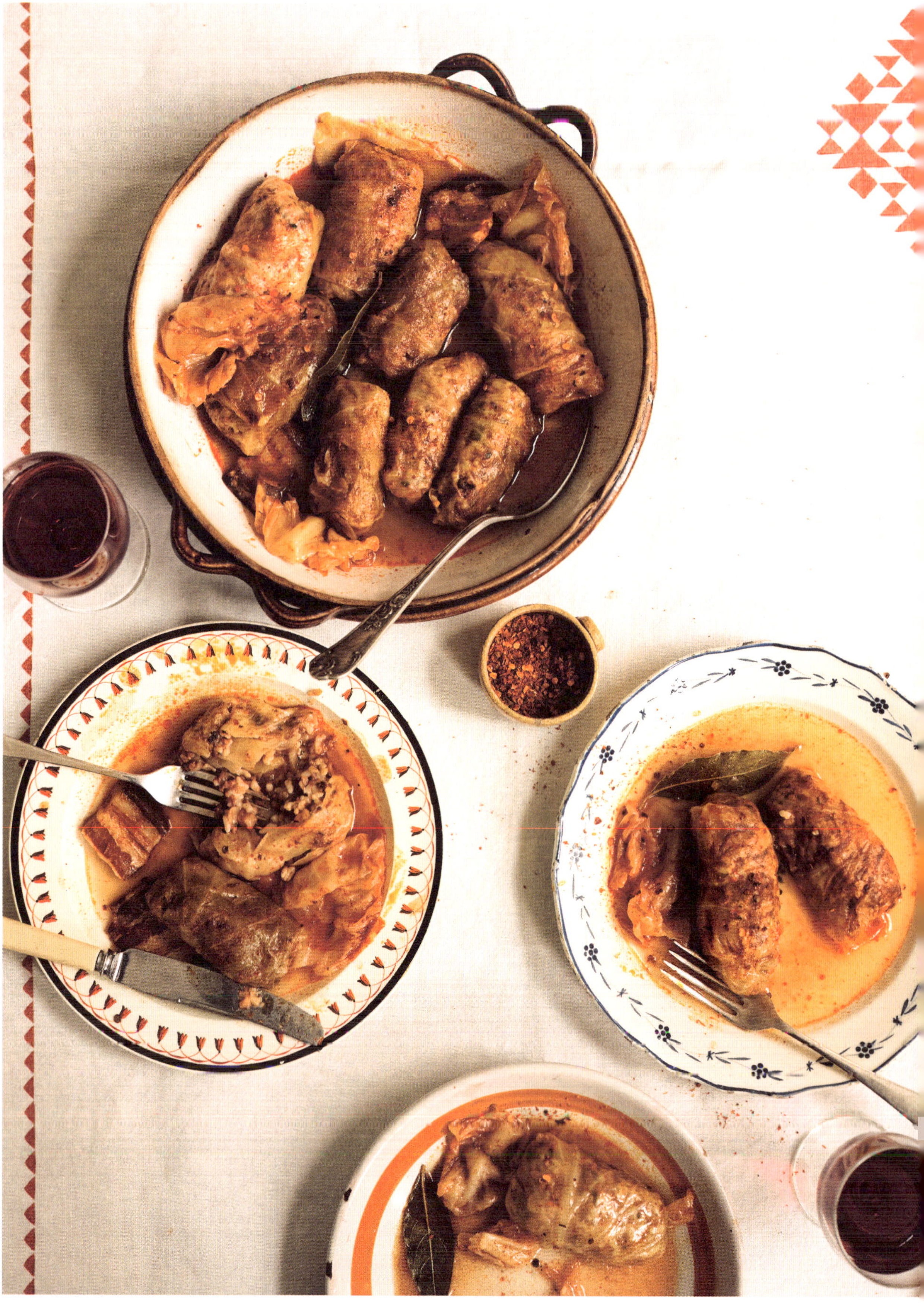

1–2 heads of Sour Cabbage (about 1.2–1.4 kg/2 lb 11 oz–3 lb total; see page 245)
50 g (1¾ oz) *slanina*, or smoked bacon (or smoked pancetta), cut into 1 cm (½ inch) thick slices
4 bay leaves
1 teaspoon black peppercorns
1 teaspoon sweet paprika
1 teaspoon Bukovo pepper (or Aleppo pepper)
200 g (7 oz) smoked pork ribs (optional)

FOR FILLING

3 tablespoons sunflower or olive oil
1 onion, finely chopped
1 leek, trimmed and finely chopped
1 teaspoon sea salt flakes
200 g (7 oz) minced (ground) beef or veal
200 g (7 oz) minced (ground) pork
¼ teaspoon ground cumin
2 tablespoons sweet paprika
½ teaspoon dried oregano
1 tablespoon vegetable bouillon powder
2–3 litres water (68–100 fl oz/ 8½–12½ cups)
200 g (7 oz/generous 1 cup) risotto rice (arborio or carnaroli), washed and drained
20 g (¾ oz) fresh parsley, leaves picked and finely chopped
freshly ground black pepper

TO SERVE (OPTIONAL)

3 tablespoons sunflower or olive oil
1 tablespoon sweet paprika
½ teaspoon Bukovo pepper (or Aleppo pepper)

Note

Feel free to use shop-bought sour cabbages. These are usually heavily brined, so before using, soak the leaves in just-boiled water for at least 5 minutes, then drain. *Sarma* is always best made the day before as the flavours develop beautifully with rest. The use of minced (ground) pork and smoked bacon and ribs is entirely optional. Substitute the minced pork with beef or lamb and the smoked bacon and ribs with other smoked meats if you prefer (or leave the bacon and ribs out entirely and add 1 teaspoon of smoked sweet paprika to the filling and substitute the salt for smoked sea salt).

Start by making the filling. Heat the oil in a large sauté pan over a medium-high heat and fry the onion and leek with the salt for 15–17 minutes until soft and jammy. Add the beef or veal and pork and cook for a further 5–7 minutes, breaking it up with a wooden spoon and stirring occasionally, until the meat is nicely browned. Reduce the heat to medium and add the cumin, paprika, oregano, vegetable powder, 2–3 tablespoons of the water and a good grind of black pepper. Stir well to combine, then add the rice and cook for a further 1–2 minutes, stirring to ensure the rice is coated in the cooking juices. Stir in the parsley, remove from the heat and set aside to cool slightly.

Next, carefully separate the leaves from the cabbage heads. Set aside the outer leaves and the smallest leaves from the hearts of the cabbages or any that are too large, small or torn. Select the best palm-sized leaves you have for rolling (ideally ones that are approximately the same size). If a leaf has a thick stem that would make rolling difficult, trim this out but keep the leaf intact (reserve any offcuts). If your cabbages have too many small leaves, you can join two leaves together to make one roll.

Line a large, heavy-based saucepan with 2–3 of the outer or torn cabbage leaves. Next, place 2–3 teaspoons of the filling along the longest side of a cabbage leaf, roll the leaf over the stuffing away from you, then fold over the sides and continue rolling. Repeat with the remaining leaves and filling. As you roll the *sarma*, pack the rolls tightly next to each other in the saucepan. Once you have a single layer, sprinkle half the *slanina* slices, bay leaves, peppercorns, paprika and Bukovo pepper on top. Cover with 2–3 outer, torn or small cabbage leaves, then place the smoked pork ribs (if using) on top. Arrange the rest of the rolls on top and finish with the rest of the *slanina*, bay leaves, peppercorns, paprika and Bukovo pepper. Cover with any remaining cabbage offcuts and leaves. Pour over enough of the water to ensure all the rolls are submerged. Weigh down the rolls with an inverted heatproof plate. Cover with a lid, then place the pan over a medium-high heat and bring to the boil. Reduce the heat to medium, then simmer gently for 3–3½ hours, or until the rolls are soft enough to slice through with a butter knife. Top up with water from time to time if needed (the *sarma* mustn't dry out).

When the *sarma* has finished cooking, prepare the topping. Heat the oil in a small frying pan over a medium heat. Add the sweet paprika and remove from the heat immediately. You are simply flavouring the oil. At this point, you can either drizzle the sweet paprika oil over the *sarma* and serve, or you can gently transfer the rolls to a large baking dish with the slanina and ribs (if used) and all the cooking juices and drizzle a little of the sweet paprika oil over each roll, then place the baking dish in the oven for 10–15 minutes at 200°C fan (425°F) to give each of the rolls a nice crisp top.

Sprinkle with a little Bukovo pepper to serve.

Lunch

SERVES 4-6

Chomlek, Ohrid Style

500 g (1 lb 2 oz) beef shin, trimmed and cut into large cubes (or any stewing cut, such as chuck steak, shank, rump or short ribs)
1 teaspoon sea salt flakes
½ teaspoon freshly ground black pepper, plus extra as needed
2 tablespoons sunflower or olive oil
200 ml (7 fl oz/scant 1 cup) water
1 tablespoon sweet paprika
2–3 bay leaves
1–2 sprigs of fresh thyme
¼ teaspoon ground cumin
500 g (1 lb 2 oz) small shallots, peeled and tops and tails trimmed
3–4 bulbs of garlic (peel the cloves from 2 and keep 1–2 whole)
500 ml (17 fl oz/generous 2 cups) beef or vegetable stock
125 ml (4 fl oz/½ cup) red wine vinegar
125 ml (4 fl oz/½ cup) red wine (optional – if not using, add 125 ml/ 4 fl oz/½ cup more stock)

This sumptuous beef stew is traditionally eaten in winter and is famously associated with Ohrid, a beautiful historic city in North Macedonia. Ohrid, one of the oldest settlements in Europe, is known as the Jerusalem of the Balkans because of its wealth of cultural and religious heritage and history. Variations of this stew are made across Serbia, Albania and Bulgaria. More contemporary versions include root vegetables, but I adore the simplicity and understated beauty of the Ohrid version, which I imagine as being most reflective of the origins of the dish – a way of using a little meat paired with some of the relatively few vegetables that would have been available in midwinter.

Chomlek is the Turkish word for an earthenware pot. This stew is traditionally cooked in exactly that and sealed round the edge with dough, then slow-baked in a wood-fired oven. It is brutally simple to put together. All you need is patience to allow it to cook slowly. Do invest in good-quality beef as it will be worth it. It sounds like a ridiculous amount of garlic, but trust me. I would also highly recommend using whole bulbs of garlic to cook in the stew – you can squeeze out the succulent garlic that has been cooked in the stewing juices and spread it on delicious bread to accompany the dish. Simple, delicious and perfectly comforting.

Preheat the oven to 180°C fan (400°F).

Season the beef all over with half the salt and the pepper.

Heat the oil in a large ovenproof casserole dish (Dutch oven) over a medium-high heat. Brown the beef for 2–3 minutes on each side, then add the water and braise the meat, uncovered, for about 5 minutes. Reduce the heat to medium, then add the paprika and cook for a further minute, stirring constantly. Add the bay leaves, sprigs of thyme, cumin, shallots, garlic (peeled cloves and whole bulbs), stock, vinegar, red wine, the remaining salt and a generous grind of black pepper.

Cover with a lid, transfer to the oven and slow cook for 3½–4 hours, checking periodically to make sure that there is sufficient liquid – if it looks like it's drying out, add a splash of water (around 100 ml/3½ fl oz/ scant ½ cup). Don't be tempted to stir too much, though, as you want the shallots and garlic cloves to stay whole.

When the juices have thickened, the meat is falling apart and the shallots are meltingly soft, the *chomlek* is ready. Check and adjust the seasoning before serving.

Lunch

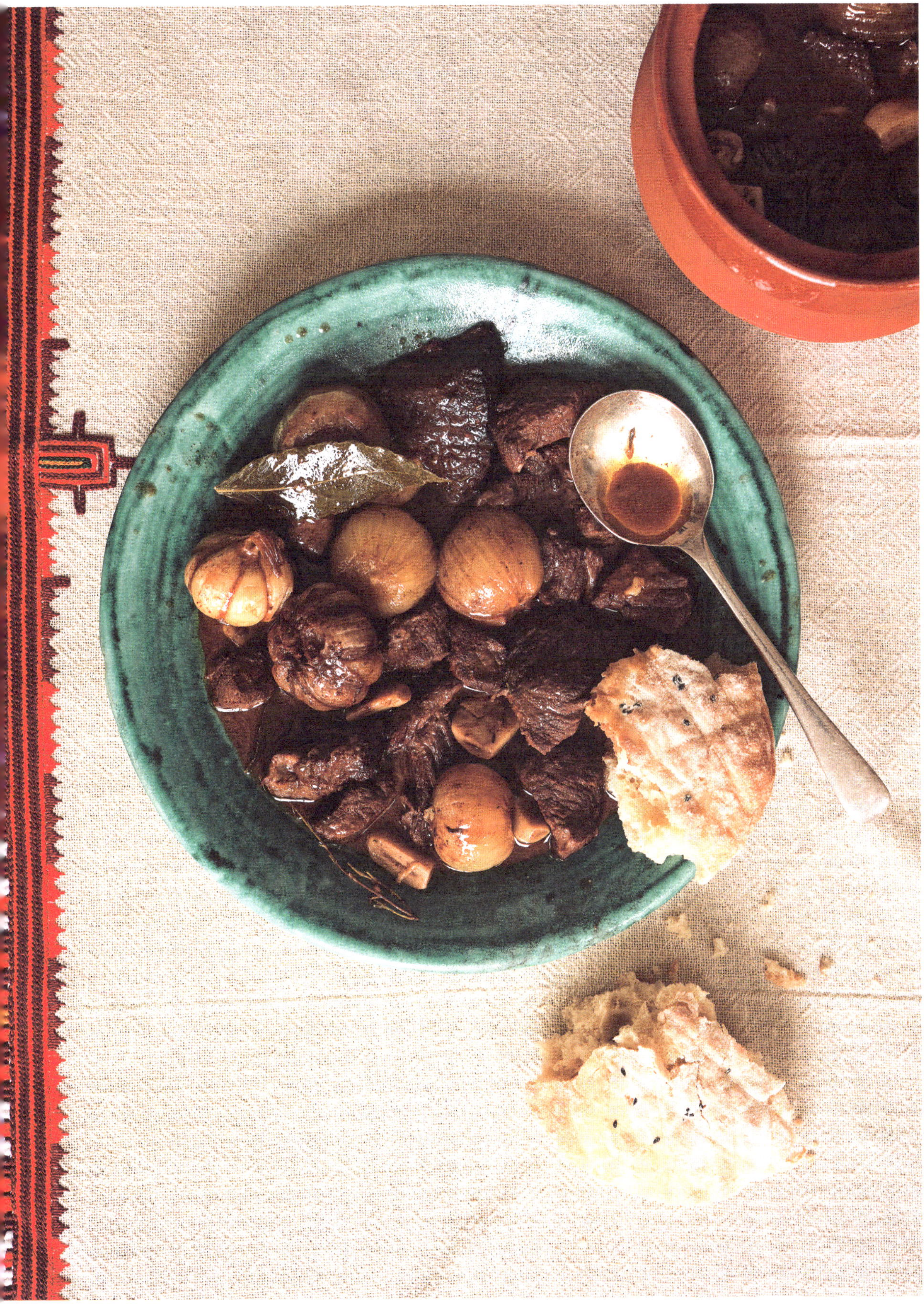

SERVES 4

Chicken Paprikaš with Noklice

1 onion, finely chopped
2 long red Romano peppers, deseeded and finely chopped
4 bone-in, skin-on chicken thighs
2 tablespoons sunflower or mild olive oil
1 teaspoon sea salt flakes, plus extra as needed
2–3 garlic cloves, crushed
3 tablespoons sweet paprika
1 teaspoon Bukovo pepper (or Aleppo pepper or ½ teaspoon chilli flakes; optional), plus extra to serve
1 tablespoon plain (all-purpose) flour
1 tablespoon vegetable bouillon powder
2 tomatoes, grated and skin discarded
1 tablespoon tomato purée (paste)
500 ml (17 fl oz/generous 2 cups) chicken or vegetable stock
freshly ground black pepper

FOR THE NOKLICE
2 medium eggs
¼ teaspoon sea salt flakes
2 teaspoons sunflower oil
60 ml (2 fl oz/¼ cup) water
140 g (5 oz/1 cup plus 2 tablespoons) plain (all-purpose) flour

TO SERVE
handful of chopped fresh parsley
sour cream or crème fraîche

When it comes to *paprikaš*, overzealousness with sweet paprika is encouraged. Famously associated with Hungary, *paprikaš* is incredibly popular across the Balkans, but especially Vojvodina, an autonomous province in northern Serbia (as it was in Yugoslavia also), which has a large ethnic Hungarian population. Famous for its excellent cuisine and cakes, Vojvodina lies on the south-eastern Pannonian Plain and is so incredibly fertile it was known as the breadbasket of Yugoslavia. The prevalent type of *paprikaš* there is *fiš paprikaš*, which is prepared with freshwater fish such as pike, catfish and carp, all cooked in a cauldron simmering over an open fire. A similar *paprikaš* is also made in Slavonia and Baranja in Croatia. In the rest of the region, *paprikaš* is an umbrella term for any meat (usually chicken or pork) or vegetable stew with a paprika broth. Other stews with a thicker paprika-based sauce that are heavier on meat (any of beef, veal, pork, lamb or game) and lighter on vegetables, fall under the umbrella of *gulaš* (particularly in Serbia). As the name suggests, they are similar to Hungarian goulash. *Paprikaš* is typically served with boiled potatoes or noklice which are little dumplings similar to Hungarian *nokedli* and German *spätzle*. Feel free to substitute them with ready-made gnocchi.

Preheat the oven to 180°C fan (400°F).

Arrange the onion, peppers and chicken pieces (skin-side up) in a casserole dish (Dutch oven). Drizzle the oil over the chicken and vegetables and sprinkle everything with the salt and a grind of black pepper. Bake in the oven, uncovered, for 25–30 minutes until the chicken skin has started to crisp and become golden and the vegetables have started to caramelise.

Remove from the oven and transfer the chicken pieces to a plate. Add the garlic, paprika, Bukovo pepper, flour, vegetable bouillon powder, tomatoes and tomato purée to the vegetables and stir well to combine. Gradually pour in the stock, stirring to loosen the vegetables. Return the chicken pieces to the dish nestling them in the liquid but ensuring the skin is not submerged. Cover, return to the oven and cook for 45–60 minutes, or until the sauce has thickened to your liking.

Meanwhile, prepare the *noklice*. Crack the eggs into a medium bowl and add the salt. Whisk with an electric whisk on high speed for 2–3 minutes, or until frothy. Add the oil and water and whisk for a further minute. Add the flour gradually while whisking to make a thick batter.

Bring a large saucepan of salted water to a simmer. Using two teaspoons, form quenelles of batter and drop into the pan. Repeat until you have used it up. Cook for 2–3 minutes, or until the *noklice* float to the top. Lift them out with a slotted spoon and place them around the chicken in the casserole. Adjust the seasoning, return the casserole to the oven, and cook uncovered, for 5-10 minutes.

Serve with fresh parsley and a dollop of sour cream or crème fraîche.

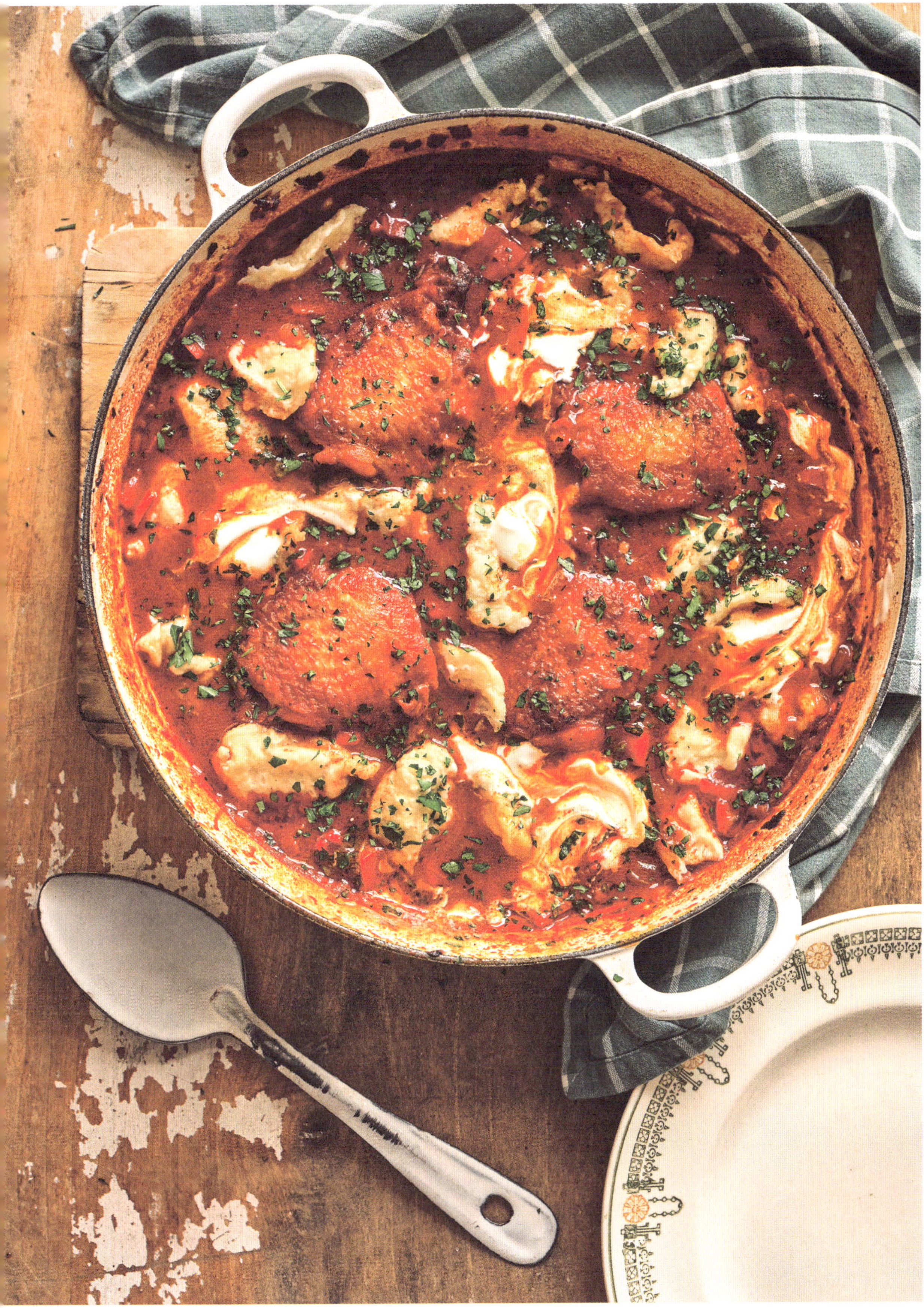

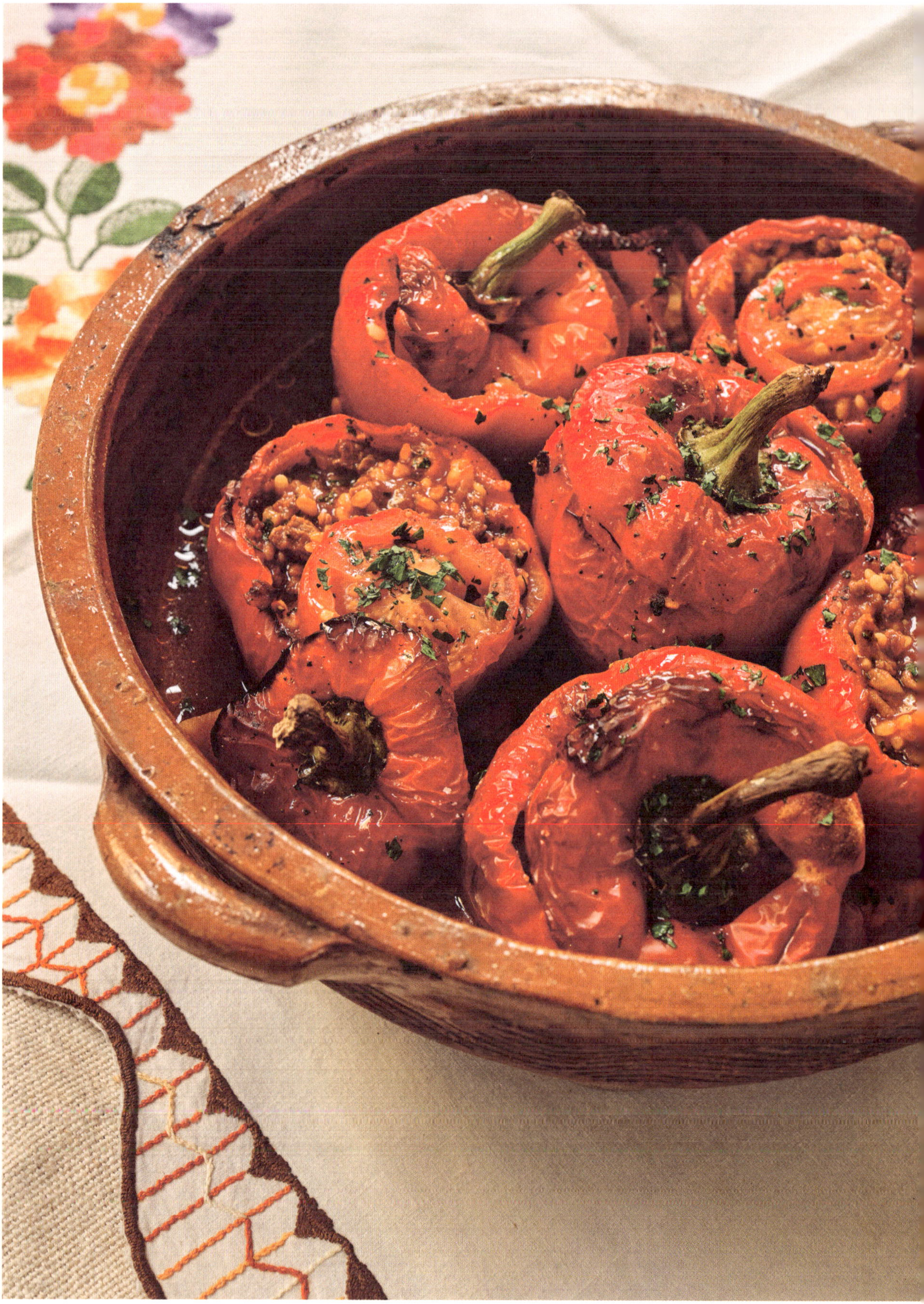

SERVES 4-6

Polneti Piperki

6 red, orange or yellow bell peppers (or 8–10 smaller yellow-green bell peppers)
3 tablespoons sunflower or olive oil
1 onion, peeled and finely chopped
250 g (9 oz) minced (ground) beef, veal, lamb or pork (or a mix of any)
1½ teaspoons sea salt flakes
1 teaspoon vegetable bouillon powder
2 tablespoons sweet paprika
1 tablespoon tomato purée (paste)
1 teaspoon dried oregano
200 g (7 oz) passata (sieved tomatoes)
125 g risotto rice (arborio or carnaroli) or pudding rice, washed and drained
1–2 large tomatoes, cut into the same amount of slices as the number of peppers you are using
400 ml (14 fl oz/generous 1½ cups) vegetable stock
freshly ground black pepper
plain set yoghurt, to serve

This is the dish my grandmother always made in summer to welcome us home. Unlike the Levantine versions of pepper *dolma* (similar versions of which you will find in Bosnia and Herzegovina), for us, stuffed peppers need to be brothy and are always served warm, topped with a generous dollop of yoghurt. The filling also greatly varies across the region – in the south, it is more likely to include rice, in the north, meat and be served with boiled or mashed potatoes. Learned wisdom on the best peppers to use for this dish differs wildly across the region. In Bosnia and Herzegovina and Croatia, small, light green bell peppers are favoured when in season (they have thinner skins). In North Macedonia and Serbia, they are more likely to use red bell peppers or the peppers for *ajvar* when they come in season (from the end of August). In the diaspora, we do not have the luxury of this debate, so I favour red, orange or yellow bell peppers. Try to find smaller specimens if you can.

Prepare the peppers by cutting around the stem of each pepper in a circle. Pull off the stem and 'lid' in one piece and trim any pith and seeds attached. Scoop out and discard the seeds and pith inside each pepper and rinse to remove any seeds. Set aside.

Next, make the filling. Heat the oil in a large sauté pan over a medium-high heat and sweat the onion for 10–12 minutes, stirring occasionally, until soft and translucent. Add the minced meat, 1 teaspoon of the salt and a good grind of black pepper and cook, stirring occasionally and breaking up the meat with your spoon, for 5–7 minutes, or until the meat is nicely browned. Add the vegetable bouillon powder, paprika, tomato purée and oregano and continue to cook for 1–2 minutes until well combined, then stir through 75 g (2½ oz) of the passata. Add the rice and cook for 1 minute more, stirring well, to coat the rice grains in the cooking juices. Remove from the heat.

Preheat the oven to 180°C fan (400°F).

Stuff the peppers with the filling, making sure each pepper is only three-quarters full. Press the filling down into each pepper with a slice of tomato. Arrange the peppers in a large, ovenproof casserole dish, big enough for the peppers to fit snugly facing upwards. Finely chop any leftover tomato and add it around the peppers. Add the rest of the passata, the stock, the remaining salt and a good grind of black pepper – the sauce should reach at least halfway up the side of the peppers – top it up with water if it doesn't. Spoon some of the sauce into each pepper, then place the pepper lids on. Soak a sheet of baking parchment in water, then scrunch it up and cover the peppers with it, making sure it fits snugly in the dish. Cover with a lid and bake in the oven for 1 hour, then remove from the oven and spoon some more cooking liquid over and into the stuffed peppers. Top up with a splash of water (around 100 ml/3½ fl oz/scant ½ cup) if there isn't enough liquid around the peppers. Return to the oven, uncovered, and bake for a further 30–35 minutes until the peppers are cooked through and blackened in places on their skins. Check the peppers from time to time and spoon some of the liquid into the peppers if they look too dry. Serve warm with yoghurt on the side.

Lunch

MAKES 48–55 SARMA (SERVES 4–6 AS A MAIN OR 8–12 AS PART OF A SPREAD)

Sarma od Lozov List

60–64 large fresh or brined vine leaves (about 300–325 g/10½–11 oz)
2 tablespoons olive oil, plus extra for brushing
1 onion, finely chopped
1½ teaspoon sea salt flakes
500 g (1 lb 2 oz) minced (ground) beef (or veal, lamb, pork or a mix of any)
2 tablespoons sweet paprika
1 teaspoon vegetable bouillon powder
20 g (¾ oz) fresh parsley, leaves picked and finely chopped
200 g (7 oz/generous 1 cup) risotto rice (arborio or carnaroli) or pudding rice, washed and drained
1 tablespoon water
400 g (14 oz) waxy potatoes, peeled and cut into 1 cm (½ inch) thick slices
2 lemons, 1 sliced and 2–3 tablespoons juice
1 litre (34 fl oz/4¼ cups) vegetable stock
freshly ground black pepper
plain set yoghurt, to serve

I never cease to be amazed by vines. Stark and bare in winter, lush and resplendent in summer. The leaves, picked at their most youthful and verdant, transformed into delicious little edible gifts filled with meat, rice and spices, that, to me, scream 'I love you' more than any other meal. How long have women from across the Balkans, the Eastern Mediterranean and the Middle East been making *sarma* (or *dolma*, or *dolmades* or *warak enab*) from vine leaves? Vines that were transported from ancient Persia across the Middle East into the Balkans. Vines that rooted in, adapted to and adopted ancient soils, surviving a millennia of winters and awakening in a millennia of springs. Gracing a millennia of summers and promising abundant grapes in a millennia of autumns (falls). An endless cycle of love and life.

Wash the vine leaves, then soak them in boiling water for about 10 minutes. Drain them and cut off any stalks. Select the largest vine leaves you have (they need to be about the size of your hand), setting aside 9–12 leaves that are too small or ripped for layering. Place the vine leaves, veins facing upwards, on a large tray and set aside.

Next, prepare the filling. Heat the oil in a sauté pan over a medium-high heat and fry the onion with the 1 teaspoon of the salt for 8–10 minutes or until softened. Add the meat and cook, stirring occasionally and breaking it up with a spoon, for about 10 minutes, or until browned. Reduce the heat to medium, add the paprika, vegetable bouillon powder, parsley and a good grind of black pepper and cook for 1 minute, stirring well to combine. Add the rice and water and cook for a further 2 minutes until the rice is coated in the cooking juices. Remove from the heat and set aside to cool slightly.

Once cooled, start to fill the leaves. Place a teaspoon of filling along the longest side of a vine leaf, roll the leaf over the stuffing, then fold over the sides and continue rolling. Place each roll on a large plate. If your leaves are small, you can place two together to make one roll. Repeat until you have used up all the filling.

Brush the base of a large, heavy-based saucepan with a little oil, then line the base with 3–4 of the reserved vine leaves. Next, layer half the potato slices on the bottom, then arrange half the rolls over the potatoes, making sure they fit snugly. Add half the lemon slices, then cover with another layer of 3–4 vine leaves. Repeat the layering process: the rest of the potatoes, then rolls, then lemon slices. Pour over the lemon juice, then cover everything with the remaining vine leaves. Sprinkle the remaining ½ teaspoon salt over the top, then pour over the vegetable stock, ensuring all the rolls are submerged; if not, top up with a little water. Cover everything with an inverted heatproof plate, then with a lid. Place over a medium-high heat and bring to the boil, then reduce the heat to medium and simmer gently for about 1 hour, topping up with water from time to time if needed, or until the rolls are soft enough to slice through with a butter knife and the stock turns a cloudy pale yellow. Allow to rest for at least 15 minutes before serving with yoghurt on the side.

Lunch

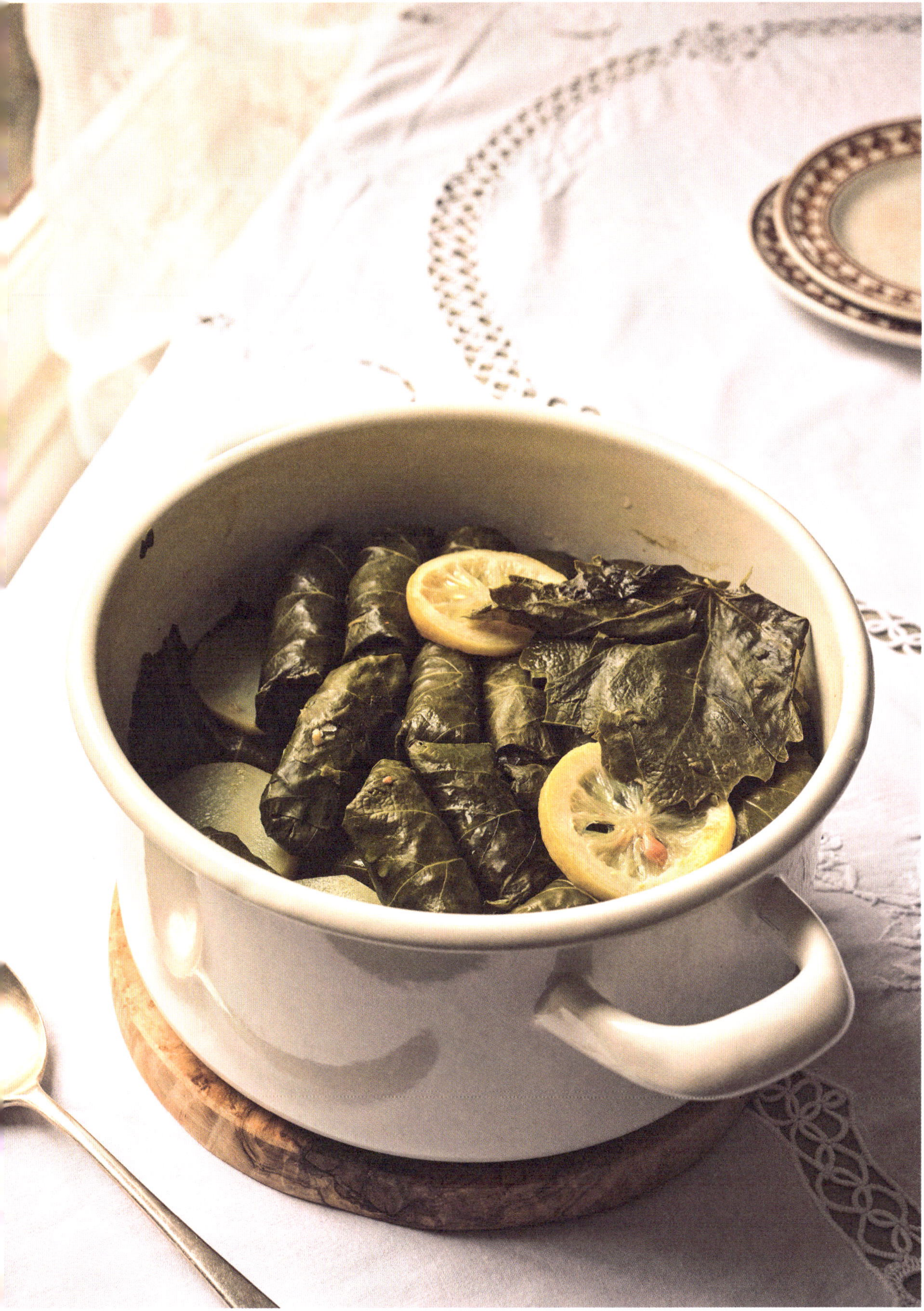

SERVES 6-8

Drob Sarma

- 1.5 kg (3 lb 5 oz) lamb's pluck (heart, lungs, liver), washed thoroughly
- 2–3 bay leaves
- ½ teaspoon black peppercorns
- 1 kg lamb's caul fat (lace fat/crépine – in as large pieces as possible)
- 2 tablespoons white wine vinegar
- 3 tablespoons sunflower or olive oil, plus extra for brushing
- 200 g (7 oz) onions, finely chopped
- 2–3 garlic cloves, finely chopped
- 1 tablespoon sweet paprika
- 1 tablespoon vegetable bouillon powder
- ½ teaspoon dried oregano
- 200 g (7 oz/generous 1 cup) risotto rice (arborio or carnaroli), washed and drained
- 30 g (1 oz) fresh parsley, leaves and tender stems picked and finely chopped, plus extra to serve
- 10 g (½ oz) fresh mint, leaves picked and finely chopped, plus extra to serve
- 200 ml (7 fl oz/scant 1 cup) vegetable stock
- ½ teaspoon sea salt flakes
- freshly ground black pepper
- thick yoghurt, to serve

Offal is used widely in Balkan cuisine and some of the greatest delicacies involve it including: Kumanovo-style mezel'k (baked stuffed tripe filled with veal or lamb head, tongue and offal), škembe čorba (tripe soup), barbecued liver, and breaded brain. Our culinary ethos continues to be: waste nothing. *Drob sarma* is one of these delicacies typical of the southern Balkans. Made in spring when lamb is in season, it is a way of using up the plentiful offal available after everyone has celebrated Easter with roast lamb. It is, I suppose, our haggis. My grandmother would typically prepare this as one big *sarma*, so I have suggested the same, but you can also make individual rolls and arrange them in a baking tray (pan), especially if can only find smaller pieces of caul fat rather than one large piece.

Bring a large saucepan of salted water to the boil, then add the lamb's pluck, bay leaves and peppercorns. Simmer, skimming and discarding scum, for around 25 minutes until there is very little scum rising to the surface. Drain well and set aside to cool. Chop the meat finely (cutting around and discarding any blood vessels, valves, sinew). Place the meat in a bowl and set aside. Wash the caul thoroughly and place it in a large bowl of cold water with the vinegar to soak while you prepare the filling.

Heat the oil in a large frying pan over a medium-high heat. Add the onion and fry for 10–12 minutes until soft and translucent. Add the garlic, paprika, vegetable bouillon powder and oregano and fry for a minute, stirring well. Add the rice and cook for 2–3 minutes, stirring to coat it in the cooking juices. Add the herbs, meat, the stock, the salt and a grind of black pepper and mix well to combine. Remove from the heat.

Preheat the oven to 180°C fan (400°F).

To assemble, drain the caul and pat it dry with paper towels. Line a medium bowl (one that fits all the filling) with reusable food wrap or a clean kitchen towel. Next, line the bowl with the caul, allowing pieces to drape over the bowl's rim. Layer as many pieces of caul as you need to ensure there is an even lining around the bowl with no gaps. You may need to trim the edges of the caul hanging over the rim – about 5 cm (2 inches) is enough. Next, place the filling into the caul-lined bowl, cover it with another piece of caul, pressing down gently to pack it in, then encase it with the caul hanging over the rim. Brush the inside of a large, round deep-sided baking dish with oil, invert it over the bowl, then carefully turn everything over. Tap the base of the bowl gently to release the *drob sarma* into the baking dish, remove the bowl, and peel off the food wrap or tea towel. You should have a sort of dome. Brush it gently all over with oil, then cover it with foil. Bake in the oven for 1–1½ hours, then remove and baste with the caul fat. If there is too much fat, remove some and reserve it. You only need about 2 cm (¾ inch) around the base of the baking dish. If there is not enough liquid, add a splash of water. Return to the oven and continue to bake, uncovered, basting with the reserved fat or adding a splash of water if needed, for a 1–1½ hours until cooked through and the caul is browned and crisp all over. Remove from the oven and rest for 10 minutes before serving scattered with the herbs and yoghurt.

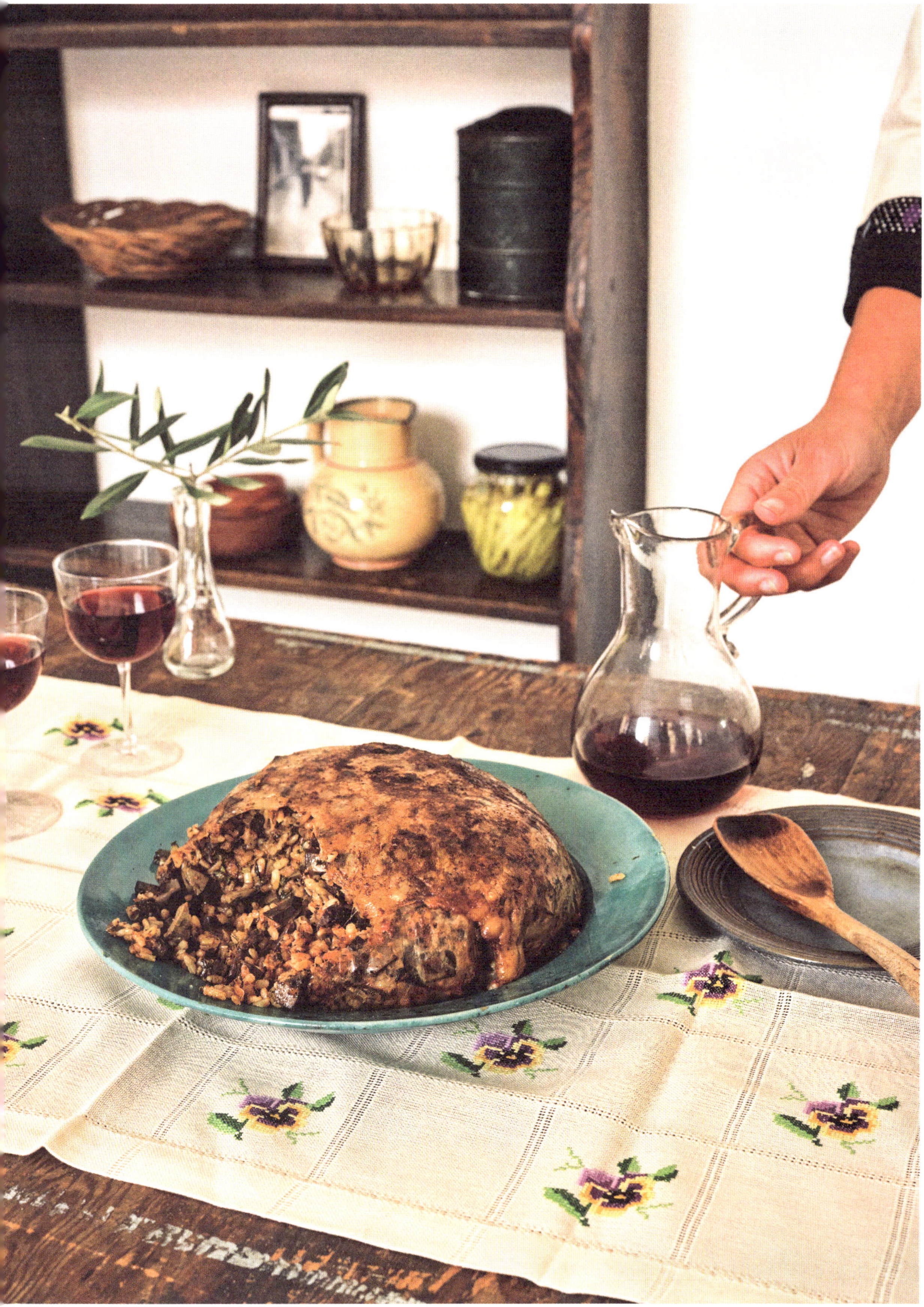

Podvarok

SERVES 4

700 g (1 lb 9 oz) Sour Cabbage (see page 245, sliced thinly (or sauerkraut), rinsed and drained
4 tablespoons sunflower or olive oil
50 g (1¾ oz) slanina (smoked and cured pork belly) or smoked pancetta
200 g (7 oz) leeks, trimmed and finely chopped
100 g (3½ oz/scant ½ cup) risotto rice (arborio or carnaroli)
1 tablespoon sweet paprika
700 ml (24 fl oz/scant 3 cups) warm chicken or vegetable stock
1¼ teaspoons sea salt flakes
4 bay leaves
4 rind-on pork chops (about 1.2 kg/ 2 lb 11 oz total)
freshly ground black pepper
Bukovo pepper (or Aleppo pepper), to serve (optional)

Note

To make this vegan, simply omit the *slanina* and pork cooking steps – you will not need the final 15 minutes in the oven with the pork chops.

One of my family's favourite festive winter dishes is *podvarok*. It is a baked casserole made from sour cabbages that was historically a vehicle for different types of meat and poultry (turkey, goose, duck or other game birds). Nowadays, it is typically prepared with pork (or beef or veal, depending on religious affiliation) or is *posen/posno* (meat-free) for certain fasting periods in the Eastern Orthodox calendar. I particularly enjoy having a meat-free version as it can be an accompaniment to anything – either roast meats, grilled whole fish (especially trout) or hot-smoked fish (again trout, or mackerel). Versions made with pork use often use *slanina* (smoked and cured pork belly) or any smoked cuts of pork (ham hock, pork hock, ribs and so on). The consistency of the *podvarok* can be anything from brothy to baked (the latter very much my family's preference). Pork chops are a firm favourite for many families in the region, including ours, so that's what I have used here.

Preheat the oven to 180°C fan (400°F).

Heat a large, dry frying pan over a medium-high heat, then dry-fry the sour cabbage for 12–14 minutes, stirring occasionally, until nearly all the moisture has evaporated and the cabbage is starting to crisp and turn lightly golden. Remove from the heat and set aside.

Meanwhile, heat 2 tablespoons of the oil in a separate frying pan over a medium-high heat. Fry the *slanina* or pancetta for 1–2 minutes, or until starting to crisp, then add the leeks and cook for a further 10–12 minutes, stirring occasionally, until softened. Add the rice and cook for a further 2 minutes, stirring to coat it in the leek mixture. Add the paprika and cook for a further minute, taking care not to burn it. Add half the stock, ½ teaspoon of the salt and a generous grind of black pepper, then stir to combine and remove from the heat.

Next, combine the leek and rice mixture with the cabbage and stir well, making sure the leeks and rice are evenly distributed. Transfer everything to a 22 x 30 cm (9 x 12 inch) roasting tin and spread it out evenly. Pour the rest of the chicken stock over the top. Place a bay leaf in each corner of the baking dish, nestled into the mixture. Sprinkle over ¼ teaspoon of the salt and a good grind of black pepper. Bake in the oven, uncovered, for 1 hour.

Meanwhile, season the pork chops all over with the remaining salt and a good grind of black pepper. Heat the remaining 2 tablespoons of oil in a large frying pan over a medium-high heat. Add the pork chops and cook for 2–3 minutes on each side until nicely browned, then remove from the heat. Remove the *podvarok* from the oven and arrange the pork chops over the top, nestling them into the mixture. If it is quite dry, add a little splash of water. Return to the oven and roast for a further 15 minutes, or until the pork is cooked through and the *podvarok* has a nice golden brown crust but is still moist underneath. Remove from the oven and rest for 10 minutes before serving. Sprinkle a little Bukovo pepper over the top to serve, if you like.

Lunch

A Bean Interlude

Beans were introduced to Europe from the Americas sometime in the middle of the 16th century, a few decades after the establishment of the Columbian Exchange. It is unclear exactly at what point they began to be cultivated in the Balkans, but it is very likely that they came via the Ottoman Empire. Over time, beans were integrated into the cuisine of the region alongside other legumes such as lentils, chickpeas (garbanzos) and broad (fava) beans. They assumed particular importance during periods of history when grain was in short supply, becoming a replacement and then a staple. It is thought that *Tetovski grav* (Tetovo beans, as they are known in North Macedonia) are one of the oldest bean varieties to have been cultivated in the Balkans. This bean variety is also sometimes referred to as Tetovac in other parts of the former Yugoslavia. They are named after Tetovo, a city in the north-western part of North Macedonia, where they are still cultivated, and were given a protected designation of origin in 2006. There are of course many other local bean varieties, but for slow-cooked, Balkan-style dishes, it is commonly accepted that *Tetovski grav* is the best bean variety to use. This is primarily to do with the beans' unique delicate flavour and cooking properties: they generally have a shorter cooking time compared to other bean varieties, becoming soft and smooth while retaining their shape. For Balkan people, beans transcend mere nourishment. They represent the cornerstone of our culinary traditions and rituals. The continuing practice of eating bean-centric meals on a Friday is deeply rooted in the region's religious heritage. Fridays were observed by Orthodox Christians as days for fasting, mindfulness and abstention from indulgence and beans – cheap, plentiful and rich in protein and nutrients – became the hearty alternative to meat. This has translated into a huge variety of so-called 'monastery' bean soups across the region. It is a practice that has surpassed religion and assumed an almost spiritual significance. A large pot of simmering beans will always be found across the Balkans – from Yugoslav-era self-management factory canteens, public institutions and offices to schools and other educational institutions, and from simple home meals to grand feasts and celebrations. Beans have become a symbol of humility, community, resilience and the celebration of the simple joy of eating together.

Lunch

SERVES 4-6

Tavče Gravče

500 g (1 lb 2 oz/2½ cups) dried Tetovo beans (or cannellini beans)
1 teaspoon bicarbonate of soda (baking soda)
3 litres (101½ fl oz/12½ cups) water
1 onion, quartered
¼ teaspoon freshly ground black pepper
2–3 bay leaves
2 tablespoons dried mint
10 g (½ oz) fresh mint, leaves picked

FOR THE ZAPRŠKA
3 tablespoons olive or sunflower oil
1 onion, finely chopped
½ teaspoon sea salt flakes
3 tablespoons sweet paprika
1 teaspoon vegetable bouillon powder

OPTIONAL EXTRAS
1 long dried red pepper
4 cooking chorizo sausages (about 250 g/9 oz total), sliced in half lengthwise and skin scored diagonally
1 tomato, sliced

Tava is the Turkish word for a baking dish or frying pan and *grav* means beans in Macedonian, hence the diminutive name of *tavče gravče*. These are thought of as the national dish of North Macedonia, though of course there are regional variations, for example in Serbia, where they are known as *prebranac*. Unlike *prebranac*, *tavče gravče* is flavoured with mint, and in my family we go overboard with it. The best beans for this come from Tetovo and the surrounding area and are known as Tetovo beans or *Tetovac*. The *zaprška* (a kind of Balkan roux) is best thickened with the bean cooking liquid and some of the crushed beans, though some people prefer to use flour. The beans are traditionally baked and served in an oval, unglazed earthenware pot. This dish can be vegan – simply top it with peppers or tomatoes – or you can add meat (typically *slanina* or smoked pork ribs for a Serbian-style *prebranac*) or sausages. My family's favoured addition is Macedonian-style *sujuk*, a spicy, paprika-infused sausage, which is longer and thinner and closer to a Spanish chorizo than a Bosnian or Turkish-style *sujuk*. This is why I have recommended using chorizo.

The day before you want to cook the beans, put them into a large, heavy-based saucepan along with the bicarb and cover with 3 litres (101½ fl oz/12½ cups) cold water. Cover and soak for 8 hours, or overnight.

The next day, drain and replace the water, then place the saucepan over a medium-high heat and bring to the boil. Boil for 10–15 minutes, after which time you should have a lot of froth and scum on the top. Drain the beans again and rinse them under running water. Return them to the saucepan, cover with the 3 litres (101½ fl oz/12½ cups) fresh water and bring to the boil again. Add the onion, black pepper and bay leaves, reduce the heat to medium and simmer, stirring occasionally, for 45–60 minutes, or until the beans are soft and cooked through but still retaining their shape. Transfer the beans to a 24 x 30 cm (9½ x 12 inch) baking dish scooping out 150 ml (5 fl oz/scant ⅔ cup) of the liquid and a few beans for the *zaprška*. Remove and discard the bay leaves. Remove the onion, finely chop it and return it to the dish.

Preheat the oven to 170°C fan (375°F).

To make the *zaprška*, heat the oil in a frying pan over a medium-high heat. Add the onion and salt and fry for 10–12 minutes until soft and translucent. Reduce the heat, then add the paprika and cook for a minute. Add the bouillon and the beans and cooking liquid, then use a fork to gently crush the beans and mix everything together. Pour the *zaprška* into the beans and add the dried and fresh mint, then stir well to combine. Transfer to the oven and bake for 45–60 minutes, or until the beans are set but there is still some liquid and an even crust on top. At this point you can either serve the beans as they are, or add any of the optional extras, nestling the pepper or sausages among the beans or arranging the tomato slices on top.

Cook for a further 10–15 minutes (if adding the pepper or tomatoes) or until the sausages are cooked (if adding chorizo). Serve warm.

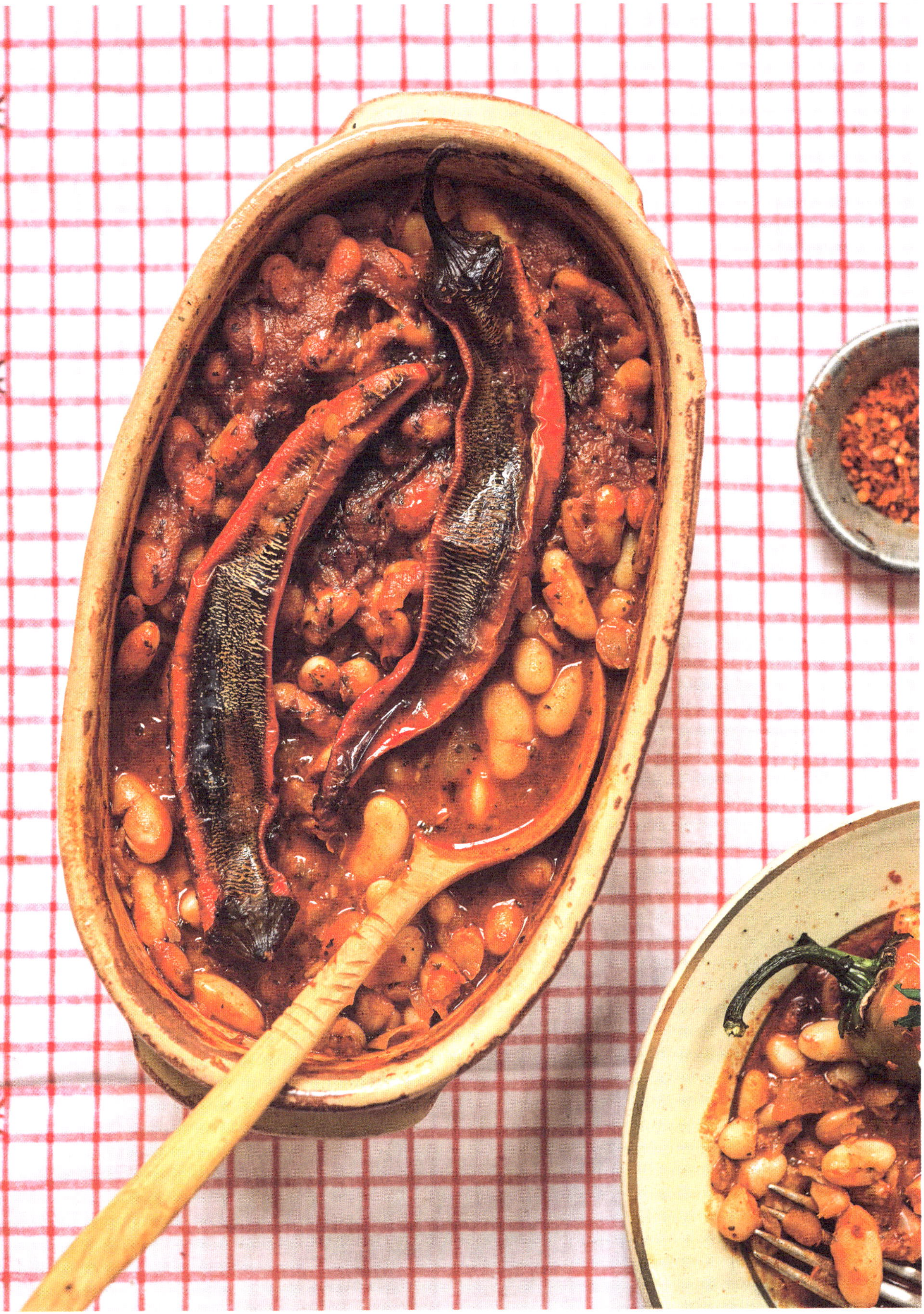

SERVES 6-8

Turli Tava

- 500 g (1 lb 2 oz) beef or veal chuck steak (or any other stewing cut), cut into 2 cm (¾ inch) pieces, trimmed
- 500 g (1 lb 2 oz) boneless pork shoulder (or any other stewing cut), cut into 2 cm (¾ inch) pieces, trimmed
- ½ teaspoon sea salt flakes
- 3 tablespoons sunflower or olive oil
- 200 ml (7 fl oz/scant 1 cup) water
- 2 tablespoons vegetable bouillon powder
- 1 tablespoon sweet paprika
- 2 onions, finely chopped
- 1 long red Romano pepper, chopped into 1.5 cm (½ inch) cubes
- 1 aubergine (eggplant), half-peeled lengthwise in stripes and chopped into 1.5 cm (½ inch) cubes
- 2 courgettes (zucchini), chopped into 1.5 cm (½ inch) cubes
- 2–3 celery stalks, chopped into 1.5 cm (½ inch) cubes
- 2–3 potatoes, peeled and chopped into 1.5 cm (½ inch) cubes
- 2–3 carrots, peeled and chopped into 1.5 cm (½ inch) cubes
- 200 g (7 oz) green beans, topped and tailed and chopped into 2 cm (¾ inch) pieces
- 20 g (¾ oz) fresh parsley, leaves picked and finely chopped
- 300 g (10½ oz) tomato passata (sieved tomatoes)
- 700 ml (24 fl oz/scant 3 cups) vegetable stock
- 100 g (3½ oz) okra, washed and topped
- freshly ground black pepper

This is very much the Balkan variant of the Turkish casserole *türlü* (meaning 'variety'). In North Macedonia it is called *turli tava*, but you will also find it called *turli đuveč* (if using an earthenware pot, rather than a baking dish), *tourlou* in Greece and *turli perimesh* in Kosovo and Albania. It is really a summer vegetable and meat casserole – often just a vegetable casserole – and the key is, as the Turkish name suggests, to use a variety of whatever vegetables happen to be in season. Where meat is used, it is usually a mix of beef or veal with either lamb or pork (depending on religious affiliation). There are so many examples on the theme of vegetable and meat casseroles across the region. In Croatia, around Zagorje, you will find *kotlovina*, a dish of grilled and stewed meat with vegetables prepared in a special standing cauldron over open fire. In Bosnia and Herzegovina, you will find *Bosanski lonac* (Bosnian pot), a dish made with lamb, potatoes and a few vegetables that is cooked in a sealed earthenware pot. All are unique and special in their own right.

Preheat the oven to 180°C fan (400°F).

Season the meat all over with the salt and a good grind of black pepper.

Heat the oil in a large, ovenproof casserole dish (Dutch oven) over a medium heat. Brown the meat for 2–3 minutes on each side, then add the water and braise the meat, uncovered, for 5 minutes. Add the vegetable bouillon powder, paprika and a good grind of black pepper and stir, then remove from the heat.

Add the onions, pepper, aubergine, courgettes, celery, potatoes, carrots, green beans and parsley to the dish, then pour over the passata and stock and stir everything well to combine and distribute the meat evenly among the vegetables. Cover with a cartouche and then the lid and transfer to the oven to bake for 1½–2 hours. After this time, remove from the oven, uncover and arrange the okra over the top, then return to the oven to bake for a further 30 minutes until the okra is cooked through and you have a nice crisp layer on the top of the casserole. Serve warm.

Lunch

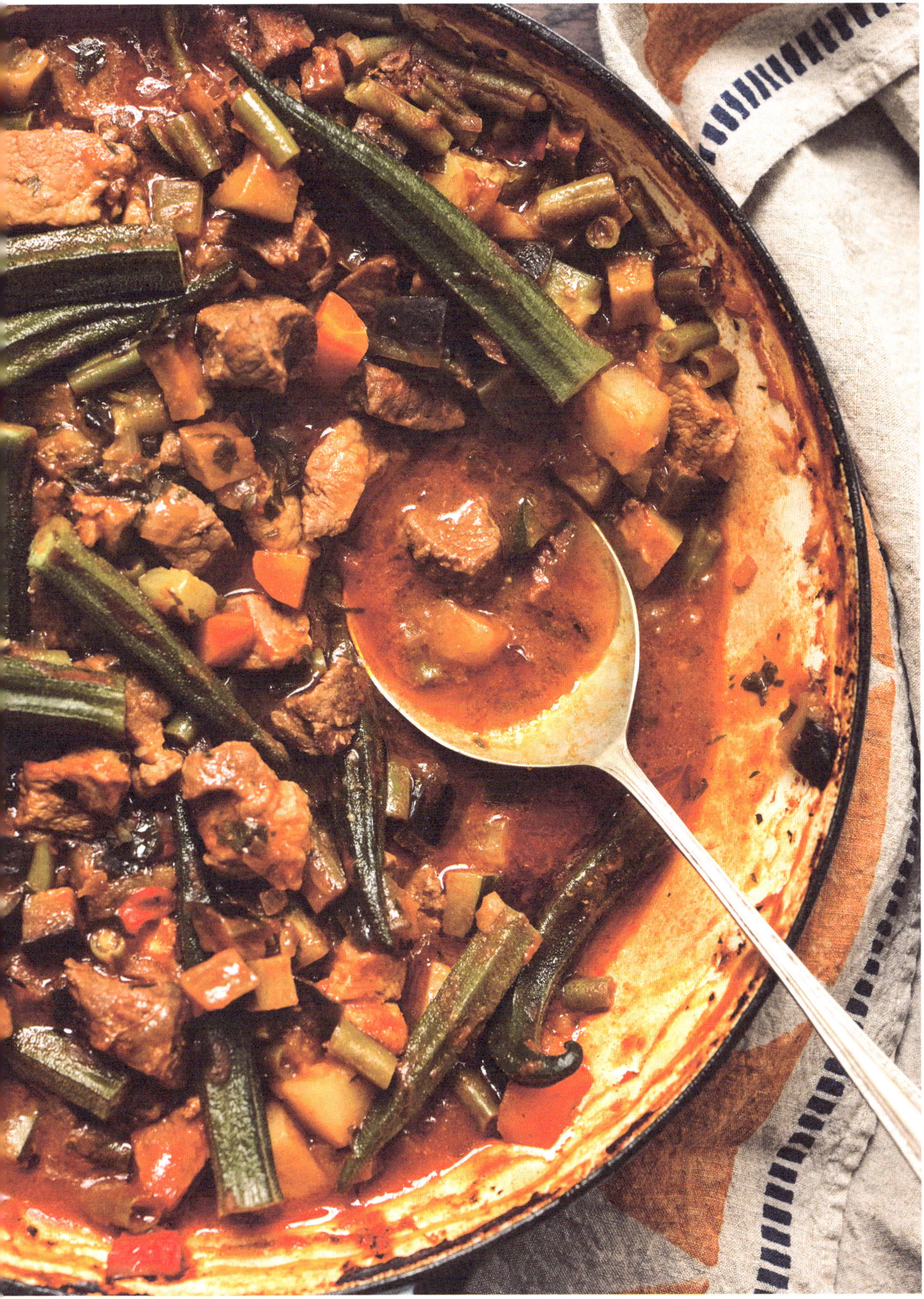

You can smell the meat grilling before you see it. Following your nose, you arrive at a restaurant or perhaps just a little hole in the wall – nothing more than a window next to a *rostilj* (grill), plumes of smoke emanating from within.

Sarajevo- or Banja Luka-style *ćevapi* or Macedonian-style *kebapcinja* (all types of oblong, skinless sausage). Spicy Leskovac-style *uštipci*, made from minced meat, onion and cheese. Glistening Srem *kobasice* (sausages). *Pljeskavice*, the Balkan hamburger. Rows and rows of *ražnjići* and various other meats on skewers. Chicken livers on skewers, either wrapped in caul fat or interspersed with smoked *slanina*, then grilled over the *rostilj*. Pork, lamb and veal chops. Everything smoking and gently whistling over a bright, dancing fire. Irresistible. Intoxicating. What to choose? It has to be *ćevapi* with a *somun* or *lepinja* flatbread, cut in half and grilled alongside on the meats. 'What would you like with it?' the grill man asks. 'Ajvar and kajmak, and the spicy dried pepper,' I respond. 'It's really spicy!' he warns. 'It's OK, I'm Macedonian.' 'Ah! Why didn't you say so!?'

Ćevapi (also known as *ćevapčići*) are beloved across the Balkans. The term starts to appear in documents relating to the former Yugoslav regions from around the 1850s within the framework of the Ottoman Empire. During this period, an early kind of fast-food industry started to develop in the territory between Istanbul and the north-western Ottoman frontiers. Balkan cities like Adrianople (Edirne), Thessaloniki, Skopje, Bitola, Sofia and Niš became the distribution centres for this nascent industry. Leskovac, part of Serbia from 1878, became an important centre for the efficient production of fried minced-meat dishes. This expertise spread quickly in several directions – towards Belgrade and the northern Balkans and towards Novi Pazar and Sarajevo and the western Balkans. Branislav Nušić – a famous Serbian playwright, writer and satirist, renowned for his sharp wit, humour and keen social commentary – was one of the first to document the arrival of the *ćevapi* industry in Belgrade from Leskovac and the southern Balkans. The population of Belgrade boomed in the late 1800s and South Serbian migrants brought their Leskovac grilling expertise with them. Special grilled meat dishes – *ćevapi* among them – became the best-selling mass-produced food in the capital. The first street hawkers in Belgrade in the 1860s could earn

FROM THE LAND
ZEMJA

a lot of money selling *ćevapi*. Slowly *ćevapi* restaurants started appearing across Belgrade, with the most renowned one, Zivko, located in the basement of the Hotel Makedonija building. *Ćevapi* do not seem to have arrived in Bosnia and Herzegovina before the 1900s. Around 1950, the historian Hamdija Kreševljaković wrote about the Sarajevo culinary crafts guilds of the Ottoman period, mentioning *ekmekcije* (bakers), *kasapi* (butchers) and *ašcije* (cooks), as well as the Sarajevo craftsmen's practice of attending *ašcinice* (restaurants), but there is no mention of *ćevapi* in his writings. Nevertheless, Sarajevo and Banja Luka took *ćevapi* in new and exciting directions and (along with Skopje, because they are the flavour I grew up with) offer some of the best *ćevapi* in the region.

Meat dishes across the Balkans are so much more than *ćevapi*, though, and meat consumption is an important aspect of the region's culinary culture, including livestock rearing and hunting in the wild forests. However, in an area plagued by poverty (and Ottoman taxation), meat was an indulgence and was therefore reserved for special occasions. There is a real ethos of nose-to-tail eating, and all parts of the animal are utilised in a variety of different ways. Meat is also used sparingly in many dishes – a little bit of meat is often heavily padded out with vegetables, legumes and grains. The type of meat preferred and consumed varies based on cultural, geographical and religious factors. The weekly fast days and four other periods of abstinence of eastern Christianity reached far beyond monastery walls, influencing the everyday diets of a significant part of the population and restricting the consumption of meat.

Lamb and mutton have always been important across the southern mountainous terrains that are more suited to shepherding and which boast hardy indigenous varieties of sheep such as the Pramenka in Bosnia and Herzegovina; the Bardhoka (or White Dukagjini, a strain of Pramenka) found in Kosovo, and some regions of Serbia, Montenegro and Albania, which and is ideally adapted to extreme low temperatures; and the Ovchepolska, Sarplaninska and Karachanka (the Macedonian strains of Pramenka*)*, used for their meat, milk, fat and wool. Their mountain grazing makes the meat incredibly delicious and while their milk production is typically low, it makes the flavour of the cheeses produced from their milk extraordinary. In spring, sheep are led to pasture in the mountains where they remain until late into autumn (fall). When they descend, mutton no longer required is slaughtered to be consumed and all parts of the animal is transformed into a variety of products to last the harsh winters, such as *pastrma*. Lamb dishes – such as roast lamb, spit-roast lamb and slow-cooked lamb – as well as various products made from lamb are then prepared in spring for Easter, Eid, the birth of a child (and/or christenings), weddings and other traditional and festive occasions and family celebrations.

Beef and veal are equally important and there are many indigenous breeds best suited to the Balkan terrains such as the Boškarin (or Istrian cattle) found in Croatia and Slovenia, the Cika in Slovenia, the Buša in Bosnia and Herzegovina, Serbia, Montenegro and North Macedonia and Podolian cattle, which are the breeds most associated with cattle production in the region.

Pork has historically been a vital part of the economy and culture across most of the region, but especially across Serbia, Montenegro, inland Croatia and Slovenia. It is a particularly important part of culinary tradition in Serbia. When the Ottoman Empire imposed excessively high taxes on the slaughter and sale of pigs in the 1880s, it sparked a series of protests in Serbia known as the Pirot rebellion. Peasants and pig farmers rebelled against what they saw as excessively burdensome taxation, which the Ottomans tried to supress with force, leading to a period of prolonged conflict that eventually ended with the Ottomans repealing the controversial taxes to end the so-called Serbian Pork War. Roast suckling pig is often the centrepiece for special occasions. More widely in the region, pigs were historically reared by richer families in the countryside, slaughtered towards the end of autumn, once again to ensure meat reserves for winter, and every part utilised from the meat to the *svinjska mast* (pork fat) and *čvarci* or *ocvirki* (cracklings). The Mangalitsa breed is found mainly in central Serbia and Vojvodina. Wild game is plentiful in the mountains and forests across the Balkans and is extensively used in the cuisine – especially venison, wild boar, hare, rabbit, pheasant and quail. If there is one thing you take away from this chapter, it should be this: meat is reserved for special occasions.

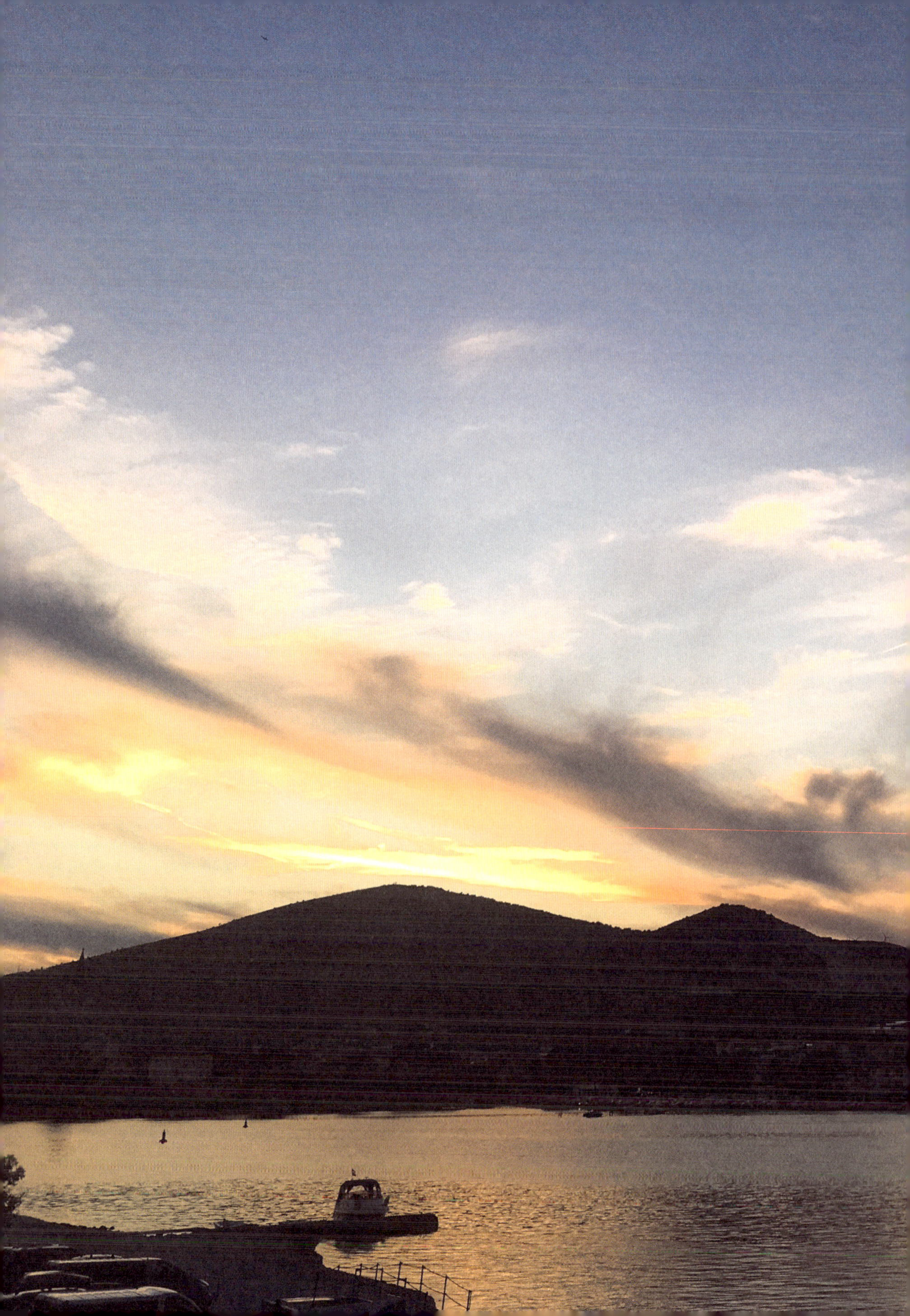

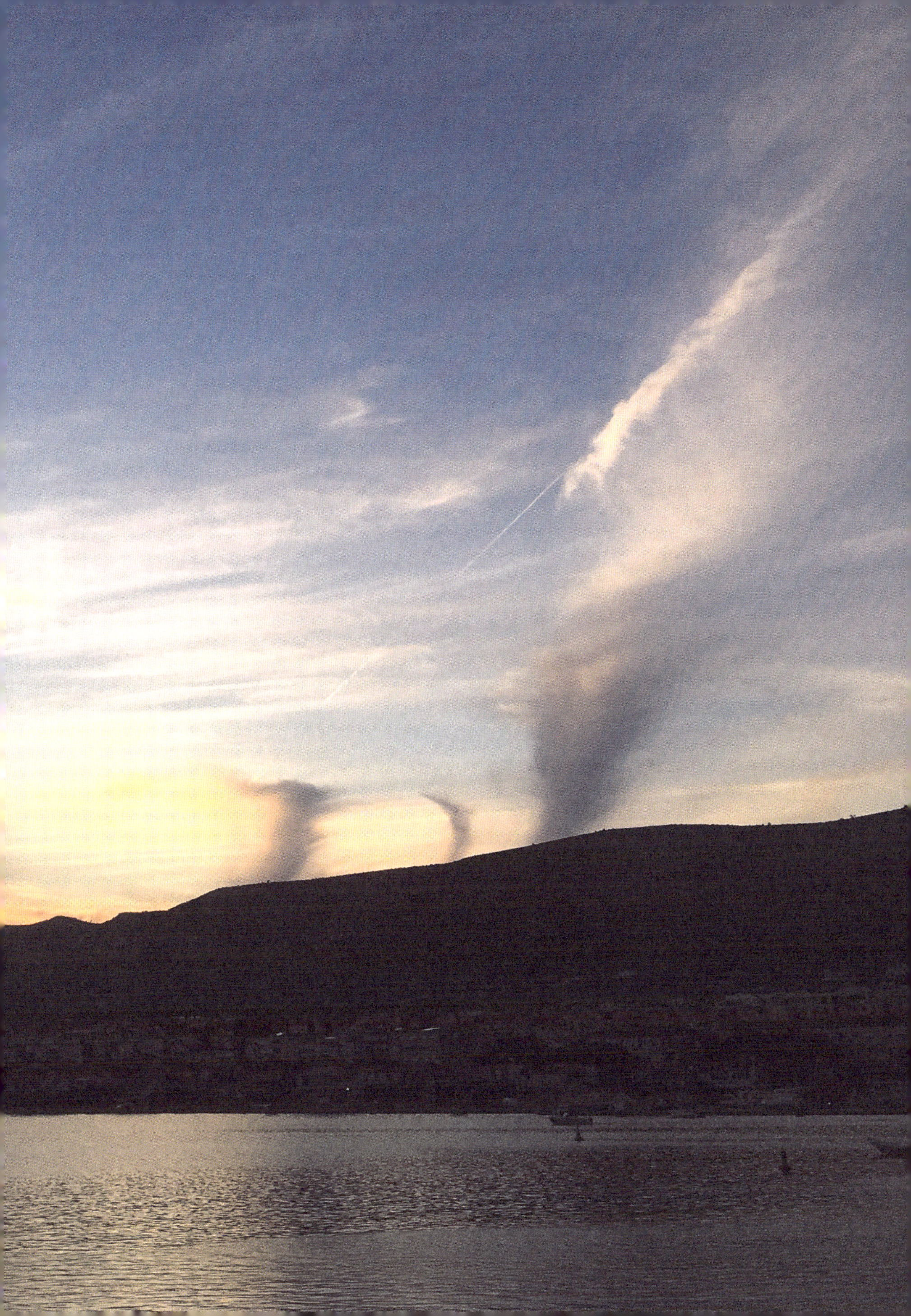

SERVES 4-6

Chicken and Rice

1.4–1.8 kg (3–4 lb) chicken, spatchcocked (backbone reserved and frozen for future stock)
2–3 potatoes, peeled and cut into 2–3 cm (¾–1¼ in) chunks
4 tablespoons vegetable oil
1 onion, finely chopped
1 leek (or 2–3 spring onions/scallions), finely chopped
1 sweet long red or green pepper, deseeded and finely chopped
3 carrots, peeled and finely chopped
½ teaspoon sea salt flakes, plus extra as needed
750 ml (25 fl oz/3 cups) warm chicken stock
2 teaspoons vegetable bouillon powder
20 g (¾ oz) fresh parsley, leaves picked and finely chopped
1–2 sprigs of fresh thyme, leaves picked and roughly chopped
250 g (9 oz/1¼ cups) long-grain rice, washed and drained

FOR THE SPICED BUTTER

40 g (1½ oz) unsalted butter, softened
2–3 garlic cloves, crushed
10 g (½ oz) fresh parsley, leaves and tender stems picked and finely chopped
1 tablespoon lemon zest
¼ teaspoon Bukovo pepper (or Aleppo pepper)
½ teaspoon smoked sweet paprika
½ teaspoon sea salt flakes
freshly ground black pepper

TO SERVE

1 lemon, cut into wedges, to serve
plain yoghurt

Baked chicken and rice is our equivalent of a Sunday roast. To me, this – what I grew up calling *tava oriz* or 'baked rice' (but is known as variations on chicken and rice in the respective Balkan languages, for example *pule me oriz* or even simply *pilaf* in Albania) – embodies the Balkan ethos of cleverly utilising a little bit of meat in a way that makes it go further. It is the go-to dish for repurposing leftovers. Often, a chicken (or chicken pieces on the bone) is used to make stock for chicken soup, then any excess stock and chicken pieces are used to make chicken and rice. Alternatively, the carcass from a roast chicken will be used to make stock and used to make chicken and rice along with the leftover meat. On more special occasions – bigger family or social gatherings – we would also use a whole chicken specifically for this, and the recipe below is that version. You can also use chicken pieces on the bone instead of a spatchcocked chicken. Try to use homemade chicken stock if you can, as it makes all the difference. Before the production of rice in the Balkans, ancient grains such as bulgur wheat and einkorn would have been used extensively. Barley, einkorn or brown rice are excellent in this and give a lovely nutty flavour (though you will need to adjust the cooking time as they take a little longer to cook).

Preheat the oven to 180°C fan (400°F).

Next, make the spiced butter. Combine all the ingredients in a small bowl and mash with a fork until well combined.

Use your hands to lift the skin of the chicken and distribute the butter under the skin. Place the chicken in a large roasting tin, breast side up, and arrange the potatoes around the chicken, then season everything with salt and black pepper and drizzle over 1 tablespoon of the oil. Roast in the oven for 30 minutes until the chicken skin has started to turn a deep golden colour and crisp up.

Meanwhile, heat the remaining oil in a large sauté pan (for which you have a lid) over a medium heat. Add the onion, leek, pepper, carrots and salt, cover and sweat, stirring occasionally, for 12–16 minutes, or until the vegetables have softened but retain some bite. Loosen the vegetables with a splash of the chicken stock if they start to stick. Add the vegetable bouillon powder, parsley, thyme, a good grind of black pepper and the rice and cook for a further 2–3 minutes, stirring to coat the rice in the vegetable cooking juices.

Remove the chicken from the oven and carefully lift it out onto a plate. Transfer the vegetable and rice mixture to the roasting tin, pour over the stock and gently stir to combine it with the potatoes and the chicken cooking juices and rendered chicken fat. Return the chicken to the roasting tin, nestling it in the rice but ensuring the skin is not submerged.

Return to the oven and bake for a further 25–30 minutes until the rice has absorbed the stock and is cooked through, and the chicken is cooked through with juices running clear if the meat is pierced in the thickest part of the thigh. Serve with lemon wedges and yoghurt on the side.

From the Land

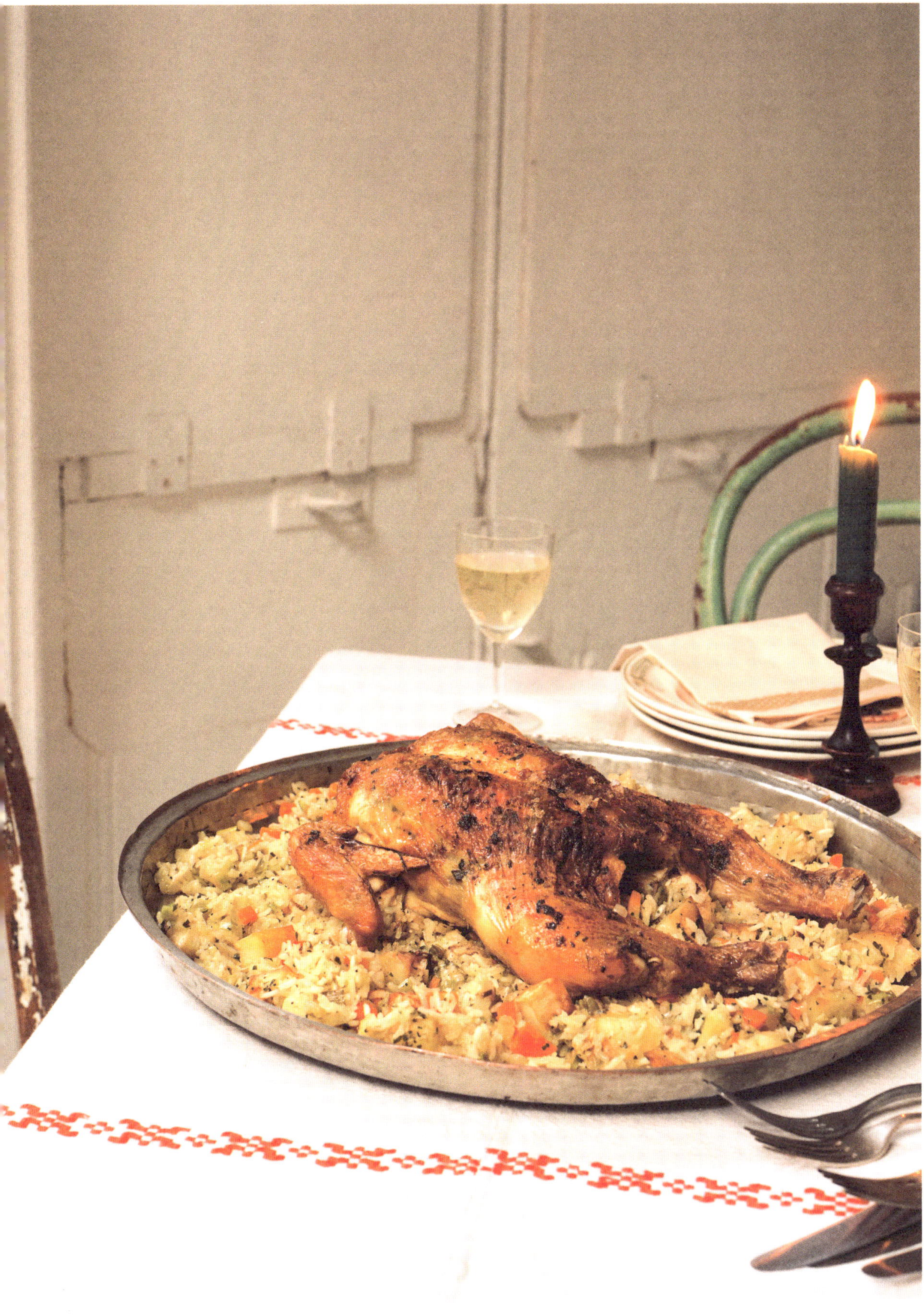

Roast Duck Legs with Mlinci and Cabbage

SERVES 4

4 duck legs (around 1 kg/2 lb 4 oz total), trimmed of any excess fat
1 tablespoon plus 1½ teaspoons sea salt flakes
3 tablespoons olive or sunflower oil
1 red onion, halved and thinly sliced
1 star anise
1 teaspoon juniper berries
1 cinnamon stick
1 small red cabbage (about 750 g/ 1 lb 10 oz), cored and finely sliced or shredded
150 ml (5 fl oz/scant ⅔ cup) red wine
600 ml (20 fl oz/2½ cups) vegetable or chicken stock
100 g (3½ oz) pitted prunes, roughly chopped
2 tablespoons dark brown soft sugar
2 tablespoons red wine vinegar
freshly ground black pepper

FOR THE MLINCI

400 g (14 oz/3¼ cups) plain (all-purpose) flour, plus extra for dusting
1 teaspoon fine sea salt
200 ml (7 fl oz/scant 1 cup) lukewarm water
2 teaspoons sunflower or olive oil

Note

You maybe able to source shop-bought *mlinci*. Alternatively, use fresh lasagne sheets, cut up into large squares and parboiled.

Martinovanje (St Martin's Day) is celebrated on 11 November every year in Slovenia, Croatia and other wine-producing regions. The autumn (fall) festival marks the moment that grape must turns into wine, and the wine is blessed. In early November 2022 I found myself swept up in the celebrations in Ljubljana and Maribor, the capital of Štajerska (Styria) – the biggest wine-producing region of Slovenia. The cities were transformed into large street parties, with wine and food producers showcasing their excellent wines and regional delicacies, and restaurants serving up seasonal St Martin's Day menus. This recipe is a recreation of a wonderful meal I had in a restaurant called Špajza in Ljubljana. *Mlinci* are a kind of pasta found principally across Slovenia, Croatia and Serbia prepared by making very thin flatbreads out of dough which are then cooked and dried for storage. When needed they are rehydrated with water or stock and used to soak up the cooking juices of roasted meats. You can make the cabbage a day ahead – it makes more than you may need, but the leftovers work very well with other smoked meats.

First, make the *mlinci*. Sift the flour and salt into a medium bowl. Add the water and oil and use a fork to bring the mixture together into a shaggy dough. Tip out onto a clean work surface (scraping down the sides of the bowl). Knead for 5–7 minutes, or until you have a soft dough. Shape into a ball, cover the dough and rest for 15 minutes. Divide the dough into four equal-sized balls. Dust the work surface and a rolling pin with a little flour and roll out each dough ball into a circle as thinly as you can (no more than 2 mm thick and 22–24 cm/8½–9½ inches in diameter).

Place a large frying pan over a high heat. When hot, add a dough circle and toast for 3–4 minutes on each side until bubbles and char marks appear. Transfer to a wire rack to cool and repeat with the remaining dough. Once cool, the *mlinci* should crack. If they do not, place them in an oven preheated to 160°C fan (350°F) and bake for 10 minutes to finish drying them out. Break the *mlinci* into pieces and store them in an airtight container until you need them. If properly dried out, they will keep like dry pasta.

If you haven't already used it for the *mlinci*, preheat the oven to 160°C fan (350°F).

Prick the skin of each duck leg all over with a sharp knife, then season with 1 tablespoon of the salt and a good grind of black pepper. Place them in a large baking dish and cook on the middle shelf of the oven for 1–1¼ hours, rotating the baking dish halfway through the cooking time, until the duck legs are tender and the skin is crisp.

To make the cabbage, heat the oil in a casserole dish (Dutch oven) over a medium-high heat. Add the onion and ½ teaspoon of the salt and fry, stirring occasionally, for 4–5 minutes until the onion has softened and started to brown and crisp. Add the star anise, juniper berries and cinnamon stick and continue to cook for 30 seconds until you start to smell the spices. Add the cabbage and stir well to coat it in the oil and combine with the onion. Add the wine, stock, prunes, sugar, vinegar, the remaining 1 teaspoon of salt and a good grind of black pepper. Transfer to the oven and cook for 1¼ hours, stirring halfway through.

From the Land

Meanwhile put the *mlinci* into a large bowl and cover with boiling water. Set aside to soak for 10 minutes, then drain.

Remove the duck and cabbage from the oven and increase the heat to 200°C fan (425°F). Remove the duck legs from the baking dish and place on a plate. Add the drained *mlinci* to the baking dish and coat well in the rendered duck fat, spreading them evenly around the baking dish. Arrange the duck legs among the *mlinci*. Return the baking dish to the oven and cook for a further 15–20 minutes until the *mlinci* crisp and brown a little. Remove from the oven and rest for 5–10 minutes before serving with the cabbage alongside.

From the Land

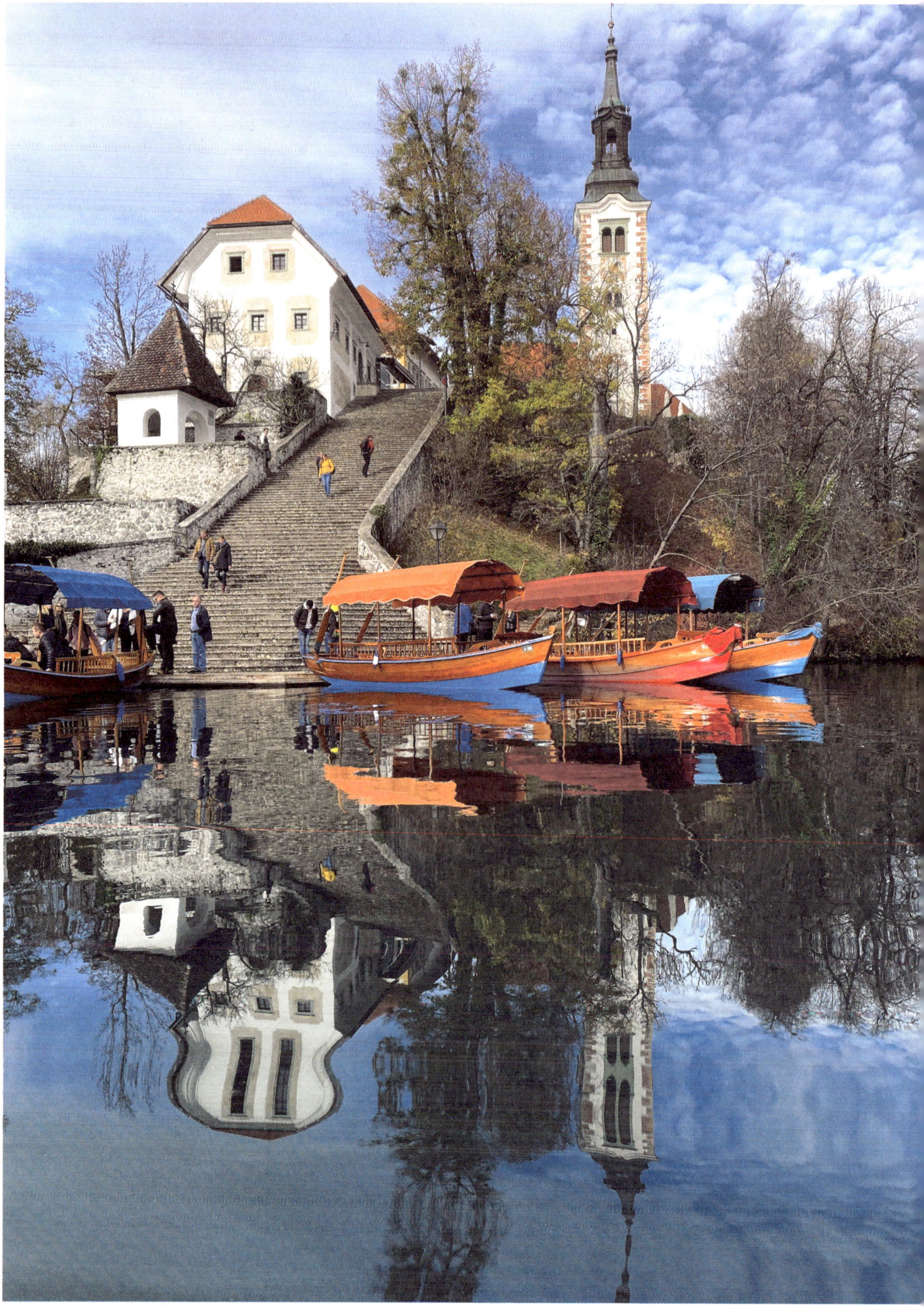

SERVES 4-6

Venison with Quince and Cranberries

1 kg venison haunch, trimmed

1½ teaspoons sea salt flakes

2 tablespoons olive oil or unsalted butter

6–8 slices of smoked streaky (side) bacon (about 120–180 g/4¼–6½ oz total), 2 slices chopped into 2 cm (¾ inch) strips, the rest kept whole for wrapping the venison

2 banana shallots, quartered

2 celery stalks, chopped into 5 cm (2 inch) batons

2–3 carrots, peeled and chopped into 5 cm (2 inch) batons

2–3 garlic cloves, thinly sliced

1–2 sprigs of fresh rosemary

1–2 sprigs of fresh thyme

½ teaspoon juniper berries, gently crushed

1 quince, peeled, cored and cut into 8–12 wedges

100 g (3½ oz) fresh or frozen cranberries

2 tablespoons red wine vinegar

1 tablespoon light brown soft sugar

250 ml (8 fl oz/1 cup) red wine

freshly ground black pepper

Wild game, and wild venison in particular, is widely used all across the Balkans. This particular dish takes inspiration from the breathtakingly beautiful area of Bohinj in Slovenia, home to Lake Bohinj and Zlatorog (Goldenhorn or Goldhorn), the legendary white buck (or perhaps Alpine ibex) from Slovene folklore that roams the heights of Mount Triglav and whose golden horns are the key to Triglav's treasure. It is very common to find wild venison prepared in a number of ways around Bohinj, but my personal favourite is slow-cooked venison paired with sour fruits, like cranberries or redcurrants. I couldn't resist adding quinces, a more southern touch. Add as much garlic, rosemary and thyme as you like. This works beautifully with steamed vegetables or a lovely creamy potato or celeriac (celery root) mash.

Preheat the oven to 170°C fan (375°F).

Pat the venison dry with paper towels, then season it all over with ½ teaspoon of the salt and a generous grind of black pepper.

Put the oil or butter and chopped bacon into a frying pan large enough to fit the venison and place over a medium-high heat. When the bacon has started to render some fat and crisp (4–6 minutes), add the venison to the pan with the bacon and brown it on all sides for about 10 minutes. Once evenly browned, remove from the heat. Transfer the venison to a large plate (reserving the oil and bacon fat as well as the bacon) and wrap it with the remaining bacon slices, overlapping them as you do and ensuring the top of the venison is fully covered.

Place the shallots, celery, carrots, garlic, rosemary, thyme, juniper berries, quince, cranberries, vinegar, sugar, the remaining salt and a generous grind of black pepper in a large casserole dish (Dutch oven) and add the oil, rendered bacon fat and chopped bacon and mix well to combine, then nestle the venison among the vegetables and fruits. Pour over the wine, cover with a lid and transfer the casserole to the oven to cook for 1–1¼ hours until the internal temperature of the venison has reached at least 70°C (158°F), checking and basting the venison with the cooking juices from time to time. Finally, remove the lid and cook for a further 15 minutes – the venison should be well done but tender and the bacon on the top should be crispy.

Remove the venison and place on a large, lipped serving platter and allow to rest for 15 minutes before carving. Remove the carrots and quinces with a slotted spoon and place around the venison. Strain the sauce into a small saucepan, taste and adjust the seasoning to your preference, and if you think it needs it, reduce it to intensify the flavour and thicken it. Serve it in a pouring jug alongside the venison.

From the Land

SERVES 6-8

Slow-roasted Easter lamb

2–3 kg (4 lb 8 oz–6 lb 10 oz) shoulder of lamb, trimmed

1 tablespoon sea salt flakes

1 bulb of garlic, half the cloves cut into 1–1.5 cm x 5 mm (½–¾ x ¼ inch) batons, the rest peeled but kept whole

2–3 carrots, peeled and 1 carrot cut into 1–1.5 cm x 5 mm (½–¾ x ¼ inch) batons, the rest cut into 10 cm (4 inch) batons

40 g (1½ oz) fresh parsley, leaves picked and stalks reserved

2 onions or banana shallots, quartered

1 leek, trimmed, sliced in half lengthwise, then sliced into 10 cm (4 inch) batons (optional)

2–3 sprigs of fresh rosemary

2–3 sprigs of fresh thyme

1–2 bay leaves

1 teaspoon freshly ground black pepper

2 tablespoons Dijon mustard

2 tablespoons extra virgin olive oil

500 ml (17 fl oz/generous 2 cups) chicken or vegetable stock

150 ml (5 fl oz/scant ⅔ cup) dry white wine, plus extra as needed

1 tablespoon plain (all-purpose) flour (optional)

Note

You can add potatoes halfway through the cooking time to roast alongside the lamb.

Eating roast lamb is how most families across the southern Balkans who celebrate Easter break the Lenten fast. *Spikovanje* or *špikanje* (larding) is a technique I first came across when watching my grandmother prepare lamb for our Easter Sunday feast. Though traditionally the term means inserting little strips of smoked pork or lard into (often lean) meat to flavour it during roasting, in the Balkans the term is also used more generally to describe flavouring the meat in other ways before roasting, mainly by using a variety of vegetables and aromatic herbs. I always thought of it as making little secret pockets bursting with flavour all over the meat. My grandmother's favoured pocket-fillers were garlic, carrots and parsley, and she often used a mustard rub over roasting joints for extra punch. This tender, slow-roast lamb is very much an homage to her.

Preheat the oven to 170°C fan (375°F). Pat the lamb dry with paper towels, then rub all over with ½ teaspoon of the salt. With a sharp knife, make 2 cm (¾ inch) deep incisions every 2–3 cm (¾–1¼ inches) all over the lamb against the grain of the meat.

Take one small baton each of garlic and carrot and one parsley leaf and insert them into an incision in the lamb. They should go all the way in and not stick out. Repeat for all the incisions you have made in the lamb.

Next, place the whole garlic cloves, large carrot batons, parsley stalks, onions, leek (if using), rosemary, thyme and bay leaves in the middle of a large, deep-sided roasting tin. Place the lamb upside down over them.

In a small bowl, combine the remaining salt with the black pepper, mustard and olive oil and mix together to create a paste. Gently brush or rub the paste over the whole surface of the lamb.

Pour half the stock and all the wine into the roasting tin. Cover the lamb first with baking parchment and then cover the roasting tin tightly with foil. Roast in the oven for 2 hours. Remove the lamb from the oven, and baste it with the cooking juices, then return to the oven, uncovered, and roast for a further 30 minutes, or until nicely browned. Next, remove the lamb from the oven again and turn it over. If there is not enough moisture in the roasting tray, add some more stock and a further splash of wine. Baste, then cover the lamb with the baking parchment and foil again and return to the oven to roast for a further 2 hours, checking periodically and basting. Finally, uncover once more and roast for a further 30 minutes, or until nicely browned. The lamb should roast for a total of at least 5 hours and up to 6 hours – the meat should be falling off the bone. Transfer the lamb to a serving dish, cover and let it rest for 30–40 minutes.

After you have removed the lamb from the roasting tin, add a splash of wine to deglaze it, then pour all the cooking juices through a sieve into a small saucepan. Allow the juices to settle and cool, then skim any excess lamb fat or oil from the top. Place the saucepan over a medium heat and add the flour, stirring to combine for 1 minute. Add the rest of the stock, stirring to avoid lumps and bring it to the boil. As soon as it boils, reduce the heat and stir until thickened to your liking. Serve with the lamb.

From the Land

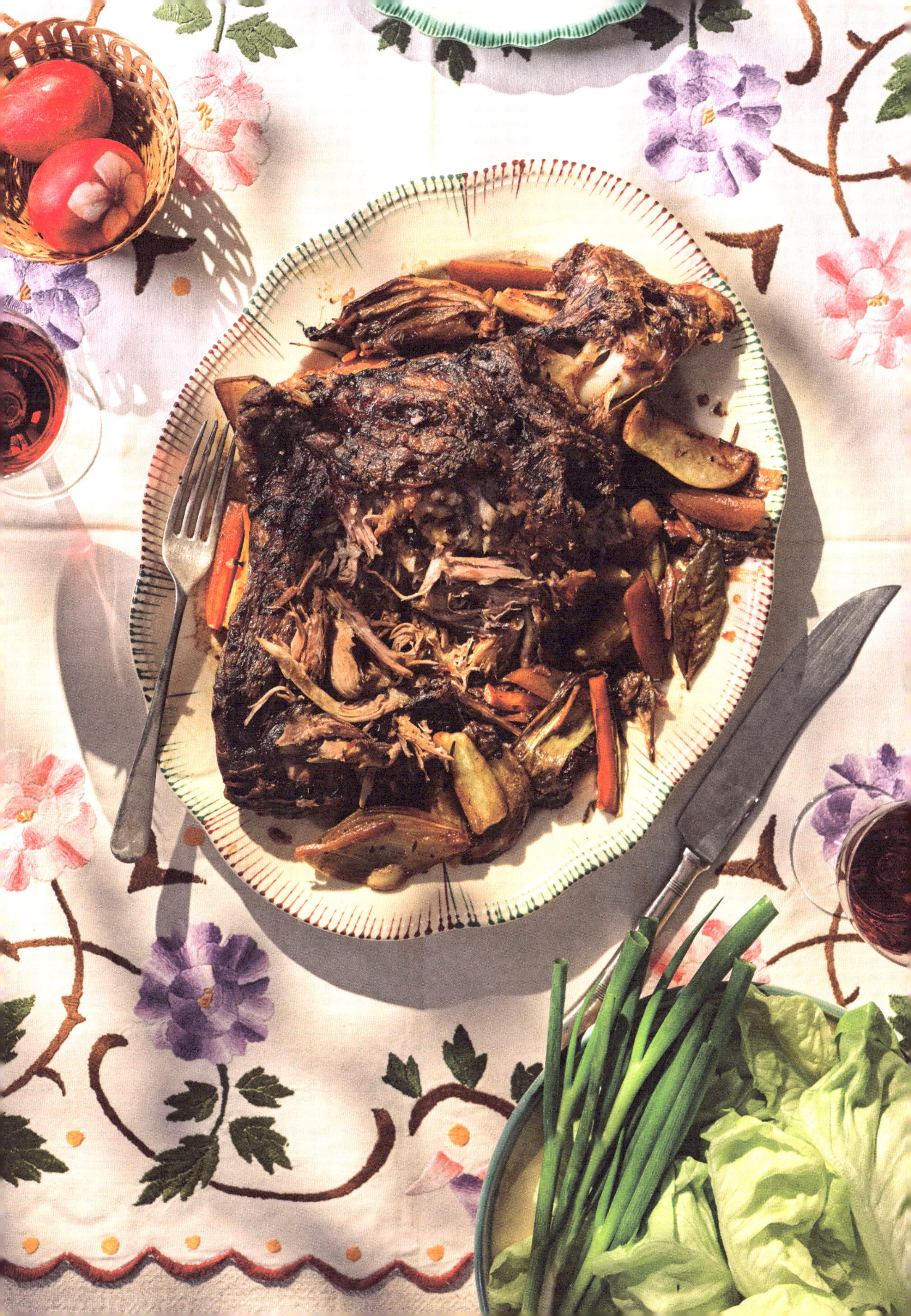

SERVES 4-6

Elbasan Tava

1 kg (2 lb 4 oz) leg of lamb, de-boned, trimmed and cut into 4–5 cm pieces
¾ teaspoon sea salt flakes
90 ml (3 fl oz/⅓ cup) olive oil
1 leek, trimmed and finely chopped
4–6 garlic cloves, finely chopped
2–3 bay leaves
2–3 sprigs of fresh thyme
700 ml (24 fl oz/scant 3 cups) beef stock
160 g (5¾ oz/generous ¾ cup) long-grain rice, washed and drained
4 medium eggs
600 g (1 lb 5 oz/2⅓ cups) set sheep's milk yoghurt, plus extra to serve
freshly ground black pepper

Once upon a time, a sultan (Mehmet II) was on a military campaign near the Albanian city of Elbasan. Local cooks preparing food for the hungry, campaigned-out, sultan used leftover lamb, beautiful rice grown in the area surrounding Elbasan and spiced yoghurt to make a baked casserole of lamb with a beautiful eggy yoghurt soufflé-like topping, and a dish known as *Elbasan tava* was born. Or, so this lovely culinary legend goes.

Elbasan tava, or sometimes yoghurt *tava* (in North Macedonia) or *tavë kosi* (in Albania), is considered the national dish of Albania. It is also eaten in various forms around Kosovo, North Macedonia, Bulgaria, Greece and Turkey. It can be made without rice, but if rice is added then it is called *Elbasan tava* as an homage to the beautiful rice of Elbasan. Originally, the topping would have been made with *kos*, a soured goat or sheep's milk, but this has given way to a mixture of yoghurt and eggs. A special thank you to our family friends Luis and Genoveva Gombar (especially Aunty Genoveva) for telling me how she prepares her *Elbasan tava*. Feel free to channel the time-pressured cooks of the sultan and use any leftover roast lamb (see page 164) to make this dish.

Preheat the oven to 180°C fan (400°F).

Pat the meat dry with paper towels, then season it all over with ½ teaspoon of the salt and a good grind of black pepper.

Heat 4 tablespoons of the oil in a large, heavy-based casserole dish (Dutch oven) over a medium-high heat and brown the meat thoroughly in batches for 4–6 minutes on each side until evenly well browned all over. Transfer the meat to a plate and set aside. Add the rest of the oil to the dish and fry the leek for 10 minutes, or until just softened. Add the garlic and cook for a further minute. Add the meat back to dish with the bay leaves, thyme and stock.

Cover with a lid and transfer to the oven to cook for about 1½ hours, or until the meat is tender and easy to cut through with a spoon. Check on the dish occasionally and top it up with more water if you need to, ensuring the meat is always partially submerged in liquid.

Remove the dish from the oven and fish out the bay leaves and sprigs of thyme, then add the rice and stir to combine. Transfer everything to a 26 cm/10¼ inch round baking dish or equivalent. Arrange the meat pieces around evenly, with the rice distributed around the baking dish. If you need to, top up with water to ensure the rice is just submerged in liquid. Bake in the oven for 15 minutes.

Meanwhile, crack the eggs into a large bowl and whisk lightly. Add the yoghurt, the remaining ¼ teaspoon of salt and a good grind of black pepper and whisk until smooth. Remove the baking dish from the oven and pour the egg and yoghurt mixture evenly over the top. Return to the oven and bake for about 20 minutes, or until the topping has set, risen and is golden brown. Serve straight away, with yoghurt alongside.

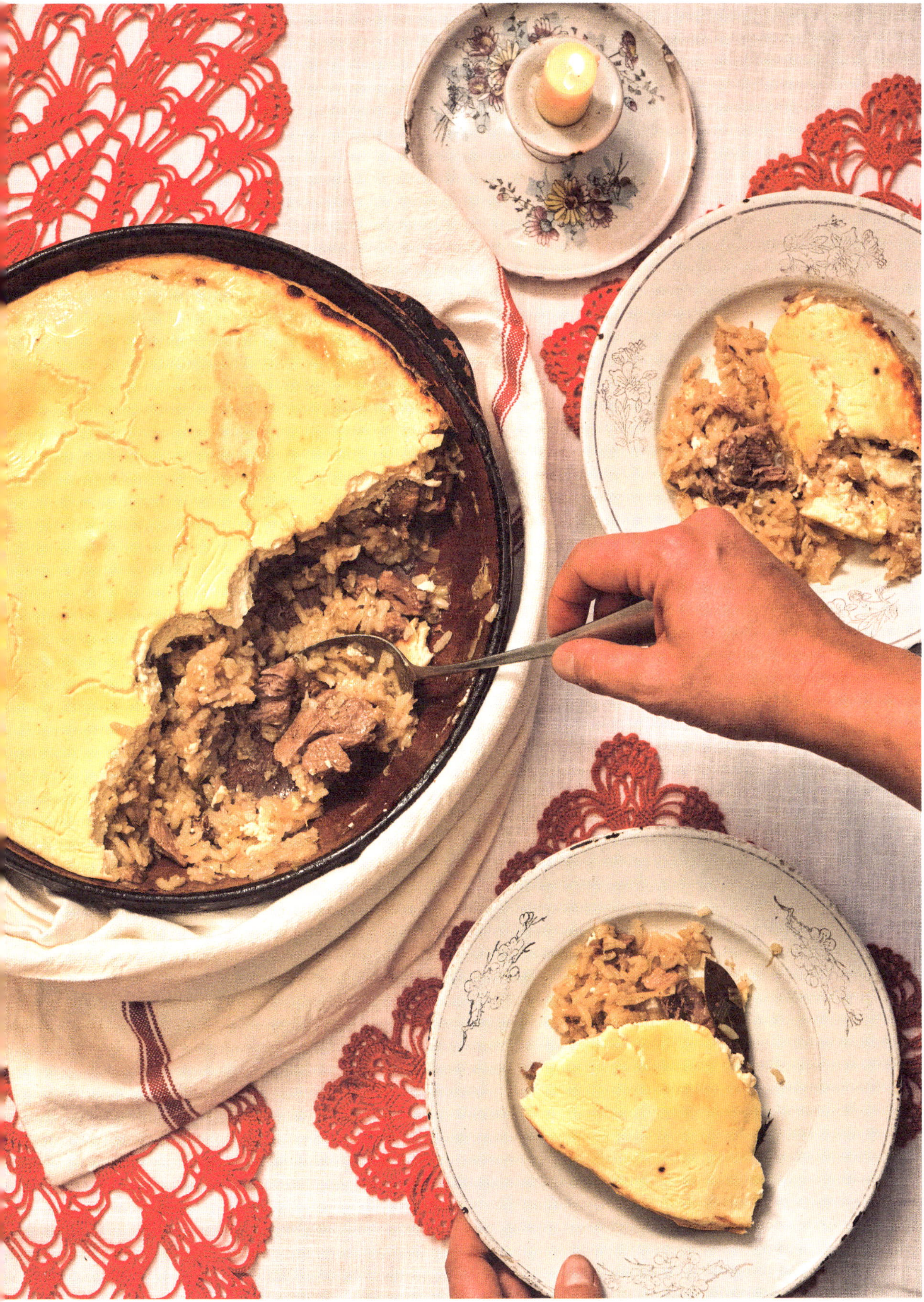

SERVES 8-10

A 'Balkexican' Pulled Pork

2–2.5 kg (4 lb 8 oz–5 lb 8 oz) boneless shoulder of pork, trimmed
2 carrots, peeled and cut into batons
1 sweet long green or red pepper, deseeded and roughly chopped
1 onion, roughly chopped
1 leek, trimmed and roughly chopped
6–8 garlic cloves, peeled
1 dried chipotle chilli (or ½ teaspoon chipotle chilli/hot pepper flakes)
1 teaspoon freshly ground black pepper
1–2 bay leaves
10 g (½ oz) fresh parsley, leaves and stalks roughly chopped
1–2 sprigs of fresh thyme
1 x 330 ml (11¼ fl oz/1⅓ cups) can of light beer (such as IPA)
brioche buns, to serve

FOR THE MARINADE

2 tablespoons sweet paprika
½ teaspoon hot smoked paprika
1 teaspoon ground cumin
2 teaspoons dried oregano
2 tablespoons Dried Pepper Paste (see page 261)
2 tablespoons apple cider vinegar
2 tablespoons dark brown soft sugar
1 tablespoon smoked sea salt flakes
½ teaspoon freshly ground black pepper

FOR THE PICKLE SALSA

2 tablespoons Pickled Chillies (see page 102), finely chopped
50 g (1¾ oz) gherkins (pickles), finely chopped
30 g (1 oz) capers (in brine), finely chopped
1 tablespoon wholegrain mustard
1 tablespoon clear honey
1 tablespoon apple cider vinegar
2 tablespoons extra virgin olive oil
20 g (¾ oz) fresh parsley and/or oregano, leaves picked and roughly chopped
¼ teaspoon sea salt flakes
freshly ground black pepper

In the wake of the fragmentation of Yugoslavia, the ongoing wars and the economic collapse of most of the former republics including North Macedonia, my mother and I moved back to Kuwait, which was recovering from its own catastrophe, the Gulf War. I was 10 and I barely remembered any English I had learned as a seven-year-old. On the first day of school, as I walked into my new class, I saw a wild-haired boy sat in the corner of the classroom, furiously drawing. I decided there and then he would be my friend. The boy's name was Anthony Pino and to this day he is still the dearest friend, a brother I never had and the best uncle to my son. He is also half Mexican, half Spanish and a fantastic cook. We often cook together, and we love to combine the flavours of Mexico, Spain and the Balkans in what we call a 'Balkexican fest'. I first made this pulled pork for one of these. While we don't generally make pulled meat across the Balkans, we do slow cook meat until it is so tender it falls off the bone. Roast pork, including roast suckling pig is loved especially across Serbia. This recipe takes inspiration from Mexican *cochinita pibil*, but with Balkan flavour. I have suggested serving it with brioche buns, but feel free to have it with fresh tortillas.

The day before you want to cook the pork, combine all the ingredients for the marinade in a small bowl and mix well to create a thick paste.

Place the pork in a large bowl and coat with the marinade, then cover and marinate in the refrigerator overnight, or for at least 8 hours.

The next day, remove the pork from the refrigerator at least 1 hour before cooking and preheat the oven to 200°C fan (425°F).

Put the carrots, pepper, onion, leek, garlic, chipotle chilli, black pepper, bay leaves, parsley and thyme into a large casserole dish (Dutch oven) and nestle the pork on top, skin side up. Pour over the beer, place a cartouche over the pork, cover with a lid and cook in the oven 45 minutes. Reduce the oven temperature to 180°C fan (400°F), then continue to cook for a further 3½–5¼ hours until the pork is falling apart. Check the pork every hour or so in case it gets dry – if it does, add 100–200 ml (3½–7 fl oz/scant ½–1 cup) water.

Meanwhile, make the pickle salsa by combining all the ingredients in a small bowl.

Once the pork is ready, remove it from the oven and transfer the meat to a large, lipped plate, leaving the liquid and vegetables in the dish. Cut off the skin, then use two forks to shred the meat, discarding any fatty bits.

Skim any excess fat from the surface of the liquid in the dish (reserve it for another use, for example frying pork chops). Remove the bay leaves and sprigs of thyme and chipotle. With a fork, mash all the vegetables into the liquid (or transfer to a blender and blend for 1 minute). Add the shredded pork back into the casserole and mix everything together so that the shredded pork is coated in the liquid. Check and adjust the seasoning, if needed.

Serve warm with brioche buns and the pickle salsa on the side.

From the Land

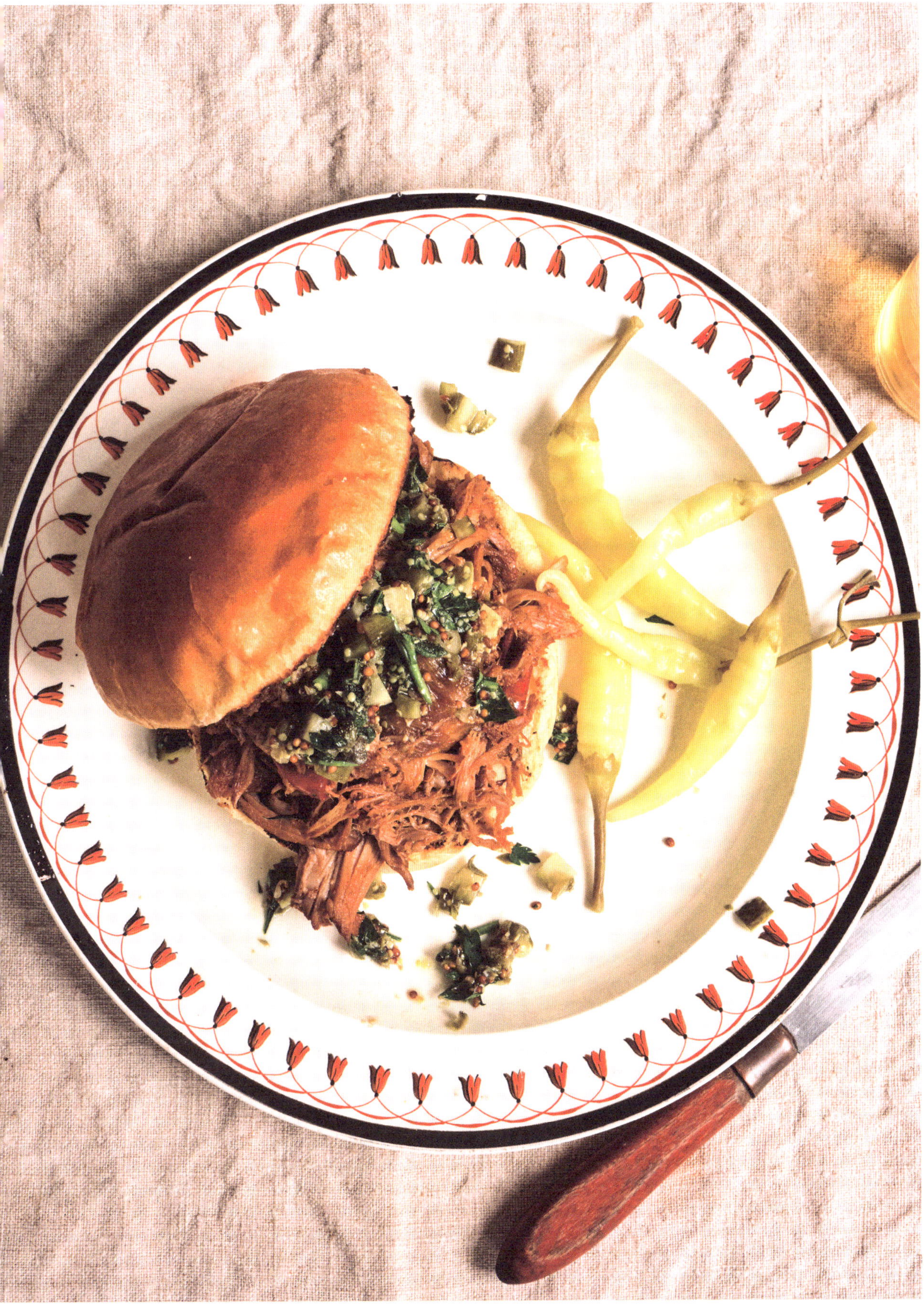

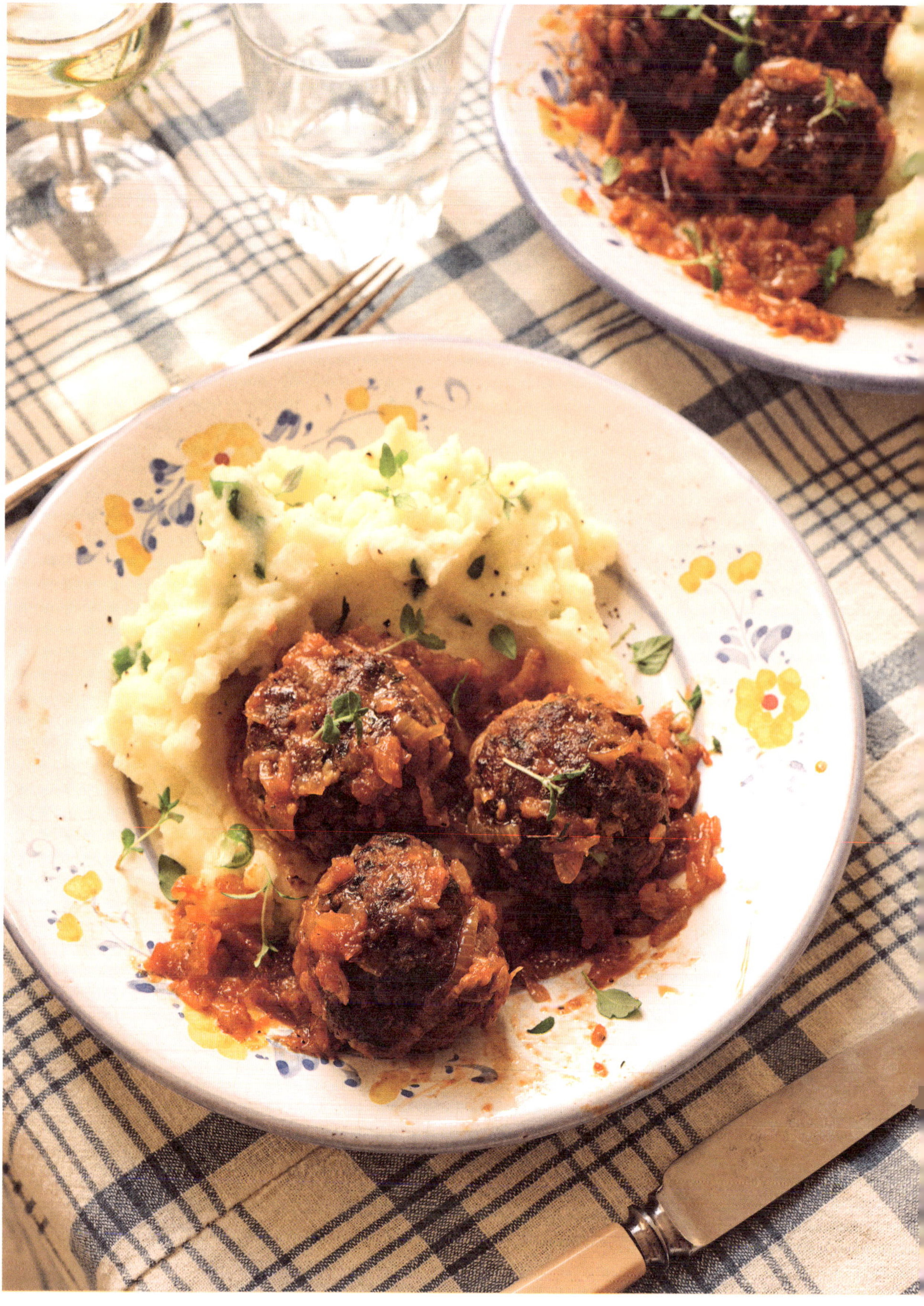

Ǩyfte, on Onions

SERVES 2-4

3 tablespoons olive or sunflower oil
700–800 g (1 lb 9 oz–1 lb 12 oz) onions, halved and thinly sliced
½ teaspoon sea salt flakes
25 g (1 oz) unsalted butter
2 tablespoons tomato purée (paste – or 1 grated tomato plus 1 tablespoons tomato purée)
¼ teaspoon ground cumin
3–4 bay leaves
100 ml (3½ fl oz/scant ½ cup) water
crusty bread, rice or mashed potatoes, to serve

FOR THE ǨYFTE

500 g (1 lb 2 oz) minced (ground) beef or veal (at least 10% fat) or lamb (or a mix of any)
1 medium egg, lightly beaten
1 onion, finely chopped or grated
1 teaspoon dried oregano
1 tablespoon sweet paprika
1 tablespoon tomato purée (paste)
4 tablespoons dried breadcrumbs (or Panko breadcrumbs)
20 g (¾ oz) fresh parsley, leaves and tender stems picked and finely chopped, plus extra to serve
½ teaspoon sea salt flakes
3 tablespoons sunflower or other neutral oil
freshly ground black pepper

Ǩyfte (or *kofte* or *ćufte*) is what we call meatballs, and there are endless versions across the Balkans. The meat is usually mixed with vegetables, spices, herbs and breadcrumbs or stale bread, as it is a very common way of stretching a small amount of meat further. There are many versions of *kyfte* on or in something, such as in tomato sauce or yoghurt sauce, or even *kyfte* made with rice, called *paša kofte*, similar to the Turkish *Hasan paşa köftesi*, which are stuffed and topped with mashed potatoes.

This version of *kyfte na kromid* – which simply means *kyfte* on onions – is one of my absolute favourites. It makes a very frequent appearance in my Balkan kitchen; my mother made them for me regularly growing up and now I do for my son.

I would suggest you seek out the best meat you can, and if you are able to, ask your butcher to double mince it for you (or if you have a meat grinder, do so yourself), as that will give you a better texture and allow you to really distribute to flavour through the meat. You can skip making the onion base entirely and just make the *kyfte*, frying them until they are cooked through and then serving them with fresh salads and crusty bread.

First, make the onion base. Heat the oil in a large sauté pan over a medium-high heat and add the onions and salt. Cover with a lid and cook, stirring occasionally, for 20–25 minutes until soft, jammy and lightly caramelised. Add the butter, tomato purée, cumin and a good grind of black pepper and cook for a further minute. Remove from the heat, add the bay leaves and the water, then transfer to a 24 x 30 cm (9½ x 12 inch) baking dish and set aside.

Meanwhile, prepare the *kyfte* Combine all the ingredients in a bowl with ½ teaspoon of the oil and a generous grind of black pepper. Knead the mixture with your hands for 2–3 minutes until well combined. Shape the mixture into 16–20 golf-ball sized balls.

Preheat the oven to 180°C fan (400°F).

Heat the remaining oil in a large frying pan and brown the *kyfte* on all sides for 3–4 minutes, just to seal them and give them a little bit of colour rather than cook them, then arrange them in the baking dish over the onion base. Bake the *kyfte* and the onions in the oven, uncovered, for 30–40 minutes, or until they are beautifully browned.

Serve warm with crusty bread, rice, mashed potatoes or other accompaniments of your choice.

SERVES 4

Pljeskavici

500 g (1 lb 2 oz) minced (ground) beef or veal (at least 10% fat; or a mix of beef, veal and pork)
1 onion, grated
1 red Romano pepper, deseeded and finely chopped
½ teaspoon bicarbonate of soda (baking soda)
1 teaspoon vegetable bouillon powder
2 teaspoons dried oregano
3 tablespoons dried breadcrumbs (or Panko breadcrumbs)
1 tablespoon olive oil, plus extra for shaping and brushing
10 g (½ oz) fresh parsley, leaves picked and finely chopped
½ teaspoon sea salt flakes
¼ teaspoon freshly ground black pepper
4 slices of sheep's milk kashkaval (or mild Cheddar; about 5 x 5 cm/ 2 x 2 inches and 1 cm/½ inch thick)
Somun (see page 66), to serve

FOR THE URNEBES
200 g (7 oz) white cheese (or feta), crumbled
200 g (7 oz) urda
50 g (1¾ oz) sour cream, or more to taste
1 tablespoon olive oil, plus extra to serve
1 tablespoon sweet paprika
1–2 tablespoon Dried Pepper Paste (see page 261) or Ljutenitsa (see page 241)
¼ teaspoon sea salt flakes, plus extra to serve
1 teaspoon Bukovo pepper (or Aleppo pepper; optional)
freshly ground black pepper

Notes
You can prepare both the *urnebes* and the patty mixture a day ahead and keep it in the refrigerator in an airtight container until you are ready to cook the burgers. Take the meat out of the refrigerator 1 hour before so it comes to room temperature.

It is easiest to think of *pljeskavica* or *pleskavica* as the Balkan hamburger. It is enormously popular in Serbia, but also across the rest of former Yugoslavia. The meat patty can be a mix of beef, veal, pork or lamb, and there are famous regional variants. To name a few: *Leskovačka* tends to be spiced with the red peppers the city of Leskovac in Serbia is famous for and served with onions; *Šarska* is stuffed with the famously delicious sheep's milk *kashkaval* from *Šar Planina* (the Šar mountains that stretch from north-western North Macedonia into southern Kosovo); *Hajdučka* (the 'outlaw's') is mixed with smoked pork meat; *Vranjanska* is topped with fried peppers and garlic. There are also all sorts of *prilozi* (accompaniments) you can choose to go with your *pljeskavica*: onions (fried or fresh), shredded cabbage, fried peppers, dried spicy peppers or spicy pepper dips, *ajvar*, *kajmak* or the *urnebes* I've suggested below. *Urnebes* means 'chaos' or 'disorder', though there is nothing chaotic about this. We call it a salad, but it is really a spread, closely related to the Liptauer spread found in Austria, Slovakia and Hungary. *Urnebes* is a winter concoction as it is made with Balkan pantry staples, and its composition varies (some include egg, roasted chopped red peppers or *kajmak*), as does its texture spectrum (from fairly dry and crumbly to creamy and smooth). It is often served with bread croutons, but in recent times it has become one of the obligatory *prilozi* for *Leskovački rostilj* (Leskovac grill). Personalisation of your *pljeskavica* is essential. I have a soft spot for *Šarska* as it is something I ate growing up in North Macedonia, and the melted cheese oozing from the centre of the meat patty is a joy.

Combine all the ingredients (except the cheese) in a large bowl. Knead the mixture with your hands until well combined.

Divide the mixture into four balls, then brush your hands with a little oil and shape the balls into burgers. Flatten one of the burgers on your palm, place a cheese slice in the middle, then fold over and cover the cheese slice in the meat mixture, ensuring the cheese is totally encased. Repeat with the remaining burgers. Once shaped, brush each patty with a little oil on both sides.

Meanwhile, prepare the *urnebes*. Place all the ingredients (except the Bukovo pepper) in a large bowl together with a generous grind of black pepper and mix well to combine. Taste and adjust the seasoning and loosen the consistency with more sour cream if you like, then arrange on a plate (feel free to serve it as ice-cream scoops, as is the fashion these days). Sprinkle some sea salt flakes and Bukovo pepper over the top and drizzle with a little more oil.

Grill the burgers on a hot barbecue (or under the grill/broiler in your oven on the highest setting) for 4–5 minutes on each side, pressing them gently as you do. Grill the *somun* on the barbecue for a minute or so to soak up the cooking juices. Serve with the *somun* and *urnebes*.

From the Land

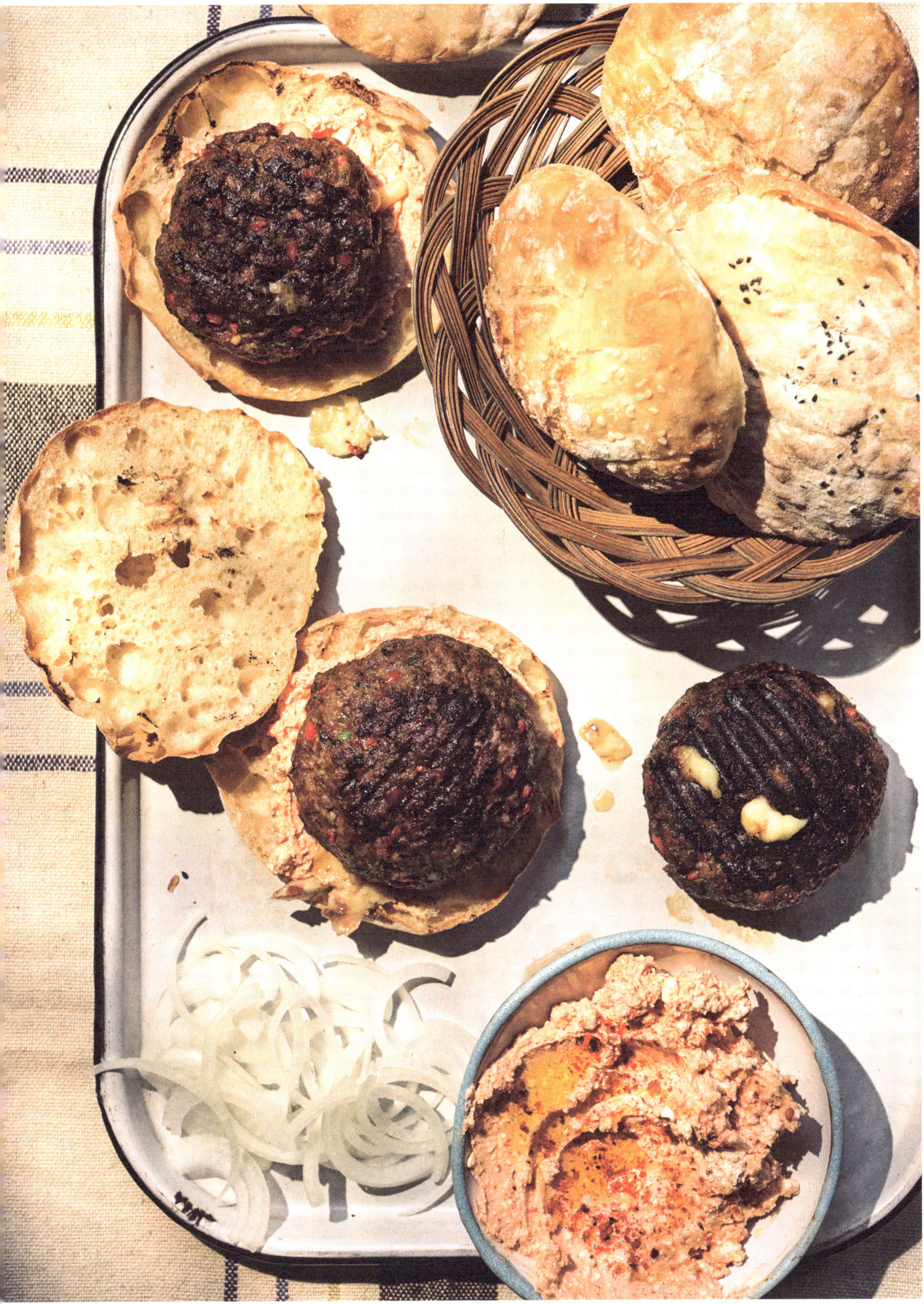

From Vardar to (Not Quite) Triglav

'Jugoslavijo' is a famous song written in 1974 by Milutin Popović Zahar and Danilo Živković. It includes the line 'Od Vardara pa do Triglava', in reference to the geographical span and diversity of the former Yugoslavia. In the early 1980s, it also became the (ironic) name of an album by the rock band Riblja Čorba. It was a phrase that was very much part of the collective consciousness of Yugoslavia – for some a positive, for many a negative.

The Vardar River flows though North Macedonia and Greece, eventually emptying out into the Aegean Sea. In the context of Yugoslavia, it symbolised the southernmost part of the federation. Mount Triglav, the highest peak of Slovenia and the Julian Alps, symbolised the northernmost part of the federation. It was a phrase I had in mind when I started travelling across the former Yugoslavia to research this book. I did make it to the source of the Vardar River in Vrutok, but I must confess I never quite made it to Mount Triglav, preferring instead to eat my way around the (what I told myself were important) culinary basecamps of Bled and Bohinj. I was often asked – by family, friends, locals – what exactly I was looking for? I didn't know exactly. Retracing childhood memories and family stories? Looking for something pre-dating former Yugoslavia? Or what, if anything, was left of it? Finding something that never existed, which I desperately wished had? Simply reminding myself of the delicious food I knew was there? Or finding other hopeless idealists like me who believed that, as well as celebrating what is unique and local across the former Yugoslavia, there is a commonality between the people from Vardar to Triglav that can bring them together and that is worth remembering.

◆◆◆

On a late afternoon on an overcast autumn (fall) day, I am climbing to the summit of Tatićev Kamen in North Macedonia, to the Kokino archaeological site. I feel as if I am ascending a stairway to a castle in the clouds, one carved into the andesite remnants of a now extinct volcano. I reach one of the four east-facing 'thrones' of what is thought to have been a sacred Bronze Age megalithic observatory. I can see why: mountainous horizon greets me in every direction I turn, and with sudden and unexpected trepidation I realise how high above that horizon I seem to be.

From the Land

My mother and I had come here on a whim – a short diversion after visiting family in Kumanovo, where my grandmother grew up. We drive past wild rose bushes bejewelled with rosehips. 'These are the kinds of rosehips your great-grandmother used to make rosehip jam,' my mother tells me, as I confess my frustration at not being able to make jam from rosehips foraged in urban London that approximates the flavour preserved in my memory. Suddenly there are oak trees – tall, resplendent, ancient. Nearing Kokino, we pass Staro Nagoričane, a small village with an 11th-century Byzantine church. My mother tells me that my great-great-grandfather, Milan, came from here. I had no idea! I am overwhelmed with the thought of him – us, me! – being descendants of the ancient inhabitants of Kokino.

Slowly I start to retrace my steps. As I turn west, I notice rays of sunlight puncturing the clouds. The sun breaks through and I am filled with inexplicable joy. The yellowed grass on the slopes, burnt by that same sun throughout summer, suddenly glimmers, golden, as if touched by Midas. I am reminded of all my summers here, the landscape like a painting etched in my mind, which I carry with me anywhere I go in the world. I think of all my other ancestors – from or living in Skopje, Bitola, Kruševo, Thessaloniki, Sarajevo, Belgrade, Ljubljana – from Vardar to Triglav. I am of all these places, of all these lands. Wherever I go, I am Balkan, and I am home.

From the Land

**MAKES
20–24 PIECES
(SERVES 4–6)**

Ćevapi

350 g (12 oz) very finely minced (ground) beef or veal (at least 10% fat)
150 g (5½ oz) very finely minced (ground) lamb
½ teaspoon freshly ground black pepper
½ teaspoon vegetable bouillon powder
1 teaspoon smoked sea salt
½ teaspoon bicarbonate of soda (baking soda)
1 onion, minced or grated
1 teaspoon sunflower oil, plus extra for brushing

FOR THE BUKOVO PEPPER SALT
1 tablespoon Bukovo pepper (or Aleppo pepper)
1 tablespoon smoked sea salt
½ teaspoon ground celery seeds (optional)

Ćevapi, also known diminuitvely as *ćevapčići* (in Bosnian, Croatian and Serbian) and *kebapčinja* (in Macedonian) are the iconic skinless, finger-sized sausages loved across the entire region. Usually made from any mixture of minced (ground) meat (beef, lamb or pork, depending on where you are in the region and on religious preference). They are considered the national dish of Bosnia and Herzegovina, but are eaten all over the region, always with *Somun* (see page 66) or *lepinja*. Some love them with *ajvar* or with *kaymak*. I grew up eating them very simply with freshly baked *lepinja*, sliced raw onion and a Bukovo pepper salt, always accompanied by chargrilled long sweet (or spicy) peppers and fresh *shopska* salad. The secret is to use very good quality meat, ground very finely – either ask your butcher to grind your meat at least twice or use a meat grinder if you have one. The best cuts of meat to use for this are chuck or flank (for beef) or neck or breast (for lamb). I often make this the night before to allow the seasoning to penetrate the meat and for the onion to tenderise it. Any form of grilled meat in the Balkans would have traditionally been cooked over smokeless embers using the old wood from grape vines or olive trees, or fig leaves, giving it a very unique flavour.

Combine all the ingredients in a large bowl and knead with your hands for 5–6 minutes until well combined and soft. Place the meat mixture in a lightly oiled piping bag. Ideally, allow the mixture to rest overnight in the refrigerator, or for as long as you can, but you can use it straightaway if you don't have time.

When you are ready to cook, cut the end off the piping bag so you have a hole with a diameter of 1–1.5 cm (½–¾ inch). Pipe out the sausage mixture onto a clean tray or baking sheet and use kitchen scissors to cut it at intervals of 8–10 cm (3¼–4 inches) to create uniform sausages. Finish shaping them with your hands a little, if necessary. Brush the sausages with a little oil, then grill on a barbecue for 4–6 minutes until nicely browned and cooked through but still moist. Alternatively, grill the sausages under a hot grill (broiler) or cook them in the oven at 200°C fan (425°F) for 10–12 minutes, rotating the them occasionally so that they brown evenly on all sides.

Serve with *somun*, *kajmak*, *ajvar* or *ljutenitsa*, sliced onions and grilled peppers, and the Bukovo pepper salt on the side.

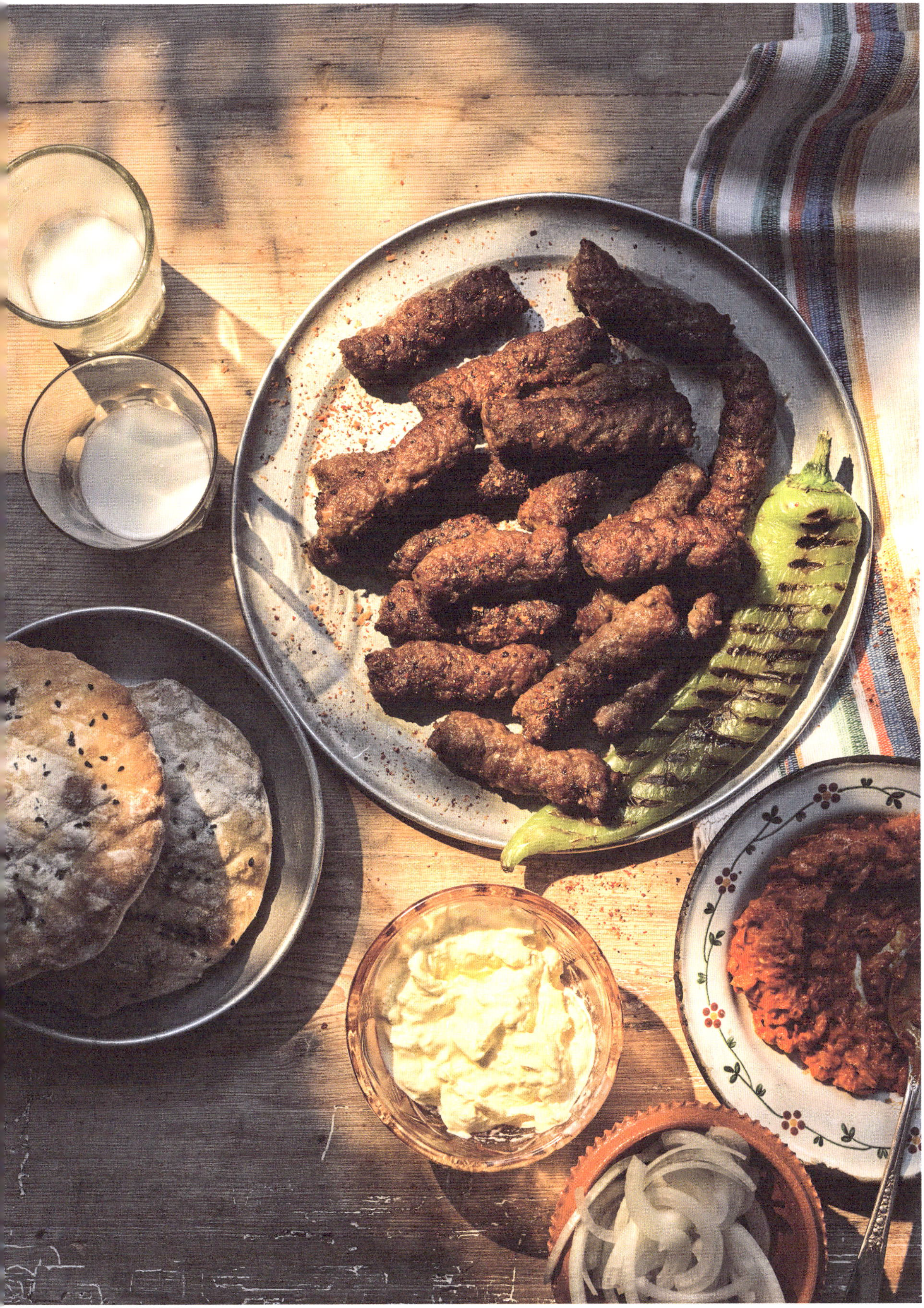

SERVES 4-6

Ražnjići

800 g–1kg (1 lb 12 oz–2 lb 4 oz) pork tenderloin, trimmed and cut into 2 cm (¾ inch) thick medallions

1 eating (dessert) apple, cored and cut into 2 cm (¾ inch) cubes

4–6 prune plums, halved and stoned

1 red onion, halved and thinly sliced, then soaked in ice-cold water for 30 seconds and drained

20g (1 oz) fresh parsley (or other soft herbs such as oregano, mint or coriander), leaves and tender stems picked

1 tablespoon olive oil

1 tablespoon apple cider vinegar

FOR THE MARINADE

2 tablespoons olive oil

3 tablespoons apple cider vinegar

30 g (1 oz) pitted prunes

3–4 garlic cloves

¼ teaspoon fennel seeds

¼ teaspoon freshly ground black pepper

½ teaspoon smoked sea salt

1 teaspoon vegetable bouillon powder

In Serbian and Croatian, *ražanj* means a barbecue spit or skewer, so *ražnjići* are meat skewers or kebabs, and are our equivalent to the better-known Greek *souvlaki* or Turkish *şaşlık*. There are many variants and different meats can be used to make them, but typically they are made from veal or pork or a mix of both, and are nothing more complicated than very good quality meat, grilled over live fire, salted and served with sliced onions. My version takes inspiration from the Balkan autumn (fall), always abundant with fruits: quinces, pears, medlars, apples and, the most highly prized of all, prune plums. Plums are used plentifully in the Balkan kitchen, both fresh and dried (or otherwise preserved), especially with meat dishes. I like to imagine a warm autumn sun setting, rows of *ražnjići* on a *rostilj* set up in the middle of the orchard, plumes of smoke caressing the now-naked apple or plum trees stripped of their fruit, the scent of the meat taunting everyone while they sit and rest a little from the harvest, eagerly awaiting some much-needed sustenance, and relaxing with a fortifying glass of *šljivovica* (plum brandy).

First, make the marinade. Combine all the ingredients in a food processor and blend to a fine paste.

Put the pork into a large container (for which you have a lid), add the marinade and toss to coat, then cover and either marinate in the refrigerator overnight or at room temperature for at least 1 hour.

Thread the marinated pork onto metal skewers (or wooden skewers that have been soaked in water for 30 minutes), interspersing them with the pieces of apple and plum.

Toss the onions with the herbs and the oil and cider vinegar and set aside.

Grill the *ražnjići* on a hot barbecue (or under the grill/broiler in your oven on the highest setting) for 3–4 minutes on each side, until the pork is cooked through. Rest for 5 minutes before serving with the onions.

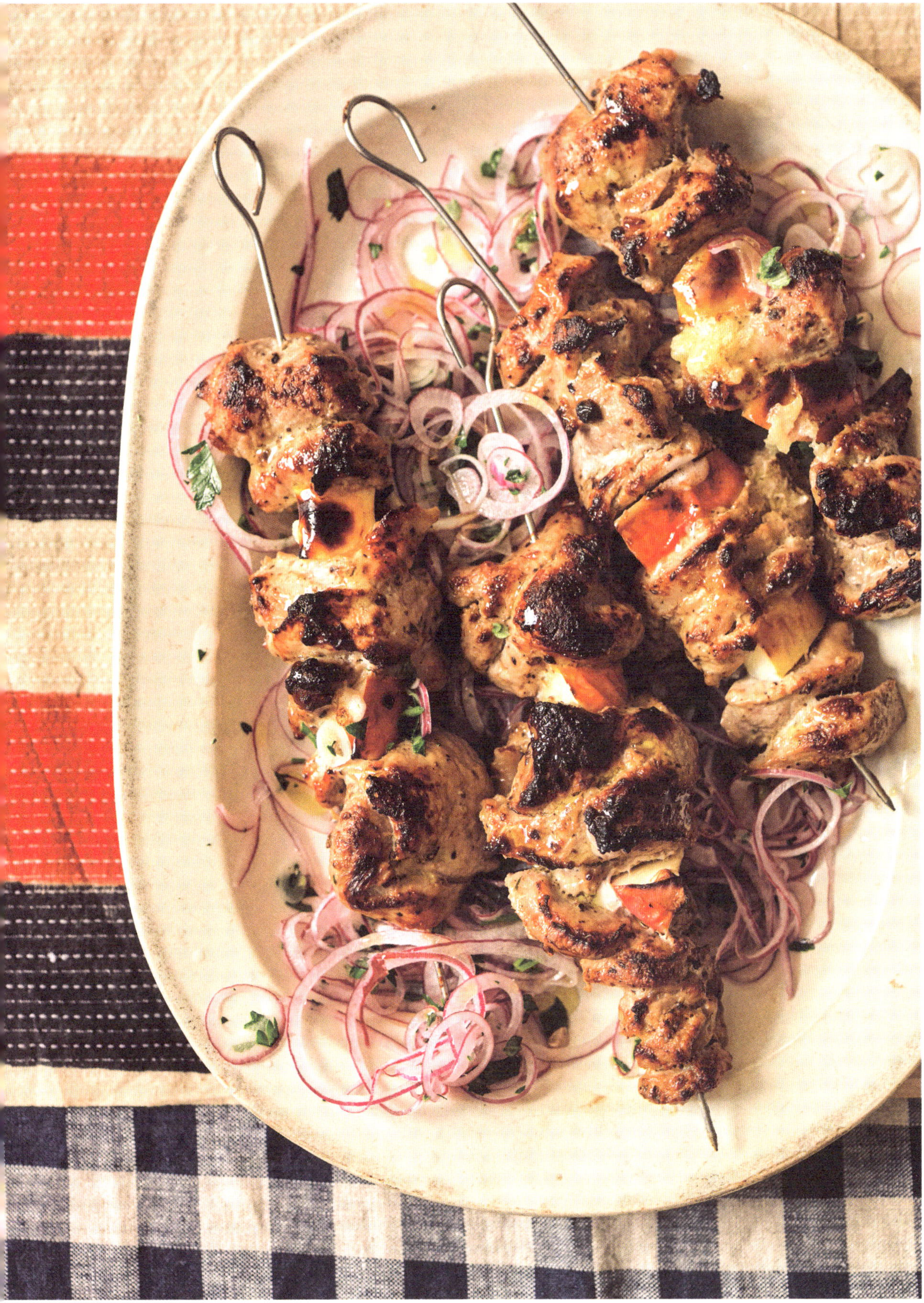

Fish and seafood is artfully integrated into the culinary heritage of the Balkans, which includes a wealth of delicacies that reflect the natural conditions and topographical diversity of the region.

Along Croatia's stunning coastline, seafood dishes showcase the freshness and abundance of the Adriatic Sea as well as local knowledge in preparation and cooking. The Adriatic Sea has an incredibly bountiful and diverse marine life. Some of the most notable native species used in the cuisine include *orada* (sea bream), which is grilled or roasted and sometimes used in soups; *lubin* (a type of sea bass), often grilled whole or filleted and highly prized for its delicate flavour and tender flesh; *sardela* (sardines), a staple of Dalmatian cuisine; *skuša* (mackerel), often smoked, grilled or pickled and used in a variety of ways, but particularly delicious in Dalmatian *pašticada*; *škarpina* (scorpionfish), as delicious as it is unusual-looking and particularly loved in fish stews; *riba-žabac* or *poša* (monkfish), prized for its firm and succulent meat and used in broths, stews, or grilled; *girici* (tiny fish, a type of whitebait); and cuttlefish, squid and octopus. Catch of the day is often simply seasoned with olive oil, salt and pepper, then grilled over live fire, with the result being a tender, smoky fish that captures the essence of the sea – *sardele na gradele* (grilled sardines) are a particularly delicious example of this. Some prefer their catch of the day coated in a light dusting of flour, dried herbs and seasoning and then fried. There are so many delicious dishes to choose from: *hobotnica* (octopus) salad, *crni rižot* (black risotto), *punjene lignje* (stuffed squid) and the iconic seafood stews, from Brudet to *Hvarska gregada*. Also notable is *buzara*, an sauce of garlic, white wine, tomato and parsley. You will rarely go wrong eating in a small *konoba* (guest house) along the Adriatic if you ask for the catch of the day and for the chef to cook it as they would for themselves.

FROM THE WATER
VODA

Montenegro's dramatic coastline offers an equally incredible selection of fish and seafood but is particularly famed for its mussels, which are farmed on ropes all around the naturally deep Bay of Kotor. Montenegro also benefits from access to inland freshwater fish to use in dishes such as *riba u maramicama* (fish in handkerchiefs), in which the fish of Lake Skadar are salt-cured or pickled in vinegar and herbs and then enjoyed as snacks or as accompaniments to main meals; *pečena ciplja* (baked bleak), which sees the small, silvery fish marinated in olive oil, garlic and herbs before baking; *jegulja s palentom* (eel with polenta), where the eel is simply grilled or roasted and served with creamy polenta – now rare given the need to protect and conserve eel stocks; and *dimljena riba* (smoked Lake Skadar fish).

Further inland and away from the glamour of the Adriatic coastline, landlocked parts of the Balkans are interwoven by fresh water: streams, rivers, lakes, waterfalls. In these areas, freshwater fish like *mekousna pastrmka* (brown trout), *pastrmka* (rainbow trout), *štuka* (European pike), *šaran* (carp), *som* (catfish), *studena* (tench), *mrena* (chub) and *lipljan* (grayling) reign supreme.

In Serbia, carp and catfish feature heavily in hearty stews and *riblja čorba* (fish soup). They are also smoked or cured and then used in a variety of dishes, one lovely example of *sarma*, made by stuffing dried red peppers with a mixture of flaked smoked carp, rice and herbs, typically prepared for periods of religious fasting. Similarly, in Bosnia and Herzegovina, freshwater fish are prominent, also often prepared as fish soup or grilled, pan-fried or roasted, as well being used for *uštipci s ribom* (small fishcakes). *Saran u rašljama* features carp butterflied and then grilled on a skewer, creating a striking dish. *Pastrmka na kamenici* involves stuffing rainbow trout with vegetables before baking it in a *kamenica* (stone oven).

Slovenia is particularly famous for its *Soška postrv* (Soča trout), a species of trout indigenous and unique to the area of the Soča River, which is highly prized for its delicate flavour and firm, pinkish flesh. It is often prepared very simply, grilled or pan-fried with olive oil, fresh herbs and lemon. The Soča trout is subject to significant conservation efforts to protect its habitat and safeguard its population.

Similar conservation efforts are in place in North Macedonia's Lake Ohrid, one of the oldest and most biologically diverse freshwater lakes in the world. It's home to a wide variety of fish species, some of which are endemic, including *Ohridska pastrmka* (Lake Ohrid trout), *belvica* (a small fish native to Lake Ohrid and connected rivers), *voultcharka* (an Ohrid nase or souffia), *pelic* (a type of roach), eel and other types of trout. Lake Ohrid trout is now a protected species due to its vulnerable status as a result of overfishing, pollution and habitat degradation, and consuming it is prohibited – though enforcement of this on both the Macedonian and Albanian sides of Lake Ohrid is … lax. Traditionally prized for its delicate flavour, Ohrid trout is either simply grilled, baked or fried and served on a bed of grilled onions. Its roe was once used for Ohrid-style fish soup – ground up with flour, herbs and various spices, then loosened with stock and padded out with flaked pieces of fish to a desired thickness. Ohrid locals now prefer *belvica* – a more sustainable species and thought to be tastier. In Ohrid, eel was prepared by baking it in an earthenware pot under ashen coals or by being smoked – but again, eels are subject to conservation efforts and there are eel passes at certain points in Lake Ohrid to improve eel migration.

Feel free to substitute the fish used in this chapter according to your personal preference and what is available where you live. I do recommend informing yourself on the latest sustainability criteria for fish and seafood.

SERVES 4-6 AS A STARTER OR SIDE SALAD

Octopus Salad with Blood Orange Dressing

4–6 octopus tentacles (about 600 g/ 1 lb 5 oz total)

1 small onion, quartered

2 bay leaves

¼ teaspoon black peppercorns

500 g (1 lb 2 oz) new potatoes, scrubbed

1 fennel bulb, thinly sliced (reserve the fronds for serving)

1 red onion, halved and thinly sliced, then soaked in ice-cold water for 1 minute and drained

20 g (¾ oz) fresh parsley, leaves and tender stems picked and roughly chopped

20 g (¾ oz) fresh mint leaves, finely sliced

sea salt

FOR THE BLOOD ORANGE DRESSING

2 blood oranges

2 tablespoons lemon juice

2 garlic cloves, crushed

90 ml (3 fl oz/⅓ cup) extra virgin olive oil

½ teaspoon Dijon mustard

1–2 sprigs of fresh thyme, leaves picked

½ teaspoon sea salt flakes

freshly ground black pepper

Octopus salad is an iconic Dalmatian treat. Usually as simple as octopus and boiled potatoes with a simple vinaigrette, this is my take on it.

First, make the dressing. Start by segmenting the oranges. Slice the tops and tails off each orange, then follow the curve to cut away the skin and pith. Holding them over a small bowl to capture all the juices, slice between the membranes to release the segments. Set them aside on a plate. With your hand, squeeze the leftover membranes to obtain all the juice.

Pour 2 tablespoons of the orange juice into a jar (reserving the rest to drink), then add the lemon juice, garlic, oil, mustard, thyme, salt and a generous grind of black pepper. Seal the jar and shake until the dressing emulsifies.

Next, cook the octopus. Put the octopus tentacles into a medium saucepan with the onion, bay leaves and peppercorns. Bring to the boil over a medium-high heat, then reduce the heat and simmer for 25–30 minutes until the octopus is tender. Drain, discarding the aromatics, and then peel off as much of the octopus skin as you can. Slice the tentacles into 1 cm (½ inch) thick rounds.

Meanwhile, cook the potatoes in boiling salted water for about 20 minutes until tender, then drain. While they are still hot, slice them into 1 cm (½ inch) thick rounds, place in a large bowl with half the dressing and mix well.

Transfer the potatoes to a serving bowl or platter and arrange the fennel, onion, orange segments and octopus over them. Spoon over the remaining dressing and scatter the herbs over the top.

Note

You can also grill the octopus tentacles on the barbecue if you prefer.

From the Water

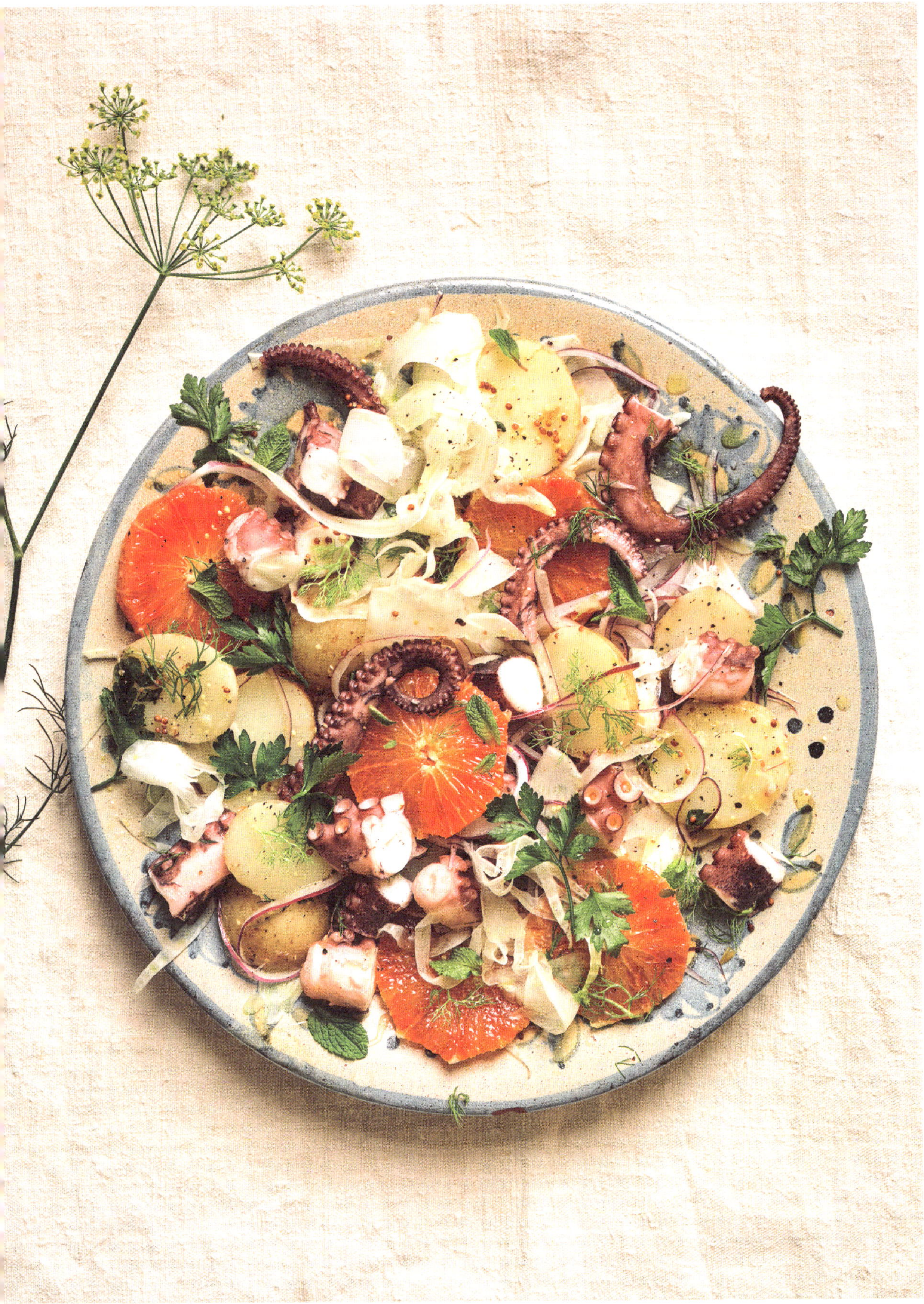

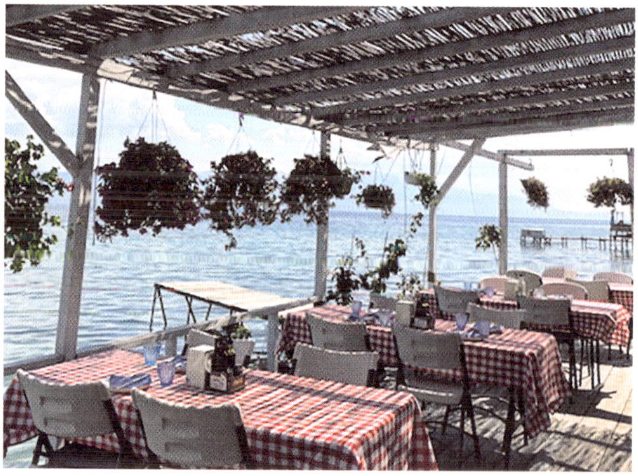

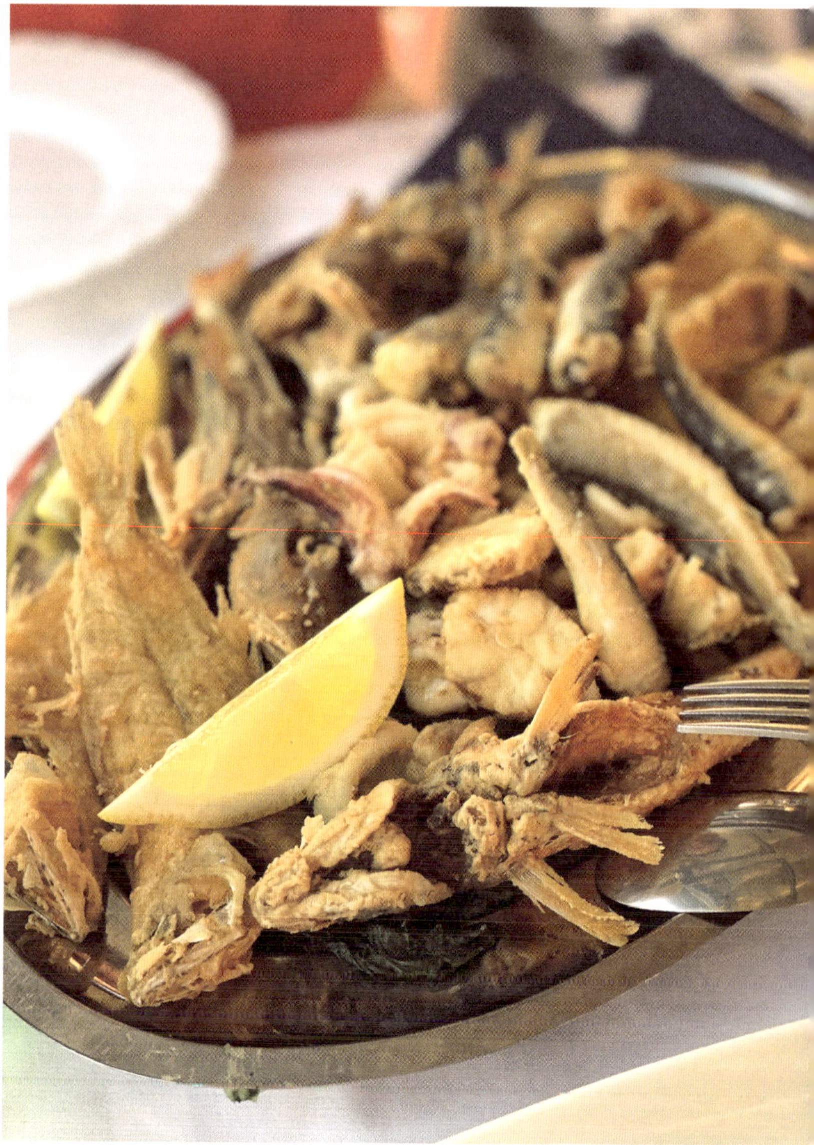

Trout with Avgolemono Sauce and Blitva

SERVES 4

FOR THE AVGOLEMONO SAUCE
- 2 medium eggs
- ¼ teaspoon sea salt flakes
- 60 ml (2 fl oz/¼ cup) lemon juice plus 1 tablespoon zest
- 300 ml (10 fl oz/1¼ cups) warm fish stock
- 20 g (¾ oz) fresh dill, fronds picked and finely chopped, plus extra to serve
- 1 tablespoon lemon-infused olive oil or extra virgin olive oil, to serve (optional)
- freshly ground black pepper

FOR THE BLITVA
- 1 large floury potato, such as Russet (about 200 g/7 oz), peeled and cut into 3–4 cm (1¼–1½ inch) pieces
- ½ teaspoon sea salt flakes, plus extra for boiling the potatoes and to serve
- 2 tablespoons extra virgin olive oil, plus extra to serve
- 500 g (1 lb 2 oz) young Swiss chard, stalks separated and chopped into 1 cm (½ inch) pieces, leaves roughly chopped
- 2–3 garlic cloves, crushed

FOR THE FISH
- 4 trout fillets, skin on
- 2 tablespoons olive oil
- sea salt and freshly ground black pepper
- lemon wedges, to serve

This dish is my fusion of the Balkan freshwater hinterland and coast, of the Adriatic and Aegean. Across the Balkans, fish are often simply coated in seasoned (and sometimes herbed) flour and then fried or grilled. *Avgolemono* (Greek for 'egg-lemon') is one of the most important Greek sauces. Used to finish any number of Greek dishes – chicken soup, meatballs, *dolmades* and so on – it is also used extensively in Balkan, Jewish, Levantine and Italian cuisine (and beyond). In the Balkans we tend to use it to thicken soups, but I love using it as a light and lemony sauce for fish. *Blitva* (Swiss chard) is the cornerstone of Dalmatian cooking, but is loved across all of Croatia, especially the coastal parts. *Blitva na lešo*, which simply means 'cooked *blitva*', is typically padded out with boiled potatoes and accompanies all of Croatia's iconic seafood but works particularly well with fried or grilled white fish and crustaceans. How *blitva* is prepared is a matter of taste; I like it heavy on the Swiss chard and garlic and easy on the potato. Young Swiss chard with thin stalks is best for this as it is less bitter, and you will not have to bother with separating leaves and stalks.

First, make the sauce. Whisk the eggs with the salt in a bowl until frothy. Add the lemon juice and keep whisking. Slowly add some of the warm stock to temper the eggs, whisking constantly as you do. It is important that the stock is warm but not too hot or else you will scramble the eggs. Continue to add the stock, and once it is all incorporated, transfer the mixture to a medium saucepan and cook over a medium-high heat, whisking constantly, for 8–10 minutes, or until the sauce has thickened to a double cream consistency. Add the zest, dill and a good grind of black pepper, then taste and adjust the seasoning as needed. Cover and set aside.

To make the *blitva*, put the potatoes into a large saucepan, cover with cold water, add a pinch of salt and then bring to a simmer over a medium-high heat. Cook for 10–12 minutes, or until cooked through. Meanwhile, heat the oil in a frying pan over a medium-high heat. Add the chard stalks and cook for 4–6 minutes, until the stalks are just starting to soften. Add the garlic and chard leaves and cook for a further 2–3 minutes until the leaves are just wilted but retaining their colour. Remove the potatoes with a slotted spoon and add them to the chard with 1–2 tablespoons of the potato cooking liquid. Add the salt and a generous grind of black pepper, then use a fork to roughly mash together until some of the potato falls apart but retains some texture. Spread the mixture over a serving plate, then drizzle with oil and sprinkle with salt.

Once the sauce and *blitva* are ready, cook the trout. Season the fillets with salt and pepper. Heat the oil in a non-stick frying pan over a medium-high heat and add the fillets to the pan, skin side down. Cook for 3–4 minutes until the skin is nice and crispy, then flip and fry for 30–60 seconds until cooked. Transfer to serving plates, add a squeeze of lemon, then spoon the *avgolemono* around each. Drizzle with a little oil and scatter some dill over the fish and serve the *blitva* on the side.

Note

You can roast or grill the fish if you prefer. Alternatively, use hot-smoked trout fillets.

SERVES 4

A Bream of the Seas

850 g–1 kg (1 lb 13¾ oz–2 lb 4 oz) wild sea bream, cleaned and descaled
2 lemons, sliced
10 g (½ oz) fresh parsley, leaves and tender stems picked, plus extra to serve
6–8 garlic cloves, quartered lengthwise
1 fennel bulb, trimmed and cut into wedges (no more than 2 cm/¾ inches thick)
1–2 beef (beefsteak) tomatoes, thickly sliced
100 g (3½ oz/⅔ cup) pitted kalamata olives, halved
½ teaspoon dried oregano
60 ml (2 fl oz/¼ cup) extra virgin olive oil
10 g (½ oz) fresh oregano, leaves picked, to serve
sea salt and freshly ground black pepper

This dish is quite simply a combination of some of my favourite ingredients from the Adriatic, Mediterranean and Aegean and, as such, it always transports me to the sea. It is very much a summertime dish, to be enjoyed on a balmy evening with a cool glass of white wine.

Preheat the oven to 190°C fan (400°F).

Using a sharp knife, score the skin of the bream on both sides. Sprinkle a pinch of salt and pepper all over and inside the cavity of the fish, then stuff 1–2 lemon slices, some of the parsley and some of the garlic inside.

Arrange the remaining lemon slices (squeezing some as you do), parsley, garlic, the fennel, tomatoes and olives in a large roasting tin. Place the bream on top, sprinkle everything with another pinch of salt and a good grind of black pepper, then sprinkle over the oregano and drizzle over the olive oil.

Roast in the oven for 25–30 minutes until the fennel is tender and the sea bream is cooked through and the skin is starting to crisp up. Scatter a little more parsley and oregano over the top to serve.

From the Water

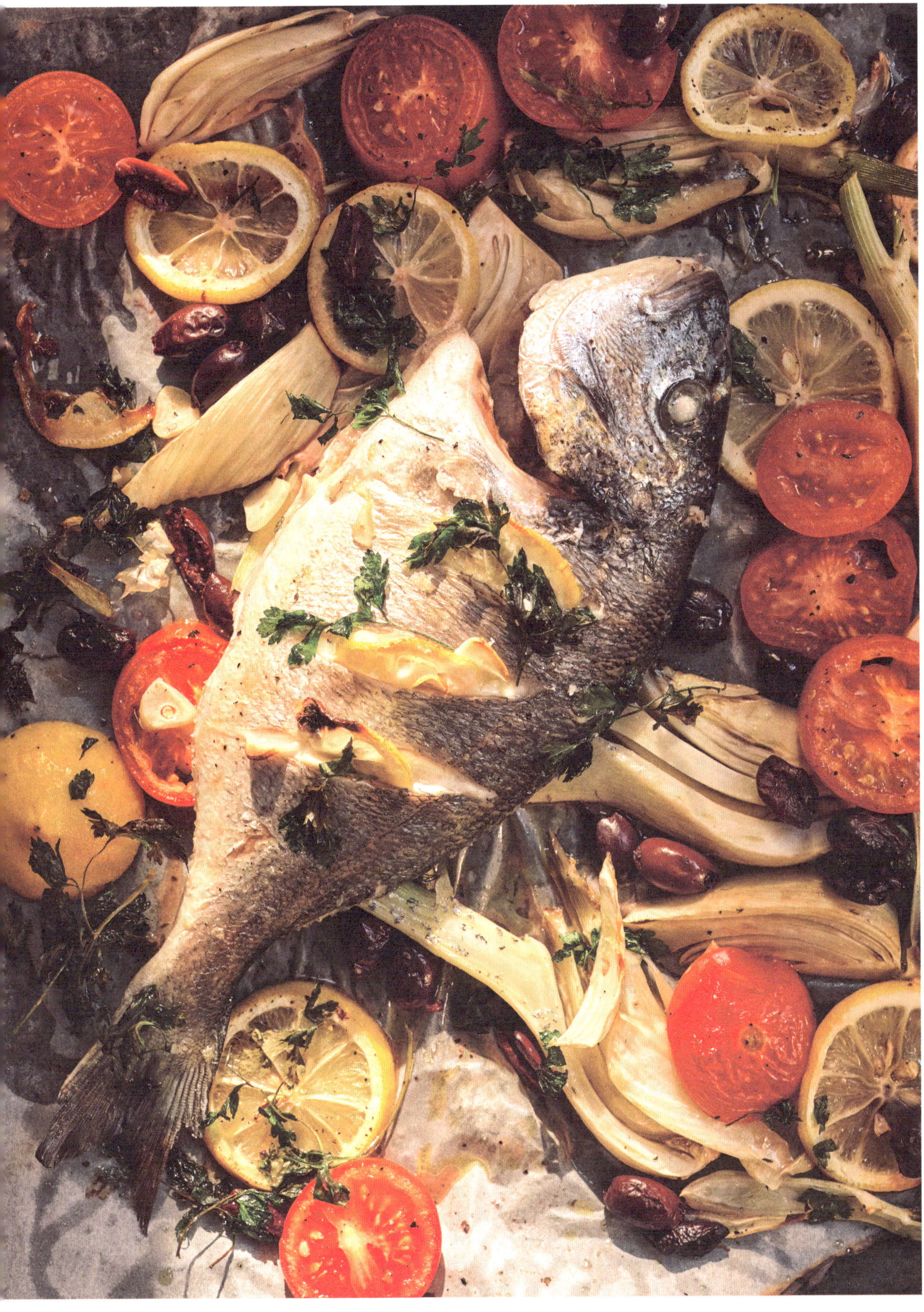

SERVES 4

Fish in Fig Leaves

12–16 fresh fig or vine leaves, washed and destalked

4 x 150 g (5½ oz) skinless cod loins or fillets

½ teaspoon salt, plus extra as needed

1 tablespoon lemon zest plus 2 tablespoons juice and wedges to serve

4–5 garlic cloves, crushed

3 tablespoons extra virgin olive oil

20 g (¾ oz) fresh soft herbs, such as parsley, dill and/or mint, leaves/fronds picked and finely chopped

freshly ground black pepper

This is an incredibly easy and effective way to cook fish that is found all over the Adriatic (particularly Dalmatia), the Aegean and the Eastern Mediterranean, again with delicious local variations. It works particularly well cooked over fire, but it is just as good when baked as parcels in the oven. The fig and vine leaves impart their own very distinctive and delicate flavours on the fish. For me, white fish like cod, sea bass or bream work beautifully with fig, and oilier fish, like mackerel or sardines, work well with vine leaves. You can do whole fish this way, too – just adjust the cooking time according to the size of your fish. I also love cooking *sirenje* or feta wrapped in fig leaves. Anything goes and I encourage you to experiment!

Blanch the fig or vine leaves in boiling water for 2 minutes, then drain and rinse under cold running water. Set aside.

Pat the fish dry with paper towels and season on both sides with a pinch of salt and a good grind of black pepper. Set aside.

Next, combine the lemon zest and juice, garlic, salt, a good grind of black pepper, oil and herbs in a small bowl and whisk well to combine.

Lay three or four fig or vine leaves in a large circle so they overlap (veins facing upwards). Place 1 teaspoon of the lemon and herb mixture in the centre, then place a piece of cod on top. Spoon 2 teaspoons of lemon and herb mixture over the cod. Wrap the fish with the leaves and tie securely with kitchen twine. Repeat with the remaining fish.

If using the barbecue, grill for 3–4 minutes on each side or until the leaves begin to scorch. If using the oven, grill (broil) under a high heat for 4–5 minutes, turning over halfway, until the leaves begin to scorch, or roast in the oven at 180°C fan (400°F) for about 20 minutes.

Serve with the lemon wedges alongside.

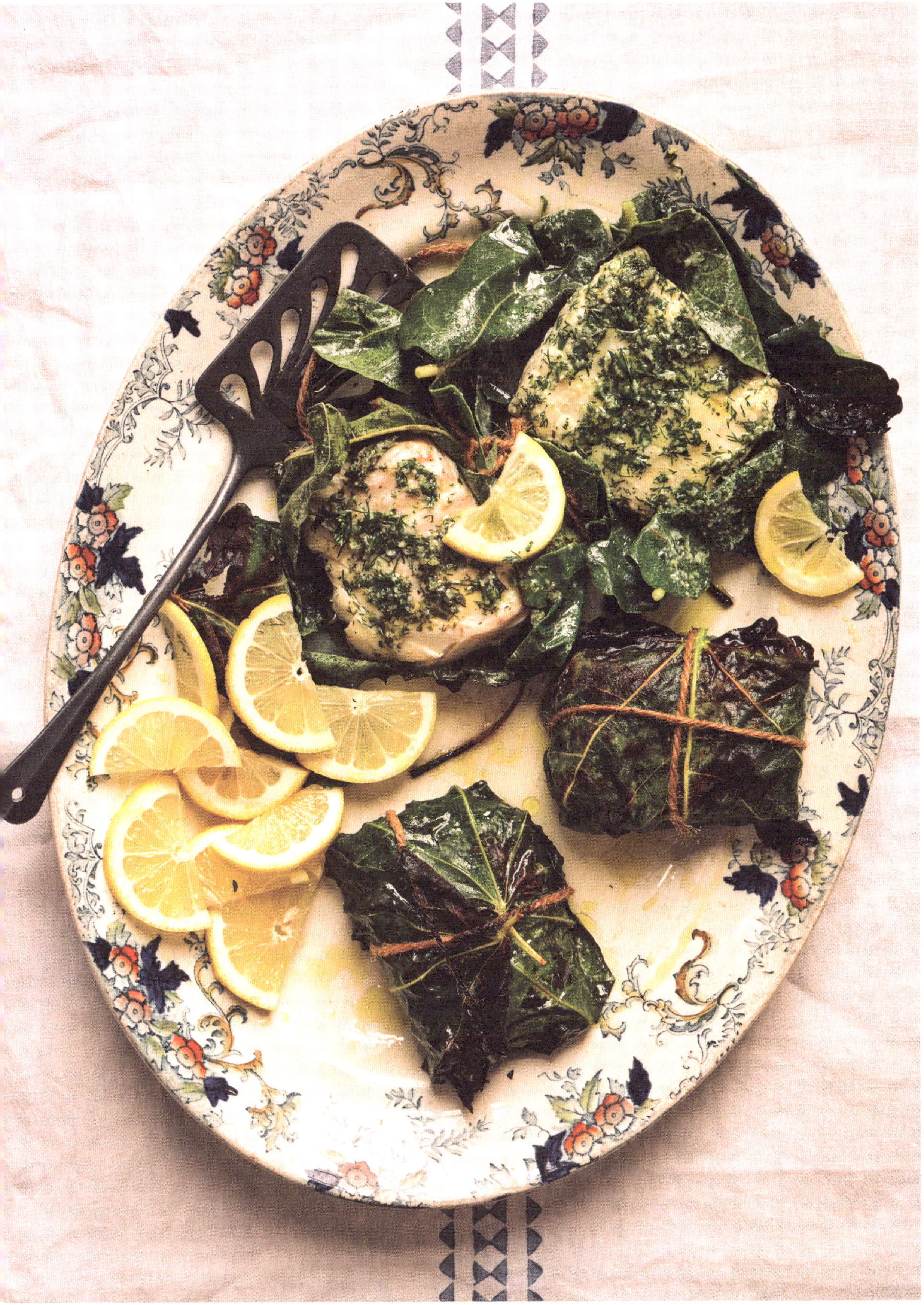

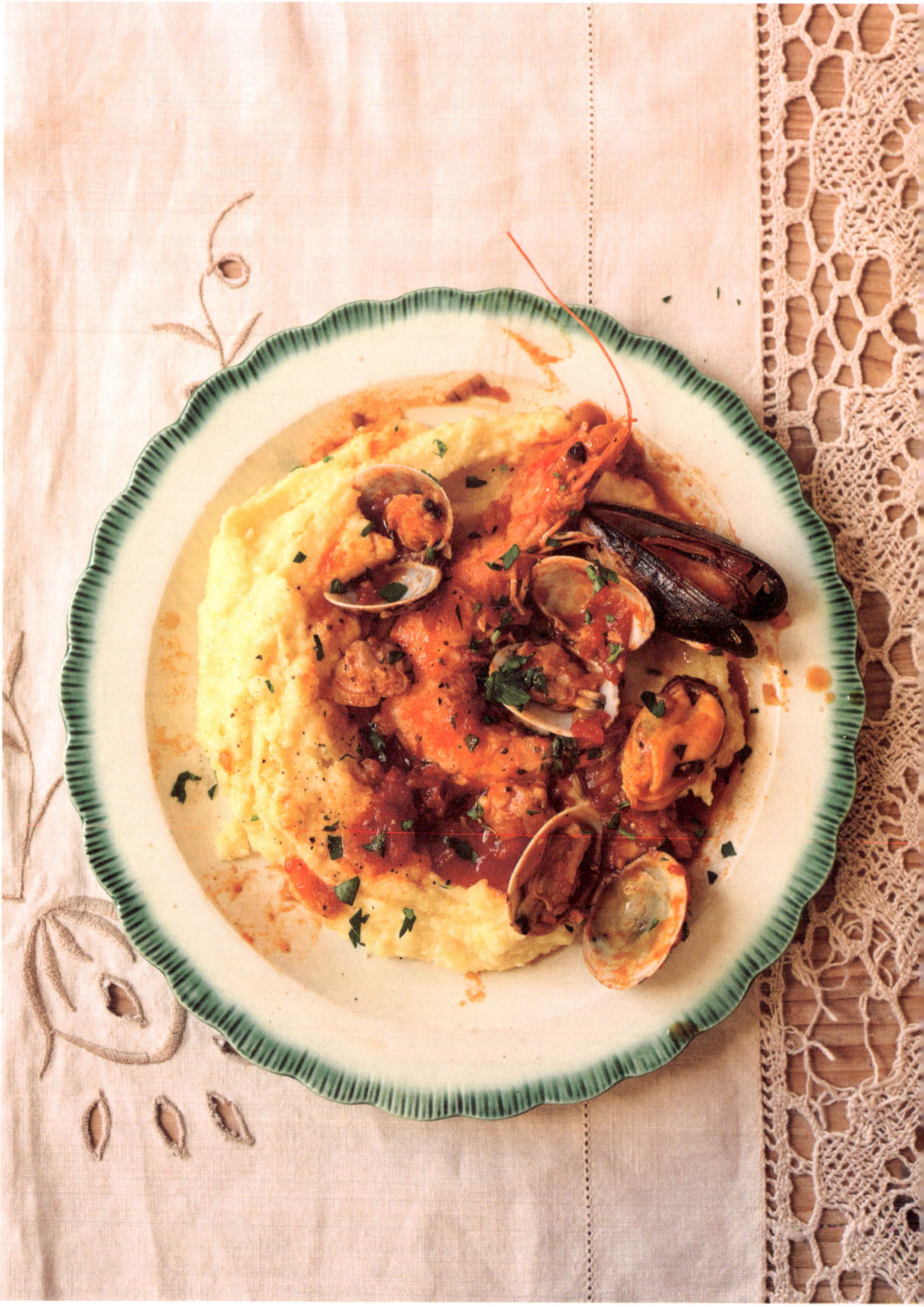

SERVES 4-6

Brodet

3 tablespoons extra virgin olive oil
1 onion, finely chopped
5–6 garlic cloves, finely chopped
½ teaspoon fennel seeds
1 lemon, 2–3 strips of zest pared, then sliced into wedges to serve
1 bay leaf
2 tablespoons tomato purée (paste)
1 x 400 g (14 oz) tin plum tomatoes (or 2–3 ripe tomatoes, roughly chopped)
100 ml (3½ fl oz/scant ½ cup) fish stock
75 ml (2½ fl oz/5 tablespoons) dry white wine (or Croatian prošek)
1 teaspoon sea salt flakes
2 tablespoons white wine vinegar
1 kg (2 lb 4 oz) mixed fish and seafood (at least three different varieties, including firm white fish, such as monkfish, and prawns/shrimp, clams, mussels, squid or cuttlefish)
20 g (¾ oz) fresh parsley, leaves picked and finely chopped, plus extra to serve
freshly ground black pepper

FOR THE POLENTA
35 g (1¼ oz) unsalted butter
700 ml (24 fl oz/scant 3 cups) fish or vegetable stock, or more if you prefer your polenta looser
2 teaspoons sea salt flakes
200 g (7 oz/1⅓ cups) quick-cook polenta (cornmeal)
2 tablespoons extra virgin olive oil
freshly ground black pepper

Brodet or *brudet* is a fish stew that for me encapsulates the Adriatic Sea. Eaten in Croatia (Dalmatia, Kvarner and Istria predominantly, but all along the coast) and Montenegro, it is a very close relative of the Italian *brodetto* eaten on the other side of the Adriatic. There are as many variants of it as there are Adriatic islands. Perhaps more. Each family has their own preference of fish, flavours and slight variations of method. Some fry the fish before making the sauce, others do not. On the Dalmatian islands, you are more likely to find it with octopus, cuttlefish and conger eel. On the mainland, you will find it made with reef fish like grouper and scorpionfish. In Montenegro, it will be very likely to include mussels, if they are in season. Really, anything goes, and the only rule is to use the catch of the day and at least three different varieties of fish or seafood. It is almost always accompanied by a bowl of golden polenta.

Heat the oil in a large sauté pan for which you have a lid over a medium heat. Add the onion and sweat, with the lid on but stirring occasionally, for 10–12 minutes, or until soft and translucent. Add the garlic, fennel seeds, lemon zest strips, bay leaf and tomato purée and cook, stirring constantly, for 1 minute until you smell the garlic and the onions are well-coated in the tomato purée. Add the tomatoes (swilling out the tin with a splash of water if using tinned), the stock, wine, salt and a good grind of black pepper. Cook, uncovered, stirring occasionally and crushing the tomatoes as you do, for 10–12 minutes, or until the tomatoes have broken down and the sauce has thickened and reduced by at least half.

Next, add the vinegar and your fish and seafood of choice. Cover with the lid and cook for 18–20 minutes, or until the fish is cooked through but still firm. If you are using clams or mussels, add these 5–6 minutes before the end and discard any that have not opened up after this time. Do not stir or you will break up the fish – just give the pan a gentle shake from time to time.

Take off the heat, remove the bay leaf and stir in the parsley.

Meanwhile, prepare the polenta. Put the butter, stock, salt and a good grind of black pepper into a large saucepan over a medium-high heat. Bring to the boil, then reduce the heat to medium and slowly add the polenta, whisking as you do. Cook, continuously whisking, for 6–8 minutes (or according to the packet instructions) until the polenta is cooked through. Loosen with more stock, if you prefer a looser consistency. Add the olive oil and whisk to combine.

Spoon the polenta immediately into individual bowls and top with the *brodet*, extra parsley and a wedge of lemon.

From the Water

Mussels 'Buzara-style', Two Ways

SERVES 4-6

2 kg (4 lb 8 oz) mussels in shells
sea salt flakes
crusty bread, to serve

ON THE RED

3 tablespoons extra virgin olive oil
1 onion, finely chopped
¼ teaspoon sea salt flakes
3–4 garlic cloves, finely chopped
30 g (1 oz) fresh parsley, leaves and stalks finely chopped
250–300 g (9–10½ oz) ripe tomatoes, grated and skin discarded
1 tablespoon tomato purée (paste)
75 ml (2½ fl oz/5 tablespoons) dry white wine
freshly ground black pepper

ON THE WHITE

3 tablespoons extra virgin olive oil
1 onion, finely chopped
¼ teaspoon sea salt flakes
3–4 garlic cloves, finely chopped
30 g (1 oz) fresh parsley, leaves and stalks finely chopped
250 ml (8 fl oz/1 cup) dry white wine
1 lemon, sliced
freshly ground black pepper

FOR THE BREADCRUMB TOPPING

3 tablespoons extra virgin olive oil
2 garlic cloves, crushed
1 tablespoon lemon zest
1 tablespoon finely chopped fresh parsley
50g (1¾ oz/scant ½ cup) dried breadcrumbs (or Panko breadcrumbs)
sea salt flakes and freshly ground black pepper

The origin of the word *buzara* (or *busara* or *buzzara*) is unknown, but it is generally thought to come from the name of the *kotlic* (pot) used in the galley kitchens of ships sailing between Dalmatia and the Veneto. It is believed that fresh *škampe* (langoustines/scampi) were taken from the Kvarner Gulf via the Dalmatian port city of Fiume (modern-day Rijeka) to Venice, and that the Dalmatian style of preparing *škampe na buzaru* (with a sauce of olive oil, garlic, white wine, various herbs and spices and much later tomatoes, after their arrival in Europe from South America) inspired Venetian cooks to create *spaghetti alla busara*.

Nowadays, *buzara* simply refers to a technique for preparing seafood along the Eastern Adriatic – specifically in the coastal regions from Croatia down to Montenegro. Seafood *na buzara* ('on buzara' or 'buzara-style') is prepared with a flavourful sauce either 'on the white', meaning a sauce made without tomato, or 'on the red', with tomato. Some say that 'on the white' is superior, but I leave it up to you to choose. *Kvarnerske škampe* (Kvarner langoustines) are still prized for their incredible flavour and eaten *na buzara*, but so are other shellfish, such as mussels. I first ate mussels like this in Perast, having seen them growing on ropes all around Kotor Bay – an incredible sight underwater. They are perfect little vessels for the delicious sauce.

Put the mussels into a large bowl and rinse them under cold running water. Gently scrub the shells to clean them and pull away the 'beard' attached to the side of each mussel. Discard any mussels with a cracked shell. Gently tap any open mussels on the side of the bowl; if they remain open, discard them. Keep them in a bowl of ice-cold water while you make the breadcrumb topping and your chosen sauce.

To make the breadcrumb topping, heat the oil in a small saucepan over a medium heat. Add the garlic, lemon zest and parsley and cook for 1 minute, then add the breadcrumbs, a pinch of salt and a good grind of black pepper. Cook for 2–3 minutes, stirring continuously, until the breadcrumb mixture is crisp and golden brown. Transfer to a serving bowl and set aside.

For the 'on the red' sauce, heat the oil in a large saucepan over a medium heat. Add the onion and salt, cover with a lid and sweat, stirring occasionally, for 10–12 minutes until the onion is soft and translucent. If the onions start to stick, add a little water to loosen. Add the garlic and half the parsley and cook for 1 minute, then add the tomatoes, tomato purée and wine and simmer gently for 8–10 minutes. Finish with a good grind of black pepper.

For the 'on the white' sauce, heat the oil in a large saucepan over a medium heat. Add the onion and salt, cover with a lid and sweat, stirring occasionally, for 10–12 minutes until the onion is soft and translucent. If the onions start to stick, add 1 tablespoon water to loosen. Add the garlic and half the parsley and cook for 1 minute, then add the wine and simmer gently for 4–5 minutes. Add the lemon slices and a good grind of black pepper.

Whichever sauce you have chosen, at this point increase the heat to high, then add the mussels and immediately cover the pan with a tight-fitting lid. Cook for 5–6 minutes, shaking the pan gently occasionally to move the mussels around. Remove the lid to check if the mussels are all open. If most are still closed, cover and cook for a further 1–2 minutes until they have opened. Check for and discard any that have not.

Transfer the mussels to a large serving bowl, pour over the sauce and sprinkle with the rest of the parsley and half the breadcrumb topping, serving the rest alongside. Serve with crusty bread to dip into the cooking liquid.

From the Water

SERVES 4

Surf 'n' Turf Peka

60 ml (2 fl oz/¼ cup) extra virgin olive oil
4 x 200 g (7 oz) cross-cut veal shanks (about 2 cm/¾ inch thick)
¾ teaspoon sea salt flakes
¼ teaspoon freshly ground black pepper, plus extra as needed
1 kg (2 lb 4 oz) waxy potatoes, peeled and quartered
2 onions, quartered
3–4 carrots, peeled and cut into chunks
2–3 red bell peppers
4–6 garlic cloves
2 sprigs of rosemary
3–4 bay leaves
800g–1 kg (1 lb 12 oz –2 lb 4 oz) octopus tentacles
200 ml (7 fl oz/scant 1 cup) white wine
crusty bread, to serve

Peka is an integral part of Croatian culinary culture, and many would say Croatia's ultimate comfort food. The name comes from *peći* (to roast or bake), but refers to both a dish typically prepared with meat (veal, lamb or pork) or seafood (specifically octopus) and a variety of vegetables and herbs, as well as the eponymous bell-shaped cast-iron dome used to cook the dish. The dome is placed over a baking tray (pan) containing the prepared ingredients like a lid, and it is then covered with hot coals, which are held in place by a metal ring fitted around the dome. The *peka* cooks in the *komin* – the fireplace or outdoor wood-fired oven of a Croatian home – benefitting from the heat of the hearth below and the live fire around and over it, which gives the dish an incredible flavour.

Peka is especially popular for family or social gatherings, and its beauty lies in the simplicity of the ingredients and the art of managing the heat around the *komin* to bring the most out of them through slow-cooking. This version combines both the inland (meat) and coastal (seafood) versions of *peka*, and is my attempt to replicate – at least a little – the flavour at home without the benefit of a Croatian *komin* or a *peka*. Feel free to adjust the quantities of the vegetables and herbs to your preference.

Preheat the oven to 200°C fan (425°F).

Brush the base of a large cast-iron casserole dish (Dutch oven) with 2 tablespoons of the oil. Season the veal with ¼ teaspoon of the salt and a good grind of black pepper on both sides, then place in the dish. Arrange the potatoes, onions, carrots, peppers, garlic, rosemary and bay leaves around the veal and place the octopus tentacles on top.

Sprinkle the remaining ½ teaspoon salt and the black pepper over the ingredients, then drizzle the remaining olive oil over the top. Press everything down gently and place a cartouche on top. Cover with the lid and cook in the oven for 45–60 minutes.

Remove from the oven and remove the cartouche. The vegetables should have created a substantial amount of liquid – spoon most of it out (reserving it in a jug), then add the wine. Give everything a gentle stir, cover again and return to the oven to cook for a further 45–60 minutes, or until the meat is tender enough to slice with a spoon. Check periodically and if it is getting too dry, spoon in some of the reserved cooking liquid. Uncover for the last 15-20 minutes to crisp everything up.

Serve warm with crusty bread for dipping in the cooking juices.

From the Water

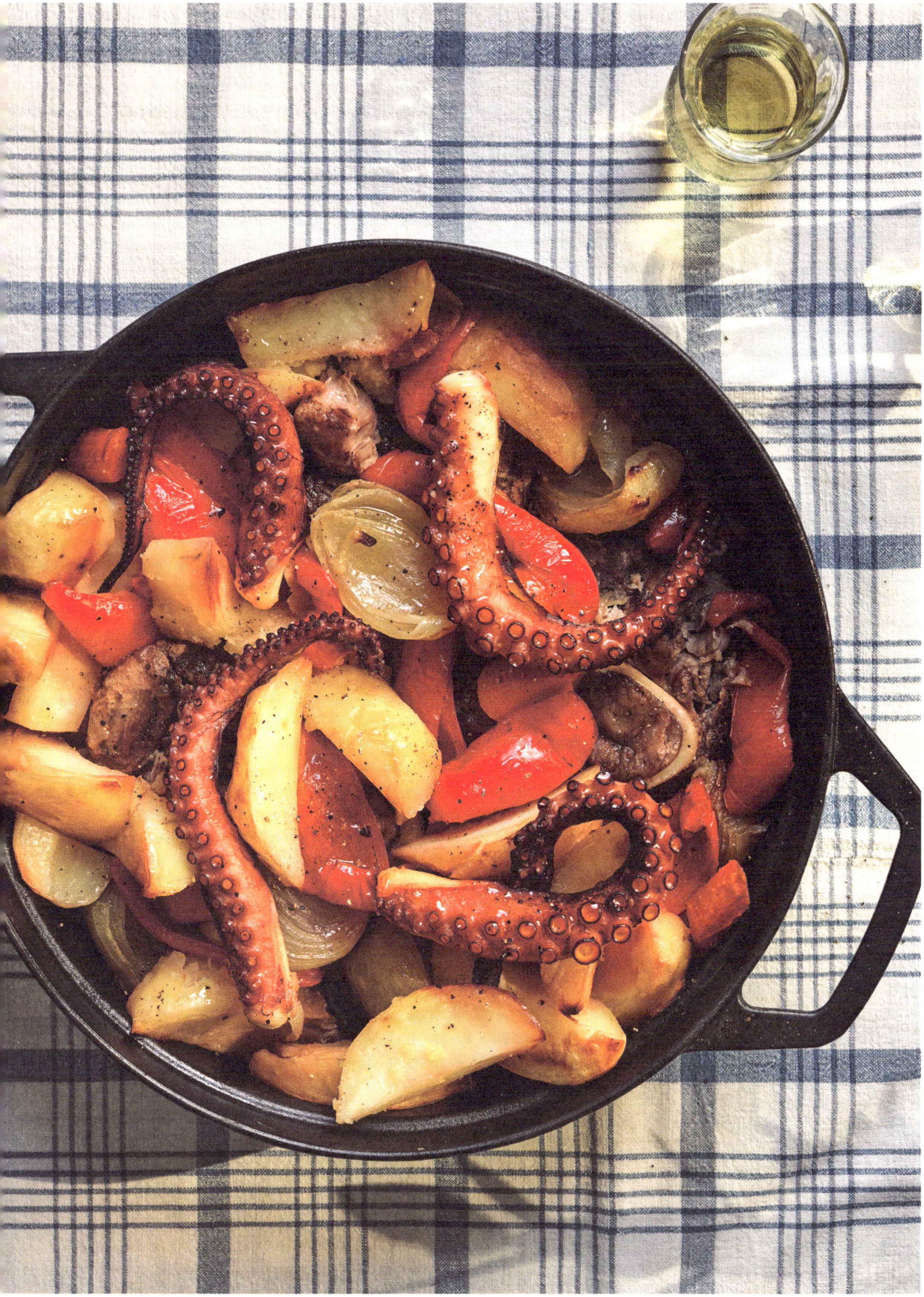

SERVES 4 AS A MAIN OR 8 AS A STARTER

Crni Rižot with Stuffed Grilled Squid

FOR THE RISOTTO
3 tablespoons olive oil
2 onions, finely chopped
3–4 garlic cloves, finely chopped
30 g (1 oz) fresh parsley, larger stalks separated and finely chopped and leaves and tender stalks also finely chopped
2 tablespoons tomato purée (paste)
1–1.2 kg (2 lb 4 oz–2 lb 11 oz) cuttlefish or squid, cleaned (for 600–800 g/1 lb 5 oz–1 lb 12 oz) final weight), bodies cut into 2 cm (¾ inch) cubes and tentacles trimmed, ink sacs reserved
150 ml (5 fl oz/scant ⅔ cup) dry white wine
800 ml (27 fl oz/3½ cups) fish stock, plus extra as needed
280 g (10 oz/scant 1¼ cups) risotto rice (arborio or carnaroli)
½ teaspoon sea salt flakes, plus extra as needed
10 ml (2 teaspoons) cuttlefish or squid ink
40 g (1½ oz) unsalted butter
freshly ground black pepper
1 lemon, cut into wedges, to serve

FOR THE STUFFED SQUID
8 medium squid (about 800 g/1 lb 12 oz total), cleaned
1 tablespoon olive oil
2–3 garlic cloves, crushed
1 teaspoon lemon zest plus 1 tablespoon juice
10 g (½ oz) fresh parsley, leaves and tender stems finely chopped
¼ teaspoon sea salt flakes
8 slices of prosciutto di speck
80 g (2¾ oz) sheep's milk kashkaval (or mild Cheddar), cut into 8 finger-sized batons
freshly ground black pepper

Crni rižot (black risotto) is an iconic Dalmatian dish that points to the historical links between Dalmatia and Venice. The stuffed grilled squid I serve with it is inspired by a delicious dish I ate in Pula, prepared by Goran Savanović, a former fisherman who now runs a lovely restaurant called Farabuto, where he prepares Istrian delicacies with whatever happens to be the catch of the day. The day we were there he made Istrian-style stuffed squid with Istrian prosciutto and delicious cheese on a bed of *buzara*-style sauce and grilled polenta. I love combining the risotto with the squid when I am trying to impress, but both elements work well on their own, too. Do ask your fishmonger to clean the cuttlefish and squid for you – you will need the bodies of the squid (for stuffing and grilling), the tentacles (trimmed), as well as all the ink sacs. Your fishmonger may have cuttlefish or squid ink sachets or jars – feel free to use these.

First, make the risotto. Heat the oil in a large, heavy-based saucepan over a medium-high heat and fry the onion for 10–12 minutes until soft and translucent. Add the garlic, parsley stalks and tomato purée and cook for a further minute. Add the cuttlefish or squid pieces and tentacles and stir to coat them in the onion mixture, then cook for 2–3 minutes until they start to turn opaque. Add the wine and stir to deglaze the base of the pan, then cover with a lid, reduce the heat to medium and gently simmer for 25–30 minutes, topping up with a little of the stock from time to time if needed, until the flesh of the cuttlefish or squid is tender.

Next, add the rice and stir until it is well coated in the cooking juices. Add about 500 ml (17 fl oz/generous 2 cups) of the stock, the salt and a generous grind of black pepper, and cook, stirring occasionally, for around 10 minutes, topping up with ladles of the stock as needed, ensuring the rice never dries out. Meanwhile, place the cuttlefish or squid ink in a small glass and dilute it with 2 tablespoons of the stock. Add it to the rice and continue to cook for 10–15 minutes, adding more stock and stirring often, until the rice is tender but is still al dente and the risotto is creamy with a loose consistency. Remove from the heat and add the butter and the rest of the parsley, stirring well to incorporate. Taste and adjust the seasoning to your taste.

Meanwhile, prepare the stuffed squid. Very lightly score the flesh of the squid diagonally with a very sharp knife on each side. Put the squid bodies and tentacles into a bowl and toss with the oil, garlic, lemon zest and juice, parsley, salt and a good grind of black pepper. Set aside while you prepare the stuffing. Roll a slice of prosciutto around a piece of cheese. Place each roll into the cavity of a squid – it should only fill it three-quarters of the way. Seal the open end with a cocktail stick.

Heat a griddle pan over a high heat and grill the stuffed squid and tentacles for 3–4 minutes on each side, or just until the flesh turns opaque and you have nice char marks all over the squid. You may need to grill them in batches.

Serve warm with the grilled squid on top and lemon wedges.

From the Water

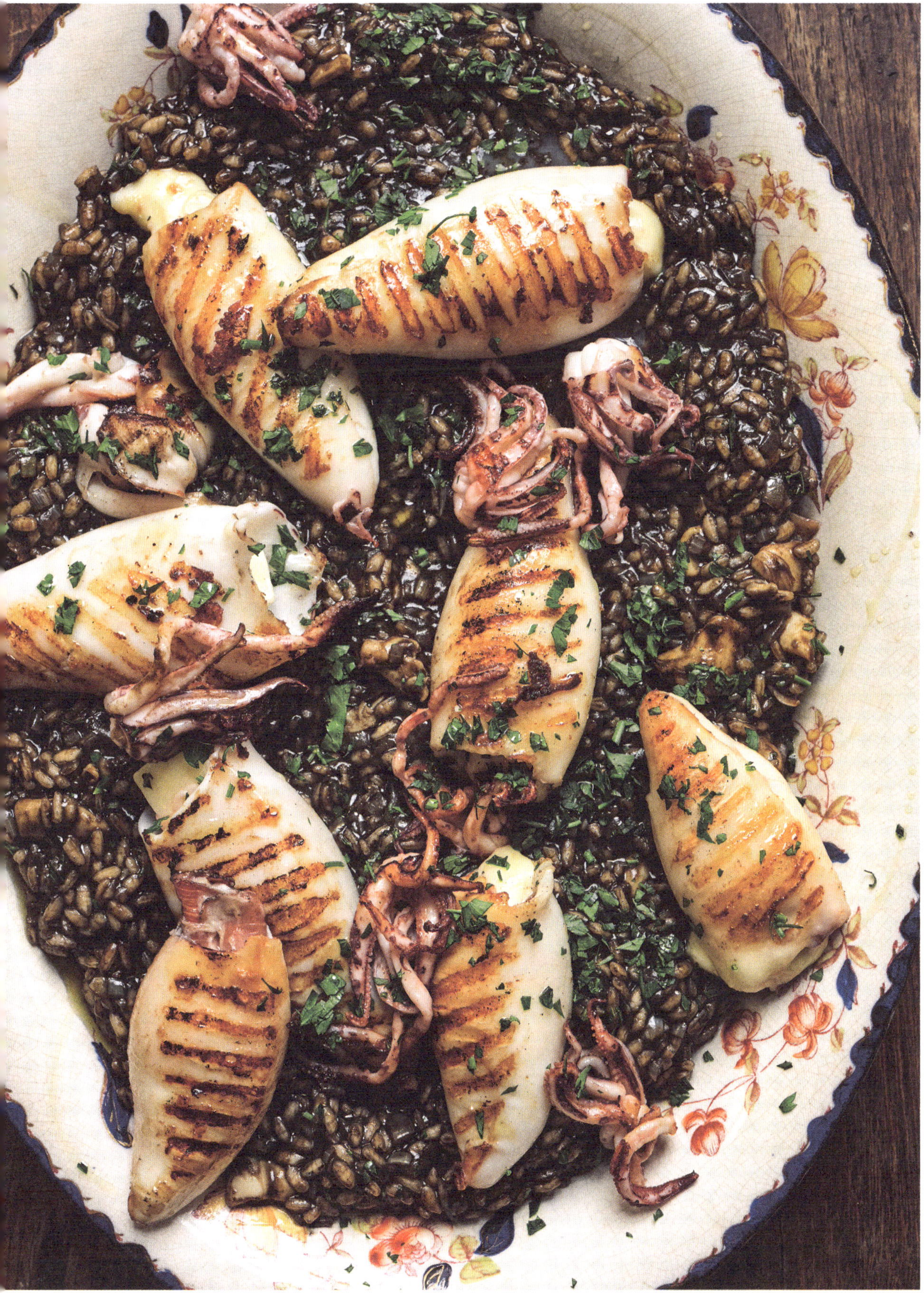

Balkan Waterscapes

Swimming has been my life-long love. Over time, it has evolved into a love of open-water swimming, which has allowed me to experience the wild beauty of Balkan waterscapes and their profound connection with our way of life, way of eating and culinary heritage. This bond is echoed in the dishes that pay homage to the bounty of Balkan rivers, lakes and seas.

My earliest memory of swimming is in the turquoise water of the Aegean on the pristine shores of Halkidiki, in northern Greece. I remember my father catching fish that day, which we grilled and ate on the beach with sandy fingers.

Then there were the summer day trips to Matka Canyon in North Macedonia, and wading in the shallows of the freezing cold Treska River. I remember my grandmother placing a large, beautifully ripe watermelon in a little backwater pool to cool, securing it in place with large river stones. We ate crisp, cold watermelon wedges, juice dripping down our arms, sat under the shade of a weeping willow.

From the Water

In Ohrid, I am always rendered speechless by the tranquil beauty of the lake, its crystal-clear water mirroring the sky, occasionally interrupted by a gentle breeze that causes little ripples to reflect the setting sun, sinking somewhere behind the surrounding mountains. Their shimmer reminds me of the scales of the *plašica* fish that are used to make the famous Ohrid pearls. I wonder if the ripples are caused by the lake's most famous inhabitant, the Ohrid trout – a species that is a living fossil, thought to have survived the last ice age. Famed for its delicately flavoured pink flesh, it is now an endangered and protected species, with many restaurants along the shore of the river now serving more sustainable species of trout.

Lake Skadar, in Montenegro, feels very different. It is verdant, with vibrant waterlilies swaying at the water's edge. In the distance, you can just about see the ruins of Grmožur, an abandoned Ottoman fortress that was later converted into an island prison, and beyond that, the fishing villages along the shores. Houses descend from the heights of Skadar down to the deep, dark blue sea of the Bay of Kotor. I once swam past a forest of ropes adorned with mussels, like jewels on a string, swinging gently to the rhythm of the Adriatic, and wondered which seaside restaurant they were destined for, no doubt to be served *buzara*-style (see page 192).

From Montenegro, the Adriatic takes me to Croatia and its magnificent coastline, where it is too easy to while away summer by the azure, sun-kissed water, with the biggest worry being which *konoba* (guesthouse) to have dinner at that night and which catch of the day to sample.

I also find myself by Lake Bled, its pristine waters breathtaking against the backdrop of emerald forests, rugged cliffs and towering peaks that seem to stand guard over the lake. I think how timeless these Balkan waterscapes are, and how they are woven into the fabric of the cuisine.

From the Water

SWEETS AND DESSERTS
BLAGO

Every home in the Balkans has, at any given point, something *blago* (sweet) to offer to guests – whether they are expected or not. It is a testament to the region's deep-rooted hospitality that within moments of guests entering a home, they are welcomed with a slice of homemade *torta* (a simple or elaborate layer cake), some kind of seasonal fruit cake, a cream cake (if you are lucky), baklava and a selection of *sitni kolaci* (tiny cakes) to accompany the obligatory coffee. *Sitni kolaci* are a category of bite-sized sweet treats like *bombici* (little 'bombs' made from any combination of fruit, nuts and chocolate) or cookies – or perhaps better to think of them as dainty confections. They are often prepared en masse to be served during celebrations, holidays and family gatherings and the selection available during festive periods increases exponentially. The diverse and tempting array of miniature desserts is perfect for satisfying a sweet tooth. They are almost always present in a Balkan home.

I was once asked: what is a uniquely Balkan cake or dessert? The subtext of this question was: aren't all Balkan cakes and desserts Ottoman or Austro-Hungarian? To a point, yes. But that is only part of the picture. What makes Balkan cakes and desserts so interesting is that they are a unique collection, reflecting the complex and rich tapestry of Balkan history. They have been shaped and adapted from ancient pagan rituals, such as *žito* or *koliva*, and centuries old traditions of using native fruits, such as *slivi* (blue plums) and figs. They have of course been influenced significantly by traversing empires: from elaborate Austro-Hungarian tortes and strudels to Ottoman baklava and syrup-drenched sweets, all adapted and given uniquely Balkan twists reflecting local tastes, traditions and ingredients. Some, like Bosnia and Herzegovina's Tufahije are an embodiment of the fusion of European and Levantine flavours and sensibilities. Other more modern innovations such as *Blejska kremšnita*, reflect these far-reaching influences and meld them into something uniquely Balkan.

Balkan *blago* is the product of a delectable journey spanning centuries. It is a category that has been shaped by a plethora of diverse peoples, cultures, religions and more. The selection included here is a miniscule morsel from the vast repertoire of the region's sweet pleasures.

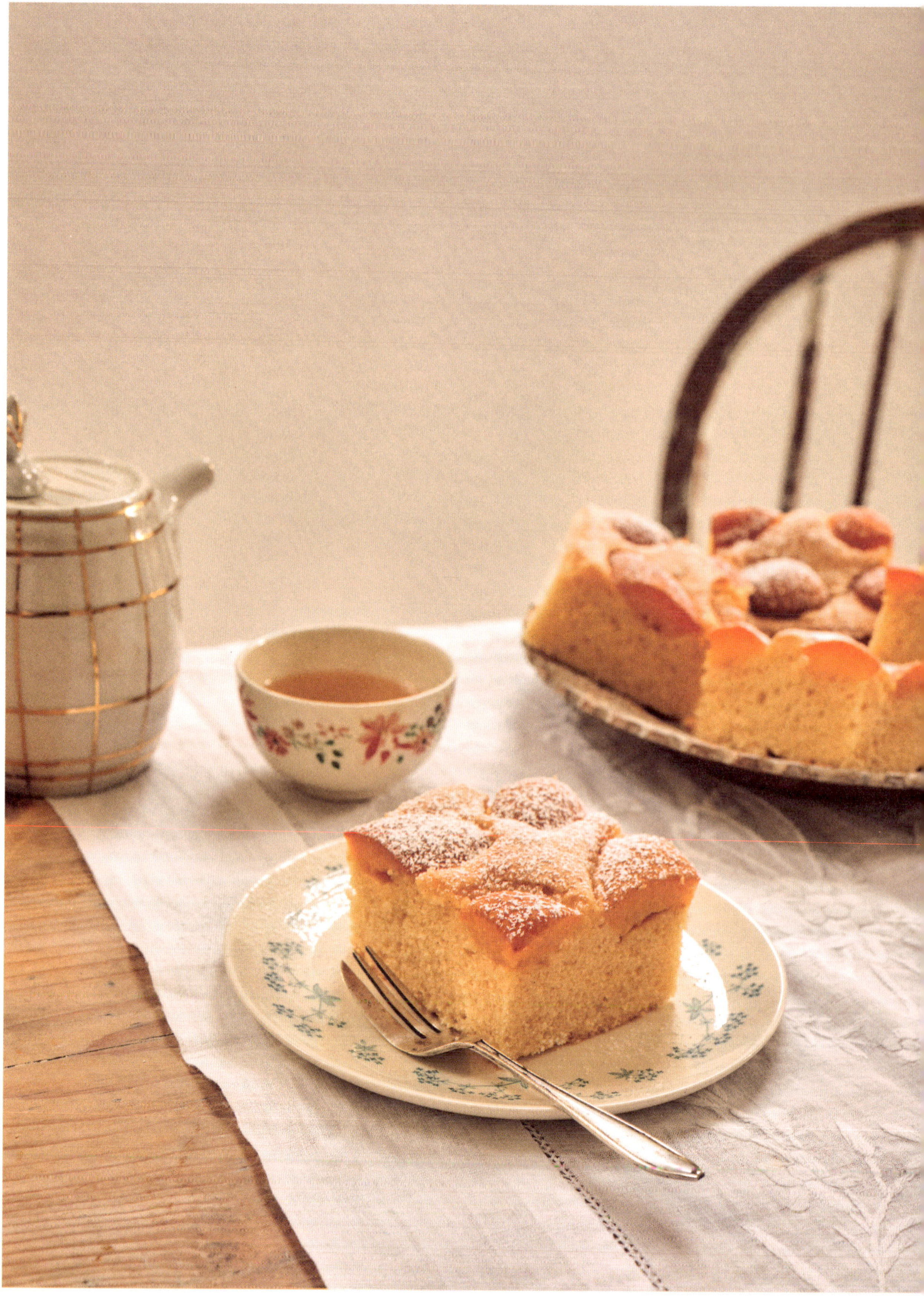

SERVES 8–12

Apricot Cake

120 ml (4 fl oz/½ cup) sunflower oil, plus extra for greasing
250 g (9 oz/2 cups) plain (all-purpose) flour, sifted, plus extra for dusting
5 medium eggs, separated
250 g (9 oz/1 cup plus 2 tablespoons) caster (superfine) sugar
2 tablespoons lemon juice plus 1 tablespoon zest
60 ml (2 fl oz/¼ cup) whole (full-fat) milk
½ teaspoon vanilla bean paste
1 teaspoon baking powder
¼ teaspoon fine sea salt
300 g (10½ oz) apricots, halved and stoned
1 tablespoon icing (confectioners') sugar, for dusting

My grandmother had a rectangular green enamel *tava* designated specifically for making *vocni kolac*, or fresh fruit cake. There would always be a weekly fruit cake, starting with sour cherries in spring and then following whichever seasonal stone fruits were available, culminating with plums in early autumn (fall). I encourage you to experiment with whatever fruit is in season. The apricot one was always my favourite. For a more indulgent treat, serve with ice cream or crème fraîche.

Preheat the oven to 170°C fan (375°F). Grease a 22 x 28 cm (8½ x 11 inch) baking dish with oil, then dust with flour and tap out any excess.

Put the egg whites into the bowl of a stand mixer fitted with the whisk attachment and whisk on a medium-high speed for 4–5 minutes, or until soft peaks form. Then start gradually adding the sugar, one tablespoon at a time, while continuing to whisk for a further 4–6 minutes or until stiff peaks form. Add the lemon juice and whisk together. Scrape the sides down with a spatula from time to time if you need to.

Next, add the egg yolks, lemon zest, oil, milk and vanilla to the egg whites and whisk on a medium speed for 1 minute to combine. Taking care not to knock out too much of the air from the egg mixture, gently fold the flour, baking powder and salt into the egg mxture until just combined with no lumps.

Spoon the mixture into your prepared baking dish, then and use a spatula or palette knife to spread the mixture out evenly. Bake on the middle shelf of the oven for 20 minutes, then remove the cake and, working quickly but carefully, arrange the apricots on top, flesh side down. Return the cake to the oven and bake for a further 30–35 minutes, or until a skewer inserted into the centre comes out clean and the cake is a light brown. Remove and set aside to cool. Once cooled, slice the cake in the dish and dust with icing sugar to serve.

Note

If your oven bakes unevenly (like mine), feel free to turn the baking dish around part way through. I find that covering the cake with baking parchment halfway through also stops the cake browning too much.

Sweets and Desserts

Prekmurska Gibanica

MAKES 16 SLICES

85 g (3 oz) unsalted butter, melted and cooled

1 x 320 g (11¼ oz) sheet of ready-rolled shortcrust pastry (you will need half)

10 sheets of filo pastry (about 175–200 g/6 7 oz total)

FOR THE POPPY SEED FILLING

200 g (7 oz/generous 1¼ cups) poppy seeds, finely ground

50 g (1¾ oz/scant ¼ cup) Vanilla Sugar (see page 261)

1 tablespoon lemon zest plus 2 tablespoons juice

FOR THE CREAM SAUCE

300 g (10½ oz/scant 1¼ cups) sour cream

3 mediums eggs

FOR THE CHEESE FILLING

275 g (9¾ oz) twaróg (not quark, as it is too wet)

100 g (3½ oz/generous ⅓ cup) sour cream

50 g (1¾ oz/scant ¼ cup) caster (superfine) sugar

FOR THE WALNUT FILLING

200 g (7 oz1¾ cups) ground walnuts

50 g (1¾ oz/scant ¼ cup) Vanilla Sugar (see page 261)

2 tablespoons rum

FOR THE APPLE FILLING

3 Granny Smith apples (about 400 g/ 14 oz total), peeled, grated and juice squeezed out

1 teaspoon ground cinnamon

Prekmurska gibanica is a speciality from a region in eastern Slovenia called Prekmurje (meaning 'over the Mur' river), but it is also made over the border in Croatia where it is known as Medimurska. Nowadays, celebrations across all of Slovenia (especially weddings) are unthinkable without it. I cheat by using ready-made shortcrust pastry and filo.

Preheat the oven to 180°C fan (400°F).

Line a 22 cm (8½ inch) square springform cake tin (pan) with baking parchment and brush the sides with some of the melted butter.

Roll out the shortcrust pastry sheet and cut out a square to fit the base of the cake tin. Prick holes over the pastry with a fork, then bake in the oven for about 6–8 minutes until just golden. Remove from the oven and set aside to cool.

Next, prepare all the fillings, by combining each one in a separate bowl.

Prepare the filo pastry by cutting the sheets down to fit exactly into the cake tin (either as one sheet or by using offcuts from ends of other sheets to make one layer).

Now start layering the cake. Brush the top of the par-baked shortcrust pastry base with a little butter, then place a filo sheet over it and brush it with butter. Spread half the poppy seed filling evenly over the filo. Drizzle 3–4 tablespoons of the cream sauce over the poppy seed filling. Place a filo sheet over the poppy seeds, brush it with butter and prick a few holes in it with a fork. Spread half the cheese filling over the filo. Drizzle 3–4 tablespoons of the cream sauce over the cheese. Place a filo sheet over the cheese, brush it with butter and prick a few holes in it with a fork. Spread half the walnut filling over the filo. Drizzle 3–4 tablespoons of the cream sauce over the walnuts. Place a filo sheet over the walnut layer, brush it with butter and prick a few holes in it with a fork. Spread half the apple filling over the filo (you do not need to add any cream sauce in the apple layer as it is moist enough). Cover it with a filo sheet, brush the filo sheet with butter and prick a few holes in it with a fork. Then repeat the layers – poppy seed, cream sauce, filo, butter, cheese, cream sauce, filo, butter, walnut, cream sauce, filo, butter, apple – ending with a final filo layer. Brush the top layer of the filo with butter, then prick a few holes in it with a fork and pour the rest of the cream sauce over the top, spreading it evenly.

Bake in the oven for 50–60 minutes until the *gibanica* is cooked through and the top is golden brown. Remove from the oven and set aside to cool completely before removing it from the cake tin. Once cool, remove, transfer to a serving board or plate and use a serrated knife to cut it into 16 square pieces.

Note

Save any excess filo pastry or offcuts to make the *Gibanica* on page 64.

Sweets and Desserts

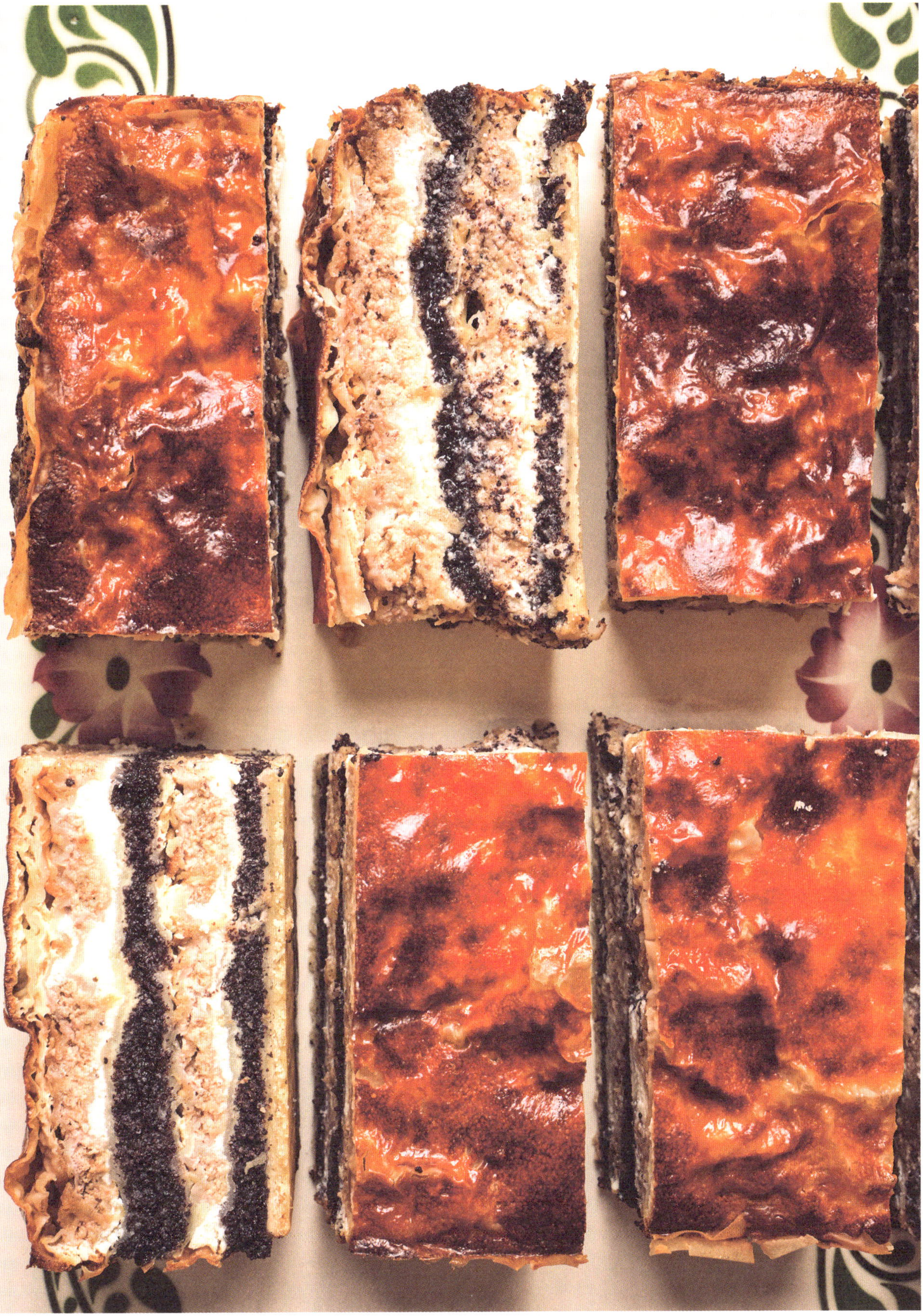

Blejska Kremšnita

MAKES 12 SLICES

2 x 320 g (11¼ oz) sheets of ready-rolled puff pastry
1.2 litres (40 fl oz/5 cups) whole (full-fat) milk
1 vanilla pod (bean) or 1 tablespoon vanilla bean paste
1 tablespoon lemon zest
8 medium eggs, separated
400 g (14 oz/1¾ cups) caster (superfine) sugar
1 tablespoon rum
120 g (4¼ oz/scant 1 cup) plain (all-purpose) flour, sifted
30 g (1 oz/¼ cup) cornflour (cornstarch), sifted
400 ml (14 fl oz/generous 1½ cups) whipping cream
50 g (1¾ oz/scant ½ cup) icing (confectioners') sugar, plus extra to serve

Blejska kremšnita or *kremna rezina* (Bled cream cake) is a truly indulgent but elegant dessert, though it is almost impossible to eat elegantly. It is essentially a custard cream slice, and versions of it are enjoyed across the Balkans, particularly in Serbia and Croatia where it is often called *krempita*, likely an adaptation of the German *cremeschnitte*, pointing to our Austro-Hungarian culinary inheritance. The Bled version of it is, however, legendary. It was created in its present form at the Hotel Park by Lake Bled in Slovenia, by Ištvan Lukačević, a pastry chef originally from Vojvodina, who went to work in Slovenia after the Second World War. Lukačević had previously worked at a bakery where he learned, among other skills, how to make vanilla pastry cream from the baker there, who had travelled and collected recipes from Austria and Germany at the turn of the 20th century. Lukačević had the idea to use this technique to make a lighter dessert for the Hotel Park menu, and the iconic *kremšnita* was born. It now has a protected designation of origin, with only patisseries from Bled permitted to make *Blejska kremšnita*. The version served at Hotel Park still tastes exceptional, especially if you have been hiking or otherwise enjoying the spectacular nature around Lake Bled. There is an urban legend that everything for the cake must come in perfect sevens – seven minutes to cook the custard, seven layers of pastry, and cut into perfect 7 cm (2¾ inch) squares. The exact recipe is a closely guarded secret, so this is my version of it.

Preheat the oven to 200°C fan (425°F) and line two large baking sheets with baking parchment.

Place the puff pastry sheets onto the prepared baking sheets and pierce holes all over each sheet with a fork. Cover with baking parchment and place another baking sheet on top. Bake the pastry sheets for 15–18 minutes, or until cooked evenly and golden brown all over. Transfer to a wire rack to cool.

Pour 1 litre (34 fl oz/4¼ cups) of the milk into a large, heavy-based saucepan over a medium heat. Slice open the vanilla pod lengthwise and scrape out the seeds, then add them to the pan along with the vanilla pod. Add the lemon zest. Heat until the milk is steaming but not bubbling, then remove from the heat and remove and discard the vanilla pod.

Meanwhile, place the egg yolks in a large bowl with half the caster sugar and use an electric whisk to beat well for 3–4 minutes, or until the yolks are fluffy and pale. Add the rum, flour, cornflour and the remaining milk and whisk until there are no lumps.

Next, using a ladle, start to gradually add the infused milk into the egg yolk mixture, whisking continuously. Don't rush or the egg mixture could curdle – you need to slowly bring the egg mixture up to the temperature of the infused milk. Once well combined, pour the egg yolk mixture back into the saucepan (if the milk has caught a little on the base of the pan, clean it before pouring the egg mixture back in). Place the pan over a high heat and bring to the boil while whisking continuously. After 2–3 minutes, the mixture should bubble and visibly start to thicken. When it does, reduce the heat to medium-high and, still whisking continuously to ensure the mixture does not catch on the base of the pan, cook for a further 8–10 minutes to cook out the flour. You should have a very thick custard.

Sweets and Desserts

Meanwhile, place the egg whites in the bowl of a stand mixer fitted with the whisk attachment and whisk on a medium-high speed for 2–3 minutes until soft peaks form. Gradually adding the remaining caster sugar, one tablespoon at a time, and continue whisking for 6–8 minutes, or until stiff peaks form.

As soon as you remove the egg yolk mixture from the heat, fold in the egg white mixture until combined.

Place one of the baked pastry sheets on a clean baking sheet and place an adjustable rectangular baking frame (at least 8 cm/3¼ inches high) around it. Spread the custard evenly over the pastry sheet. Transfer to the refrigerator and chill for 1½–2 hours, or until the cream has set.

Once the custard has set, whip the whipping cream with the icing sugar in a bowl until stiff peaks form. Spread the cream evenly over the set custard and return to the refrigerator until you are ready to serve.

Meanwhile, using a serrated knife, carefully cut the other pastry sheet into 12 squares (roughly 7 x 7 cm/ 2¾ x 2¾ inches) and set aside. When you are ready to serve, carefully arrange the pastry squares over the top. Remove the baking frame and cut out square slices. Dust liberally with icing sugar to serve.

Sweets and Desserts

Chocolate Baklava

MAKES 40 SQUARE PIECES OR 80 TRIANGULAR PIECES

FOR THE DOUGH
- 450 g (1 lb/scant 3¼ cups) plain (all-purpose) flour, plus extra for dusting
- 50 g (1¾ oz/scant ½ cup) cocoa (unsweetened chocolate) powder
- 2 medium eggs, lightly beaten
- 120 ml (4 fl oz/½ cup) sunflower oil
- 120 ml (4 fl oz/½ cup) lukewarm water
- 250 g (9 oz) margarine
- 75 g (2½ oz/scant ⅔ cup) cornflour (cornstarch), for rolling

FOR THE FILLING AND SYRUP
- 250 g (9 oz/2½ cups) walnuts, roughly chopped
- 1 tablespoon ground cinnamon
- ¼ teaspoon freshly grated nutmeg
- 25 g (1 oz) dark (bittersweet) chocolate, grated
- 60 ml (2 fl oz/¼ cup) lemon juice plus 2 tablespoons zest
- 500 g (1 lb 2 oz/generous 2¼ cups) granulated sugar
- 500 ml (17 fl oz/generous 2 cups) water

When I was little, you could buy chocolate *kore* (pastry sheets) in bakeries. Most cake shops or bakeries that sell *baklava*, especially in Bosnia and Herzegovina and North Macedonia, would have chocolate *baklava* – an intensely beautiful version, especially when made with chocolate pastry, too. This is my mother's rather clever method for *sukana baklava* (hand-rolled *baklava*), which I adapted to make this childhood favourite.

Sift the flour and cocoa powder into a large bowl. Add the eggs, oil and water, then use a fork or spatula to combine. As soon as the dough starts to come together, transfer to a lightly floured surface and knead for about 10 minutes, or until you have a soft dough that springs gently back to the touch. Divide into three equal pieces (about 280 g/10 oz each) and shape each into a ball, then cover and rest for 15–20 minutes.

Meanwhile, make the filling. Place the walnuts, cinnamon, nutmeg, chocolate and lemon zest in a small bowl and mix well to combine.

Preheat the oven to 180°C fan (400°F).

Melt the margarine in a small saucepan and set aside to cool slightly.

Returning to the dough, take one of the three balls and divide it into 12 equal pieces, then shape each into a ball. Dust your surface and a rolling pin lightly with cornflour, then roll out 10 of the balls into 7 cm (2¾ inch) diameter discs and the other two into 8 cm (3¼ inch) diameter discs. Dust one of the larger discs lightly with cornflour. Stack a smaller disc on top, dust with cornflour and repeat with the remaining small discs. Lay the second larger disc on top and dust with cornflour. Pinch the edges of the top and bottom discs together, encasing the smaller discs. Dust the work surface and your rolling pin with cornflour again, then carefully roll out the dough stack into a 22 x 32 cm (9 x 13 inch) rectangle (or the same size as a deep-sided baking tin that you'll use to cook the *baklava*). Repeat this process with the remaining two dough balls. You should end up with three layered rectangular dough sheets.

Place one rectangular dough sheet in your baking tin. Sprinkle half the filling over the top. Place another dough sheet on top, then sprinkle over the remaining filling. Top with the final dough sheet. Using a sharp knife, cut deep lines into the pastry all the way to the base to create either squares or triangle shapes. Pour the margarine over the *baklava*, then bake for 35–40 minutes. You should see the layers of the top dough sheet start to separate, and the base layer should be cooked through.

While the *baklava* bakes, make the syrup. Combine the lemon juice, sugar and water in a medium saucepan over a high heat and bring to the boil, stirring gently with the handle of a wooden spoon to help dissolve the sugar. When dissolved, reduce the heat to medium-high and simmer, stirring, until the syrup has reduced and thickened to the consistency of runny honey, 10–12 minutes. Remove from the heat and set aside.

The moment the *baklava* comes out of the oven, pour half the syrup over it, then allow to rest for 15 minutes. Pour the rest of the syrup over the top, then allow the syrup to soak in before serving. I find *baklava* is usually best the next day once the syrup has soaked through completely.

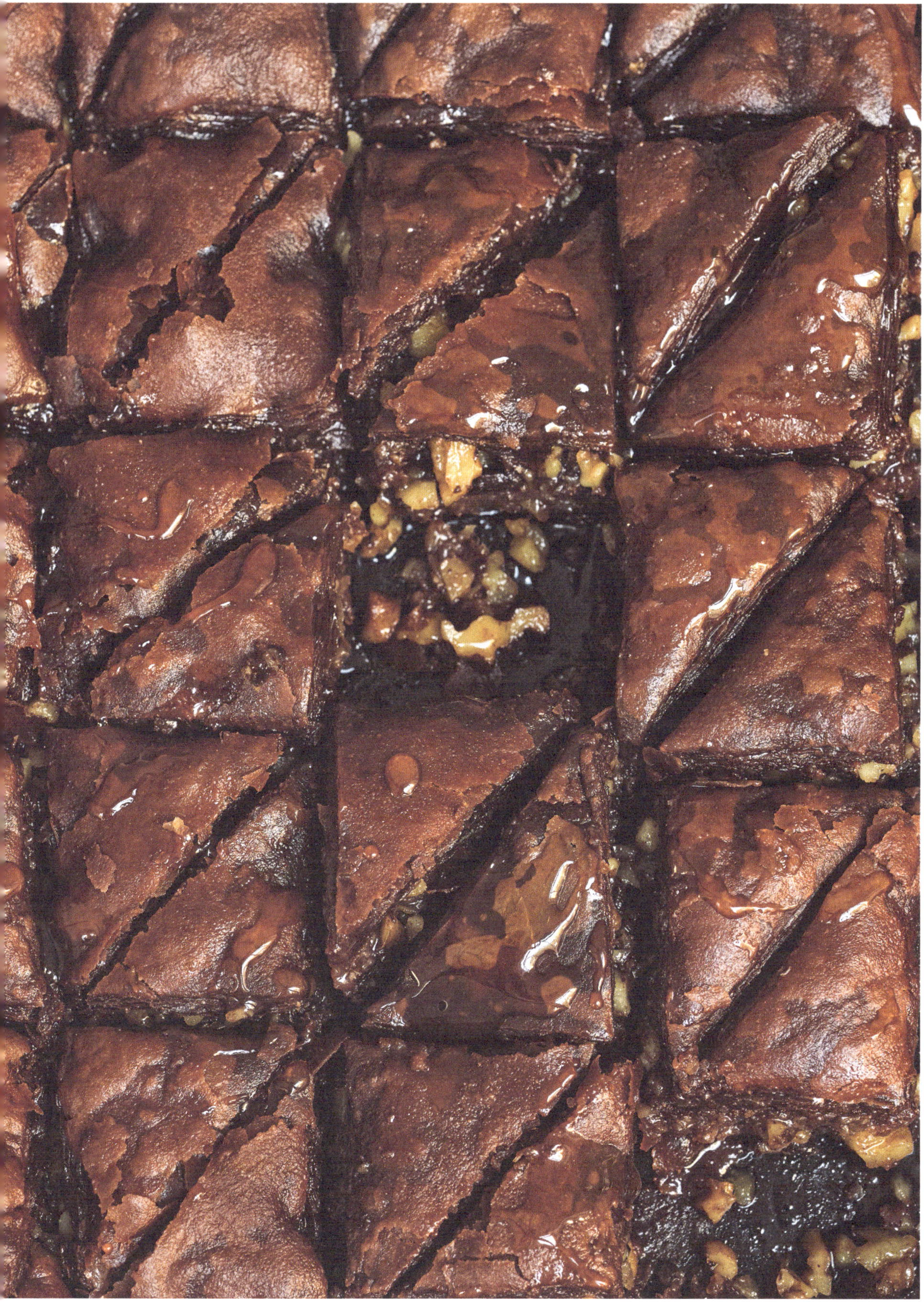

Ružice

MAKES 24 PIECES

200 g (7 oz/2 cups) ground almonds (almond meal)
300 g (10½ oz/3 cups) walnuts, coarsely ground or chopped
2 tablespoons ground cinnamon
3 tablespoons lemon juice plus 3 teaspoons zest
2 x 270 g (9½ oz) packets of filo pastry
200 g (7 oz) unsalted butter, melted and cooled
500 g (1 lb 2 oz/scant 2¼ cups) granulated or caster (superfine) sugar
350 ml (12 fl oz/1½ cups) water
1 teaspoon rose water, or to taste
dried rose petals, to serve (optional)

Note

You can use any nuts you like including hazelnuts, pistachios and pecans. Just ensure the ground half are coarser to give some texture. Use any leftover filo for the *Gibanica* on page 64.

Ružice (also known as *dul pita*) is one of the most charmingly named sweet treats from Bosnia and Herzegovina. *Ružice* means 'little roses' and *dul* also means 'roses' (derived from the Turkish word for roses, *gül*). It is essentially a type of *baklava* shaped to look like flowering roses (a marvellously easy technique, especially if you use ready-made filo). Taking inspiration from the name, I add rose water to the syrup and top them with rose petals. The strength of rose water varies greatly, so I suggest you try the quantity below but adjust it according to your taste.

Combine the almonds, walnuts, cinnamon and 2 teaspoons of the lemon zest in a large bowl and mix well to combine. You may find it helpful to divide the nut mixture in three.

Preheat the oven to 170°C fan (375°F) and line a 40 x 30 cm (15¾ x 12 inch) baking sheet with baking parchment.

Lay the filo pastry out on a work surface near the prepared baking sheet, with the melted butter and the nut mixture within easy reach.

Cover the filo sheets with a clean, damp (but not wet) dish towel while you are working to avoid them drying out and cracking.

Lay one sheet of filo on the work surface with the shorter edge at the top and brush with melted butter. Scatter some of the nut mixture evenly over the sheet. Lay a second filo sheet over the top but approximately 5 cm (2 inches) below the shorter edge of the first filo sheet. Brush it with melted butter, then scatter some of the nut mixture evenly over the sheet. Repeat with a third filo sheet, again laying it 5 cm (2 inches) below the shorter edge of the second filo sheet, brushing it with melted butter and evenly scattering with the nut mixture again. You should have used up around a third of the nut mixture. Roll the filo sheets gently upwards, starting from the bottom shorter edge of the third filo sheet. Make sure you roll tightly but be careful not to tear the filo sheets or spill too much of the nut mixture. You should end up with a *baklava* roll with the nut mixture inside.

Lay a fourth filo sheet on the work surface and brush it with melted butter. Place the roll you previously made seam side down at the bottom and roll it tightly in the filo sheet – this is to ensure the roll stays tight with the nut mixture well encased. Next, cut the roll into eight wheels or 'baklava roses', roughly 2 cm (¾ inch) thick. Place the baklava roses on the prepared baking sheet, leaving some space between each one. Repeat the above steps two more times. You should end up with 24 roses. Brush the top of each *baklava* rose with some butter and then cover with baking parchment. Bake for 25–30 minutes until the baklava roses are golden. If after 30 minutes they are not golden, remove the baking parchment and bake for up to 5 minutes more.

Meanwhile, combine the sugar, water, remaining lemon zest and the lemon juice in a medium saucepan over a high heat and bring to the boil, stirring gently with the handle of a wooden spoon to help dissolve the sugar. When the sugar has dissolved, reduce the heat to medium-high and simmer, stirring occasionally, until the syrup has reduced and thickened to the consistency of runny honey, around 10–12 minutes. Remove from

Sweets and Desserts

the heat, stir in the rose water and set aside to cool completely.

When the baklava roses are golden, remove from the oven, gently transfer to a serving platter and immediately drench them evenly with the syrup. Set aside, allowing the baklava roses to absorb all (or most) of the syrup. Serve sprinkled with rose petals, if you like.

Sweets and Desserts

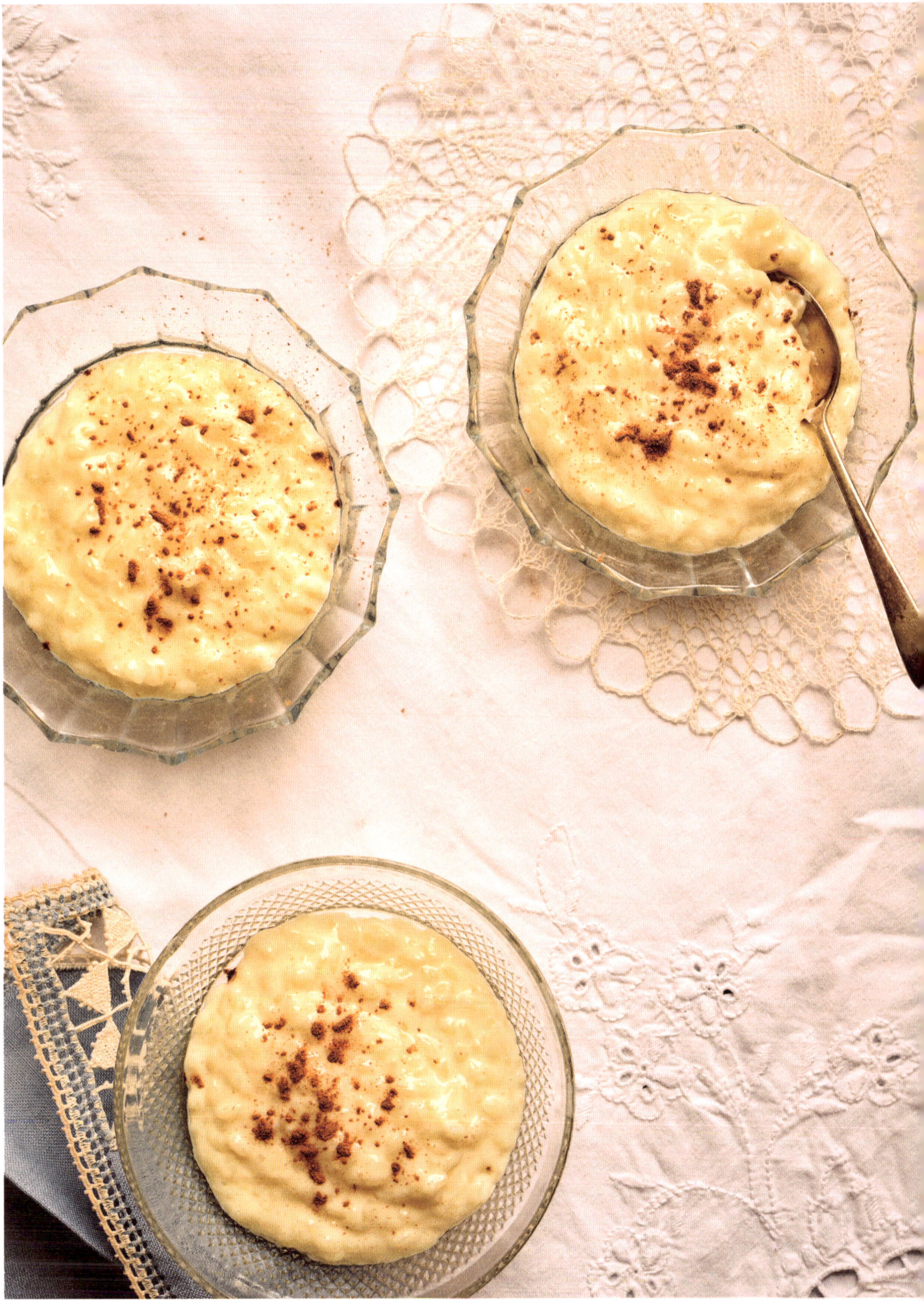

SERVES 2-4

Sutlijaš

100 g (3½ oz/generous ½ cup) risotto rice (arborio or carnaroli) or pudding rice, washed and drained
600 ml (20 fl oz/2½ cups) whole (full-fat) milk
50 g (1¾ oz/scant ¼ cup) vanilla sugar (see page 261, or 50 g (1¾ oz/scant ¼ cup) caster (superfine) sugar with 1 teaspoon vanilla bean paste)
4–6 strips of lemon zest or 1 tablespoon orange blossom water
ground cinnamon, to taste

I can still picture him sitting on a high stool in the kitchen in front of the stove, languidly holding his (ever-present) cigarette in one hand, wooden spoon in the other, gently, and lovingly stirring the *sutlijaš*, always in the same direction, never stopping because you mustn't let it stick. This was one of my grandfather's favourite things to make. A handful of honest, simple ingredients, requiring absolute concentration, patience and love. The perfect, enduring, irreplaceable union of rice, milk, sugar and cinnamon.

Sutlijaš is a sweet, cinnamon-flavoured rice pudding that is typical across the Balkans. It is a close cousin of the Turkish *sütlaç* and Greek *rizogalo*, and a more distant cousin of Indian *kheer* or the Spanish-speaking world's *arroz con leche*. A variation of it, flavoured with saffron and served with raisins and pistachios, is called *zerde* and served during Ramadan across the Balkans.

Balkan-style *sutlijaš* is typically cooked on the stove, then served cold, sprinkled with cinnamon, or in some families, topped with homemade fruit preserves. Every family will have their own way of making it, but in mine, we generally work with a ratio (my grandfather's perfect ratio), using the same *fildžan* (a Turkish coffee cup) as a measurement for everything – 1 cup rice, 5 cups milk, ½ cup sugar (less or more of the latter depending on your preference).

My mother adds lemon zest, so I do too. Sometimes I use orange blossom water. It is simplicity itself, at its most beautiful.

Put the rice, milk, sugar and lemon zest into a medium saucepan over a low-medium heat and bring to a gentle, bubbling simmer.

Cook, stirring constantly with a wooden spoon so that it doesn't catch, for 25–30 minutes, or until it reaches the consistency of a soupy risotto and the rice is cooked. It is important not to take it too far as it will thicken further once cooled.

Once ready, stir through the orange blossom water (if using) and pour it into individual heatproof serving bowls or cups and sprinkle with ground cinnamon, then place in the refrigerator. Serve chilled.

Sweets and Desserts

SERVES 4

Tufahije

750 ml (25 fl oz/3 cups) water
150 g (5½ oz/generous ⅔ cup) granulated sugar
4–6 strips of lemon zest plus 2 tablespoons juice
¼ teaspoon saffron (optional)
1 cinnamon stick
4 eating (dessert) apples, cored and neatly peeled (reserve the peel)
20 g (¾ oz/scant ¼ cup) sultanas (golden raisins)
60 g (2 oz/scant ⅔ cup) pecans, lightly toasted and roughly chopped
¼ teaspoon sea salt flakes
¼ teaspoon ground cinnamon
50 ml (1 ¾ fl oz/3½ tablespoons) whipping cream, lightly whipped

I always loved discovering how many Arabic words were appropriated and incorporated into the various languages of the Balkans via the Ottoman Empire. The name retains a whisper of *tuffaha*, the Arabic word for apple. (These words often become 'Balkanised', but always retain a vestige of their origin.) The name of this dish is a beautiful example of that and *Tufahije* is a dessert of golden apples poached in a delicate syrup then stuffed with walnuts – sometimes gently spiced, other times not – and topped with an obligatory crown of whipped cream. It is principally associated with Bosnia and Herzegovina, but is very much loved across the region in various forms (including some that use baked rather than poached apples such as *pečena yabalki* in Bulgaria). It is an unashamedly simple dessert and therefore relies on the beauty of the region's diverse produce – in this case native varieties of apples. The use of saffron here is not typical, but for me a delicious addition that brings to life the golden apples of many Balkan fairy tales.

Combine the water and sugar in a medium heavy-based saucepan (one that just fits the apples). Bring to the boil, then reduce the heat to medium. Add the lemon zest and juice, saffron (if using) and cinnamon stick.

Place the apples in the saucepan and simmer very gently for 10–14 minutes soft enough for a butter knife to easily slide 5 mm (¼ inch) into the flesh (the timing will depend on the type of apples and their size). It is important not to simmer the apples too vigorously or the apples will disintegrate. Turn them around from time to time so they cook evenly on all sides and start paying close attention after 8 minutes. When the apples are cooked, transfer them to a serving plate.

Add the reserved apple peel to the saucepan, increase the heat to high and boil vigorously for 10–12 minutes until the liquid in the saucepan has reduced by about two-thirds and you have a light syrup. Strain into a serving jug and set aside to cool.

In a small bowl, mix 3 tablespoons of the syrup with the sultanas and leave to soak for around 10 minutes until the sultanas are plump and juicy, then drain the sultanas. Add two thirds of the pecans, the salt and the cinnamon and mix well. Use this to fill the core of each apple.

To serve, place a filled apple in a dessert coupe, pour some syrup over the top and pipe a little whipped cream over the apple, then sprinkle with the remaining pecans.

Sweets and Desserts

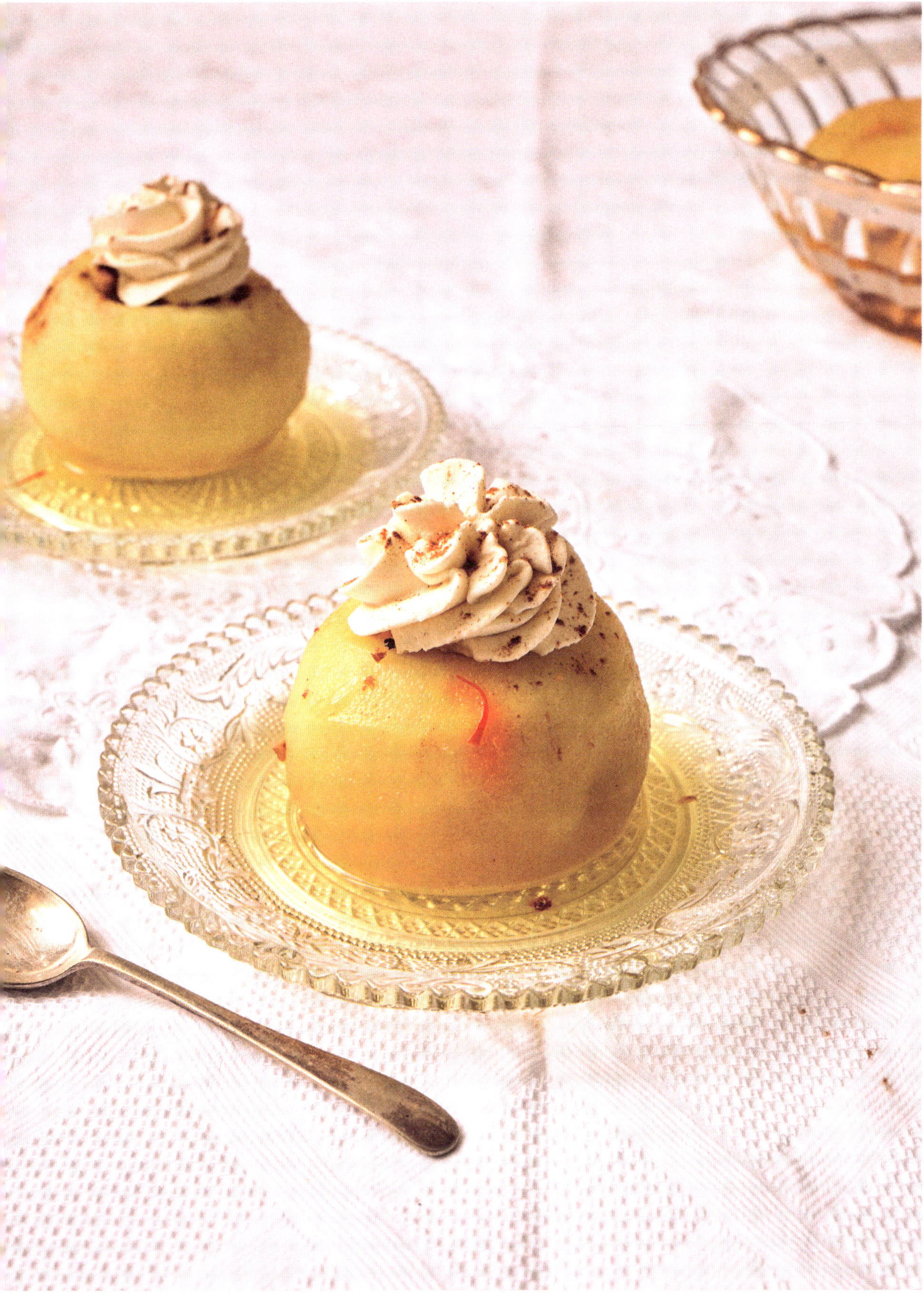

SERVES 12-16

Koh

6 large eggs, separated
90 g (3¼ oz/generous ⅓ cup) caster (superfine) sugar
60 g (2 oz/½ cup) plain (all-purpose) flour, plus extra for dusting
60 g (2 oz/½ cup) semolina
1 teaspoon baking powder
butter, margarine or neutral oil, for greasing
fine sea salt

FOR THE INFUSED MILK
1 litre (34 fl oz/4¼ cups) whole (full-fat) milk
40 g (1½ oz/3 tablespoons) Vanilla Sugar (see page 261), or more to taste
4–6 strips of lemon zest
1 cinnamon stick
4–5 cardamom pods, lightly crushed
pinch of saffron (optional)

This is a light sponge cake that if soaked with syrup is called *ravanija* (the Balkan adaptation of Turkish *revani* – a semolina cake soaked in syrup) or if soaked in milk is called *koh* (possibly an adaptation of the German *koch*, meaning 'cake'). *Koh* is an old-fashioned and simpler variant of the Balkan version of *tres leches*, which has become a modern regional obsession and can be found in any sweet or cake shop or even bakery across the Balkans. I prefer the simplicity of the one milk approach, though I do add cardamom and saffron to infuse the milk as a nod to my upbringing in Kuwait.

Preheat the oven to 180°C fan (400°F).

Place the eggs whites in the bowl of a stand mixer fitted with the whisk attachment, add a pinch of salt, and whisk on a high speed for 1–2 minutes until soft peaks form. Continue whisking, adding the egg yolks one at a time. Start to gradually add the sugar, one tablespoon at a time, and continue whisking on a medium-high speed for a further 4–5 minutes or until the mixture is pale yellow, light and fluffy and has almost doubled in size.

Sift in the flour, semolina and baking powder. Taking care not to knock out too much of the air from the egg mixture, gently fold the flour mixture into the egg mixture until just combined with no lumps.

Grease a 24 x 32 cm (9½ x 12½ inch) baking dish and dust with flour, tipping out any excess. Pour the cake mixture into the prepared dish and bake for 35–40 minutes, or until golden on top and a skewer inserted into the centre comes out clean. Remove from the oven and allow to cool for about 10 minutes.

Meanwhile, prepare the infused milk. Combine all the ingredients in a medium saucepan over a medium heat and cook, stirring occasionally, until the sugar has dissolved and the milk is steaming but not bubbling. Remove from the heat and set aside to cool and infuse until the sponge finishes baking, then strain the milk through a fine-mesh sieve.

Once the cake has cooled slightly, prick holes all over it with a cocktail stick (toothpick). Pour the infused milk over the cake and transfer to the refrigerator. Once the cake has had time to absorb the milk, cut it into rhomboid shapes and serve chilled.

Žute Dunje

I cannot remember exactly when I fell in love with quinces. Whether there was one defining moment, or whether it was the culmination of a hundred different moments, traditions and memories. Quinces placed on top of cupboards from late autumn (fall) and into winter. Their heady perfume. Their golden colour like indoor sunlight. Quinces left half-cut in the kitchen, their flesh slowly browning. My mother's habit, endearing and infuriating in equal measure, of being unable to resist them and slicing into them raw. The cut quince shrinking, slice by slice, then eventually disappearing over the course of a day or two as she steals away the slivers of beautiful and delicately fragrant fruit, savouring the extreme astringency of the raw fruit. At the *pazar* in autumn and my grandmother explaining that there are male and female quinces (the female fruit more rounded), and how the female ones were best for *slatko* (spoon sweet). Her quince *slatko* …

The first time I found quinces in London, I grabbed one and inhaled its scent deeply, provoking a knowing nod from my Turkish greengrocer. I bought as many as I could carry to make my grandmother's quince *slatko*. I planted a quince tree in our garden in London when I was pregnant with my son; I later learned that there is a Balkan custom of planting a quince tree when a baby is born as a symbol of love and life. I was heartbroken at leaving our quince tree, in full bloom, when we eventually had to move. But we planted a new quince tree in the garden of our new home.

Every time I see quinces, I hear the melody of the famous *sevdah* (traditional folk song), 'Žute Dunje' – a melancholy, soulful tune from Bosnia and Herzegovina about two star-crossed lovers who are forbidden by all around them to wed. The beautiful Fatima, her mother's only child, falls ill. All she longs for are *žute dunje* (golden quinces) from Istanbul. Her beloved sets off to bring them to her but three years pass. When he finally returns with the quinces, he finds his beloved Fatima on her deathbed, but he gives everything to see her and kiss her one last time. This beautiful song captures so many aspects of Balkan history and culture in a few melodic and poetic lines. Class structure, the inevitable voyage to seek golden quinces (a better life?) abroad, the pull to return home out of love. And, always, an indescribable longing for those beautiful fruits.

It is, I suppose, a love that has always been there, deeply and symbolically ingrained in my Balkan subconscious.

Sweets and Desserts

SERVES 4-6

Fresh Quince Kompot

800 ml (27 fl oz/3½ cups) water
100 g (3½ oz/scant ½ cup) granulated sugar
4–6 strips of lemon zest plus 2 tablespoons juice (reserve the juiced halves)
1 cinnamon stick
2–3 dried hibiscus flowers (about 1 teaspoon crushed flowers)
700 g (1 lb 9 oz) quinces
160 g (5½ oz) prune plums, halved and stoned
100 g (3½ oz) dried dates, halved and pitted
25 g (1 oz) dried sour cherries
double (heavy) cream or vanilla ice cream, to serve (optional)

The larders of Balkan homes will always contain various jars of homemade *kompot* – an umbrella term used to describe any fruit cooked in sugar and water to make what is essentially a fruit drink, which is typically consumed in lieu of dessert or, diluted with water, as a light juice like squash (cordial). *Kompot* is another way of preserving abundant seasonal fruits for winter. The jars will often be filled either with a single kind of dried or fresh fruit, or a mixture – a snapshot, if you will – of whatever happened to be in season at the time the *kompot* was made. *Kompot* can also be prepared to be consumed 'fresh' without preserving it for winter, like here. Muslims celebrating Ramadan across the Balkans will often break their fast with a freshly made *kompot* of fresh or dried fruits. In certain places, like Bosnia and Herzegovina, *kompot* is also known as *hošaf* (from the Turkish word *hoşaf*), a hark back to Ottoman times when *hoşaf* was a fruit drink served to accompany meals. It is important to allow *kompot* as much time as possible to rest in the refrigerator before serving cold – the flavours improve the longer you leave it.

Combine the water and sugar in a medium heavy-based saucepan. Bring to the boil, then reduce the heat to medium. Add the lemon zest and juice, cinnamon stick and hibiscus flowers.

Meanwhile, peel the quinces (rubbing the flesh with the reserved squeezed lemon halves as you go). Cut them into 4–6 wedges and cut out the core and seeds. Place them in the saucepan and simmer very gently for 30–35 minutes until soft enough to be pierced with a butter knife (it may take longer). Gently stir from time to time to ensure the quinces are poaching evenly on all sides. Once soft, add the plums, dates and sour cherries and continue to cook for a further 4–5 minutes until the plums are softened but retain their shape and the dried fruit has softened.

Transfer to a serving bowl and transfer to the refrigerator to cool completely. Once cold, serve it either as a drink, in cups, or as a dessert with a generous dollop of cream or a scoop of vanilla ice cream.

Note

Use apples or pears instead of quinces if you like, just reduce the cooking time to about 10 minutes – they won't need as long as quinces.

Sweets and Desserts

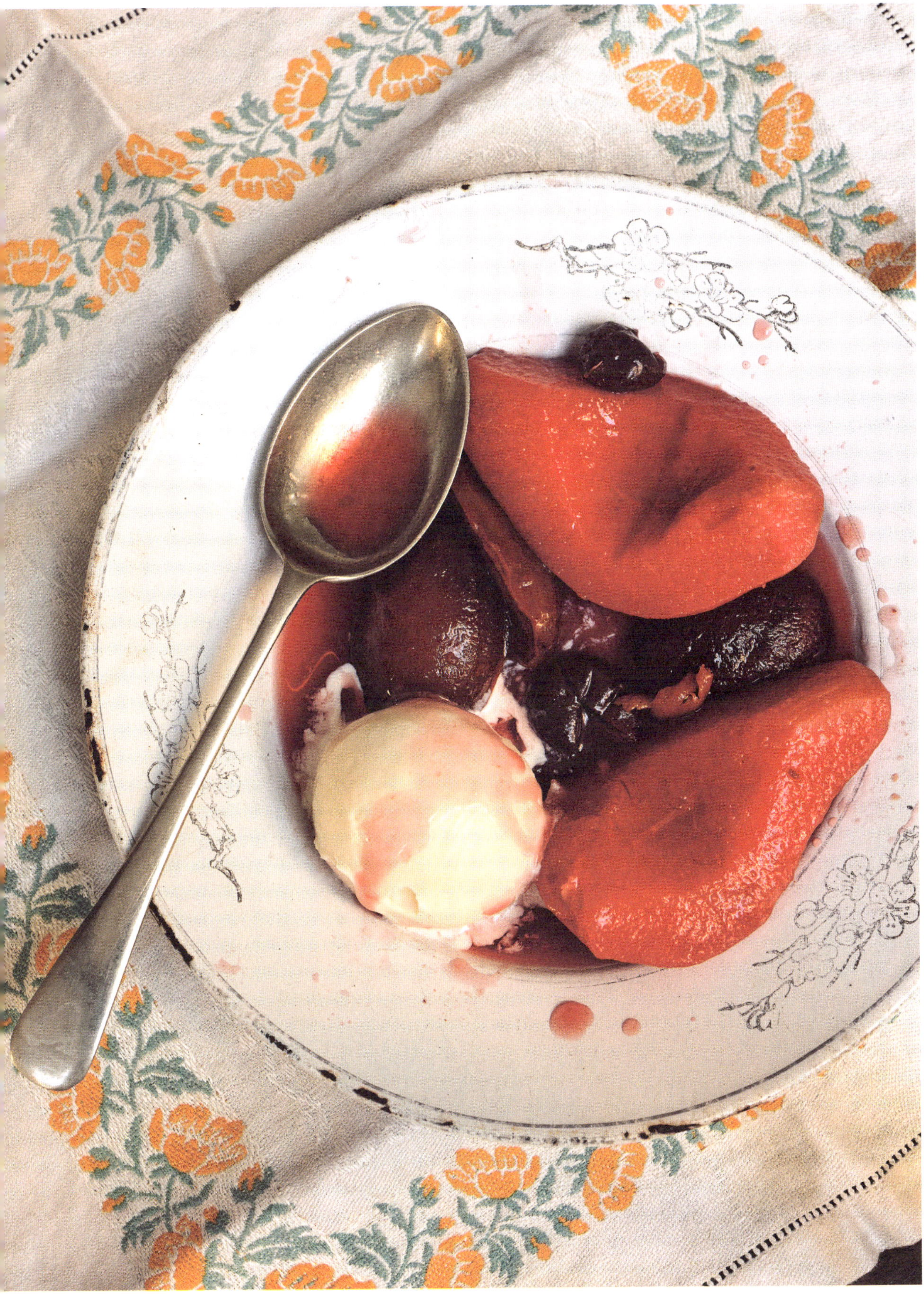

Plum Knedli

MAKES 16 DUMPLINGS (SERVES 6-8)

750 g (1 lb 10 oz) floury potatoes, peeled and cut into 4–5 cm chunks
1 medium egg, lightly beaten
¼ teaspoon fine sea salt
250 g (7–9 oz/1⅔–2 cups) plain (all-purpose) flour, sifted, plus extra for dusting
16 small ripe prune plums (no bigger than 3 cm/1¼ inches)
80 g (2¾ oz/scant ½ cup) light brown soft sugar (optional)

FOR THE TOPPING

60 g (2 oz) unsalted butter
100 g (3½ oz) fresh or dried breadcrumbs (or Panko breadcrumbs)
40 g (1½ oz/generous ⅓ cup) ground walnuts (optional)
40 g (1½ oz/scant ¼ cup) light brown soft sugar (optional)
½ teaspoon ground cinnamon (optional)

Note

You can use any small plums or apricots for this, or even strawberries, raspberries or blackberries and simply make the *knedle* smaller. You can even use a tablespoon of jam, *pekmez* or marmalade as a filling instead of fresh fruit. Feel free to use freeze-dried fruits, dehydrated fruit powders or ground nuts as a topping.

Among the most prized of the late summer fruits – and, for me, the harbingers of autumn (fall) in the Balkans – are the luscious and iconic dark blue *slivi* or *šljive* (prune plums). Some are left on the tree a little longer to develop their sugars and start their fermentation in the early autumn sun before being used to make *šljivovica* (plum brandy), but most are used for preserves such as *dzem*, *pekmez* or *slatko*. The very best ones at the peak of ripeness are used to make these plum dumplings. They are variously known as *knedle sa šljivama* (Serbia), *knedli od plavi slivi* (North Macedonia), *gomboce* (Croatia) and *slivovi* or *češpljevi cmoki* (Slovenia) and are closely related to Austrian *zwetschkenknödel*. They are really a kind of sweet gnocchi.

Making them is a little time-consuming but utterly worth it. The real secret to making them beautifully delicate and light is adding just enough flour but not too much, otherwise you end up with chewy and tough dumplings. The dough must be soft and slightly sticky but robust enough to not disintegrate while being poached.

They were very popular when I was growing up. I vividly remember my grandmother or mother walking into a room carrying a large serving plate of these, to loud cheers of appreciation and applause from everyone in the room! They temporarily fell out of fashion, but I was pleased to see they are having a renaissance across the region. Belgrade is now full of *knedle* bars, like Ferdinand Knedle, that serve every single flavour and topping combination imaginable.

Put the potatoes into a large saucepan and cover with cold water. Place the saucepan over a medium-high heat and bring to the boil, then reduce the heat to medium, cover with a lid and gently simmer until the potatoes are tender to the point of a butter knife.

Drain the potatoes well, then sit them in a colander over the saucepan to steam-dry for 3–4 minutes – this is important, as otherwise the potatoes will retain too much moisture and you will need more flour for shaping. While they are still warm, pass them through a potato ricer or food mill into a large bowl. Allow the potatoes to cool slightly (until you can touch them comfortably), then make a well in the centre and add the egg, working it through the potato with a fork. Add the salt and half the flour and work it into the potato mixture with your fingertips. Knead and gradually add more flour until you have a smooth and consistent dough that comes away from your hands and the bowl, but don't overwork the dough. You may not need all the flour, or you may need a little more – it depends on your potatoes.

Transfer the dough to a lightly floured work surface and divide it into 16 equal pieces (about 45–50 g/1½–1⅜ oz each) and roll them into balls.

Cut the plums in half and remove the stones but keep the matching halves together. If they are not that ripe, place a teaspoon of brown sugar in the stone cavity of a plum half and place the other half over it.

To assemble the dumplings, take a dough ball and flatten it into a circle on the palm of your hand. Place a plum in the middle, then encase the plum in the dough, making sure it is evenly covered on all sides. Roll it gently between your hands so it is smooth all over, then place it on a clean tray. Repeat with the rest.

Sweets and Desserts

To poach the dumplings, bring a large saucepan of water to the boil, then reduce to a gentle simmer. Carefully lower five or six dumplings into the water with a slotted spoon. Cook for 8–9 minutes (they should start to float around the 5–6 minute mark, so give them an additional 2–3 minutes after they float). Remove with a slotted spoon, draining well, then place on a large serving plate. Cook the rest of the dumplings in batches in the same way.

Meanwhile, prepare the topping by melting the butter in a small frying pan over a medium-high heat. When starting to sizzle, add the breadcrumbs and fry until lightly browned. Remove from the heat and transfer to a serving bowl. When cooled, add the walnuts, sugar and cinnamon (if using) and mix well. Sprinkle a teaspoon of the topping over each dumpling, serving the rest alongside.

Sweets and Desserts

SERVES 16-20

Slavsko Žito, A Wheat Offering

250 g (9 oz/1¼ cups) pounded split wheat, washed and drained

250 g (9 oz/2¼ cups) ground walnuts, plus extra to serve

200–250 g (7–9 oz/about 1 cup) Vanilla Sugar (see page 261), or more to taste

1 tablespoon ground cinnamon

½ teaspoon freshly grated nutmeg

1 tablespoon lemon zest

1 tablespoon vanilla bean paste

icing (confectioners') sugar, to serve

whipped cream or vanilla ice cream, to serve

Slavsko žito (also known as *slavska pčenitsa, koljivo* or *panahija*) is a dish of boiled and milled wheat, sweetened with honey or sugar and flavoured with a variety of nuts (typically walnuts), dried fruits, citrus and spices, which is prepared for *slava* or *služba* – the celebration of a family's patron saint in Eastern Orthodox Christianity. It is often served on an exquisite family heirloom tray, shaped into a dome that is elaborately decorated, usually with a stencilled icing (confectioners') sugar cross, sometimes with gold leaf, or with other more modern cake decorations.

The word *žito* is used to refer to all cereals, but it also specifically means wheat. It has the same Old Slavonic root – *žit* – as *život*, which means 'life'. The actual (sustenance) and symbolic (life, fertility, death, resurrection) importance of wheat to the region is paramount. Many ancient civilisations have used wheat (or other grains) in various forms as an offering to the gods, whichever they happened to be at the time, be it pagan, Hellenic, Slavic or Christian. Eastern Orthodox Christianity has subsumed the symbolism of *žito* into its rituals and functions, in particular in relation to those commemorating the dead. A more humble version of this dish – often just the boiled wheat kernels, unmilled and flavoured with a little bit of sugar and maybe some nuts – is prepared as part of Orthodox funerary rituals. It will often be the first thing eaten on the day of a funeral, with some left on the grave as an offering for the deceased and the family's ancestors. It is also prepared for remembrance days (and other rites and calendar days associated with the Orthodox cult of the dead), but also for baptisms and other religious customs. My earliest recollections of eating this humble wheat offering is being handed a small quantity on a napkin or a paper plate at a cemetery by various families attending either a funeral or a remembrance service that day. Like other families, we would visit the cemetery on All Souls' Day to lay flowers and light a candle on the graves of our ancestors. A swap would occur: they would give us some of their wheat for the souls of their deceased or their ancestors, and my grandmother would give them some of our own wheat for the souls of ours.

I think it a beautiful custom: exchanging food to celebrate the lives of those no longer with us, and a way to honour and preserve the memory of them. When I make it, it is rarely (if ever) for any significant *slava* or important date in the Orthodox calendar, but more of a spiritual homage` to love, remembrance and preserving the memory of those loved and lost. Feel free to decorate it if you like, or simply light a candle, enjoy it and remember.

Note

Candied peel, sultanas (golden raisins) and sour cherries all work nicely in the wheat mixture, too.

Sweets and Desserts

Put the wheat into a large, heavy-based saucepan and cover with 750 ml (25 fl oz/3 cups) water, then place over a medium-high heat and bring to the boil. Reduce the heat to medium, cover with a lid and simmer for 20 minutes. Strain the wheat (discarding the water), then return it to the saucepan and cover with 1 litre (34 fl oz/4¼ cups) fresh water. Place over a medium-high heat again, bring to the boil, then reduce the heat to medium, cover with a lid and simmer for 40–60 minutes, or until the wheat grains have fully opened up but retain a little bite. Strain the wheat through a fine-mesh sieve, rinse under cold running water, then spread it out onto a clean dish towel to dry and cool.

When dry, pass the wheat through a mincer or grind it coarsely in a food processor. Transfer to a large bowl, then add the walnuts, sugar, cinnamon, nutmeg, lemon zest and vanilla bean paste. Mix well to combine, then check and adjust the sugar and spicing to your taste. Either store it in an airtight container in the refrigerator until you are ready to serve, or use an ice cream scoop to scoop out balls of the wheat mixture onto a serving platter. Dust each scoop with icing sugar and top with more ground walnuts. Serve with whipped cream or vanilla ice cream, if you like.

Sweets and Desserts

Vanilici

MAKES 36–42 BISCUITS

250 g (9 oz/2 cups) plain (all-purpose) flour, plus extra for dusting
150 g (5½ oz) lard or ghee
125 g (4½ oz/generous 1 cup) ground walnuts
100 g (3½ oz/scant 1 cup) caster (superfine) sugar
1 medium egg plus 1 egg yolk
¼ teaspoon fine sea salt
2 teaspoons vanilla bean paste
1 teaspoon lemon zest plus 1 tablespoon juice
3 tablespoons Plum Pekmez or Apricot Dzem (see pages 247 or use shop-bought)
icing (confectioners') sugar, for dusting

Note

The use of ghee as an alternative to lard is, of course, not 'authentic', but as a vegetarian alternative, I find it provides a comparable texture to pork fat, which you do not get from butter or margarine.

Any Balkan person living abroad will tell you that homemade treats have a way of finding you, wherever you are in the world. It was the same for my mother and I living in Kuwait. When I was little, I once told my grandmother that I loved her *vanilici* more than any other *sitni kolači* (tiny sweets). This sealed their fate as the biscuit (cookie) that found me anywhere in the world. Even in the days before fast international parcel deliveries, my grandmother found ways of sending a food care package to us, stowed away in the suitcase of a kind fellow expat travelling from home to Kuwait. The care package always, always, included a small (usually repurposed ice cream) box of her *vanilici*. Her special deliveries of *vanilici* continued even after I moved to London to study, and until her passing. These will always have a special place in my heart for that reason.

Vanilici are the absolute staple of the *sitni kolači* armoury in a Balkan home. They are, I suppose, a Balkanised version of the Austrian Linzer cookie, comprised of two rich, nutty and short biscuits sandwiched together with jam, often with a small shape cut out of the middle of the top biscuit to show the jam peeking through.

Preheat the oven to 180°C fan (400°F) and line two 40 x 30 cm (16 x 12 inch) baking sheets with baking parchment.

Sift the flour into a large bowl and add the lard or ghee. Using your hands, rub the fat into the flour until the mixture resembles coarse sand (or if you have a food processor, blitz for 1–2 minutes). Add the walnuts and sugar and mix well to combine.

Whisk together the egg and egg yolk, salt, vanilla bean paste, lemon zest and juice until frothy. Add to the flour mixture and mix (or pulse) to combine.

Tip out the dough onto a lightly floured work surface and knead for 3–4 minutes until the dough comes together and is soft and pliable but not too sticky. If it is sticking to your hands or surface too much, wash your hands, dust them and your work surface with a little more flour and knead until the dough moves easily. Divide the dough into two pieces, then shape one half into a flat disc, wrap it in reusable food wrap and place it in the refrigerator while you work with the other half of the dough.

Lightly dust the work surface and your rolling pin with flour again, then roll out the dough to form a circle about 30 cm (12 inches) in diameter and 5 mm (¼ inch) thick. Use a 3 cm (1¼ inch) round cookie cutter to cut out small circles, dipping the cutter in flour between every few cuts. With a butter or palette knife, gently lift off the biscuits and place them on the prepared baking sheet. Press together the scraps of dough and roll out again, cutting out more biscuits as before. Try to cut out as many as you can to minimise re-rolling. Continue until all the dough has been used up. Repeat with the other disc from the refrigerator. Don't be afraid to flour the surface and your rolling pin, but don't overdo it or you will lose the moisture in the biscuits.

Bake on the middle shelf of the oven for about 10 minutes, or until the edges just start to turn golden and the bases are crisp.

Remove from the oven and transfer to a wire rack to cool. When cool, spread a pea-sized amount of *pekmez* or *dzem* onto the flat bottoms of half of the biscuits and sandwich them with the remaining biscuits. Roll the biscuit sandwiches in icing sugar, then store for up to 1 week.

Sweets and Desserts

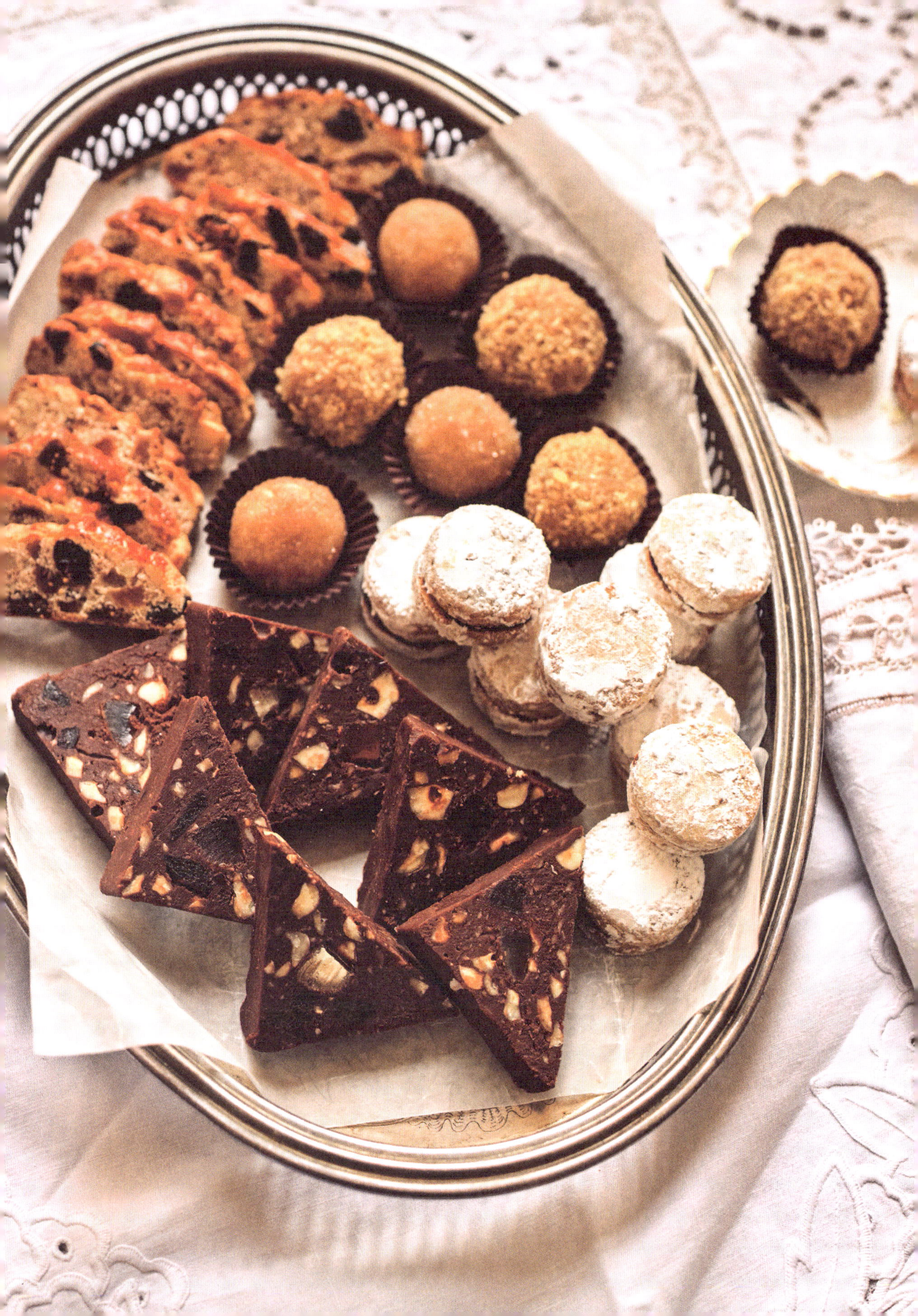

MAKES 40–48 BALLS

Apple Bombici

1 kg (2 lb 4 oz) firm eating (dessert) apples, peeled, cored and grated (for about 750 g grated apple)

350 g (12 oz/scant 1⅔ cups) caster (superfine) sugar

2–3 tablespoons lemon juice plus 1 tablespoon zest

75 ml (2½ fl oz/5 tablespoons) orange juice plus 1 tablespoon zest

1 tablespoon orange blossom water (optional)

250 g (9 oz/scant 2¼ cups) ground nuts (walnuts, almonds or hazelnuts, or a mix of any)

FOR THE COATING

100 g (3½ oz) granulated sugar, ground walnuts or hazelnuts or lightly toasted sliced almonds

Bombici or *bombice* are a whole category of *sitni kolaći* (tiny sweets) of their own. They are, as the name suggests, little taste bombs shaped like truffles. The flavour spectrum for *bombici* is wide, including any combination of dried, candied or fresh fruits (or vegetables), nuts, chocolate, biscuits (cookies) and grains. They also range from healthy (I suppose they were our protein balls long before they became a 'thing' in the world) to decadent and indulgent and there are myriad techniques for making them. The one constant, however, is their shape. This version – my mother's – is one of my favourites. It is made by candying apples and is perfect for using up a glut of the fruit in autumn. Serve these with tea or coffee, or as an after dinner sweet treat.

Put the grated apples, sugar, lemon and orange juice into a large, heavy-based saucepan and place over a medium-high heat. Cook, stirring occasionally, for 25–30 minutes, or until the apples turn translucent and most of the liquid has evaporated. Add the lemon and orange zest and the orange blossom water (if using) and continue to cook for 10–12 minutes, or until the mixture has thickened, there is little or no liquid left and you are able to run a spoon along the base of the saucepan through the mixture without it flooding back. Remove from the heat and set aside to cool slightly, then add the nuts and mix well to combine. Set aside to cool.

Next, set out petit fours cases on a tray. Place your coating of choice in a large bowl. Take a tablespoon of the cooled apple and nut mixture and roll it with your hands into a large marble-sized ball, then place it in the bowl of coating and roll to coat it evenly. Once coated, place in a petit fours case. Repeat until you have used up all the mixture. These keep well stored in an airtight container in the refrigerator for up to 2 weeks.

See photo on p. 225

**MAKES
48–52 SLICES**

Chocolate Triangle

200 g (7 oz/1 cup minus 2 tablespoons) caster (superfine) sugar

50 ml (1¾ fl oz/3½ tablespoons) water

1 tablespoon lemon zest plus 2 tablespoons juice

200 g (7 oz) dark (bittersweet) chocolate (at least 70% cocoa solids), roughly chopped

150 g (5½ oz) unsalted butter, cubed

200 g (7 oz) lightly toasted walnuts or hazelnuts, half roughly chopped and half ground

50 g (1¾ oz) dried sour cherries

50–60 g (1¾–2 oz) fruit jelly sweets (candies, similar to pâte de fruits), halved lengthwise

No-bake cakes and sweet treats are a significant part of the Balkan *sitni kolači* (tiny sweets) repertoire. *Trokut* or *triagolnik*, which simply means 'triangle' is a Balkanised version of Italian chocolate salami. It was a permanent fixture in my grandmother's kitchen because we all loved it. As far back as I can remember, it was prepared for any significant family event or important occasion. My grandmother, and one of her best friends, Aunty Lila, would start to prepare this and other *sitni kolači* days before any event – their kitchens transformed into the equivalent of an elite patisserie. I was often on 'walnut duty' as I thought of it – seated on a large wooden table, surrounded by empty bowls designated for various quantities of chopped or ground walnuts, all to be used for the various *sitni kolači* being prepared. I often think of these happy moments, quietly munching on the occasional walnut I was supposed to be chopping, observing the military precision involved in preparing the mountains of sweet treats. I remember the moment when the *trokut* was finally set and could be lifted out of the ancient triangular terrine (which I still use). I was allowed to taste test the imperfect end piece, which to me was always the most perfect.

Put the sugar, water, lemon zest and juice into a heavy-based saucepan over a medium-high heat. Cook for 2–3 minutes until the sugar has dissolved and the liquid is clear. Reduce the heat to low and add the chocolate and butter. With a spatula, stir gently until the chocolate and butter have melted. Remove from the heat, add the nuts and sour cherries and stir well to combine with the melted chocolate mixture. Set aside to cool slightly.

Meanwhile, line a 1 litre (34 fl oz/4¼ cup) V-shaped terrine mould with baking parchment and then with cling film (plastic wrap) Pour half the mixture into the mould and use a spatula or palette knife to pat it down so it is evenly distributed and there are no air pockets. Arrange the fruit jellies lengthwise down the middle. Pour the rest of the mixture over the jellies. Level out the mixture evenly then cover with cling film and chill in the refrigerator for at least 6 hours until set. Remove from the mould and and slice into 1 cm (½ inch) thick pieces to serve. Store whole in an airtight container in the refrigerator for up to 4 weeks, slicing it as you need to.

Note

If you don't have a terrine mould, use the smallest loaf tin (pan) you have. Alternatively, allow the mixture to cool slightly then spread it out onto a large sheet of baking parchment, place the fruit jellies in the middle, and roll into a salami.

See photo on p. 255

Sweets and Desserts

MAKES 4 LOGS (ABOUT 145 PIECES)

Lidia's Fruit and Nut Roll

150 g (5¼ oz/generous ¾ cup) dried apricots, chopped
200 g (7 oz/generous 1 cup) dried figs, chopped
150 g (3½ oz/⅝ cup) dried sour cherries, halved
2 tablespoons rum (optional)
4 medium eggs, 3 separated and 1 lightly beaten, for brushing
200 g (7 oz/1 cup minus 2 tablespoons) caster (superfine) sugar
200 g (7 oz/1⅝ cups) plain (all-purpose) flour, sifted
½ teaspoon baking powder
1 tablespoon lemon zest
250 g (9 oz/2½ cups) walnuts, roughly chopped

This is my mother's dried fruit and nut salami, which is a kind of cross between a fruit cake and a dried fruit salami, in that it has just enough egg, flour and sugar to bind the chopped dried fruits and walnuts. It is one of those precious old inherited recipes that as far as I'm aware doesn't have a distinct Balkan name, though it is very close to what is known in Austria and Slovenia as 'bishop's bread'. This delicious treat was a favourite of mine growing up and has now become a much-loved after school snack for my son.

Preheat the oven to 180°C fan (400°F) and line a 40 x 30 cm (16 x 12 inch) baking sheet with baking parchment.
   Combine the dried fruits in a large bowl, add the rum (if using) and mix well.
   Put the egg whites into the bowl of a stand mixer fitted with the whisk attachment and whisk on a medium-high speed for 5–6 minutes until soft peaks form. Gradually add the sugar, one tablespoon at a time, and continue whisking for 6–8 minutes, or until stiff peaks form. Add the egg yolks one at a time, whisking to combine.
   Add 2 tablespoons of the flour to the dried fruit mixture. Add the remaining flour, the baking powder and lemon zest to the egg mixture and whisk on a low speed for no more than 30 seconds just until combined.
   Add the dried fruit mixture to the egg mixture and use a spatula or metal spoon to mix well. Finally, add the walnuts and mix well to ensure they are evenly distributed through the mixture – it should be the consistency of a thick fruit cake batter
   Divide the mixture into four roughly equal pieces. With damp hands (I find it helps to have a small bowl with water and a damp kitchen towel to hand), shape each piece into a long log or salami (no more than 5 cm/ 2 inches wide and 36 cm/14 inches long). Place the salamis onto the prepared baking sheet leaving a 3 cm (1¼ inch) gap between each log to allow for expansion. Brush them with the beaten egg.
   Bake in the oven for 25–30 minutes, or until golden brown, rotating the baking sheet halfway through the cooking time. Once cooked, remove from the oven and use the parchment to transfer the salamis to a wire rack to cool completely. Slice into 1 cm (½ inch) thick slices as needed to serve.
   These keep very well for up to 4 weeks stored in an airtight container in a cool place.

Note
You can substitute the sour cherries for sultanas (golden raisins) and use any other nuts if you prefer. You can also use orange instead of lemon as your citrus flavour.

SERVES 18-24

Alexander's Cake

FOR THE WALNUT PRALINE

140 g (5 oz/scant ⅔ cup) caster (superfine) sugar

300 g (10½ oz/3 cups) walnuts, roughly chopped

FOR THE SPONGE

12 medium eggs, separated

240 g (8½ oz/generous 1 cup) caster (superfine) sugar

½ teaspoon vanilla bean paste

40 g (1½ oz/⅓ cup) plain (all-purpose) flour

¼ teaspoon fine sea salt

FOR THE FILLING AND TOPPING

4 medium eggs

160 g (5¾ oz/scant ¾ cup) caster (superfine) sugar

2 tablespoons water

200 g (7 oz) unsalted butter, softened

200 g (7 oz) dark (bittersweet) chocolate (at least 70% cocoa solids), melted and cooled, plus extra for topping

80 g (2¾ oz) Apricot Đzem (see page 247, or use shop-bought) mixed with 1 tablespoon boiling water

dark or white chocolate shavings, to decorate (optional)

This is the cake that sparked the idea for *The Balkan Kitchen*. In my grandmother's 1956 edition of the *Veliki Narodni Kuvar* (Great National Cookbook), it is called *grijaž torta s čokoladom* – praline cake with chocolate. The recipe below stays mostly true to the original, with some minor updates and adjustments.

Next to the recipe in her cookbook my grandmother had written 'Princess' and 'For Irina', with the date she had made the cake to celebrate my birth. Whenever I look at that page, I feel she is still somehow here, busily cooking something beautiful that tastes of love, longing and memories. It took me a long time to get to a place where I could make this cake, and it felt right to make it for the first time, with my mother, for my son's fifth birthday. It feels appropriate to rename the cake from 'princess cake' to 'Alexander's cake' and pass on this inheritance to the next generation. It is perhaps time for me to add my own inscription in the *Veliki Narodni Kuvar* next to the one from my grandmother.

First, make the praline. Line a large baking sheet (or heatproof tray) with baking parchment.

Place a large, heavy-based saucepan over a medium heat. When the saucepan is hot, add the sugar and shake the pan gently to ensure the sugar is distributed evenly over the base of the pan. Do not stir the sugar. When it starts to melt and colour at the edges, gently agitate it with a fork or the handle of a wooden spoon to encourage all the sugar to melt. As more of the sugar melts and colours, gently swirl the pan to ensure even colouring. When all the sugar has melted and you have a deep golden brown caramel, remove it from the heat and immediately add the walnuts. Working quickly, stir with a spatula to coat the walnuts in the caramel. Tip out the praline onto the prepared baking sheet and spread it out evenly to cool.

Once completely cooled, break the walnut praline into pieces, transfer to a food processor and blend for 1–2 minutes to a fine sand texture. Set aside.

Preheat the oven to 180°C fan (400°F). Line the base and sides of a 42 x 30 cm (16½ x 12 inch) baking tin (pan) with baking parchment.

To make the sponge, put the egg yolks into a large bowl and use an electric whisk to whisk while you gradually add 180 g (6¼ oz/generous ¾ cup) of the sugar, one tablespoon at a time. Continue whisking until the egg yolks are pale yellow and fluffy, about 6–8 minutes in total. Add the vanilla bean paste, flour and the ground walnut praline. Whisk for 10 seconds to incorporate.

At the same time, put the egg whites and salt into the bowl of a stand mixer fitted with the whisk attachment and whisk on a medium-high speed for 4–5 minutes, or until soft peaks form. Gradually add the remaining 60 g (2 oz/generous ¼ cup) of sugar, one tablespoon at a time, while continuing to whisk for a further 4–6 minutes, or until stiff peaks form. Scrape down the sides with a spatula from time to time if you need to.

Next, very gently fold the egg yolk mixture into the egg whites until well incorporated, taking care not to lose too much air. Pour the sponge batter into the prepared tin, spreading it out evenly. Bake in the oven for about 30 minutes until risen, evenly golden, slightly crinkled on the top and shrinking away from the sides of the tin. Pay close attention after 22 minutes and rotate the baking tin if you need to ensure it bakes evenly on

Sweets and Desserts   *Recipe continued overleaf*

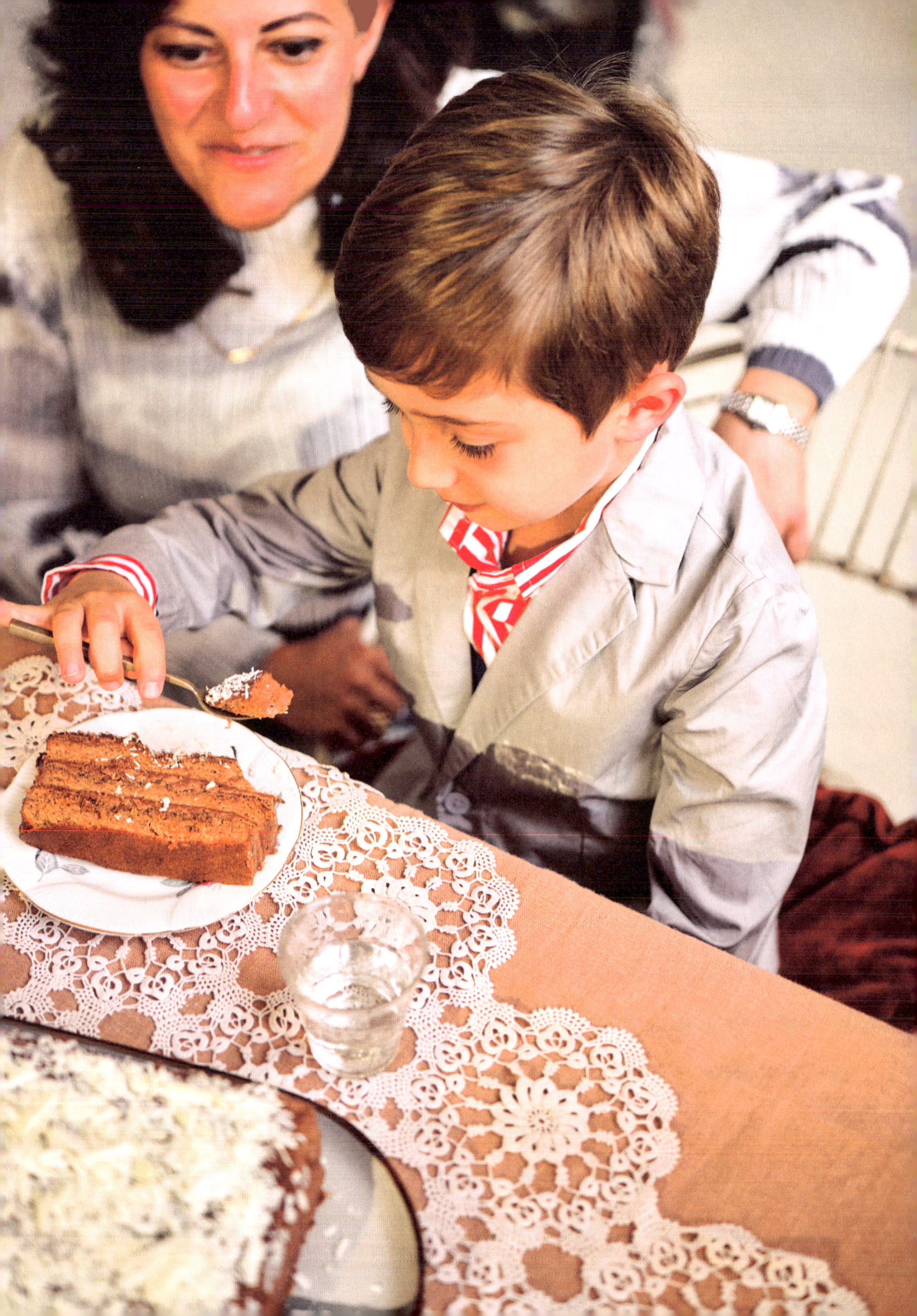

all sides. Gently press the middle of the sponge with your fingertips – it should bounce back, and a skewer inserted into the centre should come out clean. Once baked, remove the cake from the oven and set aside on a wire rack (in its tin) to cool for 2–3 minutes. Then, lay a sheet of baking parchment over the top of the sponge, place the wire rack over it and carefully invert the tin. You should be able to easily remove the tin. Carefully peel off the baking parchment. Allow the sponge to cool completely, then trim off about 1 cm (½ inch) from the edges so you have a neat rectangle. Cut the sponge, lengthwise, into three equal rectangles (about 9 x 40 cm/ 3½ x 16 inches).

While the sponge is cooling, make the filling and topping. Put the eggs, sugar and water into a large bowl and whisk to combine. Set the bowl over a saucepan of boiling water (the base of the bowl should not touch the water). Whisk continuously for at least 20 minutes until the mixture is creamy and has more than quadrupled in size. Set aside to cool.

Place the butter in a separate large bowl and use an electric whisk to beat it for 5–6 minutes until it is almost white and more than doubled in size. Add the chocolate and whisk until evenly combined. Once the egg and sugar mixture is cool, add it to the whipped chocolate butter and use a spatula to fold it in until well incorporated. Place the filling in the refrigerator and chill for at least 5 minutes before assembling the cake.

To assemble the cake, place one sponge rectangle on a serving platter (or cake board) long enough for the sponge. Using a butter or palette knife, spread half the apricot *dzem* over the top. Spread a quarter of the chocolate filling evenly over the top. Place another sponge rectangle on top and repeat, first spreading on the rest of the apricot *dzem* and a quarter of the filling, then top with the final sponge rectangle. You may want to secure the cake by placing a toothpick or small skewer at each end of the cake. Finally, cover the entire cake with the rest of the filling, spreading it neatly and evenly over the sides and the top. Finally, decorate with some dark (or white) chocolate shavings, or other cake decorations of your choice. Cut into roughly 1 cm (½ inch) thick slices to serve.

Sweets and Desserts

Slatkarnica

I am impatiently queuing at the *slatkarnica* (cake shop).

'Do you have your own bottle?'

'Yes.'

I hand over my empty, cleaned bottle. Within moments it is handed back to me, full of *boza* – a thick, sweet and lightly sour fermented drink that is the colour of rose-tinted sand.

'Anything else?'

Hesitation. Indecision. I glance across the glass display cases. Rows of different types of *baklava*. My eyes pause, tempted by the tray of chocolate *baklava*. But no, wait, they have *tulumba* (fried choux pastry dough) in glistening syrup! Then trays of *čupavci*, little sponge cakes coated in chocolate and shredded coconut. *Ravanija*, our version of Turkish *revani* (a syrup-drenched semolina cake). The always-present and hugely popular Balkan-style *tres leches* cake, covered in a dark caramel sauce. Trays of little crescent cookies – plain, with jam, walnut-covered, hazelnut-covered. Various types of *torta* – Vasina, Madarica and many other variations of thin layers of sponge or *pan di spagne*, interspersed with a creamy filling (buttercream, custard or cream), with nuts or crushed biscuits or fruit, often topped with a ganache or glaze. Then *krempita*, our version of the custard slice! Even *rožata*, a crème caramel flan! *Tufahije* (syrup poached apples, see page 214) topped with perfect swirls of cream and scatters of toasted nuts.

And then ... I see it. Something easily mistaken for a glistening block of Arctic ice, were it not for the decorative swirls around the edges.

'One *šampita*, please, and a small glass of *boza* to have with it here.'

Šampita is a mountain of Italian meringue on a very, very thin layer of sponge. The key requirement for a good *šampita*, other than the texture and delicate flavour of the meringue, is that it must be as tall as possible. As far as I am concerned, this is about the height of the expectant face of a wide-eyed, grinning small child. As I take my first bite, I am that child again.

Sweets and Desserts

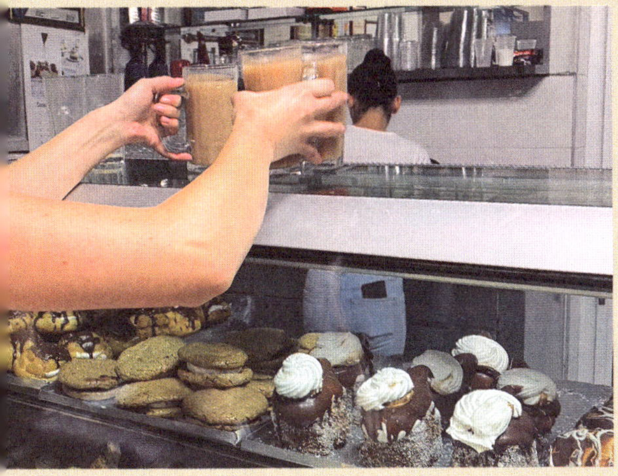

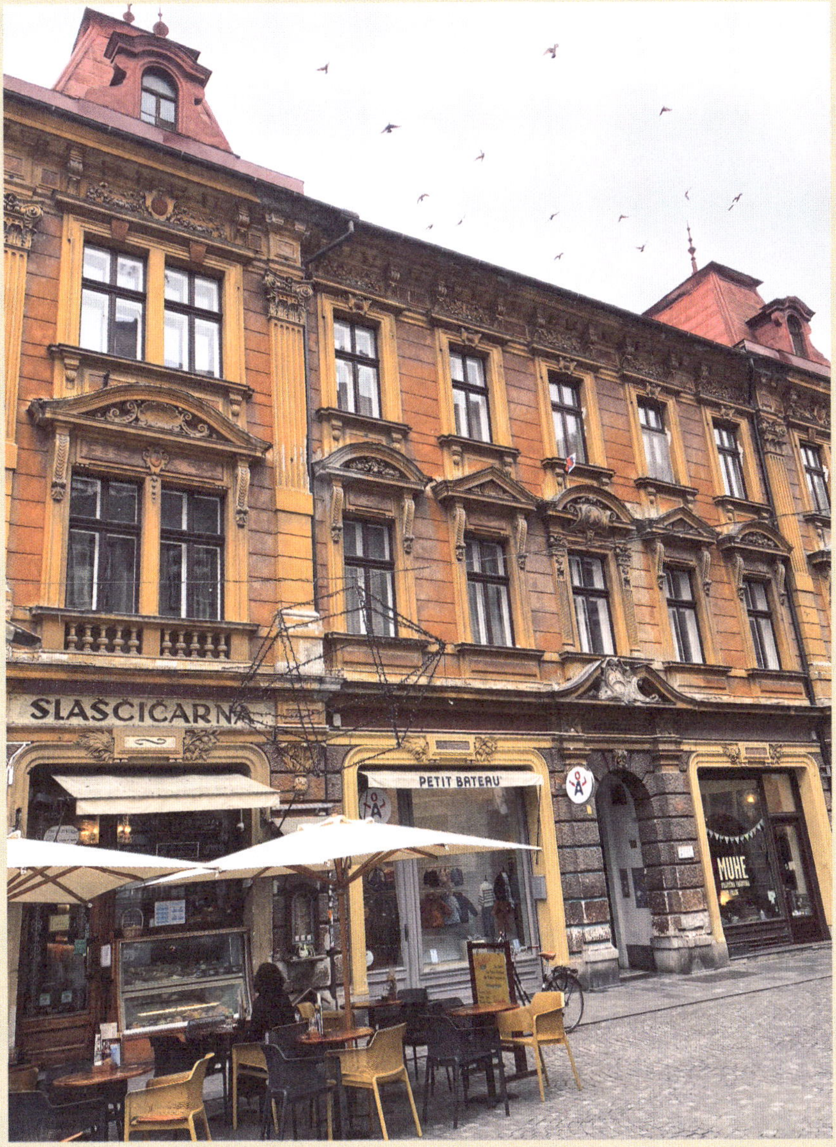
SLAŠČIČARNA
PETIT BATEAU
MUHE

Š *pajz* is a Balkanisation of the German *spiese* (food) and *spiesekammer* (food room). Colloquially, we use this to mean the Balkan larder or pantry. It is difficult to say for sure at what point *špajz* became widely used to mean larder – it could have happened either during the period of Habsburg influence or much later, during German occupation around the Second World War. What is certain is that the Balkan *špajz* is more than a food storage area, it is a way of life. Most types of traditional houses across the region – a harmonious blend of practicality and cultural identity – were built with thick stone walls and deep stone basements that were naturally cooler in the heat of summer. The basements were used for the storage of various types of food, preserves, ferments, pickles, drinks and, in times of need, as a place of refuge and safety. Houses would also feature spacious courtyards (often used for the preparation of food), overhanging eaves (for air-drying various food items such as peppers and garlic), and, often, intricate woodwork. Houses were typically oriented to maximise natural light and ventilation while offering protection from harsh weather. As life in the Balkans – and everywhere – moved from villages and towns to the cities, the idea of a space to store food moved with it. It was taken so seriously that many modernist apartment buildings constructed across former Yugoslavia from the 1960s onwards had a special *špajz* room and often a second kitchen where slow-cooking or (more 'fragrant') kitchen activities (such as frying) occurred.

FROM THE LARDER
ŠPAJZ

In my grandmother's apartment, the *špajz* was insulated from the living and dining rooms and bedrooms by a buffer, which was the bathroom. The *špajz* was a magical place, a treasure trove of wonders. It was where all the fresh and dry ingredients were stored, as well as meticulously labelled jars that stored the abundance of the preceding seasons to see us through winter. Its convenient location meant that fruit – destined for *slatko* or *dzem* – was often washed in the bathtub. I have a memory of sitting on a small stool near the tub, fishing out a perfectly ripe blue plum bobbing in the water, then stoning and peeling it to keep it whole, my grandmother instructing and supervising. My grandmother's *špajz* was what remained, and still does, long after she was gone.

The *špajz* is fundamental to the way we still eat in the Balkans – seasonally, frugally, carefully preserving the seasons, wasting nothing. Everything appropriately stored. Apples in apple crates, given space. Walnuts and other nuts still in their shells. Garlands of a hundred or more dried peppers – mild and hot. Or little packs of peppers, cored and deseeded, then flattened and tied in string in packs of 30 or 40, ready to be rehydrated and stuffed. From the start of spring, as fruits and vegetables begin to arrive, they are preserved through various methods including drying, fermenting, canning and pickling among others. In the case of fruits, they are either turned into the various types of *rakija* (fruit spirits) or destined for liqueurs. This culminates in autumn (fall) with the most beloved of all Balkan culinary rituals – the preparation of *zimnica*. *Zimnica* is a word generally used to refer to the art of preserving various fruits and vegetables to last the winter. The *zimnica* family includes perhaps the most loved and most important of all preserves in the region, *ajvar* – the Balkan caviar. From the end of summer and well into autumn, families, friends and neighbours gather together in their homes, gardens or balconies to roast hundreds of kilos of red peppers and aubergines (eggplants) over a *pećnica*. The *pećnica* is a specialised wood-fired or charcoal oven designed for roasting and charring peppers until their skins blister and blacken, a crucial step in preparing *ajvar*, as it imparts the iconic smoky flavour and makes them easier to peel. The ubiquitous and mesmerising aroma of charring peppers and aubergines elicits knowing smiles from passers-by. It truly takes an army – to peel the peppers and aubergines, to mince them and then to stew the mixture in a large cauldron-sized saucepan over a gentle wood fire for hours, stirring with a wooden spoon and adding as much sunflower oil as the vegetables will absorb until the mixture and flavour are concentrated and ready to be seasoned and stored in jars. It is these rituals, this obsession with preserving everything the land has given, that embody what the *špajz* is. A way of seeing your family through winter. Through hardships, wars, sieges. It is the art of survival.

Piperki za Ajvar!

Peppers for *ajvar*! It is early autumn (fall) and the cry echoes across the *pazar* (food market) in Skopje from nearly all the market-stall holders.

I am following my grandmother. Practically running past the iconic green metal market stands that creak under the weight of autumnal abundance, but still struggling to keep pace with my grandmother who is marching ahead with her *zembil* (woven basket) specially reserved for *pazar* trips. She knows a lady from Strumica who grows the best *ajvarki* peppers and is determined to find her. Yes, we can come back for the black grapes your mother loves, but peppers first. There she is, at last! '30 kg [66 lb] of your freshest peppers please. Also, some of your young aubergines [eggplants],' my grandmother calls. 'How are we going to carry this back, Grandma?' I ask. We will manage; we always do. I help, of course: roasting the peppers and aubergines; the endless peeling and our fingers turning a charred orange; mincing the pepper and aubergine flesh through the ancient iron grinder passed down through generations of women in my family; cooking and constantly stirring the *ajvar*; and finally placing it in jars. My grandmother considers this a small batch, *za adet* (for custom), because it is unthinkable for her not to have homemade *ajvar*. She reassures me that she knows and trusts another lady with an excellent recipe who makes and sells *ajvar* so we can top up our winter reserves. Heaven forbid we run short before next autumn. We always do.

I am now following my mother. She has seen Hamburg (Black Muscat) grapes, her favourite. A kilo, no make it two. They won't last long, they never do. Suddenly a scent overwhelms me: *dinja* (melons). All the colours on the spectrum of yellow, orange, green. All the shapes. 'Can we get some?' 'Of course.' Next to the stall there is a small van with large watermelons. 'Can we get watermelon?' I plead. 'Yes, help me pick one.' Tap, tap, tap. A heave to lift and check for the yellow patch that lets us know it has had enough time in the field to ripen to peak sweetness and crispness. Assurances from the vendor. They are *sherbet blagi* – as sweet as syrup.

From the Larder

I wonder if this time, maybe, it will be a honey-yellow watermelon. Like that one time we got one when I was little! I keep hoping …

Today, I continue these practised steps; a lifetime spent following someone in a market. Dolac Market in Zagreb. Ljubljana Central Market. Markale in Sarajevo. Kalenić Pijac (green market) in Belgrade. Tuzi Pijaca in Podgorica. The market on the edge of Kotor. In Pula. The Tregu i Gjelbërt market of Prizren. And always the Zelen Pazar (green market) and Bit Pazar in Skopje. My footsteps lead me to the mountain-herb gatherers. The grandmother with deep-set dark brown eyes, the contours of her face like the landscape of the imposing mountains she calls home. She has a vast array of herbs and medicinal plants, all meticulously labelled, as well as concoctions and ferments. The grandfather proudly wearing his *šajkača* (a traditional Serbian hat) selling his own special mountain tea mix for children. The father wearing a *tirq* (a traditional northern Albanian and Kosovan hat) selling wild herbs alongside jars of mountain honey. All gathered on different sides (Macedonian, Serbian, Kosovan) of the same Šar Mountains. They lead me to a young woman whose market stall is nestled under one of the Plecnik arcade arches, the Ljubljanica River flowing behind her. She is selling dried linden from the forests of Slovenia and herbs gathered on Mount Triglav. Then on to the ladies selling their fermented cabbage and turnip. I walk past the tomato stall with signs saying 'ancient seed'. More stalls laden with the most beautiful produce – seasonal, regional. I happen upon the Istrian lady selling a mountain of wild *šparoge* (asparagus) who tells me her favourite recipe for them. Past the stalls with artisanal produce: homemade oils, brandies, liqueurs, cured meats, cheeses, truffles, honeys, spices, herb mixes. To the earthenware stall whose owner tells me of her daughter who also lives abroad in London. Next to it, the stall with traditional handicrafts, textiles and clothing.

I am filled with the vibrancy of the atmosphere and a sense that these footsteps have been taken by generations of Balkan people. I think how deeply embedded a stroll through the market is in our lifestyle and cultural identity. At its most functional, it is a place for city-dwellers to buy the best and freshest local produce, as well as a vibrant small-scale economy and place for farmers to sell their products and wares. It is a place of cultural exchange and a microcosm of people from various ethnic and religious denominations. A place to meet and socialise while sampling unique specialities and street food. I am grateful that it remains an essential part of daily Balkan life.

From the Larder

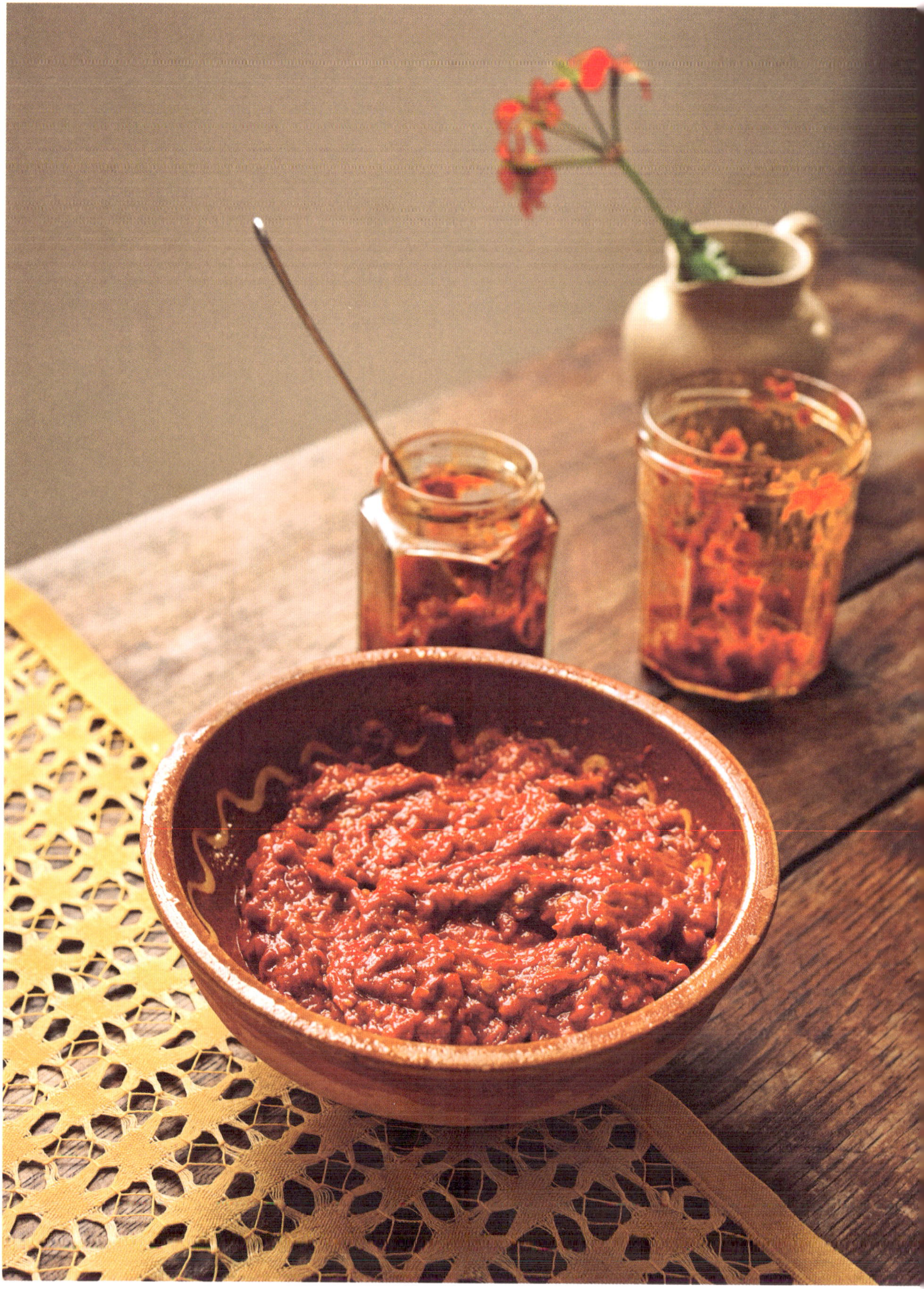

**MAKES 500–600 G
(1 LB 2 OZ–1 LB 5 OZ)**

Ajvar

Ajvar is known as Balkan caviar, and the word itself points to this as it is likely an adaptation of the Farsi word *khávyár* (caviar), brought to the Balkans via the Ottoman Empire, or perhaps before.

Historically, significant and economically important caviar production took place along the Danube River, utilising the wild sturgeon that travelled from the Black Sea up towards Vienna, but this practice eventually petered out towards the end of the 19th century for various reasons including political instability. 'Red caviar', made from more readily available and environmentally sustainable red peppers and aubergines (eggplants) – but still retaining some suggestion of exclusivity thanks to the use of sunflower oil, which was a real luxury at the time – replaced the 'real' caviar, and eventually became the one and only Balkan caviar. When exactly it became *ajvar* is the stuff of legends, but the general idea is that it was branded as such by restaurant owners in 19th-century Belgrade, most of whom seem to have come from Northern Macedonia. There is ongoing debate about who 'invented' (and therefore who can claim) *ajvar*, as well as the most 'authentic' flavours and methods of preparation.

Strumica in North Macedonia and Leskovac in Serbia are generally known for growing the best peppers for *ajvar*, called *ajvarki* or *Kurtovska kapija*. They are heart-shaped long red bell peppers with thin skins (perfect for roasting and peeling) and dense flesh (ideal for the all-important secondary cooking stage). Macedonian *ajvar* (using peppers and aubergines) and Leskovac ajvar (peppers only) are each respectively internationally registered and have protected appellations of origin. For it to be *ajvar*, there has to be a secondary cooking stage in which the roasted vegetables essentially confit in the oil. In lieu of this secondary cooking stage, some will use vinegar to preserve the roasted peppers and aubergines, but that does not quite have the same unique flavour. Having said that, *ajvar* – in all its glorious variations – is made and loved across the entire Balkan region (especially the nations and regions that formed part of Yugoslavia, and neighbouring countries like Albania and Bulgaria) and its cultural, historic and gastronomic importance transcends (or should transcend) modern political borders and debates. The only important thing to remember is that it is a delicious, addictive and incredibly versatile vegetable spread that has the potential to unite the region in its universal adulation of it.

From the Larder

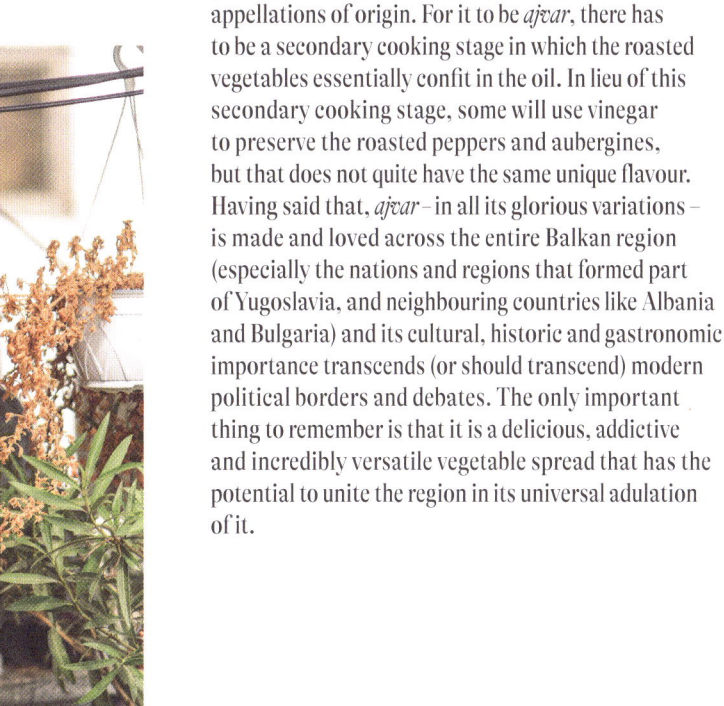

Recipe continued overleaf

- 2 kg (4 lb 8 oz) red peppers for ajvar (or long red Romano peppers)
- 300 g (10½ oz) aubergine (eggplant)
- 45–60 ml (3–4 tablespoons) sunflower or olive oil
- 1 teaspoon caster (superfine) sugar
- 1 teaspoon sea salt flakes, plus extra as needed
- freshly ground black pepper

From the end of summer and well into autumn, families, friends and neighbours gather together in their homes, gardens or balconies to roast hundreds of kilos of *Ajvarki* or *Kurtovska Kapija* red peppers and (if you find yourself in North Macedonia) aubergines (eggplants) over a *pećnica* (a specialised wood-fired or charcoal oven designed for roasting and charring peppers until their skins blister and blacken – a crucial step, as it imparts the iconic smoky flavour and makes them easier to peel. Making enough *ajvar* to last the winter takes an army: to peel the peppers and aubergines, to mince them, to stew the mixture in a large cauldron-sized saucepan over a gentle fire for hours, stirring with a large wooden spoon and adding as much sunflower oil as the vegetables will absorb until the mixture and flavour are concentrated and ready to be seasoned and stored in jars, ready for the onset of winter.

This is my base recipe for a small batch of Macedonian-style *ajvar* – scale it up if you like, and I encourage you to adapt it to your taste. Try adding some hot chilli peppers for piquancy, or use sweet long green peppers instead of red. If you love aubergines, play around with the pepper to aubergine ratio, or make a pepper-only version and add a little vinegar for Serbian-style *ajvar*. If you prefer, roast the peppers and aubergines over live fire for a smokier flavour – you will need to adjust their cooking times accordingly. The quality of the *ajvar* will depend on the quality of the peppers, so it is worth finding the best you can.

Preheat the oven to 200°C fan (425°F).

Arrange the peppers on two large baking trays (pans) lined with baking parchment. Prick the aubergine with a fork all over and nestle it among the peppers. Roast in the oven for 40–45 minutes, turning the vegetables over halfway through, until the skins of the peppers are blackened all over but the flesh is still juicy, and the aubergine is softened.

Remove the vegetables from the oven and place them in a colander set over a large bowl. Cover with a saucepan lid or reusable food wrap (this allows the peppers and aubergine to steam while cooling to make peeling easier). Set aside for 15–20 minutes.

Peel the aubergine and peel, destalk and deseed the peppers. Finely chop the pepper and aubergine flesh, then transfer it to a large, heavy-based saucepan along with any juices from your board. Place it over a medium-high heat and cook vigorously, stirring constantly with a wooden spoon, for about 10 minutes, or until the mixture bubbles and starts to thicken. When it does, reduce the heat to medium, add 30 ml (2 tablespoons) of the oil, the sugar and salt and a generous grind of black pepper and continue cooking for a further 20–30 minutes, stirring constantly. The mixture needs to gently bubble but must never stick to the bottom of the pan, so it needs constant attention. If it starts to look dry, add another 15 ml (1 tablespoon) oil and continue cooking. Depending on how your mixture absorbs the oil, you may need more.

Test the *ajvar* as you would jam – place a little of the mixture on a cold plate and run a teaspoon through the middle. If it does not flood back together and there is no oil leaking from the mixture, it is ready. If not, continue cooking for 5–10 minutes and then test again. Taste the *ajvar* and adjust the seasoning, adding more salt to your taste. When ready, spoon the hot *ajvar* into sterilised jars and seal. Once opened, store in the refrigerator and consume within 1 week.

MAKES ABOUT 750 G (1 LB 10 OZ)

Ljutenitsa

1.2 kg (2 lb 11 oz) red peppers for ajvar (or long red Romano peppers)
800 g (1 lb 12 oz) large beef (beefsteak) tomatoes
1–2 long red chillies, or more to taste
4–6 garlic cloves, finely chopped
1 tablespoon sea salt flakes, plus extra as needed
20 g (¾ oz/1½ tablespoons) caster (superfine) sugar
50 ml (1 ¾ fl oz/3½ tablespoons) red wine vinegar
100 ml (3½ fl oz/scant ½ cup) sunflower or olive oil
20 g (¾ oz) fresh parsley, leaves picked and finely chopped
freshly ground black pepper

Not to be confused with *ajvar*, *ljutenitsa* (a derivative of *ljuto*, meaning 'hot' or 'spicy') is another of the bastions of *zimnica* (winter preserves). Unlike *ajvar*, it is more of a relish than a vegetable spread, because it generally always contains tomatoes, which give it a looser consistency. Typical of North Macedonia, Serbia and Bulgaria, there are many variations. Some add cooked carrots or even apples, their sweetness helpfully offsetting the spiciness of the peppers. We typically use tiny lethal yellow or red chilli peppers called *fefferoni* (similar to Italian *pepperoncino*), but here I've gone for long red chillies as they are more widely available worldwide. The heat of *ljutenitsa* is a matter of personal preference – I like it somewhere between a gentle warmth on your palette and a cartoonesque smoke-out-of-ears moment. Although it is usually only the peppers that are roasted for *ljutenitsa*, I have suggested roasting the tomatoes and chillies alongside them out of a desire to simplify and accelerate the method and because I think it adds a nice depth of flavour.

Preheat the oven to 200°C fan (425°F).

Arrange the peppers, tomatoes and chillies on two large baking trays (pans) lined with baking parchment. Roast in the oven for 40–45 minutes, turning the vegetables over halfway through, until the skins of the peppers are blackened all over but the flesh is still juicy, and the tomatoes have softened and their skins are blistered.

Remove the vegetables from the oven and place them in a colander set over a large bowl. Cover with a saucepan lid or reusable food wrap and set aside to cool for 15–20 minutes.

Remove the cores from the tops of the tomatoes and peel them, then transfer to a food processor and blend coarsely. Scrape into a large, heavy-based saucepan and add the garlic, salt, a good grind of black pepper, the sugar, vinegar and oil. Simmer over a medium-high heat, stirring occasionally, for 10 minutes.

Meanwhile, peel, destalk and deseed the peppers and chillies. Finely chop the pepper and chilli flesh and add to the saucepan with the tomatoes. Reduce the heat to medium and continue to cook, stirring occasionally, for 30–40 minutes, or until the *ljutenitsa* has reached the consistency of a thick sauce. Finally, add the parsley and cook for a further 1–2 minutes. Taste and adjust the seasoning to your preference. When ready, spoon the hot *ljutenitsa* into sterilised jars and seal. Once opened, store in the refrigerator and consume within 1 week.

See photo on p. 90

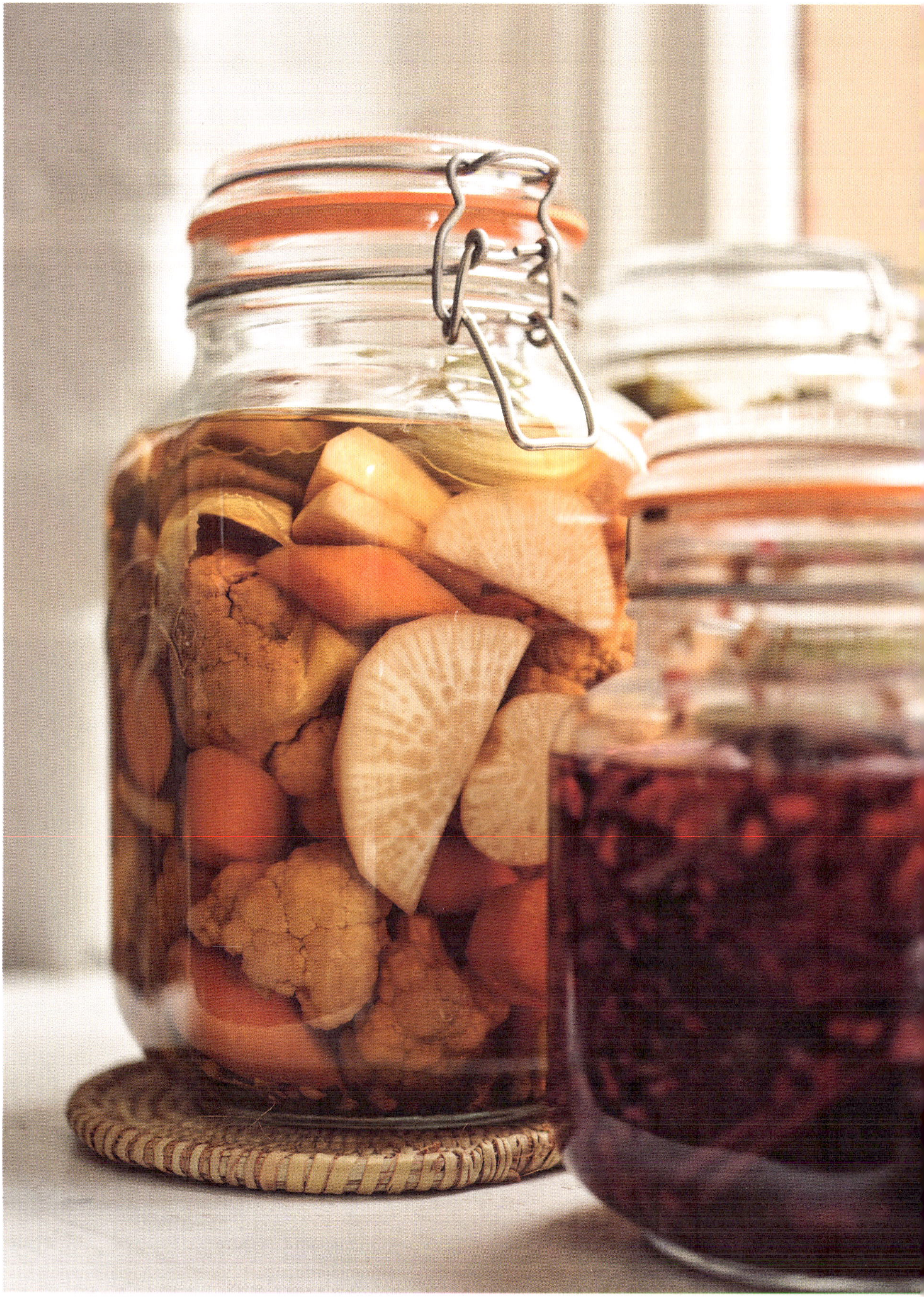

Turšija

In the Balkans *turšija* (derived from the Persian *torshi* and Turkish *turşu*, meaning 'sour') has, like its Persian, Levantine and central Asian cousins, become the umbrella term used to describe any vegetables that have been either fermented or pickled (typically in a vinegar-based solution) or otherwise soured and preserved.

There are hundreds of types of *turšija* according to regional (and family) preferences. They are typically prepared from late summer and into autumn (fall) to act as an appetizer, accompanying the various brandies of the region, but it is also seen as a kind of winter 'salad' to accompany heartier winter dishes. The fermentation liquid (or pickle juice) is infamously thought of as a hangover cure after a night of heavy drinking, but also a useful vitamin and gut-health booster shot!

Any combination of vegetables will work, and with any of the methods below – either a gentle pickle such as the cauliflower, carrot and turnip, or a pure 2–5% brine based ferment such as the sour cabbage. Feel free to play around with different flavour combinations. The pickled baby aubergines are a rather elegant version that is closely related to Turkish *patlıcan turşusu*. My grandmother made it and served it for special occasions to impress guests because it looks rather beautiful. If you use red cabbage, as I have, the pickle will turn a lovely fuchsia.

Cauliflower, carrot and turnip

MAKES 1 X 2 LITRE (68 FL OZ) JAR

- 700 g (1 lb 9 oz) cauliflower, cut into small florets
- 200 g (7 oz) carrots, peeled, topped and tailed, then sliced into 1 cm (½ inch) thick diagonal slices
- 200 g (7 oz) small/baby turnips, peeled, halved lengthwise and thickly sliced
- 1 sweet long green pepper, stalk trimmed
- 1–2 young vine leaves (optional)
- 650 ml (22 fl oz/2¾ cups) white wine vinegar
- 300 ml (10 fl oz/1¼ cups) water
- 2–3 bay leaves
- 1 teaspoon coriander seeds
- 125 g (4½ oz/generous ½ cup) granulated sugar
- 30 g (1 oz) sea salt flakes
- ¼ teaspoon black peppercorns

Plunge the vegetables into a saucepan of boiling water and blanch for 1 minute, then drain. Arrange the vegetables in a clean, sterilised 2 litre (68 fl oz/8½ cup) capacity clip-top jar.

To make the brine, combine the remaining ingredients in a saucepan and bring to the boil, then reduce the heat and simmer for 5 minutes. Remove from the heat and set aside to cool slightly before pouring the liquid and aromatics into the jar over the vegetables. Seal the jar immediately and place in a cool, dark spot away from direct heat. Allow to pickle for at least 4 weeks before using. Once opened, store in the refrigerator for up to 6 months

Pickled baby aubergines

MAKES 1 X 1 LITRE (34 FL OZ) JAR

300–350 g (10½–12 oz) baby aubergines (eggplants), stalks trimmed

4–5 thin celery stalks (or thicker stalks sliced lengthwise – no thicker than 5 mm/¼ inch)

10 g (½ oz) fresh parsley, leaves picked and finely chopped, stalks reserved

75 g (2½ oz) white or red cabbage, finely shredded

75 g (2½ oz) carrots, finely chopped

30 g (1 oz) celery leaves, finely chopped

1 tablespoon plus 1 teaspoon sea salt flakes

4–5 garlic cloves, halved

250 ml (8 fl oz/1 cup) white wine vinegar

1 tablespoon caster (superfine) sugar

½ teaspoon black peppercorns

100 ml (3½ fl oz/scant ½ cup) water

1 long red or green chilli pepper (optional)

freshly ground black pepper

Keeping them intact, slice the aubergines lengthwise 3–4 times from just below the green stem where the flesh begins so you have 1–1.5 cm (½–¾ inch) thick slices that are held together by the stem.

Place the sliced aubergines in a small saucepan and cover with water. Bring to the boil, then reduce the heat to medium and simmer gently for 20–25 minutes until the aubergines are soft but still holding their shape. Drain and set aside to cool.

Plunge the celery or parsley stalks (or both) into a large bowl of boiling water and blanch for 1 minute until soft. Drain and set aside.

To make the filling, combine the cabbage, carrots, celery leaves and parsley leaves in a bowl with 1 tablespoon of the salt and a generous grind of black pepper and mix well.

Next, make the brine. Combine the garlic, vinegar, sugar, 1 teaspoon of salt, peppercorns and water in a small saucepan over a medium-high heat and simmer for 1 minute, just until the brine is hot and the sugar and salt have dissolved. Remove from the heat and set aside to cool slightly.

Now assemble the pickle. Place some of the filling between each slice of the aubergine, then, using the celery or parsley stalks, tie the layers together so that the aubergine is held together in its original shape. Place any remaining filling in the base of a sterilised 1 litre (34 fl oz/4¼ cup) jar. Put the aubergine parcels in the jar, packing them in tightly. Add the chilli, if you like. Pour over the warm brine. Place any remaining celery or parsley stalks on the top to secure the aubergines in the jar and press them down so they are submerged in the brine. Seal the jar and store in a cool, dark place. Leave to develop its flavours for at least 30 days before using. Once opened, store in the refrigerator for up to 6 months.

MAKES 1 X 5 LITRE (1¼ GALLON) BUCKET

Sour Cabbage

2–3 white cabbages (about 3 kg/ 6 lb 10 oz total)
165 g (6 oz/1¼ cups) sea salt flakes, plus extra as needed
1 beetroot, peeled and quartered
3.5 litres (118 fl oz/14¾ cups) distilled or dechlorinated water (or tap water that has been boiled and then cooled to room temperature)
2–3 tablespoons lemon juice

Kisel, *kiseli kupus* or *kiselo zelje* – fermented whole sour cabbages – is more of an art form than an exact science. Every family across the Balkans has their own techniques and recipes. My grandmother always added beetroot, which gave the cabbage a delicate flavour and a lovely pink hue.

For whole cabbage heads, I have found the best brine percentage to be 3–5 per cent. With the salt in the cores and the 3 per cent brine, this recipe lands at just over 4 per cent.

Prepare the cabbages. Using a sharp paring knife, remove the outer leaves and the cores of the cabbages, cutting conically almost halfway into the cabbage. Place 2 tablespoons of the salt (about 20 g/¾ oz) into each cabbage core.

Pack the cabbages tightly into a sterilised 5 litre (1¼ gallon) capacity transparent lidded tub or bucket, wedging them with each other and keeping the salt-filled cores facing upwards. Add the beetroot.

To make the brine, dilute the remaining 105 g (3¾ oz/generous ¾ cup) of salt in the water and pour it around the cabbages, taking care not to wash out the salt from the cores. Add the lemon juice. The brine should cover the cabbages; if it doesn't, make a little more using 15 g (½ oz) salt for every 500 ml (17 fl oz/generous 2 cups) water. Weigh the cabbages down with a sterilised fermentation weight or heavy plate which should also be submerged in the brine. Secure the lid and set aside at room temperature away from direct sunlight.

For the first week, check the ferment daily to 'burp it' and release gas build up. You need to circulate the water daily by scooping the brine with a sterilised ladle and pouring it back in and repeating this several times to create a gentle vertical whirlpool. Around day 4, taste the brine – it should taste like sea water, and you should start to detect a gentle fizz and sourness. If not, add another 1–2 tablespoons salt and taste again the next day. After the first week, check and circulate the brine every 2–3 days. After 2 weeks at room temperature, transfer the container to a garage or cellar, and continue to taste and circulate the brine every 2–3 days. The water should stay fairly clear throughout the ferment. The cabbages will naturally release more liquid and shrink slightly as they ferment. If you see a white bloom of (harmless) kahm yeast on the surface of the brine, remove it, taking care not to mix it with the brine below, then clean the rim of the bucket, and re-sterilise the fermentation weight and lid. A bloom of any other colour – red, blue, green, grey or black – will mean the ferment has gone bad and you need to discard it and start over. The best way to avoid this is to ensure everything is always submerged in the brine.

The ferment will be ready anywhere between 4–6 weeks or once the flavour is as you like it. When ready either use the sour cabbage, or transfer it to the refrigerator to stop (or slow) the fermentation where it can keep for around 4 weeks.

**MAKES ABOUT
1.2 KG (2 LB 11 OZ)**

Three-citrus Marmalade

700 g (1 lb 9 oz) unwaxed organic citrus fruits (1 pink grapefruit, 1 blood orange and 1 lemon)

1.8 litres (61 fl oz/7½ cups) water, or more or less as needed (see method)

1 kg (2 lb 4 oz/4½ cups) granulated sugar, or more or less as needed (see method)

Marmalade is a term used across the Balkans to refer to a fruit preserve made from any fruit ground into a pulp, then cooked down with sugar and some form of citric acid (usually lemon juice). It is mostly a term used for peaches, apricots and other stone fruit, but also, confusingly, for marmalade made from citrus. This is my mother's rather clever method for citrus marmalade, which involves minimal effort, maximum flavour and is relatively quick. Importantly for me, the end result is pleasingly sour and not overly sweet.

Wash the citrus fruits well, then trim the ends of each and slice into quarters lengthwise. Trim the central column of white pith from each quarter, then remove all the pips. Place all the trim, pith and pips in a pieces of muslin (cheesecloth), tie it securely and set aside.

Slice the citrus quarters into thin wedges (no more than 2 mm thick). Weigh the fruit (and any juices) and place in a large saucepan. Add three times the weight of water (for example, for 600 g/1 lb 5 oz fruit, that is 1.8 litres/61 fl oz/7½ cups water). Add the muslin bag containing the pips and submerge it. Cover and set aside for 24 hours.

The next day, remove the muslin bag, squeezing out as much of the pectin-rich juice as you can into the fruit and water mixture, then discard it.

Place the saucepan over a medium-high heat and simmer for 2 hours, or until the fruit is soft and the peels are translucent. Skim off any froth from time to time as the mixture simmers. It should reduce by about half.

Carefully weigh the cooked mixture again and, if you like your marmalade sweeter, add the same weight of sugar. I prefer mine a little less sweet, so I reduce the sugar by one-sixth – so for 1.2 kg (2 lb 11 oz) mixture, I add 1 kg (2 lb 4 oz/4½ cups) sugar.

Return to the heat and simmer until the marmalade thickens and reaches setting point. Once it has, remove from the heat, skim off any froth gathered at the top with a clean spoon, cover with a damp dish towel and leave to rest for 15–30 minutes. Spoon the marmalade into sterilised jars and seal.

Note
As this is a method that works by volume, feel free to play around with the citrus you use, though always include at least one lemon as it helps the marmalade to set.

Apricot Dzem

**MAKES ABOUT
400–500 G
(14 OZ–1 LB 2 OZ)**

1 kg (2 lb 4 oz) apricots
300–400 g (10½–14 oz) caster (superfine) sugar
2–3 tablespoons lemon juice

Unlike marmalade or *slatko* (see pages 246 and 249), for *dzem*, fruit is halved or quartered and cooked in such a way as to ensure that the fruit pieces keep their shape and texture, somewhat. Typically, this is made on the stove, but baking the jam is much easier and gives a more interesting flavour, with a slight edge of caramelisation. When I was little, I used to crack apricot stones with a large rock and eat them like almonds. Using them for this *dzem* gives it a nice almond flavour and is, I suppose, the grown-up version of that. Though I confess, when I make this, a few stones do make their way into the garden where I still crack them with a large stone and for a few moments relive my childhood.

Preheat the oven to 180°C fan (400°F).

Halve and stone the apricots and weigh them. Place them in a baking dish large enough that you have no more than two layers of apricots. Carefully break open 10–12 apricot stones, trying to keep the kernels whole. Peel the kernels as much as possible (the skins can be slightly bitter) and add them to the baking dish with the apricots. Add half the weight of the stone apricots in sugar (for example, for 800 g/1 lb 12 oz apricots, add 400 g/14 oz sugar). Add the lemon juice and bake, uncovered, for 1–1½ hours, stirring occasionally, until the jam has reached your preferred consistency. Remove from the oven, cover with a damp dish towel and leave to rest for 15–30 minutes. Spoon the jam into sterilised jars and seal.

Note

Feel free to play around with flavours. I occasionally add a sprig of rosemary or orange blossom 10–15 minutes before the end of the cooking time. This method works well with all stone fruits – if they are not as juicy, add 1–2 tablespoons water before you bake them.

Plum Pekmez

**MAKES ABOUT
200–300 G
(7–10½ OZ)**

1 kg (2 lb 4 oz) prune plums, halved and stoned
2 tablespoons water
1–2 tablespoons caster (superfine) sugar
2–3 tablespoons lemon juice

Unlike Turkish *pekmez* (fruit condensed to a molasses-like syrup), Balkan *pekmez* is even more condensed and more of a fruit butter or spread. Fruits with high natural sugar are perfect for this, and the most ideal (and favoured) candidate for *pekmez* is the iconic prune plum also used to produce *šljivovica* (plum brandy). Other blue plum varieties such as Victoria plums work well also. You will need very ripe plums – if they are not quite there yet, place them in a paper bag at room temperature for a day or two to ripen.

Place the plums in a large, heavy-based saucepan with the water and cook over a medium heat, stirring continuously with a wooden spoon, for 10–15 minutes until the skins of the plums have separated. Strain the plums through a fine-mesh sieve, pressing the pulp through with your spoon, to remove the skins. Discard the skins and return the pulp to the saucepan along with the sugar and lemon juice. Cook over a medium heat for 1–½ hours, or until the pulp has reduced by over half and is a thick, spreadable consistency. Spoon the *pekmez* into sterilised jars and seal.

From the Larder

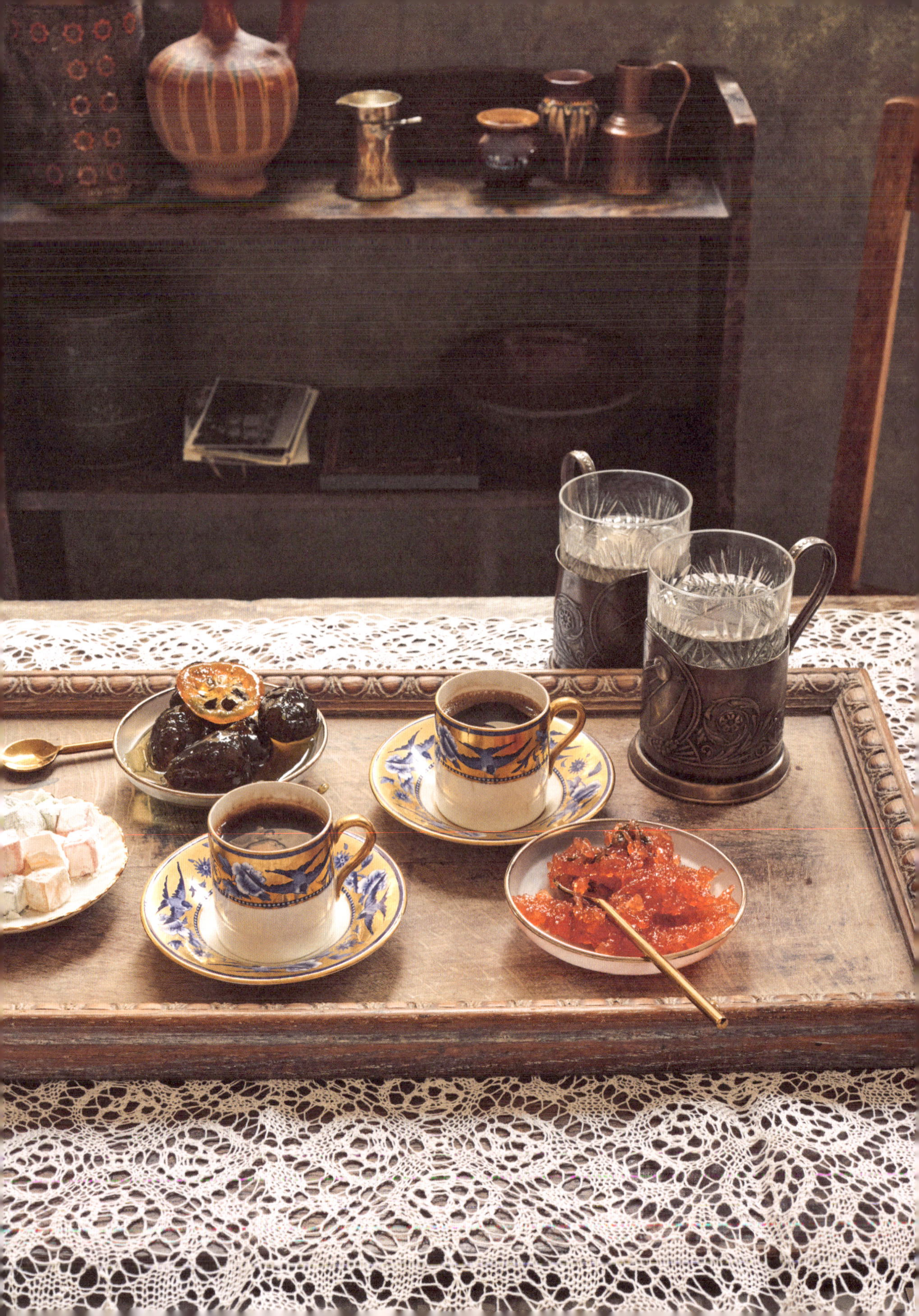

Slatko

Slatko translates literally as 'sweet', but here it refers specifically to spoon sweets, which are whole fruits (or fruit pieces) cooked in sugar syrup. *Slatko* is always served with a glass of cold water and Turkish coffee, to welcome guests to a home. Green fig and quince *slatko* are my favourites – very closely followed by sour cherries or yellow cherries (which are difficult to source in the UK) and wild strawberries.

MAKES ABOUT 1 KG (2 LB 4 OZ)

1 kg (2 lb 4 oz/4¼ cups) granulated sugar
300 ml (10 fl oz/1¼ cups) water
1 lemon, thinly sliced
3–4 quinces (for 700-800 g/1 lb 9 oz– 1 lb 12 oz grated quince)
1–2 lemon-scented geranium (*Pelargonium citrosum*) leaves (optional)

Quince

After my grandmother passed away, one of the many painful things my mother and I had to do was to go through her *špajz*, which was stocked full of her beautiful homemade preserves, so lovingly prepared and ready to give us a taste of the seasons we had missed while living abroad. We shared as many as we could with our loved ones. I came back to London with a suitcase full of them, and most were her quince *slatko* – always my favourite. Over the years, they have been opened for special moments – my wedding, the birth of my son, moving to a new home. I have one jar of quince *slatko* left, which I will perhaps never open because, through this jar, my beloved grandmother is somehow still feeding it to me. This is her recipe.

Put the sugar and water into a large, heavy-based saucepan over a medium-high heat and simmer for 10–15 minutes until the sugar has dissolved and a thin syrup has formed.
 Meanwhile, fill a large bowl with water and add the lemon slices. Peel and grate the quince, dropping the grated quince into the lemon water as you go to avoid it discolouring. When the syrup is ready, drain the grated quince and and transfer it and the lemon slices to the syrup. Simmer over a medium-high heat for about 1 hour, stirring occasionally with a wooden spoon and skimming off the froth from time to time (clean your skimming spoon each time). When the quince has turned a pale peach colour, remove the pan from the heat and cover with a damp dish towel. Set aside to rest for 15–30 minutes to allow the quinces to release any retained moisture.
 Place the saucepan over a medium-high heat again, add the geranium leaves (if using) and continue to cook, skimming off any froth from time to time, for a further 20–25, or until it reaches setting point. When it's ready, remove the pan from the heat, cover again with the dish towel and allow to rest for about 15 minutes. Spoon the *slatko* into sterilised jars and seal.

From the Larder

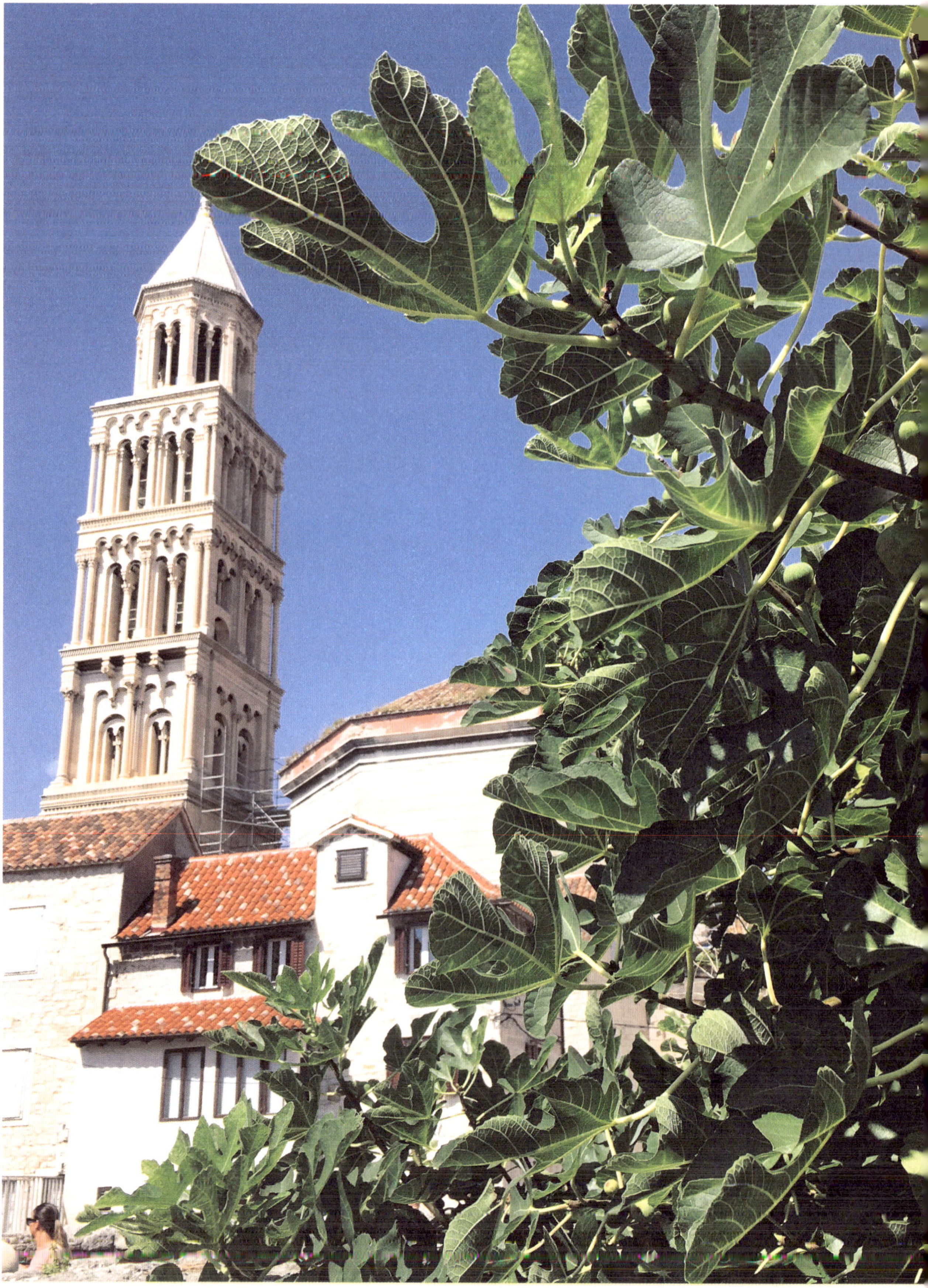

Green fig

1.5 kg (3 lb 5 oz) green (unripe) figs (no larger than 2–2.5 cm/¾–1 inch), tops trimmed

1 teaspoon bicarbonate of soda (baking soda)

3 lemons (1 sliced, 5–6 strips of zest and 60 ml/2 fl oz/¼ cup juice)

3 kg (6 lb 11 oz/13½ cups) granulated sugar

1.5 litres (50¾ fl oz/6⅓ cups) water

In our garden there is a very old and wild fig tree. It is one of the reasons I fell in love with our current home. It produces an incredible number of figs, but few ever ripen, and when they do, I rarely get to them before the local London gangs of pigeons and parakeets. I preempt them by using the green figs in spring. This particular *slatko* takes a lot of time and patience but is truly worth it. My grandmother, and every maker of green fig *slatko* I have spoken to, swears by the 'nine waters rule' – the figs need to cook in nine waters. It has, as far as I can discover, no scientific basis other than to ensure the figs are soft enough. My grandmother used to add bicarbonate of soda (baking soda) during the middle simmer to soften the figs, so I do too, and I have found that they are usually soft enough by the sixth simmer.

Skewer each fig with a cocktail stick (toothpick) from the stalk through to the bottom. Place them in a large, heavy-based saucepan, cover with 3 litres (100 fl oz/12½ cups) cold water, then place over a high heat and bring to the boil. Reduce the heat to medium and simmer gently for 10–15 minutes. Carefully and gently (without breaking up the figs) strain through a colander. Return to the saucepan, add 3 litres (100 fl oz/12½ cups) fresh cold water and repeat the process: bring to the boil, reduce to simmer for 10–15 minutes, strain. Repeat the process four more times (six batches of water in total). For the fourth repetition, add the bicarbonate of soda with the water. For the final repetition, add the lemon zest. Very carefully strain the figs and set them aside. Discard the lemon zest.

Clean the saucepan, then add the sugar and 1.5 litres (50¾ fl oz/6⅓ cups) water, place over a medium-high heat and simmer until the sugar has dissolved (agitate the sugar gently with a spoon to encourage it to dissolve). Next add the figs, lemon slices and lemon juice and simmer gently over a medium heat for 30–40 minutes until the syrup thickens to the consistency of honey. Remove from the heat, cover with a damp dish towel and leave to rest for about 15 minutes. The figs will release any retained moisture and dilute the syrup, so resting allows you to control the final consistency of the syrup. Return the *slatko* to the heat and bring back to the boil, then simmer gently to thicken the syrup to your taste – bearing in mind the syrup will thicken further as it cools (I suggest 10–15 minutes). Skim any froth with a clean spoon. Test the *slatko* to make sure it's set and when ready, remove from the heat, cover again with the dish towel and leave to rest for about 15 minutes. Spoon the *slatko* into sterilised jars and seal.

From the Larder

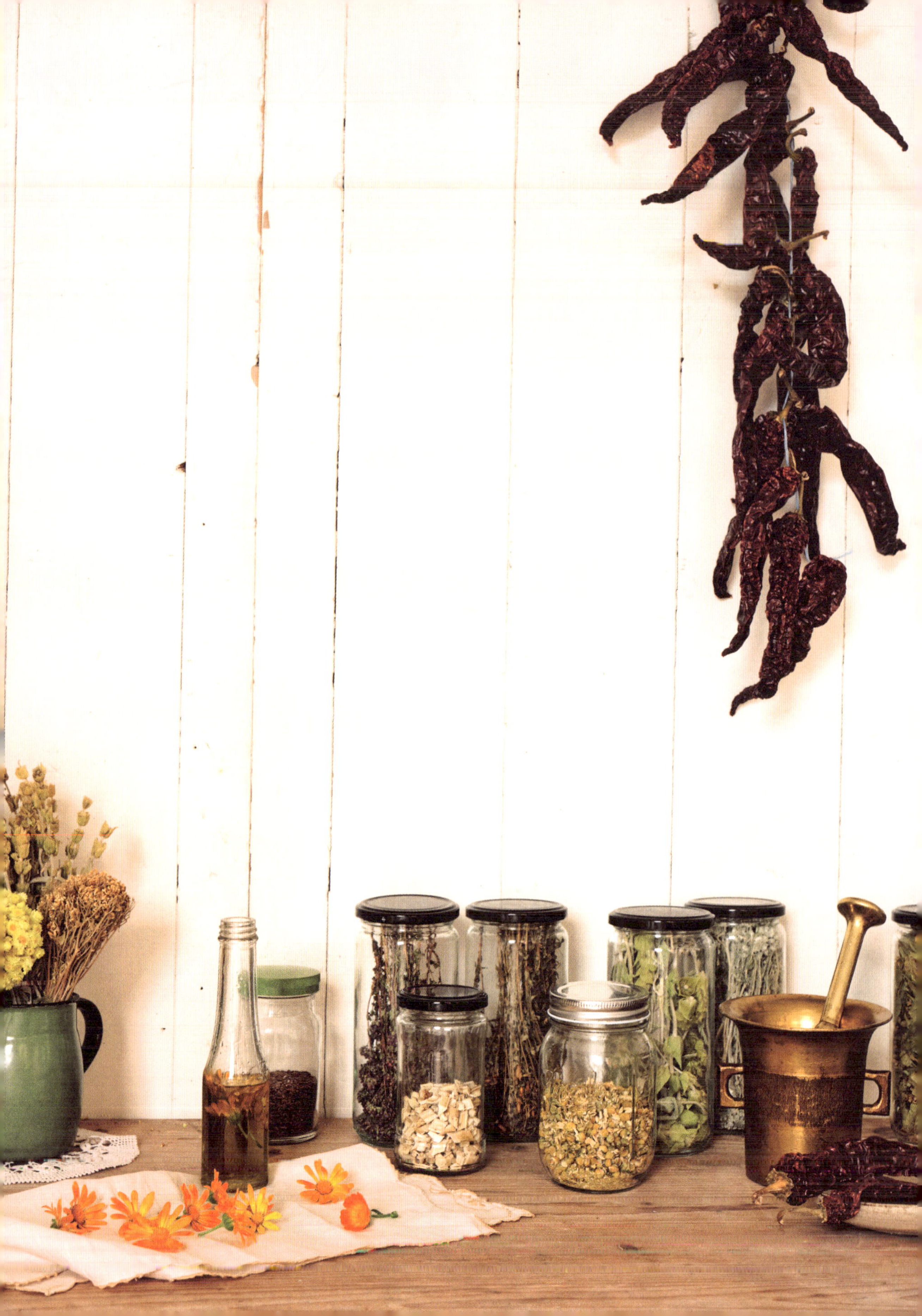

MAKES ABOUT 500 ML (17 FL OZ/GENEROUS 2 CUPS)

Linseed Tea

1 tablespoon brown linseeds (flaxseeds)
1 litre (34 fl oz/4¼ cups) boiling water, plus extra as needed
honey, to taste

The diverse Balkan landscape is a treasure trove of *lekovite biljke* (medicinal plants) that have been used for generations to make home remedies for treating most common ailments (from digestive issues and common colds to fevers) and for promoting general well-being and health. Reliance on locally available, natural resources and traditional medicinal knowledge has been crucial to survival in the region over centuries. Accordingly there is a rich tradition - very much still alive - of carefully collecting various herbs, including chamomile, mint, sage, thyme and oregano, as well as native plants, such as the leaves, flowers and fruits of the European linden or lime (*Tilia x europea*), nettles, calendula and rosehips, and wild mountain plants, such as yarrow, *planinski čaj* (mountain tea, also known as *sideritis* or ironwort), *kantarion* (St John's wort) - typically infused in oil and used for all manner of cuts, bruises, muscle aches and pains and joint dislocations, and tubers of certain species of wild orchids (*Orchis mascula* or *Orchis militaris*) are collected, dried and ground to produce a flour that is mixed with sugar, flavourings, and liquid (such as water or milk) to produce a thick drink called *salep* – though the latter are now protected species, due to depletion of the population. Roots of other plants are utilised, too, for example a tisane - made by steeping marshmallow root, then mixed with lemon juice and honey is a favoured home remedy for alleviating respiratory illnesses. In our home, coughs are cured with this linseed tea - which is really more of a homemade cough syrup than a tea. I recommend you use organic, brown linseeds if you can.

Put the linseeds and water into a medium heavy-based saucepan over a medium-high heat and simmer for 25–30 minutes until the water becomes a translucent reddish brown and has thickened to a syrupy consistency. Remove from the heat, cover and leave to cool slightly. The liquid will thicken further as it cools and become gloopy. Don't let this put you off. Pass the mixture through a fine-mesh sieve and discard the linseeds. Add honey to taste. If you cannot get past the consistency, loosen it with a little boiling water before serving.

From the Larder

Rada's Šumadijski Čaj

SERVES 6–8

- 100 g (3½ oz/scant ½ cup) caster (superfine) sugar
- 500 ml (17 fl oz/generous 2 cups) good-quality šljivovica (ideally meka šljivovica if you can find it, but any rakija or šljivovica will work)
- 300 ml (10 fl oz/1¼ cups) water, or more if you prefer it a little weaker
- 1 cinnamon stick (optional)
- 1 vanilla pod (bean), split (optional)
- 8 prunes, to serve (optional)

Šumadijski čaj simply means 'Šumadijan tea', but tea this is not. It is cooked *rakija* (fruit brandy) – and it is therefore also called *kuvana rakija*. This is very much a winter warmer for when the snow and frosts arrive – our version of a hot toddy – but it is also served to welcome guests to the home during the festive winter season. Šumadijan tea is typically made with *meka* (soft) *rakija* or *šljivovica* (plum brandy). Soft *rakija* is the 'first cook' of fermented fruit and is therefore a weaker or softer brandy (typically around 20 per cent alcohol) than what is known as *prepečenica* (overbaked), which is the 'second cook' *rakija* (typically 40–50 per cent alcohol, or stronger if homemade).

Šumadija is a historically and economically important region in central Serbia, named so because of the once dense and almost impenetrable forests (*šuma*) which have now given way to large-scale food production thanks to the area's incredibly fertile soils that are especially suited to fruit production. Unsurprisingly, some of the best *rakija* and *šljivovica* the Balkans has to offer comes from here. My friend Ivan Marković, a self-professed gastrophile who has travelled Serbia (and the rest of the Balkans extensively) in search of forgotten and unique dishes, hails from Šumadija and he kindly shared his tips and his mother's – Mrs Rada Marković from Gornji Milanovac – recipe for *Šumadijski čaj*. The recipe comes with a warning – do not inhale the fumes when you cook it, or ... you will be incapacitated. He also suggested adding prunes to serve, which is a lovely touch. I hope they will both forgive my addition of some atypical aromatics ...

Start by making a caramel: place a medium heavy-based saucepan over a medium heat. When the saucepan is hot, add the sugar and shake the pan gently to ensure the sugar is distributed evenly over the base of the pan. Do not stir the sugar. When it starts to melt and colour at the edges, gently agitate it with a fork or the handle of a wooden spoon to encourage all the sugar to melt. As more of the sugar melts and colours, gently swirl the pan to ensure even colouring. When all the sugar has melted and you have a deep golden brown caramel, reduce the heat to medium and very carefully (as the caramel will splutter), pour in the *šljivovica* and water, and swirl the pan to dissolve the caramel. Add the cinnamon stick and vanilla pod (if using) and cook for 3–4 minutes, just until the liquid starts to bubble – don't let it simmer. Remove from the heat and strain into a heatproof serving jug (pitcher).

To serve, place a prune in a small heatproof cup (such as an espresso cup), then pour in some of the hot *Šumadijski čaj*.

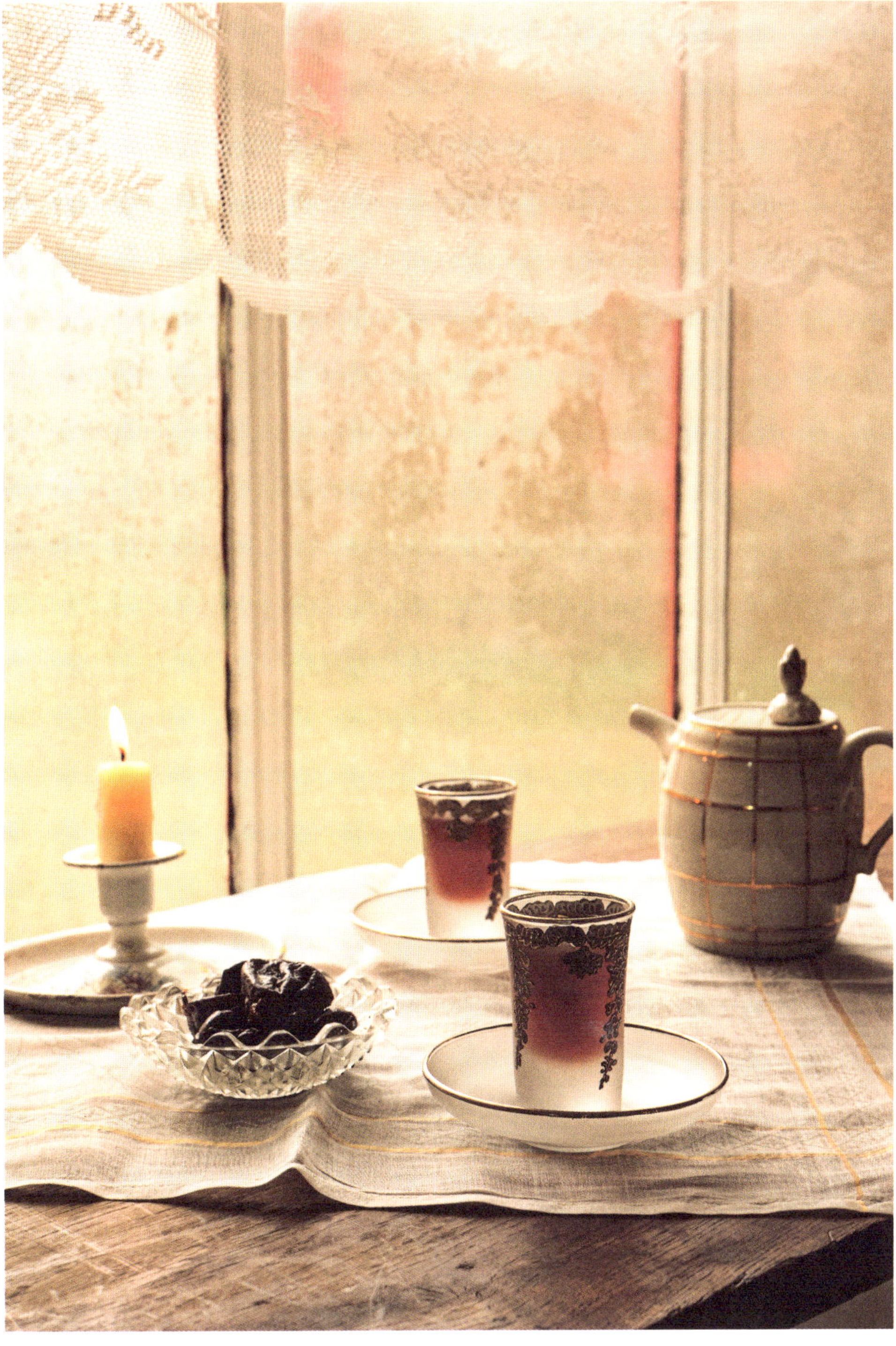

Red Fruit Liqueur

MAKES ABOUT 1 LITRE (34 FL OZ/4¼ CUPS)

- 600 g (1 lb 5 oz) red fruits, such as strawberries, raspberries, redcurrants, blackcurrants, sweet or sour cherries, loganberries and blackberries (one or a mix of any), stalks and leaves removed, pitted if necessary and halved or quartered if large
- 300 g (10½ oz/scant 1⅓ cups) caster (superfine) sugar, plus extra to taste
- 1 litre (34 fl oz/4¼ cups) good-quality lozova rakija (or grappa), plus extra as needed

In a bygone era when family doctors still made house calls, my great-grandmother Olga (in)famously feigned a malady every time the family doctor visited their house in Pajkomaalo (the old city centre of Skopje, sadly destroyed in the 1963 earthquake) to attend to someone in the family. The cure for her 'sickness' was always a prescription for a litre of pure alcohol, which she would use to make the most incredible orange or mandarin liqueurs. One of the other family recipes for liqueur passed down to me (orally) is no more than an instruction to steep red fruits with sugar in alcohol as the fruits come into season – starting with wild strawberries and carrying on through to blackberries. I do it all in one go, at the perfect moment when a few of my favourite red fruits overlap in summer, but I do top it up with a handful of foraged blackberries at the end of summer. You can use any combination of fruits, or indeed stick to one fruit. Whichever mixture you use, do always include at least one naturally sweet red fruit like strawberries, to balance the sourer ones. I typically use *lozova rakija* (grape brandy) – similar to Italian *grappa* – to make liqueurs, as I find the flavour of whatever I am infusing it with tends to come out better.

Layer the fruit with the sugar in a 1.5 litre (50¾ fl oz/6⅓ cup) sterilised clip-top jar. Close and set aside to rest overnight. The next day, the fruit should have released some of its juices. Top with the *rakija*. There should be about 2 cm (¾ inch) of liquid above the fruit – top up with more *rakija* if not.

Wipe any residue from the rim of the jar with a clean cloth, close, then set aside in a spot that gets direct sunlight for 1 month, giving it an gentle swirl every 4–5 days.

After a month, check the flavour. If you like it, strain most of the liquid through a fine-mesh sieve (reserve enough to just cover the fruits), sweeten it further if you like, then pour it into a sterilised bottle, close and store it as you do all other alcohol. As for the reserved fruits infused with *rakija* – store them in clean airtight container in the refrigerator submerged in a little bit of the alcohol for up to 4 weeks. They work wonderfully as a last-minute dessert spooned over some amaretti or lady fingers biscuits, served with ice cream or double (heavy) cream and dark (bitterwsweet) chocolate.

From the Larder

MAKES ABOUT 1 LITRE (34 FL OZ/4¼ CUPS)

Orahovača

600 g (1 lb 5 oz) green (young) walnuts, washed, patted dry and quartered
250 g (9 oz/scant 1¼ cups) granulated sugar, or more to taste
5–6 strips of lemon zest
1 cinnamon stick
1 vanilla pod (bean), halved lengthwise
750 ml (25 fl oz/3 cups) good-quality lozova rakija (or grappa)
honey, to sweeten (optional)

I've lost track of the reasons why walnuts are integral to the Balkan way of life. The obvious ones are the use of walnut wood (for medicinal purposes, as well as for anything from kitchen utensils to furniture) and the ripe nuts, the latter of which are the bastions of Balkan baking. The spiritual reason is the shade of a walnut tree – the deepest, most cooling and most precious of all tree shades in the summer sun. The practical one is the walnut leaves, gathered, dried and stored around cupboards to protect clothes and linen from moths. The alchemical reasons: to make various concoctions, from young green walnut preserves and pickles to walnut leaf honey and homemade hair moisturisers. It is commonly thought that walnuts originated in Asia and were dispersed through migration into Europe, but recent evidence of the presence of walnut trees in glacial refugia across the Balkans suggests a more complex picture of the evolution of these bountiful trees. Suffice it to say, our love affair with walnuts is unsurprising and ancient. If you are lucky to have a walnut tree in your garden or your vicinity and you can bring yourself to sacrifice a few, precious green walnuts, do make *orahovača* (or *orahovac*) – a wonderful liqueur, which is very much a cousin to French *liqueur de noix* and Italian *nocino*. Use green walnuts from the common European walnut (*Juglans regia*). They are usually in season from late June through to early July in the northern hemisphere. After this, they harden into the ripe fruits. It goes without saying that the better quality of *rakija* you use, the better the outcome will be.

Put the walnuts, sugar, lemon zest, cinnamon stick and vanilla pod into a 1.5 litre (50¾ fl oz/6⅓ cup) sterilised clip-top jar and cover with the *rakija*.

Sit the jar by a window that gets direct sunlight for 3–5 days, giving the contents of the jar a gentle stir with a clean spoon once a day, every day, until the sugar dissolves.

Next, place the jar somewhere dark and leave it for at least 21 days. After this time, taste the liqueur. If you are happy with the depth of flavour, strain it through a fine-mesh sieve into a sterilised bottle (or bottles – they make excellent presents). If you prefer a deeper flavour, leave it for a few more days, but no longer than 30 days. Check the sweetness, too – if you prefer your liqueur sweeter, add some honey or extra sugar after straining the liqueur.

Note

Feel free to play around with different flavourings: orange, star anise, cloves and so on. When cutting green walnuts, use gloves and cover the surface or you will never get rid of the stains. The flavour deepens and develops beautifully over time after straining – if you can, leave it out of direct sunlight for at least a year (ideally two), then taste and adjust the sweetness before you start using it. I like to round off the flavour by sweetening it with honey.

From the Larder

**MAKES ABOUT
1.5 LITRES
(50¾ FL OZ/6⅓ CUPS)**

Boza

100 g (3½ oz/¾ cup) organic millet flour
2 litres (68 fl oz/8½ cups) spring water (or water that has been boiled and then cooled)
150 g (5½ oz/generous ¾ cup) light brown soft sugar, plus extra to taste
1 teaspoon fast-action dried yeast

Boza is a malted drink made by fermenting millet (thought of as the most prized), maize, wheat, bulgur, barley, rice or even chickpeas (garbanzos). In the Balkans, as elsewhere in the world, malted drinks made from fermented grains date back to when humans started gathering the grains. It is very likely that some form of *boza* came to the region via the Levant. Whether it retained its original form or was adapted into what was already being produced in the region is difficult to say. Undoubtedly it was popularised by the Ottomans – it was famously a drink favoured by the Janissary corps, who were prohibited from drinking alcohol, but who could indulge in this (mildly alcoholic) beverage. *Boza* is still enjoyed in its various forms all over Turkey and the Balkans and is thought of as a power drink, high in vitamin B and often recommended to breastfeeding mothers. The colour varies according to the flour used – anything from light beige to brown. The consistency varies according to regional preferences. Of course, the preparation methods vary, too. For example, in Bulgaria, the flour is toasted before cooking and then fermented, which gives a nuttier flavour and darker colour. In Serbia, it is often thinner and paler. This version is what I grew up drinking in sweet shops in North Macedonia, usually served cold, as an accompaniment to a delicious cake or *baklava*. The flavour varies greatly depending on the method used as well as the flour, but it will always be what most would call an 'acquired taste' – somewhere between mildly alcoholic, sour beer and sweet and malty.

Put the flour into a large, heavy-based saucepan and pour in the water, stirring well. Bring to the boil, then reduce the heat to medium-high and simmer for 25–30 minutes, stirring to ensure there are no lumps and the flour does not stick. You should have a thick soup texture. Remove from the heat, cover and set aside to cool to room temperature.

Pour the mixture into a large sterilised plastic bowl. Spoon a little of the mixture (around 50 ml/1¾ fl oz/3½ tablespoons) into a small bowl, add 1 tablespoon of the sugar and the yeast, stir and set aside for 5–10 minutes until the yeast froths. Once it has, add it to the large bowl with a further 100 g (3½ oz/generous ½ cup) of the sugar, stirring well to combine. Cover the bowl with a sterilised plastic cover and set aside somewhere dark to ferment at room temperature for 12–48 hours. Start to check, stir and taste the mixture occasionally after 12 hours – you should start to see air bubbles and detect a gentle fizz, a slightly sweet smell and a tinge of sourness. Stop the fermentation when you like the flavour – if you prefer sweeter *boza*, shorten the fermentation process, if you prefer it more acidic, go beyond the 48 hours. I tend to stop after 36 hours.

When you like the flavour, strain the mixture through a muslin. Add the rest of the sugar, mix it well and decant it into sterilised bottles. Place the bottles in the refrigerator – it will fizz for the first 12–24 hours until it settles, when it is ready to be consumed. Serve as is or sweetened to taste.

Note

If you prefer your *boza* thicker, reduce the amount of water when you cook the millet flour. Equally, feel free to dilute the *boza* with water if you prefer it thinner.

Consume within 3–5 days once its ready; after that it turns slightly too acidic.

MAKES 1 COCKTAIL

Lilac Gin and Tonic

50 ml (1¾ fl oz/3½ tablespoons) floral gin
20 ml (1½ tablespoons) lilac syrup, or more to taste (see below)
125 ml (4 fl oz/½ cup) tonic water (I like Fever-Tree Indian tonic water)
lilac flowers and a lemon wedge, to garnish

FOR THE LILAC SYRUP

20 g (¾ oz) lilac (*Syringa vulgaris*) flowers (4–6 clusters of flowers), rinsed and patted dry
3–4 blackcurrants or blueberries (fresh or frozen)
200 g (7 oz/1 cup minus 2 tablespoons) caster (superfine) sugar
200 ml (7 fl oz/scant 1 cup) boiling water

Spring days when the lilacs bloom are fleeting, their heady, ethereal scent immediately transports me to streets across the Balkans lined with lilac, branches bursting with abundant clusters of flowers, from white to purple and every shade between. Lilac flowers fall like snow with even the gentlest gust of wind. Children making garlands from the tiny blooms. Young and old lovers sit on benches under the overburdened branches, intoxicated with each other, intoxicated with the unmistakeable scent. 'How can I go on without you, when difficult days come, when old friends are gone, and when the lilacs begin to smell,' sang Vesna Zmijanac and Dino Merlin, alluding to our almost mythical love of lilacs. It is a love that has stayed with me, and for a few days (if we are lucky, weeks) in early May, I roam the streets of London searching for the scent of lilac and come home laden with stolen branches of blooms. This syrup is the best way I have found to preserve that scent for just a little longer, as I await the return of the lilac blossom the following year. Pick lilac clusters that are fully in bloom but not yet browned or discoloured and, ideally, pick them first thing in the morning when the nectar is most potent. The berries are there to give a rather elegant lilac colour to the syrup.

First, make the lilac syrup. Gently pick off the small lilac flowers from the clusters, taking care to pull out the base of each little flower but discarding any green or woody parts.

Place the lilac flowers, blackcurrants or blueberries and sugar in a medium bowl and pour over the boiling water. Stir gently to dissolve the sugar, then cover and allow to infuse for around 3 hours (don't be tempted to leave it longer, there is a tipping point beyond which the syrup will turn bitter). Strain through a fine-mesh sieve into a sterilised bottle. The syrup will keep in the refrigerator for up to 4 weeks, but I do also freeze it in ice cube trays.

To make the cocktail, combine the gin, lilac syrup and tonic water in a chilled highball glass filled with ice cubes. Garnish with lilac flowers and a lemon wedge.

Note
This syrup also works beautifully with Palačinki (see page 32) and a little squeeze of lemon.

From the Larder

MAKES 175–190G (6–6 3/4 OZ)

Tarana

125 g (4½ oz/1 cup) plain (all-purpose) flour, plus extra for dusting
½ teaspoon fine sea salt
1 medium egg
1 teaspoon water

There comes a point at the height of summer where in every Balkan household, cotton tablecloths or bedsheets, reserved for this special purpose alone (or the shared purpose of preparing *pita* and *burek*), emerge and are placed on every available surface. For those living in houses with gardens, all outdoor tables and flat surfaces are covered. For those in apartments, it is every table, sofa and unused bed. Living spaces are transformed to act as drying canvases for what is essentially Balkan pasta, which is traditionally made in summer and dried in the sun (or very well-aerated rooms) so it may be stored for the winter.

Tarana or *tarhana* is one of these pastas. It is not to be confused with its cousins, Greek *trahanas* or Central Asian and Levantine *tarhana*, which include other flavours and a fermented dairy element. Balkan *tarana*, like the region itself, sits squarely between these influences and Italian influences in that it is made with eggs and flour. In Bosnia and Herzegovina you can also find *kisela* (sour) *tarhana* flavoured with fresh tomatoes. It can be used fresh in soups and stews or baked with meat or vegetables (or both), or dried and stored. It is often eaten for breakfast or a light dinner, cooked very simply and topped with a little butter or oil and, of course *sirenje* cheese. This version is a little more elaborate and includes baked *sirenje* – variations of which you will find in the cuisine of most of south-eastern Europe and the eastern Mediterranean, the Greek dish *bouyourdi* being one of them.

Sift the flour and salt into a medium bowl. Crack the egg into a separate small bowl and lightly beat with the water. Pour the egg into the flour and use a fork to bring the mixture together into a shaggy dough. Tip out onto a clean work surface (scraping down the sides of the bowl). Knead for 5–7 minutes – this is intentionally a very hard dough. Keep going until the egg and flour are well combined into a dough with an even yellowish colour. Place a clean dish towel on a large tray and generously dust the middle of it with some flour. Using a box grater, shred the dough over the flour-dusted dish towel. Pause periodically and use the dish towel to roll the *tarana* around so it gets coated in the flour as you grate. When you have finished grating the dough, spread it out evenly over the tea towel. Either use immediately in soup or as pasta or dry it out as follows: place the tray in a well-ventilated and dry part of the kitchen and dry for about 2 days. Once dry, it can be stored in an airtight container or jar like dry pasta.

Kajmak

MAKES 100–120 G (3½–4¼ OZ)

1 litre (34 fl oz/4¼ cups) raw (unpasteurised) whole (full-fat) milk
sea salt flakes

Pour the milk into a large, heavy-based saucepan over a medium-high heat. Bring to a gentle simmer (taking care the milk does not froth and spill out), then remove from the heat and allow the milk to cool to room temperature. Once a layer of thick cream (this is the *kajmak*) has formed on the cool milk, use a slotted spoon to carefully collect it and place it in a sieve placed over a bowl. Return any liquid that has passed through the sieve into the bowl to the saucepan and place the sieve with the *kajmak* over the bowl in the refrigerator. Return the saucepan to a medium-high heat and repeat the process: bring the milk to a gentle simmer, allow it to cool and develop the *kajmak*, skim the *kajmak*, add it to the sieve with the other *kajmak*, allow it to drain, return any drained liquid to the saucepan. You will need to repeat the process in total about 4–6 times.

Reserve the depleted milk to use for baking. Transfer the drained *kajmak* to a sterilised airtight container and weigh it, then add 1–1.5 per cent of the weight in salt – for example, for 100 g (3½ oz) *kajmak* add 1–1.5 g salt. Gently stir it in, but try to keep some of the *kajmak* layers. It will keep in the refrigerator for 7–10 days.

Dried Pepper Paste

80 g (2¾ oz) dried long red peppers
2 garlic cloves, peeled
60 ml (2 fl oz/¼ cup) extra virgin olive oil, plus extra to top
½ teaspoon sea salt flakes
freshly ground black pepper

Put the dried peppers into a large saucepan and cover with water. Place over a medium-high heat and bring to the boil, then reduce the heat and simmer for 10–12 minutes, or until the peppers are rehydrated. Drain the peppers, remove the stalks and seeds, then, with a teaspoon or a butter knife, scrape out the flesh of the peppers and discard the skins.

Place the flesh of the peppers, the garlic, oil, salt and a good grind of black pepper in a food processor and blend until smooth. Transfer to a sterilised jar, top with a little extra oil and store in the refrigerator to use as needed. The paste will keep for up to 4 weeks in the refrigerator.

Vanilla Sugar

MAKES 500 G (1 LB 2 OZ)

500 g (1 lb 2 oz/scant 2¼ cups) caster (superfine) sugar
1–2 vanilla pods (beans), halved lengthwise

Put the sugar and vanilla pods into a large, sterilised, dry jar for which you have a lid. Close tightly with the lid and give it a gentle shake. Store in a cool, dry place and allow to infuse for at least 4–5 days before you use it. Shake the jar from time to time and top it up with more sugar every time you use some. Replace the vanilla pods after 2 months.

From the Larder

Glossary

INGREDIENTS	EXPLANATION	SUBSTITUTION
Ayran or airan	A yoghurt drink, made by diluting natural set yoghurt with water and salt.	• Kefir or drinking yoghurt (see below)
Blue plums	Means *plave šljive* (in Bosnian, Croatian, Serbian and Montenegrin) or *plavi slivi* (in Macedonian). These are medium-sized (3-5cm/1¼-2 in), oblong-shaped, blue-skinned plums common across the Balkan region. In appearance their skin ranges from purple to deep blue, with a firm and juicy yellow-orange flesh. Native cultivars are all part of the family of plums (l. *prunus domestica*) and include *Požegača, Crvena Ranka, Čačanska Lepotica, Čačanska najbolja, Valjevka*.	• Prune plums • Victoria plums
Bukovo pepper	Known as Bukovec or Bukovka, this is a pepper seasoning made from dried and crushed long red peppers (from a variety of cultivars) grown around a small village called Bukovo near Bitola in southern North Macedonia. It is intensely red in colour, pleasantly aromatic, often contains the seeds of the peppers, and can be either sweet or spicy.	• Aleppo pepper • Pul biber
Cacao powder	Finely ground powder made from raw cacao beans that have been cold-pressed to remove the cacao butter, resulting in a powder with an intense flavour and higher nutritional content. Look for labels that include words such as raw, unprocessed and unsweetened cacao powder.	• Cocoa powder, although it may yield a slightly different result and flavour profile due to the differences in processing. • Carob powder (see below)
Carob powder	Finely ground powder made from the dried and roasted pods of the carob tree (l. *Ceratonia siliqua*). Historically it was widely used in Balkan cuisine as a more local and affordable alternative to cocoa powder. It is naturally sweet and less bitter than cocoa powder or cacao powder, with an earthy flavour, subtle notes of caramel and molasses, and a milder, more subdued chocolate-like taste.	• Cacao powder (see above) or cocoa powder, but you may need to make adjustments. • Carob powder tends to be naturally sweeter than cacao or cocoa powder and thickens mixtures more due to its high fibre content.
Cornmeal	Fine flour made by grinding dried corn kernels.	• Fine maize flour
Čvarci	*Čvarci* (in Bosnian, Croatian, Serbian and Montenegrin), *ocvírki* (in Slovenian), *čvarki* or *dzimirinki* (in Macedonian) are somewhere between pork cracklings and pork rinds. They are prepared by rendering pork fat very slowly until little bits of meat and skin, cooking in the rendered fat, turn golden brown, light and crunchy. They are typically seasoned just with salt, but sometimes also garlic or sweet paprika or other spices and aromatics. They are typically enjoyed as a snack alongside *rakija*, but also used as an ingredient in baking or as topping or garnish to add texture and flavour to dishes.	• Pork rinds or pork crackling
Čvarci, duvan	*Duvan čvarci* are a speciality version of *čvarci* from the city of Valjevo in western Serbia. *Duvan čvarci* are cooked longer than *čvarci* until almost all the fat is extracted leaving delicate crackling fibres which look like shredded tobacco (*duvan* meaning tobacco in Serbian).	• Pork rinds or pork crackling, finely chopped

Drinking yoghurt	Different to *ayran*, drinking yoghurt (called simply *jogurt* or sometimes *tekući* (liquid) *jogurt* is simply natural fermented yoghurt in liquid form. A very traditional dairy beverage popular across the region and made from fermented milk, it has a tangy and slightly sour flavour. Almost always served as a chilled refreshing drink alongside pastries, breads, or with main dishes, it is also extensively used in baking and cooking, for example as a base for sauces or for thickening soups or stews.	• Kefir
Griz	Wheat grits or fine semolina, made from durum wheat. Used in both sweet and savoury dishes, or simply cooked with milk to make a creamy wheat porridge or pudding.	• Semolina rimacinata or cream of wheat
Kajmak	*Kajmak* is a dairy product made by heating unpasteurized whole (full fat) milk and allowing it to ferment, after which the cream is skimmed off the top. It is then either layered or lightly churned to give it a smoother, thick, creamy texture with a consistency similar to clotted cream or soft butter. Kajmak can be either "young" meaning freshly skimmed and typically unsalted, or "aged" which typically means salted and allowed to ferment after it is skimmed, giving it a more sour and thicker consistency. It ranges in colour from pale ivory to golden yellow, depending on the type of milk and the fermentation process used.	• Clotted cream. For "aged" kajmak, mix clotted cream with flaked sea salt and store in the refrigerator, allowing it to gently ferment and develop flavour.
Kaškaval or kashkaval	*Kaškaval* is a type of semi-hard cheese made from cow's, sheep's, or goat's milk, or a combination. It is typically firm and smooth but slightly elastic in texture, and pale yellow, but it can range in both colour as well as texture from semi-soft to semi-hard, with older varieties being firmer and crumblier. It is rich and nutty with savoury undertones, but the taste varies depending on the type of milk used, the length of ageing, and regional variations in production methods. Aged *kaškaval* can be tangier and sharper.	• Mild cheddar, or a mix of mature cheddar and mozzarella • Italian caciocavallo
Kiselo mleko	This translates to sour milk but is a natural set (plain) yoghurt.	• Natural set (plain) yoghurt
Linden	European linden or lime (*l. Tilia x europea*)	
Lozovača or lozova rakija	Rakija made from grapes	• Grappa
Njeguški pršut	Njeguški pršut is a traditional air-dried ham from the village of Njeguši in Montenegro. Made from high-quality pork, it is salted, cured, and aged for several months, and famously in the mountain air of Njeguši which gives it its distinct flavour and texture. Njeguški pršut is renowned for its rich, savory taste, delicate marbling, and slightly smoky aroma, making it a prized delicacy in the region often enjoyed thinly sliced as an appetizer or paired with local cheeses and wines.	• Smoked prosciutto
Peppers, for pickles	Small spicy cayenne / chilli peppers, know colloquially as 'fefferoni'.	• Italian pepperonicini
Peppers, long green	There are many long green pepper cultivars across the region of every shape, each of which have a distinct flavour profile. Long green peppers can be both sweet and spicy. Generally, if they are rounder, plumper and pale green, they will be sweet. If they are longer, thinner and a darker green, they will be hotter. However that is not always the case. All long green peppers - either mild and sweet or fiery hot are favoured for roasting, grilling, salads, stuffing and pickling, depending on personal preference and heat tolerance.	• Turkish Carliston peppers • Banana peppers • Anaheim peppers (spicy) • Cubanelle peppers • Friggitelli peppers • Sweet Italian peppers
Peppers, long red	There are many long red pepper cultivars across the region of every shape, each of which have a distinct flavour profile. Long red peppers can be both sweet and spicy. Notable varities include Zlatna Žetva and Pirot peppers from Serbia, Kurtovska Kapija, Ajvarki and Vezenki peppers from North Macedonia.	• Romano peppers • Piquillo peppers

Glossary

Term	Description	Equivalents
Peppers, long dried red	Any long red peppers which are dried at the end of summer to be rehydrated and consumed over winter.	• Spanish Ñora pepper • Gujillo pepper
Peppers, Vezenki	Translates loosely to 'embroidered' peppers. These are a rather unique varietal, typically red, but known for their distinctive pattern on the skin which looks like embroidery.	
Peppers, Ajvarki or Kurtovska Kapija	Heart-shaped long red pointed bell peppers with thick skins and dense flesh. The cultivars used for making *ajvar* are known colloquially as *ajvarki* or *Kurtovska Kapija*.	• Red bell peppers
Rakija	A traditional fruit brandy widely produced and consumed throughout the Balkans. It is typically prepared by distilling fermented fruit. It can be made from any fruits, including blue plums, grapes, apricots, apples, Williams pears, cherries, and quinces. *Rakija* is known for its high alcohol content. It is typically served neat accompanied by mezes or appetizers, or it forms part of any large social or family gatherings and celebrations.	
Sitni kolači	Bite-sized sweet treats	
Skuta	A young curd/cottage cheese made from cow's milk or sheep's milk whey. Mild and faintly sweet, it is typically used in baking and desserts around Slovenia and Croatia.	• *Twaróg* • Ricotta
Slanina	Salt-cured and dried, or salt-cured and smoked pork belly or pork fatback. It can be simply salted, or flavoured with various spices and aromatics, such as garlic, black pepper, and sweet paprika. *Slanina* is often sliced thinly and eaten as a savoury snack or appetizer, but it is also used extensively in baking and cooking.	• Smoked streaky bacon • Smoked pancetta
Sujuk or sudžuk	A spicy, sweet paprika-infused sausage, made from beef, lamb or pork.	• Chorizo
Suvomesnati or suho meso	Meaning dry meat, the term is used to describe a range of meats (typically pork, beef, lamb or game) preserved through curing, air-drying and sometimes smoking. Includes *slanina* (see above), *pršut* (Balkan-style prosciutto), dry-cured sausages such as kulen or *sujuk* (see above). These are typically served on a meat platter as an appetizer or as an accompaniment to main meals.	
Tomatoes	There are many cultivars of tomatoes across the Balkans, and the most prized are large tomatoes with beefy flesh. Notable varieties include Volovo Srce (bull's heart) or Jabučar (apple). In the green markets they are often marketed as 'old/heirloom seeds'.	• Beef (beefsteak) tomatoes • Bull's Heart (oxheart) tomatoes • San Marzano tomatoes
Šljivovica or slivova rakija	*Rakija* made from blue plums.	
Urda	A fresh, creamy, mild-tasting cheese made from whey. It can be "young" and be more soft and creamy, or "aged" and therefore tangier and crumblier.	• Ricotta • Turkish '*harika cökelek*'
Vegetable bouillon powder	One of the most highly used all-purpose vegetable seasonings across the Balkans is a brand called Vegeta (produced by the Croatian food company, Podravka). It is commonly used as a substitute for salt and consists of a blend of dehydrated vegetables including carrots, celery, onions, peppers, parsley and various other herbs, spices and sometimes MSG or other flavour enhancers.	• Vegetable bouillon / stock powder (ideally reduced or no salt)
White cheese	Refers to *beli sir* (in Bosnian, Croatian, Serbian and Montenegrin) or *belo sirenje* (in Macedonian and Bulgarian) and means a type of cheese made from cow', sheep's or goat's milk, or a combination – depending on regional preferences and availability. It can be "young", and have a mild, creamy and delicate texture, or it can be "aged", typically in brine, and develop a more complex, tangy flavour and crumbly texture.	• Feta

Cook's Notes

Black pepper Always freshly ground black peppercorns, but feel free to substitute to whatever you have or like and adjust it to your taste.

Butter Always unsalted, unless otherwise specified.

Eggs I buy free-range organic mixed eggs which come in various sizes. For the recipes I used average or medium-sized ones which weigh between 50-55g.

Flour Across the Balkans it is milled and categorised differently and comes as T-types, the number broadly indicating how much of the wheat kernel is included in milling, from T-400 (pure white), T-500 and T-550 (some wholemeal), T-850 (half-white, half wholemeal), T-1100 (wholemeal).

White wheat flour will then be either *meko / glatko* (soft / smooth) or *oštro* (sharp). *Meko/glatko* is more finely milled and typically used for certain types of enriched breads, pastries and cakes, layered/stretched pastries (such as pita or burek), and pastas. *Oštro* is slightly rougher and works well in wetter doughs, such as for certain breads, but also with cakes, biscuits and cookies requiring other raising agents like baking powder. It is also used for thickening. They do not have exact equivalents in internationally available flour types.

For me, the following work best: a combination of plain and strong white flour for the layered/stretched Balkan breads and pastries, strong white flour for enriched bakes, and plain flour for all other cakes and bakes.

Lemons Always unwaxed.

Measuring Spoons Always level, not heaped, unless otherwise specified.

Milk Always whole/full fat, unless otherwise specified.

Oil I either use a good quality cold-pressed sunflower oil or an everyday, good quality extra virgin olive oil for cooking.

For salads, mezes and finishing dishes, I use more special, single-origin extra virgin olive oil.

Salt For baking and boiling (for example, salted water) I use a fine sea salt. For everything else (cooking and finishing) I use flaked sea salt (typically Maldon).

I have suggested exact quantities of salt for everything except salted water which for boiling should be salty enough to taste of the sea. For the baking recipes, please do follow the recommended amount as it will impact the result. For everything else, feel free to taste and adjust according to your preference or simply leave it out.

Sourcing ingredients sustainably and responsibly I advocate for sourcing ingredients responsibly and sustainably.

The meat, eggs and dairy I use are always from organic, free-range, high welfare and sustainable suppliers.

I purchase seafood from responsible and sustainable sources and try to use whatever is in season. If the types of fish or seafood I have suggested are not locally available to you, please feel free to substitute them for ones that are.

As much as possible I source fruit and vegetables seasonally and where possible locally, opting for organic and sustainably farmed as much as possible.

Weights All the recipes in the book were tested in metric. I weigh everything, including liquids, on an electronic scale as I found there was a slight variation between this and standard measuring jugs.

Index

A

ajvar 236, 239–40
Alexander's cake 229–31
almonds: *ružice* 210–11
apples: apple *bombici* 226
    apples in *šlafor* 37
    prekmurska gibanica 204
    ražnjiči 178
    štrudla 50
    tufahije 214
apricots: apricot cake 203
    apricot *džem* 247
    Lidia's fruit and nut roll 228
Ariadne's nettle *chorba* 117
aubergines (eggplants): *ajvar* 239
    aubergines in walnut sauce 102
    imam bayildi 126–7
    pickled baby aubergines 244
    pindzur 92
    turli tava 152
avgolemono sauce, trout with 185

B

bacon: a bean *čorba* 120
    sarma od kisel kupus 135–7
    venison with quince
      and cranberries 163
bake, cauliflower 129
a 'Bakexican' pulled pork 168
baklava, chocolate 208
the Balkan Kitchen 10–13
Balkan penicillin 110
the Balkans 14–27, 198–9
barley: meatball soup 116
beans 149
    a bean *čorba* 120
    tavče gravče 150
beef: *ćevapi* 176
    chomlek, Ohrid style 138
    juha with *knedle* 112–13
    klepe 132–4
    kyfte, on onions 171
    meatball soup 116
    pljeskavici 172
    polneti piperki 143
    Sarajevo-style *burek* 54–7
    sarma od kisel kupus 135–7
    sarma od lozov list 144
    turli tava 152
beer: a 'Bakexican'
    pulled pork 168
biscuits (cookies): *vanilici* 224
blejska kremšnita 206–7

blitva, trout with avgolemono
    sauce and 185
bombici, apple 226
boza 258
bread: Grandma's savoury cake 68
    milibrod 74–5
    old bread bake 67
    somun 66
a bream of the seas 186
brodet 191
buckwheat flour: pumpkin *štruklji* 39–41
burek 54–60
    Sarajevo-style *burek* 54–7
burgers: *pljeskavici* 172

C

cabbage: a bean *čorba* 120
    podvarok 148
    roast duck legs with *mlinci* and
      cabbage 160–1
    sarma od kisel kupus 135–7
    sour cabbage 245
cakes: Alexander's cake 229–31
    apricot cake 203
    kob 216
cannellini beans: *makalo* 91
carob bean powder: *potica* 76–7
carrots: cauliflower, carrot and turnip
    pickle 243
    ruska salata 84
    surf 'n' turf *peka* 194
casseroles *see* stews and casseroles
cauliflower: cauliflower bake 129
    cauliflower, carrot and turnip pickle 243
ćevapi 176
chard: *soparnik* 62
cheese: *crni rižot* with stuffed
    grilled squid 196
    Galička salata 89
    gibanica 64
    Grandma's savoury cake 68
    kačamak 44–5
    kifli 70
    klepe 132–4
    old bread bake 67
    pita 53
    pljeskavici 172
    prekmurska gibanica 204
    ruska salata 84
    shopska salata 82
chicken: Balkan penicillin 110
    chicken and rice 158
    chicken *paprikaš* with *noklice* 140
    ruska salata 84

chillies: pickle salsa 168
chocolate: Alexander's cake 229–31
    chocolate baklava 208
    chocolate triangle 227
chomlek: Ohrid style 138
chorba, Ariadne's nettle 117
cinnamon: *ružice* 210–11
citrus fruit: three-citrus marmalade 246
corn cobs: street corn 106
cornmeal: Grandma's savoury cake 68
    kačamak 44–5
courgettes (zucchini):
    Balkan penicillin 110
    courgettes in yoghurt sauce 105
    turli tava 152
cranberries, venison with
    quince and 163
cream: *blejska kremšnita* 206–7
    prekmurska gibanica 204
crepes: *palačinki* 32
crni rižot with stuffed grilled squid 196
cucumber: *shopska salata* 82
    tarator 86
čvarci: eggs and tomatoes 43
    kačamak 44–5

D

dates: fresh quince *kompot* 218
drinks: *boza* 258
    lilac gin and tonic 259
    linseed tea 253
    orahovača 257
    Rada's *šumadijski čaj* 254
    red fruit liqueur 256
drob sarma 146
duck: roast duck legs with *mlinci*
    and cabbage 160–1
dumplings: *klepe* 132–4
    noklice 140
    plum *knedli* 220–1
džem, apricot 247

E

Easter lamb, slow-roasted 164
eggs: *blejska kremšnita* 206–7
    cauliflower bake 129
    eggs and tomatoes 43
    Elbasan tava 166
    pastrmajlija 78–9
    ruska salata 84
    spinach and rice 130
Elbasan tava 166

F

fennel: a bream of the seas 186
    Mejrema's fish soup 119
fig leaves, fish in 188
figs: green fig *slatko* 251
    Lidia's fruit and nut roll 228
filo pastry: *gibanica* 64
    prekmurska gibanica 204
    ružice 210–11
    štrudla 50
fish: a bream of the seas 186
    brodet 191
    fish in fig leaves 188
    Mejrema's fish soup 119
    trout with avgolemono sauce and *blitva* 185
flatbreads: *somun* 66
fruit liqueur, red 256

G

Galička salata 89
garlic: *chomlek*, Ohrid style 138
    slow-roasted Easter lamb 164
gherkins (pickles): *Galička salata* 89
    pickle salsa 168
    ruska salata 84
gibanica 64
gin and tonic, lilac 259
Grandma's savoury cake 68
graškok 124
green beans: *turli tava* 152

H

ham: a bean *čorba* 120
    Galička salata 89
    Grandma's savoury cake 68
hazelnuts: chocolate triangle 227

I

imam bayildi 126–7

J

jam: apricot *džem* 247
juha with *knedle* 112–13

K

kačamak 44–5
kajmak 261
    street corn 106
kebabs: *ražnjiči* 178
kifli 70
klepe 132–4
knedle: *juha* with *knedle* 112–13
    plum *knedli* 220–1
koh 216
kompot, fresh quince 218
kufer 99–100
kyfte, on onions 171

L

lamb: *ćevapi* 176
    Elbasan tava 166
    klepe 132–4
    polneti piperki 143
    šketo 114
    slow-roasted Easter lamb 164
lamb's pluck: *drob sarma* 146
leeks: leek, lemon and olive *salata* 88
    podvarok 148
lemons: leek, lemon and olive *salata* 88
    Lidia's fruit and nut roll 228
lilac gin and tonic 259
linseed tea 253
liqueurs: *orahovača* 257
    red fruit liqueur 256
ljutenitsa 241
lozova rakija: *orahovača* 257
    red fruit liqueur 256

M

makalo 91
markets 236–7
marmalade, three-citrus 246
mayonnaise: *ruska salata* 84
meatballs: *kyfte*, on onions 171
    meatball soup 116
    Mejrema's fish soup 119
milibrod 74–5
milk: *blejska kremšnita* 206–7
    kajmak 261
    koh 216
    sutlijaš 213
millet flour: *boza* 258
mlinci: roast duck legs with *mlinci* and cabbage 160–1
mussels 'buzara-style', two ways 192–3

N

nettles: Ariadne's nettle *čorba* 117
    pita 53
noklice, chicken *paprikaš* with 140
nuts: apple *bombici* 226

O

octopus: octopus salad with blood orange dressing 182
    surf 'n' turf *peka* 194
okra: *turli tava* 152
old bread bake 67
olives: a bream of the seas 186
    leek, lemon and olive *salata* 88
onions: *drob sarma* 146
    kyfte, on onions 171
    orahovača 257
oranges: blood orange dressing 182

P

palačinki 32
paprikaš: chicken *paprikaš* with *noklice* 140
parsley: *šketo* 114
parsnips: *juha* with *knedle* 112–13
pasta: Balkan penicillin 110
    mlinci 160–1
    tarana 260
pastries: *kifli* 70
    pita 51–3
    potica 76–7
    Sarajevo-style *burek* 54–7
    solenki 73
pastrmajlija 78–9
patties: *pljeskavici* 172
peas: *graškok* 124
    ruska salata 84
pecans: *tufahije* 214
peka, surf 'n' turf 194
peppers 95
    ajvar 236, 239
    chicken *paprikaš* with *noklice* 140
    dried pepper paste 261
    fried and marinated peppers 97
    ljutenitsa 241
    pindzur 92
    polneti piperki 143
    shopska salata 82
    stuffed and baked peppers 95
    surf 'n' turf *peka* 194
pickles: cauliflower, carrot and turnip pickle 243
    pickle salsa 168
    pickled baby aubergines 244
pies: *gibanica* 64
    pita 51–3
    Sarajevo-style *burek* 54–7
    soparnik 62
pindzur 92
pita 51–3
pljeskavici 172
plum pekmez 247
    kifli 70
    vanilici 224
podvarok 148
polenta (cornmeal): *brodet* 191
polneti piperki 143
poppy seeds: *milibrod* 74–5
    prekmurska gibanica 204
pork: a 'Bakexican' pulled pork 168
    pastrmajlija 78–9
    podvarok 148
    ražnjiči 178
    sarma od kisel kupus 135–7
    turli tava 152
porridge: *kačamak* 44–5
potatoes: Balkan penicillin 110
    blitva 185
    juha with *knedle* 112–13
    octopus salad with blood orange dressing 182
    plum *knedli* 220–1
    ruska salata 84
    Sarajevo-style *burek* 54–7
    sarma od lozov list 144
    surf 'n' turf *peka* 194
potica 76–7

praline, walnut 229–31
prekmurska gibanica 204
priganice 34
prosciutto di speck: *crni rižot* with stuffed grilled squid 196
prune plums: fresh quince *kompot* 218
   plum *knedli* 220–1
   plum *pekmez* 247
   ražnjići 178
prunes: roast duck legs with *mlinci* and cabbage 160–1
puff pastry: *blejska kremšnita* 206–7
pumpkin *štruklji* 39–41

Q

quinces 217
   fresh quince *kompot* 218
   quince *slatko* 249
   venison with quince and cranberries 163

R

Rada's *šumadijski čaj* 254
raisins: *milibrod* 74–5
ražnjići 178
red fruit liqueur 256
rice: chicken and rice 158
   crni rižot with stuffed grilled squid 196
   drob sarma 146
   Elbasan tava 166
   Mejrema's fish soup 119
   podvarok 148
   polneti piperki 143
   sarma od kisel kupus 135–7
   sarma od lozov list 144
   spinach and rice 130
   sutlijaš 213
risotto: *crni rižot* with stuffed grilled squid 196
ruska salata 84
ružice 210–11

S

salads: *Galička salata* 89
   leek, lemon and olive *salata* 88
   octopus salad with blood orange dressing 182
   ruska salata 84
   shopska salata 82
   spring onion salad 129
salami, fruit: chocolate triangle 227
   Lidia's fruit and nut roll 228
salsa, pickle 168
Sarajevo-style *burek* 54–7
sarma: *drob sarma* 146
   sarma od kisel kupus 135–7
   sarma od lozov list 144
sausages: *ćevapi* 176
shallots: *chomlek*, Ohrid style 138
škeketo 114
shopska salata 82
skewers: *ražnjići* 178
slanina: a bean *čorba* 120
   podvarok 148

slatkarnica 232
slatko 249
   green fig *slatko* 251
   quince *slatko* 249
slavsko žito 222–3
šljivovica: Rada's *šumadijski čaj* 254
solenki 73
somun 66
   a 'Bakexican' pulled pork 168
   pljeskavici 172
soparnik 62
soups: Ariadne's nettle *chorba* 117
   Balkan penicillin 110
   a bean *čorba* 120
   juha with *knedle* 112–13
   meatball soup 116
   Mejrema's fish soup 119
   škeketo 114
sour cabbage 245
   a bean *čorba* 120
   podvarok 148
   sarma od kisel kupus 135–7
sour cherries: chocolate triangle 227
   Lidia's fruit and nut roll 228
   štrudla 50
spinach: *pita* 53
   spinach and rice 130
spring onions (scallions): *soparnik* 62
   spring onion salad 129
squid: *crni rižot* with stuffed grilled squid 196
stews and casseroles: *brodet* 191
   chomlek, Ohrid style 138
   grašhok 124
   podvarok 148
   turli tava 152
street corn 106
štrudla 50
štruklji, pumpkin 39–41
sugar, vanilla 261
sultanas (golden raisins): *potica* 76–7
surf 'n' turf *peka* 194
sutlijaš 213
sweets: apple *bombici* 226
   chocolate triangle 227
Swiss chard: *blitva* 185
   soparnik 62

T

tarana 260
tarator 86
tava, Elbasan 166
tavče gravče 150
tea, linseed 253
teškoto 47
Tetovo beans: a bean *šorba* 120
   tavče gravše 150
tomatoes: *brodet* 191
   chicken *paprikaš* with *noklice* 140
   eggs and tomatoes 43
   grašbok 124
   imam bayildi 126–7
   ljutenitsa 241
   mussels '*buzara*-style', two ways 192–3
   pindzur 92
   polneti piperki 143
   shopska salata 82
   turli tava 152

tonic water: lilac gin and tonic 259
Triglav 174–5
trout with avgolemono sauce and *blitva* 185
tufahije 214
turli tava 152
turnips: cauliflower, carrot and turnip pickle 243
turšija 243
twaróg: *prekmurska gibanica* 204

U

urda: *pljeskavici* 172
   stuffed and baked peppers 95
urnebes 172

V

vanilici 224
vanilla sugar 261
   milibrod 74–5
   slavsko žito 222–3
Vardar 174–5
veal: *ćevapi* 176
   pljeskavici 172
   surf 'n' turf *peka* 194
venison with quince and cranberries 163
vine leaves: fish in fig leaves 188
   sarma od lozov list 144

W

walnuts: aubergines in walnut sauce 102
   chocolate baklava 208
   chocolate triangle 227
   Lidia's fruit and nut roll 228
   orahovača 257
   potica 76–7
   prekmurska gibanica 204
   ružice 210–11
   slavsko žito 222–3
   štrudla 50
   tarator 86
   vanilici 224
   walnut praline 229–31
wheat: *slavsko žito* 222–3
wild garlic (ransoms): *soparnik* 62

Y

yoghurt: courgettes in yoghurt sauce 105
   Elbasan tava 166
   Galička salata 89
   kačamak 44–5
   klepe 132–4
   old bread bake 67
   tarator 86

Z

zaprska, tavče gravče 150
žute dunje 217

SOURCES AND FURTHER READING

Allan, Nicholas, When Dreams Collide: Travels in Yugoslavia with Rebecca West, Nine Elms Books: 2022.

Alacki, Adrijana, *Macedonian Traditional Cookbook*, Skopje : Vincent grafika. 2010

Andreevski, Petre M. *Izbrani dela : vo šest knigi*, Skopje: Tabernakul, 2002.

Andreevski, Petre M. *Tunel*, Skopje: Libris, 2020.

Andrić, Ivo, *The Bridge on the Drina*, Chicago: University of Chicago Press, 1977.

Barbieri, Veljko, *Epitaf carskog gurmana*, Zagreb: August Cesarec, 1983.

Bisenić, Ljiljana, *Yugoslav Specialities*, Zagreb: Znanje (English Edition), 1984.

Bracewell, Wendy, 'Eating Up Yugoslavia: Cookbooks and Consumption in Socialist Yugoslavia', in Paulina Bren, and Mary Neuburger (eds), *Communism Unwrapped: Consumption in Cold War Eastern Europe*, New York, NY: Oxford University Press, 2012.

Bracewell, Wendy. *Orientations : An Anthology of East European Travel Writing, ca. 1550-2000*. Budapest: Central European University Press, 2009.

Bren, Paulina., and Mary Neuburger, *Communism Unwrapped : Consumption in Cold War Eastern Europe*, New York, NY: Oxford University Press, 2012.

Buchanan, Meriel, *Good Food from the Balkans*. London: F. Muller, 1956.

Chloupek, Drago (ed) *Knjiga Za Svaku Ženu, Uzorna Domácica*, Zagreb: 1952.

Chomsky, Noam. Yugoslavia : Peace, War, and Dissolution. Ed. Davor Džalto. Oakland, CA: PM Press, 2018.

Cohen, Lenard J., and Jasna. Dragović-Soso, *State Collapse in South-Eastern Europe : New Perspectives on Yugoslavia's Disintegration*. West Lafayette, Ind: Purdue University Press, 2008.

Flandrin, Jean-Louis, Massimo Montanari, and Albert. Sonnenfeld. *Food : A Culinary History from Antiquity to the Present*, New York ; Columbia University Press, 1999.

Davies, Tricia., Lesley. Chamberlain, and Catherine Atkinson, *The Balkan Cookbook : Traditional Cooking from Romania, Bulgaria and the Balkan Countries*, London: Southwater, 2000.

Drulović, Anja. *Titov kuvar*. Beograd: Laguna, 2005.

Fotiadis, Ruža, Vladimir Ivanović, and Radina Vučetić (eds), *Brotherhood and Unity at the Kitchen Table : Food in Socialist Yugoslavia*. Zagreb: Srednja Europa, 2019.

Gavrilović, Žarko, *Srpski pravoslavni posni kuvar*. Beograd: Grmeč : Privredni pregled, 2001.

Glenny, Misha. *The Balkans, 1804-1999 : Nationalism, War and the Great Powers*. London: Granta, 2000.

Glenny, Misha. *The Fall of Yugoslavia : The Third Balkan War*. 3rd ed. London: Penguin, 1996.

Grubačić, Andrej. *Don't Mourn, Balkanize! : Essays after Yugoslavia*. Oakland, Calif: PM Press, 2010

Howe, Robin, *Balkan Cooking*, London: André Deutsch, 1965.

Ivanišević, Jelena, *Od kuharice do književnosti : ogledi o kulinarskoj prozi*. Zagreb: Institut za etnologiju i folkloristiku, 2017.

Ivanova, Mariya et al. (eds), *Social Dimensions of Food in the Prehistoric Balkans*, Oxford; Oxbow books, 2018.

Ivanovska, Sonja and Djimrevska, Irena (eds), *Food Beyond Borders*, Project publication for 'Support to Economic Diversification of Rural Areas in Southeast Europe (SEDRA) implemented by GIZ and the Standing Working Group for Regional Rural Development in South Eastern Europe (SWG RRD).

Ivković, Bosa. *Lovačka Kuharica*. Zagreb, 1954.

Kaneva-Johnson, Maria. *The Melting Pot : Balkan Food and Cookery*, Prospect Books, 1995.

Kaplan, Robert D, *Balkan Ghosts : A Journey through History*, New York: Vintage, 1994.

Kapor, Momo, *Vrlo Krake Priće*, Zagreb: Znanje, 1983.

Karačić, Ivanka. *Domaća kuhinja*, 5th Edition, Zagreb: Znanje, 1979.

Koneski, Blaže, *Poezija*, Skopje: MANU, 2011.

Koneski, Blaže, *Vezilka*, Skopje, 2021.

Lee, Alexander, "A History of Börek" in *History Today*, Volume 69 Issue 9 September 2019.

Marjanović, Radica (Dika), *Dalmatinska kuhinja*, 2nd Edition, Split, 1951.

Marković, Spasenija-Pata, *Yugoslav Cookbook*, Belgrade: Vintage, 1966.

Marković, Spasenija-Pata, Велики народни кувар (*Great National Cookbook*) Belgrade: Narodna Knjiga, 1956 plus subsequent editions.

Matić, Terezija, *Biseri Stare Kuhinje*, Zagreb, 1987.

Mirodan, Vladimir. *The Balkan Cookbook*. Wheathampstead: Lennard, 1987.

Mlekuž, Jernej. *Burek: A Culinary Metaphor*, Budapest-New York: CEU Press, 2015.

Novačić, Dejan. *Emigrantski kuvar : sve što ste oduvek hteli da znate o jugoslovenskoj kuhinji, ali nemate više koga da pitate*. Novi Sad: Stylos art, 2009.

Novak-Markovic, Olga, *Jugoslavenska kuhinja (Yugoslav Cookbook)*, Ljubljana: Cankarjeva Založba, 1984.

Ognjenovic, Gorana, and Jasna Jozelic, eds. *Nationalism and the Politicization of History in the Former Yugoslavia*, Basingstoke: Palgrave Macmillan, 2021.

Peštek, Almir, Marko Kukanja, and Sanda Renko, eds. *Gastronomy for Tourism Development : Potential of the Western Balkans*. United Kingdom: Emerald Publishing, 2020.

Pilcher, Jeffrey M. *The Oxford Handbook of Food History*. Oxford; Oxford University Press, 2012.

Polese, Abel, ed. *Informal Nationalism after Communism: The Everyday Construction of Post-Socialist Identities*. London: I.B. Tauris, 2018.

Prazmowska, Anita. Eastern Europe and the Origins of the Second World War. Basingstoke: Macmillan, 2000.

Rajak, Svetozar et al., eds. *The Balkans in the Cold War*. London: Palgrave Macmillan, 2017.

Ramet, Sabrina Petra, *Balkan Babel : The Disintegration of Yugoslavia from the Death of Tito to the Fall of Milošević*. 4th ed. Boulder, Colo. ; Westview, 2002.

Silber, Laura, and Allan. Little, The Death of Yugoslavia. London: Penguin, 1995.

Singleton, Frederick Bernard. A Short History of the Yugoslav Peoples. Cambridge: Cambridge University Press, 1985.

Todorova, Maria, *Imagining the Balkans*. Updated ed. Oxford: Oxford University Press, 2009.

Vučetić, Mira, *Kubarstvo ... Prerađeno Izdanje*, Zagreb: N.p., 1952.

Vučetić, Mira. *Zlatna knjiga kuharstva*. Zagreb: Nakladni zavod Matice hrvatske, 1976.

Wachtel, Andrew. *The Balkans in World History*. Oxford; Oxford University Press, 2008.

West, Rebecca. *Black Lamb and Grey Falcon*. S.l: MacMillan, 1942.

West, Richard, Tito and the Rise and Fall of Yugoslavia, London: Sinclair-Stevenson, 1994.

About the Author

Irina Janakievska is a Macedonian-British writer and recipe developer. Irina was born in Skopje, North Macedonia (then one of the republics of former Yugoslavia) but grew up in Kuwait from the late 1980s onwards. In 2001 she moved to London to complete her undergraduate and masters degrees at the London School of Economics in international relations and history. After university, a large corporate law firm sponsored her through law school and Irina became a solicitor. In 2020, Irina left her successful career in corporate and finance law to follow her passion for sharing her love of Balkan cuisine, the Balkans and its people with the world. Irina completed her culinary training at Leiths School of Food and Wine. She has contributed to the Guardian, Foodnetwork US, Whetstone Magazine and Mediterranean Lifestyle magazine. The Balkan Kitchen was shortlisted for the Jane Grigson Trust Award in 2023.

Irina lives in London with her husband Peter and young son Alexander, cooking, researching and writing about Balkan history, food culture and culinary traditions.

Acknowledgements

This book has written itself many times in my heart over the past twelve years. It has been a privilege and dream come true to bring it to life on paper and share the love I have for the Balkans with the world.

First and foremost, my beautiful and extraordinary mama, Lidia Janakievska. I owe you more than I can ever articulate. None of this would have been possible without you and your support. Your love and courage continues to inspire me every day. You braved the unknown and sacrificed everything to seek a better life for us and to give me an exceptional education, without which I would not be where I am. You taught me to be fearless, to trust myself, to dream and to work hard to make my dreams a reality, while always staying true to who I am, where I come from, and doing the right thing. Thank you for everything, I love you.

Emily Sweet, my lovely agent – thank you for discovering me, believing in my dream and helping me turn it into reality. I am so lucky I get to work with you.

Eve Marleau, my incredible editor – a heartfelt thank you for everything: the opportunity of a lifetime to write my love letter to the Balkans, your advice, creativity, ideas, patience, and general brilliance. Above all thank you for giving me the creative freedom and working tirelessly to bring this book to life. Huge thanks to Sarah Lavelle, Kajal Mistry and the rest of the team at Hardie Grant and Quadrille who have worked tirelessly in the background. Lucy Kingett, I am so grateful for your thoughtful, sensitive and thorough copy editing. Working with you all has been an absolute pleasure.

To the dream team who helped wrap my words with exquisite beauty, thank you: Liz Seabrook and her stunning, gentle photography; Tabitha Hawkins for her considerate and culturally sensitive art direction and the most gorgeous props; Esther Clark and her assistant Caitlin [MacDonald] for cooking and styling the food so wonderfully; Evi O. Studio for all their hard work and patience on the design of this book; Stuart Hardie, for magically extracting the vision for the book cover from my mind and [translating my love for the art of Macedonian painter, Dimitar Kondovski] into the most beautiful and iconic book cover.

I am profoundly grateful to Olia Hercules and Tara Wigley for their beautiful words that grace the cover of this book. I am also forever grateful to Joudie Kalla for being the first to champion an unknown, aspiring food writer. [My love, hope and support for peace and freedom in your respective homes, always.] A heartfelt thank you also to Helen Goh, Jenny Linford, Melissa Thompson and Özlem Warren for their generosity of spirit and kind words of support when this book was no more than a beautiful dream. To Ravneet Gill and the amazing Countertalk team – thank you for everything you do, especially for the invaluable events and resources you provide for novice food writers; I benefitted greatly from them. To everyone involved with the Jane Grigson Trust Award – thank you for the honour of shortlisting this book in 2023 and for your invaluable support. Michael Harding – thank you for teaching me everything I know about food photography – it was what ultimately led to people noticing my writing.

I am forever grateful to several editors who were the first to commission pieces from me: Andy Pietrasik at the *Guardian*, Elena and Melisa Koyunseven at *The Mediterranean Lifestyle*, Layla Schlack at *Whetstone Magazine*, Michelle Baričević at *Foodnetwork* (US), and Arbër Gashi at *Balkanism*.

To everyone I met travelling through the Balkans who opened their hearts to me, to everyone from the Balkans or the Balkan diaspora who has connected with me and shared their experiences and stories with me – thank you, I wish I could name you all here. In addition to those I have named throughout the book I would like to thank the following: Jelena Belgrave, for her friendship and our fermentation and all things Balkan chats; Aleksandra Aleksandrova Oberstar, for her friendship, our unforgettable trip to Istria, and all her advice on Dalmatian and Slovenian cuisine; Stevo Stepanovski, the bibliophile of Babino, for reminding me of the beautiful poetry of Blaže Koneski; Mirčeta Konatar in Kotor and Njeguši, Snježana and Mers Filiplić in Pula; Anna Colquhoun, for letting me take over her kitchen for a day in Bolara 60 and for our insightful chats about Istrian cuisine.

To my dearest friends and neighbours – you know who you are – for your friendship, love and support and above all for eating all the food I cooked while testing the recipes. To the Murray-kievski-Kofoed-Eatons – my adopted Anglo-Irish-Danish family. Thank you for being so willing to be Balkanised, for being my number one super-fans, taste testers, and an invaluable support network. Sue and Neil, my wonderful parents-in-law, an especially huge thank you for looking after Alexander and for always being readily available to help - most of my research trips would not have happened without you. You are all simply the best, and I love you all so very much.

My final thanks goes to two people. My husband Peter, my greatest champion who has given me unwavering love and support as I embarked on the insanely risky endeavour of abandoning a secure career to follow my heart and leap into the unknown. Our souls are lucky to have found each other in this lifetime. I love you, forever. And my son Alexander, my greatest joy, who inspires me with his beautiful heart every day. My love for you is infinite.

Published in 2024 by Hardie Grant Books (London)

Hardie Grant Books (London)
5th & 6th Floors
52–54 Southwark Street
London SE1 1UN

hardiegrantbooks.com

All rights reserved. No part of this publication may be reproduced, stored in a retrieval system or transmitted in any form by any means, electronic, mechanical, photocopying, recording or otherwise, without the prior written permission of the publishers and copyright holders.

The moral rights of the author have been asserted.

Copyright text © Irina Janakievska
Copyright Photography © Liz Seabrook
Copyright photography © Irina Janakievska pages 7, 8, 9, 10, 11, 13, 16, 17, 23, 27, 29, 38, 46, 47, 52, 58, 61, 94, 98, 99, 100, 101, 118, 149, 162, 174, 175, 184, 186, 187, 198, 199, 217, 232, 233, 236, 237, 239, 250, 251
Copyright photography © Stefan Samandov pages 237, 239
Copyright photography © Stephanie McGehee page 270

British Library Cataloguing-in-Publication Data. A catalogue record for this book is available from the British Library.

The Balkan Kitchen
ISBN: 978-1-78488-685-1

10 9 8 7 6 5 4 3 2 1

Publishing Director: Kajal Mistry
Commissioning Editor: Eve Marleau
Internal layout design: Evi.O-Studio | Emi Chiba & Susan Le
Typesetting: Evi.O-Studio | Doreen Zheng
Cover design: Stuart Hardie
Copy editor: Lucy Kingett
Proofreader: Kathy Steer
Photographer: Liz Seabrook
Food stylist: Esther Clark
Prop stylist: Tabitha Hawkins
Indexer: Vanessa Bird
Production Controller: Martina Georgieva

Colour reproduction by p2d
Printed in China by Leo Paper Products Ltd.

MIX
Paper | Supporting responsible forestry
FSC® C018179